The Obama Presidency

The Obama Presidency

Appraisals and Prospects

Editors

Bert A. Rockman

Purdue University

Andrew Rudalevige

Dickinson College

Colin Campbell

University of British Columbia

Los Angeles | London | New Delhi
Singapore | Washington DC

CQ Press
2300 N Street, NW, Suite 800
Washington, DC 20037

Phone: 202-729-1900; toll-free, 1-866-4CQ-PRESS (1-866-427-7737)

Web: www.cqpress.com

Cover design: Mike Pottman, M Design & Print
Cover photos: © Pete Souza/White House/Handout/CNP/Corbis
Composition: C&M Digitals (P) Ltd.

♾ The paper used in this publication exceeds the requirements of the American National
Standard for Information Sciences—Permanence of Paper for Printed Library Materials,
ANSI Z39.48-1992.

Printed and bound in the United States of America

15   14   13   12   11   1   2   3   4   5

Library of Congress Cataloging-in-Publication Data

The Obama presidency : appraisals and prospects / Bert A. Rockman, Andrew
    Rudalevige, Colin Campbell, editors.
    p. cm.
Includes bibliographical references.
ISBN 978-1-60871-685-2 (alk. paper)
    1. United States—Politics and government—2009- 2. Obama, Barack. I. Rockman,
Bert A. II. Rudalevige, Andrew, 1968- III. Campbell, Colin.

E907.O226 2011
973.932092—dc23

2011022129

Contents

BERT A. ROCKMAN, PURDUE UNIVERSITY

ANDREW RUDALEVIGE, DICKINSON COLLEGE

Barack Obama's ascension to the president was historic and seemed to defy the "facts" of American politics. But the heady success of the 2008 election was mirrored by the 2010 midterm "shellacking" as the president had to argue that his consequential, but controversial, policy agenda had prevented disaster even if it had not restored economic boom times. A 50-50 nation is the result as 2012 approaches.Counter-factual will need to become factual for the Obama administration to live up to its transformative potential.

JOEL D. ABERBACH, UNIVERSITY OF CALIFORNIA, LOS ANGELES

How have President Obama's actions matched up to candidate Obama's vision of large-scale change? The record is mixed, owing to a combination of historical circumstance, robust partisan opposition, and the president's own choices. Yet perhaps the most fascinating thing about the Obama administration after two-plus years in office is the utter confusion about what it is.

GEORGE C. EDWARDS III, TEXAS A&M UNIVERSITY

Presidential success rests not upon persuasion of legislators or the public, but upon the presidents' facilitation of policy change within the constraints of the political context they inherit: they cannot create new opportunities, but only take best advantage of those that exist. Obama (hardly alone among presidents) misread his electoral mandate and overestimated his own persuasive abilities, given a hugely divided country.

Preface and Acknowledgments

The presidency of Barack Obama will surely be regarded as one of the most conse-quential, and controversial, in American history. It deserves sustained study along many lines—after all, Obama's would be a landmark administration if only for the multiracial background of the president himself, the first person of African Amer-ican descent to hold America's highest office. But the crisis-wracked times in which Obama took office, and his ambitious response to them, have been hugely impor-tant in their own right. Rather than peace and prosperity, Obama inherited war and recession—and the administration's struggles against both, while simultane-ously establishing its own agenda, have been marked by a complicated sequence of successes and setbacks.

These have not always been easy to track, nor have they always worked in tandem. Even as Obama and the nation reveled in the dramatic announcement of the death of Osama bin Laden, Washington politics continued as usual. Jubilant crowds gathered; the president urged Americans to "think back to the sense of unity that prevailed on 9/11."[1] But within two days the House had returned to its consid-eration of contentious measures banning abortion funding and repealing parts of the 2010 health care reform law while the Senate had stalled once more over judicial nominations and competing jobs bills.[2]

Indeed, Obama's presidency has unfolded in a savagely polarized partisan set-ting. The "Obama doctrine," it has been observed, is that he doesn't have one—and while this pragmatism has real advantages it also offers ammunition to both ends of that spectrum. His critics on the right call him "the most radical president we've ever had,"[3] and suggest he is practically (sometimes literally) un-American.[4] His critics on the left wish he was far more radical, on issues ranging from health care and entitlement reform to the legal regime underpinning the "war on terror"—a phrase that has been downplayed by the administration, but a reality its policies reflect. Some decry Obama's "no drama" deliberative style as dithering indecisive-ness; others applaud the president's unwillingness to embrace dogmatic certainty and his predilection to suit policy to situations as they arise.[5] Some argue that the president's policy plans are out of touch with the public mood; others charge instead that the administration simply lacks a readily comprehended overarching narrative that might have anchored its legislative victories in the political arena. The last Gallup approval poll of April 2011 showed 46 percent approving of Obama's performance and 46 percent disapproving: a 46-46 president in a 50-50 nation.[6]

Sorting out these divisions and contradictions, and linking them to what political scientists know about presidential behavior and American politics, is the task of this book. This volume provides one of the first systematic assessments of the Obama presidency. It offers appraisals of the administration's tactics and strategies as it took office and transitioned from the historic 2008 campaign; of the policy agenda it developed; and of its legislative strategy and its interbranch relations more generally. And it suggests how past policy—and politics—may affect the administration's prospects, not least for 2012.

To be sure, no matter when a project like this goes to press, it cannot keep up with the news.

As of this writing, debates over the impact and meaning of bin Laden's death dominate the airwaves. Southern states struggle to clean up after violent tornadoes that killed more than three hundred people. American and allied warplanes fly sorties over Libya. Neighboring Tunisia and Egypt struggle to effect a transition to democratic rule. Japan tries to recover from a horrific earthquake and tsunami— and to prevent nuclear reactors damaged by those blows from becoming their own disasters. A divided European Union seeks to shore up its weakest economies. Oil prices rise. Meanwhile, the president and Congress struggle to negotiate the coming year's budget after finally completing the current year's, six months late—with the real possibility of a government shutdown or even default lurking in that impasse. Meanwhile the Iowa caucuses, lurching ever closer, remind us that electoral imperatives are never far from Washington minds.

In short (as Richard Neustadt wrote long ago), "by present standards, what would once have been emergency is commonplace." Yet "politics as usual" continues unimpeded.[7] Presidents must be multitaskers, and we don't know what challenges will come to the forefront of the White House agenda.

Thus the value of this book, we hope, lies in illuminating the politics and governance strategies that undergird the Obama administration, and how they might be applied to the tests that await. How has President Obama reacted to the "political time" in which he finds himself?[8] How does he make decisions? How does he make policy, communicate, campaign, lobby, persuade? Our goal here is to balance detailed coverage of contemporary events with the ways those events fit—and can be explained by—generations of scholarship regarding presidential behavior and the American political system. As such, it is designed for scholars and students alike, especially as a supplementary text for courses on American government or the US presidency. It is both accessible and accurate; we look forward to the conversations its chapters should spark.

We are grateful to all those who have helped bring this project to fruition. First and foremost, of course, that means the contributing authors, whether veterans of this series or newly recruited for this volume. As in previous iterations, we have tried to provide a generational and topical mix that illuminates new research on the presidency, and we are delighted that a wide range of top-notch scholars from around the world have once again agreed to lend their seasoned judgments to this volume.

Special thanks must go to our extraordinarily supportive (and patient!) team at CQ Press, especially editorial director, editorial assistant Nancy Loh Charisse Kiino, production editor Elizabeth Kline, copy editor Kathryn Krug, and those on the marketing team, including Erin Snow, Chris O'Brien, and Chloe Falivene.

And finally, our deep thanks to our families and colleagues. Your support and sacrifices often go unnoted—but never unappreciated.

Notes

1. "Remarks by the President on Osama bin Laden," Office of the Press Secretary, The White House, May 2, 2011.
2. Jennifer Steinhauer and Carl Hulse, "Good Feeling Gone, in Congress Anyway," *New York Times*, May 4, 2011.
3. See Matthew Continetti, "The Paranoid Style in Liberal Politics," *The Weekly Standard* 28 (April 4, 2011).
4. In response to the "birther" movement noted in this volume, the president ultimately felt compelled to respond to "this silliness" by requesting that the state of Hawaii waive normal procedure and release his long-form birth certificate. See Michael D. Shear, "With Document, Obama Seeks to End 'Birther' Issue," *New York Times*, April 27, 2011.
5. Timothy Egan, "In Defense of Dithering," *New York Times*, March 24, 2011, available at http://opinionator.blogs.nytimes.com/2011/03/24/in-defense-of-dithering/ (accessed March 31, 2011).
6. See http://www.gallup.com/poll/113980/Gallup-Daily-Obama-Job-Approval.aspx (accessed May 4, 2011). While the killing of Osama bin Laden gave Obama's ratings a significant boost in early May, it seemed unlikely that rally effect would be sustained long.
7. Richard E. Neustadt, *Presidential Power and the Modern Presidents* (New York: Free Press, 1990), 5.
8. Stephen Skowronek, "Presidential Leadership in Political Time," in Michael Nelson, ed., *The Presidency and the Political System*, 8th ed. (Washington, DC: CQ Press, 2005), 89-135.

CHAPTER 1

Introduction:
A Counterfactual Presidency

Andrew Rudalevige and Bert A. Rockman

IF F. SCOTT FITZGERALD was right that the mark of a first-class mind is the ability to hold two contradictory ideas at once, then understanding the Obama adminis-tration must require something akin to genius.

The competing narratives that accompany the past few years might bring on whiplash. Is Obama too liberal, too activist, too eager to drive the nation toward some sort of socialist paradise? Or is he too moderate, too conciliatory, too willing to sell out his base? Is he too eager to be a "movement leader" rather than a politician—or is he too far down in the partisan muck his campaign promised to transcend? His administration was attacked both for its efforts to expand the size and scope of government and the inability of the government to command the creation of new jobs or plug underwater oil wells. Praised as a great communicator, he was upbraided for failing to provide a "master narrative for his presidency."[2] Hailed as a pioneering and inspiring president for his multiracial background and multinational upbringing, he was reviled and doubted for the very same reasons.

Surely Barack Obama arouses both adulation and—not to put too fine a point on it—hatred. And these contradictory critiques run in parallel with contradictory behavior by voters—or, if not contradictions exactly, sharp reversals in rapid sequence so precipitous that they might as well be contradictions. We find our-selves examining a presidency that is distinctly historic, yet very much constrained by its times, that of a polarizing figure in a polarized world, with a consequential but hugely contentious record at the midterm.

The goal of this volume is to begin to unravel the complexities of policy, poli-tics, and polemics that have marked the last few years and that shape the challenges of governance through (and well beyond) the 2012 election. The goal of this prefa-tory chapter, fortunately, is less ambitious. In what follows we seek to provide some historical context, to lay out the plan of this book, and to lay out some thematic ammunition to give readers a consistent frame across the chapters.⟩

Getting Elected, Taking Office: What (Political) Time Was It?

The notion of "political time," advanced by the political scientist Stephen Skowronek, hinges on the broader historical context of a given presidency. ⟨For Skowronek a president's "warrant" to reshape the American state depends on his relationship to the dominant governing coalition and the strength and cohesiveness of that coalition. Presidents who enter office as defenders of an established order that has grown unpopular may find themselves merely presiding over its dissolution. But presidents elected when an old regime has grown weakened and divided have the opportunity to "reconstruct" politics and establish a new relationship between the government and the people.[3]⟩

Many people expected that Barack Obama was at least potentially a "president of reconstruction," in these terms. After all, in the 2008 election he carried twenty-eight states and won a higher percentage of the two-party vote than any candidate for two decades (and a higher share than any Democratic candidate since 1964). He captured "red" states such as Indiana and made significant inroads into the long-Republican south, winning Virginia and North Carolina along with Florida. Democrats netted twenty-one new seats in the House and eight in the Senate, even reaching the magic number of sixty members for cloture.[4]

The outlines of Obama's "back story" are well-known.[5] For our purposes it is enough to begin in 2004, when a little-known candidate from the US Senate, a self-described "skinny kid with a funny name," gave the keynote address at the Democratic National Convention. His stirring call to national unity—a call admittedly unheeded in the 2004 campaign and its aftermath—suggested the rise of a new, unpolarized politics, a vision that was post- or perhaps supra-partisan. "There are those who are preparing to divide us, the spin masters and negative ad peddlers who embrace the politics of anything goes," he said. "Well, I say to them tonight, there's not a liberal America and a conservative America—there's the United States of America. There's not a black America and white America and Latino America and Asian America; there's the United States of America."[6]

The speech caused a sensation (far outshining that of the party's presidential nominee, Senator John F. Kerry) and Barack Obama was on the national map. He won his Senate seat that November; Kerry lost; and by 2007, Obama had decided to run for president, taking on far more experienced and well-known candidates. Most prominent among them was the embodiment of the Democratic Party establishment, Senator and former first lady Hillary Rodham Clinton. Clinton had the experience, the name recognition, and (at least to start with) the cash—Obama had the story, the oratory, and a savvy grasp on local organizing. He knew both the fine print of the delegate selection rules (as it would turn out, Clinton's high-priced consultants did not) and how to use new technologies for tried and true purposes: namely, for getting out the vote. After a long, drawn-out primary fight, he defeated Clinton to become the Democratic nominee—and the first African American candidate nominated by a major party for national office.

And then, of course, he won. In the wee hours of election night, as Obama's victory became clear, crowds gathered spontaneously in American cities to celebrate, as if it were New Year's Eve. Tears were shed and backs were slapped. All this, coming on top of the 2006 gains that had restored their majority to both chambers of Congress, sparked high hopes among giddy liberal activists (and not a few academics) for a new, lasting Democratic majority. Though son of one president, George W. Bush had cast himself as heir to another, Ronald Reagan; but in the wake of the 2008 election, what historian Sean Wilentz had termed the Age of Reagan seemed complete, and the Age of Obama begun. As it polled in late 2008, Gallup found only four states it could rate as "solid[ly] Republican" and one more leaning that way.[7]

This optimism was artificial, of course, and events proved it to be misleading. In November 2010 the Republican party swept to widespread congressional (and state house) victories, swamping the blue map with red. The GOP went from 179 House seats to 242, a gain of 63 House seats; the Democratic majority in the Senate shrank to 53. Obama himself termed the results a "shellacking."

In some ways this result was shocking—the House swing was the largest at the midterm since 1938. In some ways, though, it was predictable. After all, the Democratic moment of good feeling went against the deeper grain of partisan identification: some fifty House districts that had voted for John McCain in 2008 had Democratic members of Congress in 2010, and most returned to Republican control. And Obama and the Democrats had benefited from a particularly unpopular predecessor, even in 2006 but especially in 2008.[8] Immediately prior to the latter election, more than nine in ten Americans felt that the country was "on the wrong track,"[9] and George W. Bush left office with a paltry 22 percent approval rating. In a national poll conducted a month after the election, when public sympathy for an outgoing incumbent often kicks in, large majorities criticized Bush's handling of the economy, foreign policy, and the Iraq war; only 18 percent of respondents said they "were going to miss him" when he left office.[10]

There were reasons for this. The economy was shedding jobs at an enormous rate, while most investment indices had plummeted 40 percent or more in 2008 alone. Two wars were ongoing, in Iraq and Afghanistan, as well as a broad array of controversial initiatives aimed at the wider "war on terror." Efforts to deal with pressing issues such as entitlement reform and the immigration system had fallen well short of success and even, arguably, been counterproductive.

* Economic unrest and foreign conflict perpetuated nat'l disapproval of the Bush administration

This inheritance placed the Obama presidency—in sharp contrast to the Obama campaign—in a particularly intractable governance environment. White House chief of staff Rahm Emanuel would later sardonically comment on the Bush "gift bag" to the new administration: it included an "automobile industry that was on its back, a country that had almost doubled the national debt on his watch, an economy that was now experiencing the deepest recession in history since the Great Depression, and a financial system that was in its worst contraction in fifty years. That is exactly the gift bag that was left."[11] In his inaugural address, Obama counseled patience: "the challenges we face . . . are serious and they are many. They will not be met easily or in a short span of time." And he claimed that, contrary to those who might "question the scale of our ambitions, . . . the stale political arguments that have consumed us for so long no longer apply."[12]

But patience is not one of the strong points of American politics. And if the long-standing rancor of political discourse had likewise tried the public's tolerance, that hardly meant it had dissolved into the ether. The president soon realized the challenges. "I've been running for this bus," he said; "And now I've caught it. And it's a big bus."[13]

Driving the Bus

If it was a big bus, Obama had big plans. By the end of 2010, a trio of statutes with immense impact—a $787 billion package to stimulate the economy, the most comprehensive changes to Wall Street regulation since the Great Depression, and an ambitious extension of health care coverage to thirty million uninsured Americans—had become law. So had a variety of other measures, from the repeal of the military's "don't ask, don't tell" policy, to new regulation of the credit card industry, to overhaul of the student loan industry. Billions of dollars had been pumped into the American automotive and financial industries. Two new justices had joined the US Supreme Court. A new strategic arms treaty with Russia had been ratified. The 2001 tax cuts—and a wide range of unemployment benefits—had been extended in a second effort at economic stimulus at the end of 2010.[14] Further, Obama had begun to withdraw troops from Iraq, while beefing up the US and NATO military presence in Afghanistan. He had issued executive orders affirming the Freedom of Information Act, barring torture, and erasing the Bush-era legal precedents governing detainee treatment. He had even won the Nobel Peace Prize.

Yet for all the activity, public discontent continued and even expanded, as the midterm election results made consequentially clear—the 111th Congress held "the odd distinction of being both historically busy and epically unpopular."[15] In the spring of 2011, the Dow Jones Industrial Average had topped 12,000, after dipping below 7,000 in March 2009; but job growth remained painfully slow and the unemployment rate had lingered above 9 percent for the longest stretch since the early 1980s (it finally fell to 8.9 percent in February 2011). Though GDP was growing, slowly, and had been since late 2009, two thirds of the public felt the economy was still in recession in 2011.[16] The stimulus boosts had helped open record short-term budget deficits, and no progress had been made toward reforming the spending on entitlement programs that made closing the long-term structural deficit increasingly implausible. Immigration reform and climate change legislation failed to gain traction. An underwater oil well explosion in the Gulf of Mexico spewed pollution for more than three months, exposing the rickety regulatory regime for such drilling and reopening old debates between environmentalists and those seeking energy independence. The president had ordered the closure of the detention center at Guantanamo Bay, Cuba, but it remained open; and many of the administration's tactics in the war on terror were reminiscent in practice, if not exactly parallel in rationale, of its predecessor's.

Thus liberals complained from the left; conservatives complained from the right; and a new populist anti-tax movement sprang loudly to life. The promise of partisan unity had been achieved only within each party—polarization in Congress reached new heights by 2010.[17]

A new call for civility in public discourse was sparked by the murder in Tucson of six people and the critical wounding of the congresswoman they were waiting to meet—with one of the deaths a young girl who had been born, with heartbreaking irony, on September 11, 2001. But even as Obama's calls to make government worthy of the victims' best hopes garnered widespread acclaim, and his approval ratings rose back past 50 percent in early 2011, Senate minority leader Mitch McConnell (R-KY) laid down a new marker for the president's efforts to shift to centrist ground in the 2010 lame-duck session and in the 112th Congress. "We will see," McConnell said, "if he actually wants to work with us to accomplish things that we're already for."[18] Such were the constraints on the president's power to persuade as the nation began a new era of divided government.

The Plan of the Book

This volume presents a roster of distinguished scholars with dual assignments. They aim to step back, to view these developments from the broader perspective of how historical context, and research on the presidency, can inform our understanding of ongoing events; and to zoom in, to detail the substance of the policies traced above and the notable institutional developments and inter-branch relationships of the Obama administration.

The chapters that follow start with the wider angle. Leading off, Joel Aberbach provides a broad overview of the administration to date and an update on the progress of the 2008 campaign promise to provide "change we can believe in." How have President Obama's actions matched up to candidate Obama's vision? Where they have fallen short, Aberbach argues, this is partly due to circumstances, partly to robust partisan opposition to the president, and partly to Obama's own choices. "Perhaps the most fascinating thing about the Obama administration after two years in office is the utter confusion about what it is," he notes.

A systematic evaluation of the opportunities facing Obama upon his accession to the presidency, and his strategic response to them, is provided in the next chapter by George Edwards. Less sanguine than Aberbach, Edwards argues that presidents cannot create new opportunities; they must take advantage of those that already exist. They facilitate, rather than forge, policy change. Obama (hardly alone among presidents) misread his electoral mandate and overestimated his own persuasive abilities given a hugely divided country.

The next chapters expand on some of these themes. James Campbell, for instance, examines the 2008 elections, to see why Obama won—and their aftermath, as he sought to govern. Campbell argues that Obama's general policy strategy was to appeal to his left-leaning base, not to the middle; but that in a country that remains to the center-right of the ideological spectrum, this was not an approach that was likely to be successful. Obama will need to move back to centrist ground—perhaps forced there by the 2010 midterm results—in order to win back majority support for 2012. But Gary Jacobson's subsequent analysis makes clear how polarized the nation is, and thus how difficult building a majority coalition has become. In a detailed disaggregation of public opinion, Jacobson pays close attention to the components of presidential and policy approval, as well as the Tea Party phenomenon and the attitudes of its adherents.

From these systematic takes on public opinion, the analysis moves to the intersection where that public meets presidential institutions. Diane Heith discusses the Obama administration's quest for the politician's holy grail: the ability to communicate directly with the mass public without mediation or commentary. She concludes that the tools of social media and outreach were successful in reaching the White House's supporters, but perhaps not the wider public; and that competing voices still threatened to drown out Obama's efforts. Further, traditional media outlets resented the efforts of the administration to evade their scrutiny. Larry Jacobs, by contrast, suggests that the direct outreach efforts launched through the new Office of Public Engagement suffered for another reason: they were, to some extent, disingenuous. Interest group connections, as exhibited in interactions on issues ranging from health care to financial reform, remained an "inside game."

The next group of chapters builds on this institutional lead-in. The structure of the White House, and the information flow of Obama's advising structures, is examined by Andrew Rudalevige. He notes Obama's efforts to gain leverage over the tough choices he had to make, and argues that for various reasons Obama did not fully implement his campaign endorsement of Abraham Lincoln's "team of rivals" model. Barbara Sinclair details Obama's legislative strategy and his relations with a Congress that successfully enacted large-scale new laws but whose makeup and rules encouraged minority recalcitrance—and, in the Senate, empowered it. David Yalof turns to Article III, assessing how the administration dealt with the judiciary and with the legal issues it inherited from George W. Bush. He suggests that Obama's approach to judicial restraint led to a relatively hands-off approach to this aspect of inter-branch relations, a recalcitrance that he may have cause to regret.

Finally, three chapters detail the substance and success of the Obama agenda in three key areas. As suggested above, in a wide variety of arenas, this has been a consequential period in American policymaking. Christopher Foreman, Robert Singh, and Stephen Weatherford guide the reader through recent developments in domestic policy, foreign policy, and economic policy, respectively. Foreman chronicles the ambitions of the Obama domestic agenda—along with the structural obstacles facing its implementation. His efforts to shape long-term change while dealing with short-term crisis inevitably walked a tightrope. Likewise Singh, writing from London with a transatlantic eye on the administration's foreign relations, notes its difficult balancing act between acknowledging the constraints of a globalized world and a commitment to continued American leadership thereof. Replacing "Wilsonian militarism" with "restrained pragmatic realism" had important consequences, he argues, but was not brand new—in some ways Obama's term was perhaps more like the second term of George W. Bush, than Bush's second term was like his first. Weatherford seeks to lay out Obama's economic policy and his hopes to reduce American income inequality. He brings the volume full circle by arguing (contra Edwards) that the 2008 electorate supported major change in economic policy but (agreeing with Edwards) that Obama's election did not overthrow the dominant conservative ideology. Positive policy change did not lead to political reward; "in today's polarized political environment, no good deed goes unpunished."

The last chapter, by Bert Rockman, Eric Waltenburg, and Colin Campbell, provides a contextual coda that prompts us to consider both the situational and institutional aspects of the Obama presidency. Rahm Emanuel famously exhorted the administration not to let a crisis "go to waste"; but how much discretion—how many degrees of freedom?—did President Obama, no matter his talents, have in setting his own course? They assess the aims and strategies of the administration to date with an eye toward the interaction of the president as a person, the presidency as an institution, and the office's place in the wider system of American governance. What happens when exalted expectations meet political realities?

Looking Back, and Forward

No reader will agree with everything these authors conclude (for that matter, nor do we). Some of their assessments of the administration's thoughts and efforts are quite positive, others far less so. Consequential presidencies are likely to be controversial. We are confident that readers will find the vast array of information provided here invaluable in shaping their own informed judgments about the Obama administration's past, and its likely future.

In so doing it is tempting, of course, to seek a presidential analogue. The economic ravages facing Obama upon taking office inevitably occasioned references to Franklin Roosevelt. The potential clash between an expansive domestic agenda, the necessities of war, and the dictates of budget deficits perhaps suggested instead the trials of Lyndon Johnson. *Congressional Quarterly* asked the question "Truman, Reagan, or Clinton?" with reference to Obama's legislative strategy facing a newly divided Congress.[19] And the demands of the administrative presidency and homeland security brought to mind, sometimes uncomfortably for the administration, echoes of George W. Bush.[20]

Obama's administration did, of course, echo earlier themes from earlier presidencies. If history does not repeat itself, perhaps at least it rhymes.[21] And the post-midterm era certainly hinted of Clinton-era "triangulation," complete with the former president at the press secretary's podium and his staffers returning to key positions—though apparently the term itself was verboten in the White House.[22] Still, in his 2011 State of the Union address, Obama urged an aggressive program of long-term investment in education, research, and infrastructure, even in the face of rising pressures to control federal spending. Incrementalism would not solve national needs, he suggested: "We do big things."[23]

Whether a polarized polity hamstrung by deficit and debt can still do "big things" is an open question. To be sure, that Barack Hussein Obama became president in the first place was (as Vice President Biden might have put it) "a big [expletive] deal."[24] But that affirming counterfactual was matched by the administration's need (and inability) to achieve other counterfactuals that proved even stickier. Obama adviser David Axelrod observed that "the hardest argument to make in politics is that things could have been worse, when they're not good."[25] Yet that is where the president found himself with regards to economic policymaking. Abroad, he found himself walking a tightrope between American interests, constrained resources, and a range of problems from Japanese natural (and nuclear) disaster to newly unleashed revolution in the Middle East. And, having pledged his "brand" to a uniting vision of bipartisanship, the simple reality of contemporary politics—that well-honed party discipline is the key mechanism for legislative success—meant that even policy victories threatened to undercut Obama's broadest appeal.

Plato's perfect Republic exhibited the perfect balance between reason and passion, with reason firmly in control. "No drama Obama" would surely sympathize. But the American republic in the twenty-first century showed the continuing power of political passion and the claims of fear over hope, and even over Hope. Counterfactual will need to become factual—and the "professor-in-chief"[26] will need to reclaim the power of the presidential pulpit—for the Obama administration to live up to its transformative potential.

Notes

1. Mike Allen and Jim VandeHei, "Obama Isolated Ahead of 2012," *Politico*, November 8, 2010.
2. Timothy Egan, "A Big Idea," *New York Times*, December 7, 2010.
3. Stephen Skowronek, *The Politics Presidents Make* (Cambridge, MA: Harvard University Press, 1994); Skowronek, *Presidential Leadership in Political Time: Reprise and Reappraisal*, rev. ed. (Lawrence: University Press of Kansas, 2011).
4. That figure was not official until the long recount process to determine the result of the Minnesota Senate race confirmed the victory of Al Franken over incumbent Norm Coleman in July 2009.
5. For details, see Barack Obama's own autobiographies, the pre-political *Dreams from My Father* (New York: Times Books, 1995) and the more conventional *The Audacity of Hope* (New York: Crown, 2006); David Remnick, *The Bridge: The Life and Rise of Barack Obama* (New York: Knopf, 2010); Richard Wolffe, *Renegade: The Making of a President* (New York: Crown, 2009); and, on the 2008 election, Michael Nelson, ed., *The Elections of 2008* (Washington, DC: CQ Press, 2009).
6. Speech delivered at the Democratic National Convention, Boston, Massachusetts, July 27, 2004. Transcript available at http://www.barackobama.com/2004/07/27/keynote_address_at_the_2004_de.php (accessed March 22, 2011).
7. Sean Wilentz, *The Age of Reagan: A History, 1974–2008* (New York: Harper, 2008); Gallup, "State of the States: Political Party Affiliation," January 28, 2009. The states identified as "solid[ly] Republican" were Idaho, Utah, Wyoming, and Alaska, with Nebraska "leaning Republican." Twenty-nine states were rated as "solid[ly] Democratic" and six as leaning Democratic, leaving ten as competitive. Available at http://www.gallup.com/poll/114016/state-states-political-party-affiliation.aspx (accessed March 22, 2011).
8. President George W. Bush was, of course, hugely popular at other points in his administration. For an assessment of his complex and consequential presidency, see the essays in Colin Campbell, Bert A. Rockman, and Andrew Rudalevige, eds., *The George W. Bush Legacy* (Washington, DC: CQ Press, 2008).
9. See *New York Times*/CBS poll results, as published at http://documents.nytimes.com/latest-new-york-times-cbs-news-poll#p=1 (accessed March 22, 2011).
10. Nearly half of those asked said that Bush would be remembered as "definitely worse than most" of the recent presidents and another 30 percent said he would be remembered as

"not as good as most." Just 2 percent said he was "one of the very best." Hart/McInturff, Inc., *Survey #6091* conducted for NBC News/*Wall Street Journal* (Washington, DC: December 5–8, 2008), Questions 3, 4a, 4b, 4c, 4d, 26, 27, 28a.

11. Richard Wolffe, *Revival: The Struggle for Survival inside the Obama White House* (New York: Crown, 2010), 283.

12. President Barack Obama, Inaugural Address, January 20, 2009, available at http://www.whitehouse.gov/blog/inaugural-address/ (accessed March 22, 2011).

13. Quoted in Bob Woodward, *Obama's Wars* (New York: Simon & Schuster, 2010), 34.

14. Lisa Lerer and Laura Litvan, "No Congress since '60s Makes as Much Law as 111th Affecting Most Americans," *Bloomberg.com,* December 22, 2009; available at http://www.bloomberg.com/news/2010-12-22/no-congress-since-1960s-makes-most-laws-for-americans-as-111th.html (accessed March 22, 2011).

15. David Fahrenthold et al., "Stormy but Highly Productive 111th Congress Adjourns," *Washington Post*, December 23, 2010.

16. According to the Rasmussen Consumer Index, January 31, 2011. Available at http://www.rasmussenreports.com/public_content/business/indexes/rasmussen_consumer_index/rasmussen_consumer_index (accessed March 22, 2011).

17. See, e.g., Joseph J. Schatz, "2010 Vote Studies: Presidential Support," *CQ Weekly*, January 3, 2011, 18.

18. Jeff Winkler, "McConnell 'Skeptical' about Obama's Centrist Rhetoric ahead of State of the Union," *Daily Caller*, January 25, 2011, available at http://dailycaller.com/2011/01/25/mcconnell-skeptical-about-obamas-centrist-rhetoric-ahead-of-state-of-the-union/ (accessed March 22, 2011).

19. Schatz, "2010 Vote Studies: Presidential Support," 24.

20. See, e.g., Charlie Savage, "Obama's War on Terror May Resemble Bush's in Some Areas," *New York Times*, February 17, 2009; Andrew Rudalevige, "Bureaucratic Control and the Future of Presidential Power," *White House Studies* 10 (2010): 139-57.

21. This observation is often attributed to Mark Twain.

22. Ari Berman, "Obama: Triangulation 2.0?," *The Nation*, February 7, 2011.

23. "Remarks of the President in the State of the Union Address," Office of the White House Press Secretary, January 25, 2011.

24. Rachel Weiner, "Biden to Obama: 'A Big [Expletive] Deal,'" *Washington Post*, March 23, 2010, available at http://voices.washingtonpost.com/44/2010/03/did-biden-tell-obama-signing-w.html (accessed March 22, 2011).

25. Quoted in Wolffe, *Revival*, 158.

26. Jonathan Alter, *The Promise: President Obama, Year One* (New York: Simon & Schuster, 2010), 267.

CHAPTER 2

"Change We Can Believe In" Meets Reality

Joel D. Aberbach

THE OBAMA ADMINISTRATION IS CLEARLY HISTORIC and represents a remarkable change in a nation that only a half century ago permitted legal racial discrimination in much of its territory. But the change was advertised as going well beyond an ascriptive characteristic of the president. The administration entered office in the midst of a huge financial crisis, with promises to bring substantial changes to the nation. Its major campaign document was titled *Blueprint for Change*,[1] its campaign book was titled *Change We Can Believe In*,[2] and its initial budget document was titled *A New Era of Responsibility: Renewing America's Promise*. As President Obama said in his message accompanying the budget:

> The time has come to usher in a new era of responsibility in which we act not only to save and create new jobs, but also to lay a new foundation of growth upon which we can renew the promise of America.[3]

My mission in this chapter is to focus on the executive branch under Obama, with emphasis on the philosophy and style of the Obama presidency, the extent to which the Obama administration has been similar to or different from its predecessors—especially its immediate predecessor, Obama's appointments strategy, and what has happened so far in his attempts to implement his program. My

This chapter is a much-revised version of a lecture given at the Rothermere American Institute at the University of Oxford. I thank the director of the Institute, Nigel Bowles, for inviting me and members of the audience for their questions. Thanks also to Bert Rockman and Andy Rudalevige for their comments and suggestions and to Tiffany Chow for coding the data in tables 2.1 and 2.2.

approach here is to look first at what Obama promised during the campaign in order to give an indication of what people expected of him and, to the degree one can rely on such things, what he expected of himself; second, at the appointments strategy he followed (with its attendant opportunities and problems) and the way he has organized his administration; and finally at what has happened so far in his attempts to implement his program. I'll conclude with an overall evaluation of the administration so far, with emphasis on what its experiences imply for presidential power and for the future of the Obama presidency.

Before getting into the core of the chapter, let me make a few brief comments on the unique nature of Obama the man. In his nomination and general election campaigns, he communicated hope for significant change and yet reassuring calm in the eye of the storm (and he had the advantage of a primary opponent who did not take him all that seriously at first as she positioned herself for the general election). One might characterize the situation as hope plus a bit of an enigma—the promise of significant change symbolized by his complex racial identity and suggested in the soaring rhetoric of his speeches, mixed with his reassuring calm and coolness and strong suggestions of pragmatism.

Peter Baker, writing in the *New York Times* on inauguration day 2009, gave a quite good description of the enigmatic side of Obama as exemplified in the transition period:

> He remains hard to read or label—centrist in his appointments and bipartisan in his style, yet also pushing for the broadest expansion of government in generations. He has reached across old boundaries to build the foundation of an administration that will be charged with hauling the country out of crisis, but for all the outreach he has made it clear he is centralizing policy making in the White House. He will eventually have to choose between competing advice and priorities, risking the disappointment or anger of constituencies that for the moment can still see in him what they hope to see.[4]

Still, over and over again he signaled his pragmatism, saying in his inaugural address, for example: "The question we ask today is not whether our government is too big or too small, but whether it works, whether it helps families find jobs at a decent wage, care they can afford, a retirement that is dignified. Where the answer is yes, we intend to move forward. Where the answer is no, programs will end." This sentiment was reiterated in his budget report,[5] and is a recurring theme in writings about him, at least by those who do not label him a dangerous radical of one sort or another.

Finally, and not necessarily consistent with his pragmatism in the long run, the Obama team early on signaled again and again that it regarded the current economic crisis as a golden opportunity as well as a tremendous challenge. What is now known as Rahm Emanuel's doctrine has been widely quoted: "You never want a serious crisis to go to waste. What I mean by that is that it's an opportunity to do things you could not do before." Or, as Larry Summers, the first head of the Obama administration's National Economic Council put it: "The recession is a critical economic problem—it is a crisis. But a moment when there are millions of people who are unemployed, when the federal government can borrow money over the long term at under 3 percent, and when we face long-run fiscal problems is also a moment of great opportunity to make investments in the future of the country that have lagged for a long time."[6] This is a classic "garbage can" situation, an opportunistic wedding of a problem to a policy preference that may not be particularly appropriate to solving the problem at hand.[7] An example would be the numerous policy changes or modifications that were matched to instruments like the stimulus package ostensibly meant to address the economic crisis. Perhaps pragmatist or centrist pragmatist is not adequate to describe Obama. Another possibility is that he is—dare I make up a label?—a "visionary pragmatist," someone who is a moderate or centrist for the most part but who knows how to seize the moment for proposing and implementing changes that have substantial impact on society. That characteristic has many virtues, but leaves him open to misinterpretation by friend and foe alike.

What Was the "Change We Can Believe In"?
What Did Obama Promise?

Obama promised a huge array of things, as most presidential candidates do. At the risk of being biased in some way in my selection, let me emphasize some that were particularly prominent. These are taken from the *Blueprint for Change* and *Change We Can Believe In: Barack Obama's Plan to Renew America's Promise*.[8] He promised to make the government more effective and to cut wasteful spending; to restore fiscal discipline to the federal government and to provide immediate and more effective relief from the economic crisis with an emergency economic plan; to make the federal government more open and transparent; to free the executive branch of special interest influence; to make sure that Americans had an affordable health care system that improved (but maintained) the current private insurance system, preserved Medicare, and provided coverage for those who could not afford it through a tax subsidy program; to add new jobs through investment in national infrastructure; to promote energy independence and create a clean energy future and five million green jobs; to ensure the freedom to unionize (the Employee Free Choice Act); to protect Social Security; to reform the No Child Left Behind Act by improving its assessments and accountability systems; to provide effective pay equity for women; to provide stronger border and workplace enforcement and also a plan for eventual citizenship for those in the United States illegally; to strengthen enforcement of civil rights through ending politicization in the Civil Rights Division of the Department of Justice; to end the war in Iraq through "a responsible, phased withdrawal"; to finish the fight against Al Qaeda and the Taliban in Afghanistan; to expand the American military; to reaffirm US values in the conduct of the struggle against terrorism; to support Israel; to support veterans; and to restore respect for the rule of law and America's values. And lots more. One can argue that it was an admirable platform and certainly a change in direction or emphasis from many of the policies of the Bush administration, but for the most part it was not a platform of radical change or even one—with the possible exception of Iraq, where Obama had more credibility—that was much different than what Hillary Clinton or most mainstream Democrats had to offer. (And, indeed, she might have been more to the left on domestic policy, especially on health.) The change was, to a large degree, represented by the man himself. Because of his racial background, life story, and perhaps even the thing the Republicans mocked him for at their convention—his experience as a community organizer—he was demonstrably different, a change just by being himself. Better yet, he communicated brilliantly, at least in set speeches, and always projected a calm that reassured a public looking for something different after both the failed Bush presidency and the financial meltdown.

So what has his administration produced so far?

Appointments

If personnel are policy, appointments are an important gauge of at least potential policymaking.[9] One way to assess the nature and significance of Obama's appointments is to look at them in comparison to earlier administrations. Table 2.1 presents

TABLE 2.1   Traditional Cabinet Appointees:
Obama, Bush II, and Clinton Administrations

	Obama	Bush II	Clinton
% Female	26.7	21.4	21.4
% African American	6.7	14.3	28.6
% Latino	13.3	7.1	14.3
% Asian American	20.0	14.3	0
% Ivy League Education	33.3	14.3	21.4
% Other Private Education	46.7	7.1	50.0
% PhD	13.3	7.1	21.4
% Lawyers	40.0	50.0	71.4
% Republican	13.3	92.9	0
% Served in Clinton Administration	40.0	—	—
	(N=15)	(N=14)	(N=14)

[handwritten note:] ✱ Obama's apointees were not that radical (this certainly wasn't part of his 'change')

TABLE 2.2   Top Appointees (Includes Traditional Cabinet):
Obama, Bush II, and Clinton Administrations

	Obama	Bush II	Clinton
% Female	38.2	23.1	29.6
% African American	14.7	11.5	14.8
% Latino	5.9	3.8	7.4
% Asian American	11.8	7.7	0
% Ivy League Education	29.4	15.4	22.2
% Other Private Education	44.4	23.1	55.6
% PhD	17.6	15.4	22.2
% Lawyers	35.3	42.3	62.9
% Republican	5.9	88.5	0
% Served in Clinton Administration	50.0	—	—
	(N=34)	(N=26)	(N=27)

a comparative view of Obama's cabinet appointments as of March 4, 2009, in contrast to the early appointments of George W. Bush ("Bush II" in the table) and Bill Clinton, his two immediate predecessors. Table 2.2 broadens the perspective by including top appointees to positions that do not have cabinet status.

A look at the tables will show that Obama's cabinet and top officials were not all that unusual, at least demographically. In fact, if one was looking for change or something unusual about the Obama administration, this is clearly not the place to find it. Obama's cabinet was just a bit more female than those of his predecessors, had the smallest representation of African Americans (especially noticeable when compared to the Clinton cabinet), and had a higher percentage of Asian Americans and a lower percentage of lawyers than those of his predecessors. Other figures that stand out are the high percentage of Ivy League educated cabinet members (one-third) and the extraordinary percentage of those with degrees from private institutions (fully 80 percent of his cabinet). All in all, if one was to look at the cabinet in terms of change, the direction is toward a traditional definition of elite.

The data in table 2.2 add some valuable perspective, but do not alter the general view. The percentage of African Americans among Obama's total top appointees is now up to the level of the Clinton administration and Obama's administration has the most minorities overall among its top appointees—32.4 percent versus about 23 percent for Bush II and Clinton. However, there is little change among the rest of the categories, so the overall impression remains one of a more or less traditional set of elite appointees, with fewer lawyers than served at the top of previous administrations. If any administration stands out (aside from Obama's in the relatively low percentage of lawyers in top posts), it is the Bush administration, which had an unusually low percentage of top appointees with degrees from Ivy League or private institutions. Finally, while Hillary Clinton was the most notable Clinton person appointed to the Obama administration, fully 50 percent of Obama's appointees had served in the Clinton administration.

The initial appointments came fast and furious in the postelection period, but various ethics-related problems caused major embarrassment and, in at least the case of Tom Daschle, potentially with dire implications for the health care reform effort that was a major initiative of the administration. The effort at post-partisanship was also a mixed success at best, with an embarrassing withdrawal by Judd Gregg, apparently over an effort by the Obama White House to control preparations for the politically sensitive upcoming census. And there were also some complaints from liberals because of the many appointees from the political center. As one newspaper story noted of the foreign policy appointees: "Many liberal loyalists anticipated jobs in the new administration, but the president has filled out his foreign policy team largely with centrists connected to Clinton and the GOP. . . . The new president gave control of the three biggest national security fiefdoms to Clinton as his new secretary of State, holdover Robert M. Gates as Defense secretary, and retired Marine Gen. James L. Jones Jr. as national security advisor." Indeed, the account noted, one disappointed foreign policy intellectual said about his fellow job-seekers: "If they're not running into Hillary people, they're running into Republicans."[10]

Complaints from liberals were not confined to the composition of the national security team. Frank Rich of the *New York Times*, for example, in a column arguing that "The Brightest Are Not Always the Best" emphasized what he considered the less than stellar record of the Obama economic team. As he put it, "It's the economic team that evokes trace memories of our dark best-and-brightest past." Rich then went on to give his negative views on the records of Lawrence Summers, the new top economic adviser, and Timothy Geithner, the nominee for secretary of the treasury, both of whom he described as protégés of former treasury secretary Robert Rubin. Rich saw Rubin, along with Summers, as leading figures in the repeal of the Glass-Steagall Act and other decisions that contributed to the financial meltdown.[11]

There was also concern about other appointees. For example, another *Times* story focused on the mixed reviews that environmentalists gave to the appointment of Ken Salazar as secretary of the interior. One environmentalist described him as "a right-of-center Democrat who often favors industry and big agriculture in battles over global warming, fuel efficiency and endangered species." He went on to say of Salazar: "He is very unlikely to bring significant change to the scandal-plagued Department of Interior. It's a very disappointing choice for a presidency which promised visionary change."[12] The *Times* editorialized that Mr. Salazar might be "too nice" for the job, characterizing him as a "genial compromiser."[13]

My purpose here is not to endorse or criticize those who characterized some of Obama's appointees this way, but to emphasize that from the start of the administration there were doubts about just how much change it represented and criticisms of some of its most important personnel selections.

And that was just from the liberal side of the spectrum. Aside from the usual problems in making appointments and securing confirmations that have beset American administrations for years now—the Obama administration actually was slightly ahead of his two predecessor administrations in percentage of Senate-confirmed appointees at the 100-day mark, although it lagged badly compared to the four previous administrations in the percentage of appointees it had in place after one year, and in the time the Senate took to confirm nominees[14]—the Republican opposition made strong efforts to demonize some key appointees. Obama ended up giving recess appointments to individuals such as Craig Becker, accused of being too close to the labor unions (to the National Labor Relations Board) and to Dr. Donald M. Berwick, accused of being in favor of rationing health services (to run Medicare and Medicaid). He also had a high-profile nominee to run the Office of Legal Counsel at the Justice Department (Dawn Johnsen) withdraw from consideration in a dispute over her work for an abortion rights group.[15]

Finally, in a case I will touch on later concerning the nature of presidential power, President Obama gave a staff appointment (assistant to the president) to Elizabeth Warren, a move designed to bypass delaying tactics and then a battle over whether or not she should be the administrator of the new Consumer Financial Protection Bureau that she was instrumental in getting included in the 2010 financial reform bill. Opposition was more widespread in this case than in the other two, and there were serious concerns about a maneuver that went beyond a recess appointment in its implications for presidential power.

In short, the appointments process under President Obama did not produce a radically changed set of appointees compared with those of his predecessors (certainly in terms of demographic characteristics) and the process continued to be slow and conflictual. The latter is not particularly the fault of the administration, but a result of a system that has not adapted to political polarization in a Senate governed by rules that make controversial political appointments exceedingly difficult to get approved, and even noncontroversial appointments difficult to get approved in a timely manner.

On broader issues with respect to the bureaucracy, the huge economic problems the administration has faced tend to obscure its efforts to reform administration. The effort is in the usual areas and does not suggest much that is new or particularly innovative—eliminating "wasteful redundancy," streamlining procurement, reforming contracting and acquisition, and focusing on performance (with appointment of a chief performance officer)[16]—although final judgment should await more definitive study. Actions taken in these areas thus far, plus an announced federal pay freeze unlikely to improve the morale of federal workers, suggest not hostility to the bureaucracy and the civil service it employs but that the administration in its first two years felt that it had bigger fish to fry. Perhaps the reorganization effort President Obama announced in the 2011 State of the Union address portends a major emphasis on the bureaucracy, but early reactions by experts are highly skeptical that the administration's efforts will, when the smoke clears, be judged successful.[17]

Implementing the Obama Program

In this section I select from a list of the most significant promises made by President Obama and examine his administration's effectiveness in shaping or implementing the programs, policies, or approaches connected to those promises or to situations that have arisen during the first two years or so of its tenure. The list is necessarily incomplete and the analysis necessarily limited by the fact that in many areas the process is ongoing, but is meant to make a start toward an overall evaluation of the administration's effectiveness in conceiving and implementing what it promised to do or, by necessity, was forced to do.

Promote the highest ethical standards and free the executive branch of special interest influence: This was one of the key elements of Obama's pledge to bring change to Washington. Typical of the statements in his major campaign document was the following: "We are in this race to tell the corporate lobbyists that their days of setting the agenda in Washington are over."[18] It was an unequivocal statement, but the realities of life in Washington and the career experiences of many of those with political or policy expertise soon intruded. The aforementioned Tom Daschle, who was to be secretary of health and human services and a key player in health care reform, withdrew because of tax payment problems and Tim Geithner, confirmed as secretary of the treasury (the department in charge of the Internal Revenue Service), also faced confirmation criticism because he neglected to pay taxes that he clearly should have paid.[19] Bill Richardson, a likely secretary of commerce, withdrew because of an investigation connected to state contracts.[20] And then there was William J. Lynn, an ex–Raytheon lobbyist nominated for deputy defense secretary, whose nomination meant the rules about lobbyists issued on January 21, 2009, had to be waived only two days later, on January 23.[21]

Liberal critics were dismayed: "This is exactly why people are skeptical of politicians, because change we can believe in is the same thing as business as usual."[22] And conservatives were gloating: "After Obama's miraculous 2008 presidential campaign, it was clear that at some point the magical mystery tour would have to end. The nation would rub its eyes and begin to emerge from its reverie. The hallucinatory Obama would give way to the mere mortal. The great ethical transformations promised would be seen as a fairy tale that all presidents tell—and that this president told better than anyone. I thought the awakening would take six months. It took two and a half weeks."[23]

Make government more effective also got off to a less than auspicious start: The cause was with the administration's first choice for chief performance officer (Nancy Killefer). This was another tax problem, with the nominee to head this effort in trouble because of unpaid payroll taxes for a household employee.[24]

But there is potentially a more general problem with the policy czars (an informal term for someone appointed by the president to oversee administration in a given area and provide coordination across the government). They are meant to make policymaking and governing more effective, yet are just as likely to exacerbate internal friction. An excellent article by James Pfiffner analyzes the policy czar situation in the Obama administration, where "by one count, Obama had even more 'czars' than the Romanoffs, the Russian royal family that dominated Russia from 1613 to 1918, which produced 18 monarchs."[25] Pfiffner points out general problems with this system, such as unclear accountability and the fact that "czars are often frustrated because they are supposed to be in charge of policy, yet they do not have authority commensurate with their responsibilities." He cautions that even when czars do not use their influence in a heavy-handed manner, other White House staff may step in and complicate the situation even further.[26]

It is too early to judge just how effective this system has been. Administration records and participant memoirs will be needed to get a definitive answer. But as Pfiffner notes, "the larger the White House staff and the more czars that the president designates, the more likely the White House will be difficult to manage, and relations between the cabinet secretaries and White House staff will be strained."[27] The czar system can lead to embarrassing moments like one where the secretary of Health and Human Services (Kathleen Sibelius) had to admit in congressional testimony that she was not in charge of policy. However, Pfiffner says, neither was the health care czar, Nancy-Ann DeParle. The person really in charge, he says, was White House chief of staff Rahm Emanuel.[28] In the end, the administration did get a health care reform bill passed, so perhaps, for whatever reason, the system worked in this case.

But one thing is certain: the czars threaten Obama's transparency goal, where the overlapping portfolios (often across czars and certainly with the departments and agencies, let alone within the White House itself) promote the kind of opaque administration with complex lines of authority that Franklin Delano Roosevelt ran. The latter reveled in such a system, and it can work, but it's not the transparent system that Obama promised.

Cut wasteful spending: This will be a long slog, complicated by the initial need to get spending done under the stimulus package. In President Obama's February 24, 2009, address to the nation he mentioned savings of $2 trillion over ten years already identified by his budget team. He also stated the usual things about stopping fraud, waste, and abuse in federal expenditures. According to its first budget document, the administration had begun "an exhaustive line-by-line review of the Federal Budget,"[29] one that is actually scheduled to continue for some time. Cynics will remain skeptical until the cuts are fully identified and actually made. Many of the cuts in this document, it turns out, were projected savings from ending the war in Iraq, savings that have probably been offset by the unstable situations there and in Afghanistan and Pakistan.[30]

Restore fiscal discipline to the federal government, while making major program changes in health care, energy, and education: Obama promised this in his initial budget; he vowed, as just mentioned, to cut expenditures in Iraq, allow taxes on those earning above $250,000 to return to their pre-2001 rates, while cutting the budget deficit in half within a decade. As the *New York Times* account noted at the time, the budget document "contains many ambitious and costly programs that would have to be approved by Congress, including some that Republicans and fiscal hawks are likely to oppose."[31] The efforts to invest in clean energy, reform the health care system, and lift standards in the schools were, as the *Times* noted, both ambitious and costly. Whether and in what form these efforts, and the changes in taxes proposed, survive the internal bargaining and congressional processes over the years will determine what we actually see in the end. Experience so far (such as the trade-offs made to get health care reform through Congress and to get unemployment insurance extended in the lame-duck session in late 2010) suggests that the process (and product) is likely to be messy, convoluted, and strongly influenced by key stakeholders in and out of government.

With the budget deficit careening out of control, President Obama proposed a bipartisan panel to make recommendations for reducing annual deficits and addressing long-term budget problems. The proposal for a bipartisan commission to report after the 2010 elections did not receive the necessary number of votes in Congress, and the president then set up a commission by executive order. This commission made recommendations to cut deficits by almost $4 trillion in the next decade, but there is no guarantee that the recommendations will be voted on, let alone pass.[32] The basic problem is that Democrats do not want to endorse cuts in entitlements such as Social Security and Medicare, and Republicans find tax increases anathema. Indeed Republicans want to focus exclusively on spending cuts, though most are not anxious to be too specific on the cuts they have in mind. The Congress elected in 2010 promises much heat on deficit reduction, especially with Republicans in control of the House and under some pressure to craft legislation in this area, but the prospects for agreement on significant changes do not, as of this writing, appear bright.

Make affordable health care available to all: Obama's plan, as outlined in his campaign documents, seemed quite convoluted, something to worry about politically in light of the failure of the earlier Clinton administration plan that was significantly hurt by the difficulty in explaining it to the public. He attempted to offset the concerns of those already insured by promising to maintain the current system of private insurance for those who have it. While his initial budget proposal to set up a $634 billion "reserve fund" for transforming and modernizing America's health care system suggested the lack of a clear set of programs, it could reasonably be read as an appeal for pragmatic deal-making, evidenced by its language about "explor[ing] all serious ideas" and working with Congress while adhering to eight laudable principles.[33]

The history of the administration's effort to get health care reform enacted is covered in other parts of this volume. Suffice it to say, a reform bill was passed after an epic struggle and numerous deals and compromises that did relatively little to mollify opponents and has done relatively little for the president's standing with the public. It did, however, bring him recognition from many, particularly within his own political base, as someone who can accomplish big things. As the *New York Times* editorialized: "Barack Obama put his presidency on the line for an accomplishment of historic proportions. . . . Over time the reforms could bring about sweeping changes in the way medical care is delivered and paid for. They could ultimately rival Social Security and Medicare in historic importance."[34]

More will be known in the years ahead, and it will be a long time before many of the provisions of the bill are implemented, but as of late 2010 children will be able to remain on their parents' health insurance policies until they are twenty-six; children will no longer be denied coverage because of pre-existing conditions; people will no longer be dropped from insurance because of illnesses; and there will be access for the uninsured with pre-existing conditions through a subsidized high-risk pool.[35] The length of time that will elapse before full implementation of all the provisions of the bill leaves it vulnerable to sabotage by its opponents or even to repeal, legislatively or judicially. Still, there is a good chance that the public will find many, if not most, of the actual provisions much to its liking in practice, and that the reform will endure. If so, despite the initial absence of a public option and the sweetheart deals made with the drug companies, the *Times* prediction about the probable significance of the bill will become a reality.

Provide immediate and increased relief from the economic crisis with an emergency economic plan, and provide new jobs through national infrastructure investment: Like health care reform, this is an area where the Obama administration scored a significant legislative victory.[36] In the end, the stimulus plan Congress enacted may be regarded as the piece of legislation that did much to hold off a depression but, again like health care reform, the stimulus package has been highly controversial because it has not lived up to expectations.

When Mr. Obama signed the bill in February of 2009, he carefully announced that it would "not mark the end of our economic troubles," but he went on to say that it did "mark the beginning of the end" and that "we are putting Americans to work doing the work that America needs done in critical areas that have been neglected too long—work that will bring real and lasting change for generations to come."[37] Administration officials initially forecast that unemployment would peak at about 8.5 percent, forecasts that have been far off the mark and have come back to haunt them. While probably the best analysis so far of the effects of the stimulus (done by two respected economists, Alan Blinder and Mark Zandi) concluded that "the effects of the fiscal stimulus alone appear very substantial, raising 2010 real GDP by about 3.4%, holding the unemployment rate about 1½ percentage points lower, and adding almost 2.7 million jobs to U.S. payrolls,"[38] the failure of the overall situation to improve as expected and the underestimation of the course of the total unemployment figures have made the stimulus look like a huge failure to much of the public. As James Surowiecki argued in *The New Yorker*, "the stimulus—which, to begin with, was too small to completely offset the economy's precipitous drop in demand—was oversold. The Administration's forecasts about the recession (particularly regarding job losses) were too optimistic, and so its promises about what the stimulus would accomplish set the public up for disappointment."[39]

The bottom line is that the Obama stimulus package, inevitably a series of compromises as passed like most other American legislative packages, may have been a huge success in the eyes of some analysts professionally qualified to judge—and, according to a White House study at least, effective and relatively free from fraud[40]—but, due to inaccurate initial estimates and overselling, it is not given much credit by the public. It has been derided by opponents on the right as a waste of money and on the left for falling short of what was needed.

Work for a clean energy future: There was spending on this through the stimulus package (over $50 billion). There was also a firm promise by President Obama's nominee to head the Environmental Protection Agency (EPA), Lisa Jackson, to put science first in making decisions on environmental issues,[41] and a directive from President Obama to the EPA that it reconsider whether to grant California and other states waivers to regulate tailpipe emissions linked to global warming and to the Department of Transportation (DOT) to issue revised guidelines on fuel efficiency.[42] However, Obama in office has also been clear that there will be no "quick fix" to problems such as the US dependence on foreign oil. Rather he pledged on January 26, 2009, to "commit ourselves to the steady, focused, pragmatic pursuit" of energy independence,[43] and he committed to a cap-and-trade system that will net $150 billion over ten years to fund clean energy investments by fiscal year 2012.[44] This is perhaps the most promising (in terms of likely success) of his major initiatives, but the legislation establishing cap and trade, after passing the House, has been stalled in the Senate and unlikely to see action in the 112th Congress. Administrative action through EPA seems the most likely avenue for regulating CO_2 emissions, but will be controversial. Indeed, in the spring of 2011 the EPA announced new emission restrictions, even as a Republican-led House committee voted to strip the agency of the authority to do so.

While the BP oil spill was obviously not contemplated in Obama's campaign documents, I take this up here because of its relationship to energy and administrative problems. An oil well blowout in April of 2010 caused a huge problem for the Gulf Coast and for the Obama administration. The details are beyond the scope of this chapter, but from an administrative point of view the spill highlighted severe problems in the Interior Department agency in charge of such matters (the Minerals Mining Service, MMS) that the Obama administration had not corrected. The frustrating inability of the government to estimate correctly the extent of the spill, to get a well-coordinated response to the spill going immediately, and to solve the problem quickly, all damaged Obama politically. While much of this, with the exception of the inadequacies of the MMS,[45] was arguably not the fault of the administration and there was improvement once the "incident commander" (Admiral Thad Allen of the Coast Guard) began to fully assert himself, the agonizingly long process to cap the well did little to improve the image of the administration as an efficient and effective operation. President Obama attempted to recoup from the blow by dismissing the head of the Minerals Management Service (her resignation was requested by the Interior secretary) and by very publicly forcing BP to set up a $20 billion compensation fund that will be administered by Kenneth Feinberg, the mediator who successfully oversaw the compensation fund for victims of 9/11.[46] The whole incident—while probably handled reasonably well given the horrible circumstances, the constant gaffes by BP, and the long-standing (and embarrassing and uncorrected) problems in the MMS—did not cover the administration in glory.

Handle the bank bailout and related issues better than the Bush administration did: One would think that this would have been the proverbial "slam dunk." But, as the *Washington Post* said of Secretary Geithner's plan to overhaul the financial rescue effort of the Bush administration, "according to a wide consensus on Wall Street, in Washington and beyond," it lacked "freshness and clarity." As the story indicated, "Many of the specific policies Geithner offered were tweaks, adjustments or continuations of Paulson's strategy. And the more novel elements of the Geithner plan—the creation of an entity with public and private money to buy up bad assets from banks, a 'stress test' of 20 or so of the nation's largest banks, and $50 billion to prevent foreclosures—originally came with so few details about how they would work that it contributed to the very public anxiety and investor uncertainty that Geithner criticized."[47] There were also debates within the administration, won by Geithner (he favored limited restrictions), on how closely the government should dictate how banks spend government-provided money.[48] Soon there arose a marked disagreement between the administration and Congress over the stringency of executive bonus limitations contained in the stimulus bill, with the administration dismayed by strict language in the bill passed by Congress.[49] Liberal critic Paul Krugman summed up one perspective on policy in this area as follows: "The real question is why the Obama administration keeps coming up with proposals that sound like possible alternatives to nationalization, but turn out to involve huge handouts to bank stockholders."[50] All in all, not a strong performance to start, especially in light of the fact that most of the issues involved have been obvious since the fall of 2008.

However, in the end one can argue that the administration turned a situation where it received almost universal criticism into one that may have positive, lasting results. Much of the TARP money has been repaid to the Treasury. And in 2010 the administration achieved passage of a financial regulatory reform bill that "would limit some of the riskiest activities of banks and regulate the multitrillion-dollar market in over-the-counter securities. It would [also] give federal regulators the tools, if they need them, to shut failing large banks and financial firms instead of bailing them out."[51] There were criticisms of the limitations and exceptions in the bill, and a strong recognition that its effectiveness would in large part be determined by the way regulations implementing it are eventually written. With powerful interest groups lined up to influence the rule-making process, the outcome is far from clear,[52] but President Obama's action in making sure that Elizabeth Warren would have a large impact on the initial consumer regulations (see above) indicates a strong posture on the part of the administration and at least could eventually make the financial reform legislation close to what the president said it would be—part of "a new foundation" for the economy.[53]

Inaugurate a post-partisan era: One can argue that reaching out to Republicans did not generally work well for the first two years of the administration, but Obama did try at the start—and, with more success, at the end, during the 2010 lame-duck session of the Congress. The net result in the stimulus package was a greater emphasis on tax reductions (and alternative minimum tax [AMT] relief) than might otherwise have been the case and cuts to funds earmarked in the original bill for family planning. Critics (and Obama himself, later) faulted Obama for "compromising in advance" on the stimulus. In the end, he got no Republican votes in the House, but three crucial votes in the Senate. The same sorts of criticisms are easy to make about health care reform and the financial reform package, to take two prominent examples, but gestures to the opposition won a few votes on the financial reform and, perhaps just as important, did keep several crucial conservative Democrats, many of whom were swept into office when Obama was elected, on the administration's side in key votes in Congress.

Joel Achenbach argues that the kind of post-partisanship promised in Obama's book, *The Audacity of Hope*, is now as dated as *The Iliad*. "The common ground that Obama hoped for has turned out to be the size of a bathroom scale," Achenbach wrote, and his image, while not the most poetic, is surely correct.[54] The hope and the reality turned out to be nearly 180 degrees apart for most of the first two years.[55] On the other hand, during the 2010 lame-duck session, Obama managed a "surprising success," with ratification of the nuclear treaty with the Russians as well as repeal of "don't ask, don't tell," an extension of unemployment benefits, and a deal of sorts on tax cuts and inheritance taxes.[56] Many liberal Democrats were less than happy with the deal on taxes, but the public approved.[57] It is unlikely that this spirit of bipartisanship will last long in the new Congress, but for Obama himself it could be an image-restorer and certainly provided a temporary lift.[58] His speech in Tucson after the attempted assassination of the local congresswoman, Gabrielle Giffords, was well-received and boosted his call for "civility."

Restore America's place in the world: The administration's early foreign policy decisions and pronouncements caused tensions with President Obama's liberal base, particularly over aspects of policy on Iraq and, more vaguely, on Afghanistan.[59] Where to start? Perhaps with the appointment of Hillary Clinton, one of whose major policy differences with Obama was over Iraq. Then came a set of orders to close Guantanamo (but not immediately) and to use only the limited interrogation methods outlined in the Army Field Manual. That made his liberal critics somewhat happier, but this was somewhat offset by a court case in which the administration, much to the shock of the judges hearing the case, invoked the state secrets argument used by the Bush administration to withhold information. To quote the ACLU director about the case: "This is not change."[60] And a _New York Times_ story by Charlie Savage titled "Obama's War on Terror May Resemble Bush's in Some Areas," noted that "In little-noticed confirmation testimony recently, Obama nominees endorsed continuing the CIA's program of transferring prisoners to other countries without legal rights, and indefinitely detaining terrorism suspects without trials even if they were arrested far from a war zone."[61] The administration in May of 2009 said that it would use the military commission system to prosecute detainees and also refused to release photographs documenting detainee abuse.[62] The tension abated somewhat over time, but then in March of 2011, President Obama issued an executive order "that will create a formal system of indefinite detention for those held at the U.S. prison at Guantanamo Bay," the result of a complex set of events that left civil libertarians disappointed and the Republican chairman of the House Homeland Security Committee (Peter T. King) elated.[63]

On the wars in Iraq and Afghanistan, the administration unveiled and then followed through on plans to withdraw most (but not all) troops from Iraq by 2010, although between 35,000 and 50,000 will remain until at least the end of 2011 (with a reported promise to revisit the plan if circumstances change).[64] In the meantime, more troops have been sent to Afghanistan, with an exit plan aiming at July 2011 that the secretary of defense said would proceed in a way (pace and size) "to be determined in a responsible manner based on the conditions that exist at that time."[65] The Iraq decision did not play well with many liberals in Congress and the Afghanistan decision has also been a source of concern among liberal Democrats.[66] A book by Bob Woodward documents Obama's frustrations with the military leadership,[67] but at this point these are—as Woodward's book title suggests—"Obama's wars." The president is in a situation where, should the war continue to go poorly, the announced decisions on the war in Afghanistan (and the situation in Pakistan), whatever his behind-the-scenes reservations, can come back to haunt him in the future.

It is still too early to gauge the results of the president's efforts to change the views of the United States in much of the world. Ultimately, however, the course of the war in Afghanistan and the future situation in Iraq, as well as the development of the complex policies connected to the counterterrorism effort, will have a huge impact on the entire effort. The outcome is hardly assured, and the outbreak of revolutionary fervor in the Middle East in early 2011 only made matters more complicated.

Restore respect for the rule of law and America's values: This pledge was extraordinarily important to many of Obama's followers, a prime example of the kind of change that they expected from the new administration. It intersects with many of the other items already covered.

Early in the administration, Charlie Savage, the noted *New York Times* reporter who specializes in issues connected to presidential power, wrote: "Within days of his inauguration, Mr. Obama thrilled civil liberties groups when he issued executive orders promising less secrecy, restricting C.I.A. interrogators to Army Field Manual techniques, shuttering the agency's secret prisons, ordering the prison at Guantanamo Bay, Cuba, closed within a year and halting military commission trials. But in more recent weeks, things have become murkier."[68] What made things murkier were such things as statements by Elena Kagan, then the nominee for solicitor general and later named to the Supreme Court, that those accused of helping Al Qaida (in particular in the finance area) should be subject to indefinite detention without trial; the invocation of "state secrets" by the Obama Justice Department to shut down a lawsuit; and a clear signal on executive privilege that, in the words of then White House counsel Gregory Craig, the "president of the United States [should be mindful] not to do anything that would undermine or weaken the institution of the presidency."[69] In September of 2009 the Justice Department announced plans "to impose new limits on the government assertion of the state secrets privilege" by imposing a review by the attorney general "if military or espionage agencies wanted to assert the privilege to withhold classified evidence sought in court or to ask a judge to dismiss a lawsuit at its onset."[70] The *New York Times* and others denounced this as "An Incomplete State Secrets Fix" because so much rested on the willingness of the Justice Department to stand up to the intelligence agencies. As Senator Russ Feingold (D-WI) put it, without a mandate for a court review, it amounted to a policy of "just trust us."[71]

In one of the more bizarre cases of the assertion of executive power, the administration refused to allow its social secretary to testify before Congress on an incident involving gate-crashing at a White House dinner. To quote Mark Rozell, a noted scholar who writes on executive privilege, the administration's argument "doesn't even pass the laugh test, to be quite blunt about it. . . . This definitely goes against the president's own pledge for a more open administration, and to move beyond the secrecy practices of the Bush era." Emily Berman, of the Brennan Center for Justice at NYU School of Law, said that Obama "in many ways [has] fallen into the trap that a lot of leaders do. They come in with the best of intentions and the most forceful rhetoric. But they find that the temptations of governing push quite a bit against the initial statements."[72]

In March of 2010 the administration suffered the embarrassment of having a federal judge rule that "the National Security Agency's program of surveillance without warrants was illegal, rejecting the Obama administration's effort to keep shrouded in secrecy one of the most disputed counterterrorism policies of former President George W. Bush."[73] As James Risen and Charlie Savage note, candidate Obama had declared it "'unconstitutional and illegal' for the Bush administration to conduct warrantless surveillance of Americans. . . . But since Mr. Obama won the election, administration officials have avoided repeating that position."[74]

About a month later, James Risen was subpoenaed by the Justice Department (something that had to be approved by the attorney general) to testify about confidential sources he used in a 2006 book on the CIA and the Bush administration. The executive director of the Reporters Committee for Freedom of the Press said of this: "The message they are sending to everyone is, 'You leak to the media, we will get you.'"[75] The administration later took a hard line in another case, indicting a National Security Agency employee, Thomas A. Drake, for leaking information related to his conclusion that the NSA was squandering money. The reporter covering the case said the following: "The indictment of Mr. Drake was the latest evidence that the Obama administration is proving more aggressive than the Bush administration in seeking to punish unauthorized leaks to the press."[76]

It's not my purpose here to give a full account of all these incidents—one might add the Wikileaks spectacle to the list—or to say that the actions were uncalled for in light of the realities that the administration might have felt it faced, or even to endorse the views of many in these cases that the Obama administration has gone as far as or further than the Bush administration in these areas. I note simply that the administration's actions in these values-laden areas have often been a far cry from the change that it promised.

Teaching Realism

A prime element of Richard Neustadt's model for an effective president is the need to teach realism. Neustadt argues, "Because he cannot control happenings, a President must do his best with hopes. His prestige is secure while men outside Washington accept the hard conditions of their lives, or anyway cannot blame him. If he can make them think the hardship necessary, and can make them want to hear it with good grace, his prestige may not suffer when they feel it."[77]

President Obama entered office at a devastatingly difficult moment, with the economy in tatters and wars in both Iraq and Afghanistan. He had the further misfortune to inherit an economic crisis that, at least in its public manifestations, was relatively recent, making it almost inevitable that he would not be able to blame his predecessor for long once he assumed office. The economic problem would become his if not solved in relatively short order.

Further compounding the problem is the fact that he ran as a candidate of change. "Change we can believe in" indicates that something better is coming. Making that happen in the economic circumstances Obama inherited required a delicate approach that both taught realism about the amount of time change would take and presented evidence that change for the better was on the way. In the non-economic (great recession) sphere it required the president to satisfy the desire for his constituency for change in many of President Bush's policies while, ideally, making the post-partisan era he envisioned seem more than a dream.

Initially, there seems little doubt that Obama was quite effective in communicating to the public the seriousness of the economic situation and the time that it would take for his efforts to bear fruit. His critics, indeed, said that he had been so "realistic" that he was helping to depress the markets and depress consumption. Obama's address to the nation on February 24, 2009, was an attempt to add some optimism to the realism. As time went on, however, and especially when the unemployment rate did not go down as promised in conjunction with the economic stimulus, the public mood began to sour. Critics on the right claimed the stimulus was an ineffective device, while those on the left argued that it was inadequate. Neither interpretation did much to help the administration. It had tried to both set a sober tone and provide optimism, but the seriousness of the recession and its own inaccurate predictions on the impact of the stimulus on unemployment rates made its major policy to deal with the problem look like a failure even though, as Blinder and Zandi argue, the stimulus package may have actually been quite successful.

Beyond that, the record is hard to categorize. On the one hand, the administration has done what no predecessor managed: secured passage of a major health care reform. It signed into law a major reform of the financial system and appointed, though by means that skirt the usual procedures for filling major positions, a noted advocate for tough enforcement of the law. It has drawn down the troop level in Iraq, as promised, though now the question remains whether the situation is sustainable. In the 2010 lame-duck session it had additional successes in both foreign and domestic affairs, including the nuclear treaty with Russia and the repeal of "don't ask, don't tell." And it has made many sound appointments and issued regulations in many areas that at least its supporters should find vast improvements over what his predecessor did.

However, the administration has also disappointed many of its supporters. Part of this is due to compromises that are inevitable in the complex political system of the United States, especially as in the case of the Obama administration where, even though the majority Democrats had a big margin in the 111th Congress, nearly fifty conservative "Blue Dog" Democrats held the balance of power and Republicans would basically not cooperate at all. But another part, as documented in this chapter, is due to decisions made by the administration. Inevitably there were pressures of all sorts, but the administration made the choice to follow the course it did on such matters as state secrets and surveillance without warrants. One can say, as with the closing of Guantanamo, that reality (and Congress) intervened, but that is the core of Obama's current dilemma in dealing with those who supported him in the election—"change we can believe in" has often been either not the change that had been hoped for or, sometimes, little change at all. This has disillusioned some supporters and de-energized others, while doing little to attract anyone from the opposition.

So the record is mixed. Lots of admirable plans and goals, many of which an objective critic could pick apart in terms of design, likely effectiveness, or compromised nature, were all attempted against a backdrop of severe economic dislocation and a public that expected great change. Within a year, the bloom was off that rose, though successes in the lame-duck session and in early 2011 at least temporarily re-energized the administration and, it appeared, restored some of its public support.[78]

Conclusion

Perhaps the most fascinating thing about the Obama administration after two-plus years in office is the utter confusion about what it is. The right is convinced that Obama is, from its perspective, a dangerous socialist of some sort. While the more temperate among them do not describe him as a Muslim or as foreign born, they do seem to regard him as imbued with a kind of otherness that may be a not-too-subtle reflection of his race or, more charitably, a reflection of what they see as a genuine (and wrong-headed) desire to truly change the way the country works and the way its bounty is distributed. Liberals, on the other hand, see him as much too prone to compromise and, overall, every bit the pragmatist he said in his campaign coexisted with the change agent that he advertised to the Democratic Party. Indeed, to counteract what they perceived as Obama's tendency to temper "some of his liberal previous positions," a group called Accountability Now was formed by groups from organized labor, liberal bloggers, and MoveOn .org.[79] They were countered from the moderate right by people like columnist David Brooks who argued, after the introduction of Obama's initial budget, that he has "an agenda that is unexceptional in its parts but that, when taken as a whole, represents a social-engineering experiment that is entirely new." Brooks went on to say that moderates are now "forced to confront the reality that Barack Obama is not who we thought he was. His words are responsible; his character inspiring. But his actions betray a transformational liberalism that should put every centrist on notice."[80]

So what Obama is remains in the eye of the beholder, a product of the man, his sometimes colliding goals, his promises of change, his oft-repeated rhetoric/ mantra of pragmatism, and the stark realities of the political and economic landscape he must traverse.

It is probably fair to say that "Obama [continues to be] a work in progress,"[81] that he is a moderate in many, if not most areas, a pragmatic practitioner of what he calls "a new era of responsibility," but also demonstrably capable of proposing major changes when he believes the moment is right or necessity demands it. His administration has not had the smooth and cooperative course he probably hoped it would, but it must be graded against the enormity of the task it faced and credited with using the economic crisis effectively to get elements of its program enacted quickly through the stimulus bill and later through a highly polarized Congress.

Is it "change we can believe in"? For many who supported him, certainly not yet,[82] although there have been some big changes from his predecessor. For those who hoped for a truly fundamental revamping of the political and social order in their preferred direction, their disappointment is likely to last as long as Obama is president. Indeed, for many liberals, to quote Charles M. Blow from a June 2010 column in the *New York Times*, "the thrill is [already] gone." (Blow, by the way, pragmatically advises Democrats: "We have to stop waiting for him to be great and allow him to be good.")[83] Ironically, for those on the other side, like Newt Gingrich, who apparently believe, in contrast to critics on the left, that America under Obama has become a "secular-socialist machine," the change has gone far too far already. There is probably nothing Obama can realistically do that will give them pause.[84]

Richard Stevenson argued tellingly that "a year into his presidency, Mr. Obama [had] lost control of his political narrative, his ability to define the story of his presidency on his own terms. . . . The novelty factor has worn off, along with the power of his positioning as the not-Bush."[85] That is an excellent summary of the difficulty Obama faced at the time of the midterm elections, and I submit that his actions, both administratively and in purely policy terms, contributed to the problem. Some of it was probably inevitable: reality and "change we can believe in" often do not mesh well, especially in such a difficult economic environment—and, particularly among the committed, any change is likely to be too much modest for many on one side and much too radical for those on the other. Add the initial tendency to see what one wanted to see in Mr. Obama and to envision that he would do great things to transform the nation and its politics as one wanted them changed—then throw in the cold fact that the recession has been stubbornly deep and that Obama has kept policies in some sensitive and highly emotional areas that were more like those of Bush than many were led to expect—and the letdown should be no surprise.

But it is important to remember that Obama's situation is, to say the obvious, far from hopeless. He is *the president* and, as such, well positioned to use the office to reinforce the positives that go with the title, as he did in his speech in Tucson following the shootings there in January 2011. Going forward, he also has the advantage of a Republican-controlled House that he can make into a whipping boy if the opposition is too shrill and its threatened investigations of his administration too obviously partisan,[86] and a Republican Party that may go through divisive agony in choosing its nominee to oppose him. Countering this is the likelihood that, as a leading scholar of American politics notes, with the "prospects for bipartisan cooperation during the 112th Congress . . . not bright," Obama will act "more on his own authority and initiative within the executive than is desirable,"[87] a reality that, especially if his actions do not please them substantively, would continue to strain relations with his more liberal supporters. The good news for President Obama is that these supporters have nowhere else to go.

Notes

1. *Blueprint for Change*, www.barackobama.com, accessed 2/12/08.
2. *Change We Can Believe In: Barack Obama's Plan to Renew America's Promise* (New York: Three Rivers Press, 2008).
3. Office of Management and Budget, *A New Era of Responsibility: Renewing America's Promise* (Washington, DC: Office of Management and Budget, 2009), www.whitehouse.gov/omb/, p. 1.
4. Peter Baker, "Transition Holds Clues to How Obama Will Govern," *New York Times*, January 20, 2009, www.nytimes.com, accessed 10/6/10.
5. *A New Era of Responsibility*, p. 3.
6. Both quotes are from David Leonhardt, "The Big Fix," *New York Times*, January 27, 2009, www.nytimes.com, accessed 10/6/10.

7. The best study in American politics employing an approach derived from the "garbage can" model is John W. Kingdon, *Agendas, Alternatives, and Public Policies*, 2nd ed. (New York: Longman, 2003).

8. See notes 1 and 2 for complete citations.

9. See also the Rudalevige chapter in this volume.

10. Paul Richter, "For Obama Campaign Advisors, There's No Sure Thing," *Los Angeles Times,* February 11, 2009, www.losangelestimes.com, accessed 2/12/09.

11. Frank Rich, "The Brightest Are Not Always the Best," *New York Times*, November 7, 2008, http://www.nytimes.com/2008/12/07, accessed 12/8/08.

12. Kieran Suckling, quoted in "Environmentalists Wary of Obama's Interior Pick," *New York Times*, December 18, 2008, www.nytimes.com, accessed 12/17/08.

13. "Is Ken Salazar Too Nice?," *New York Times*, January 2, 2009, www.nytimes.com, accessed 1/2/09.

14. See Anne Joseph O'Connell, "Waiting for Leadership," Center for American Progress, April 2010, www.americanprogress.org, pp. 1-2.

15. See "Politics 1, Rule of Law 0," *New York Times*, April 13, 2010, www.nytimes.com, accessed 4/13/10. The story indicated that the White House was unwilling to get into a battle over Johnsen's appointment prior to President Obama's making his second nomination to the Supreme Court.

16. This list comes from the White House web page. It is not a featured section, but comes under "issues" of "Fiscal Responsibility." See www.whitehouse.gov/issues/fiscal, accessed 1/17/11.

17. See Robert Brodsky, "The Rocky Road to Reorganization, from Nixon to Obama," *Government Executive,* March 8, 2011, www.govexec.com, accessed 3/15/11; and Karen Tumulty and Ed O'Keefe, "History Shows Obama's Effort to Reorganize Government Could Be an Uphill Battle," *Washington Post*, January 27, 2011.

18. *Blueprint for Change*, p. 5.

19. Jeff Zeleny and David Stout, "Daschle Withdraws as Cabinet Nominee," *New York Times*, February 4, 2009, www.nytimes.com, accessed 2/3/09.

20. Jeff Zeleny, "Gregg Ends Bid for Commerce Job," *New York Times*, February 13, 2009, www.nytimes.com, accessed 2/13/09.

21. William Matthews, "Lynn Gets Waiver from Obama Lobbyist Rules," *Federal Times*, January 26, 2009, www.federaltimes.com, accessed 2/13/2009. Waivers were also issued for staffers such as Mark Patterson who represented Goldman Sachs and became chief of staff at Treasury, and others.

22. Melanie Stone, Citizens for Responsibility and Ethics in Washington, quoted in Peter Baker, "Obama's Promise of Ethics Reform Faces Early Test," *New York Times,* February 3, 2009, www.nytimes.com, accessed 10/6/10.

23. Charles Krauthammer, "The Fierce Urgency of Pork," *Washington Post*, February 6, 2009, www.washingtonpost.com, accessed 2/6/09.

24. Zeleny and Stout, "Daschle Withdraws as Cabinet Nominee."

25. James P. Pfiffner, "President Obama's White House 'Czars,'" *PRG Report*, Newsletter of the Presidency Research Group of the American Political Science Association, Spring 2010, p. 5.

26. Ibid., p. 6.
27. Ibid., p. 7. See also Anne E. Kornblut, "White House Moving to Repair Troubled Relationship with Cabinet," *Washington Post,* March 9, 2011, www.washingtonpost.com, accessed 3/9/11. A quote in the article from a person described as a "senior Democratic official" is quite revealing: "The czars keep people from getting in. The level of frustration is pretty high."
28. Pfiffner, "Czars," p. 7.
29. *A New Era of Responsibility,* p. 34.
30. See Singh's chapter in this volume.
31. Jackie Calmes and Robert Pear, "Obama Plans Huge Shifts in Spending," *New York Times,* February 27, 2009, www.nytimes.com, accessed 2/26/09.
32. See, among others, Brady Dennis and Lori Montgomery, "Deficit Plan Wins 11 of 18 Votes; More than Expected, but Not Enough to Force Action," *Washington Post,* December 3, 2010, www.washingtonpost.com, accessed 12/3/10.
33. *A New Era of Responsibility,* p. 27.
34. "Health Care Reform at Last," *New York Times,* March 22, 2010, www.nytimes.com, accessed 3/22/10.
35. Nancy-Ann DeParle, "What Happens Next," The White House, March 23, 2010, Internet message received on 3/23/10.
36. See the Weatherford chapter in this volume.
37. "Obama's Remarks at Stimulus Signing," *New York Times,* February 17, 2009, www.nytimes.com, accessed 3/22/10.
38. Alan S. Blinder and Mark Zandi, "How the Great Recession Was Brought to an End," July 27, 2010, p. 1, www.economy.com/mark-zandi/documents/End-of-Great-Recession.pdf, accessed 3/26/11. The raid that killed Osama bin Laden in May 2011 also produced at least a temporary bump-up in public approval for President Obama.
39. James Surowiecki, "Second Helpings," *New Yorker,* September 20, 2010, p. 52.
40. Lori Montgomery, "Report Gives Stimulus Package High Marks," *Washington Post,* October 1, 2010, www.washingtonpost.com, accessed 9/30/10.
41. John M. Broder, "E.P.A. Pick Vows to Put Science First," *New York Times,* January 14, 2009, www.nytimes.com, accessed 10/6/10.
42. A presidential memorandum to the Department of Transportation and other agencies dated May 21, 2010, outlined new steps for the appropriate agencies to take "to produce a new generation of clean vehicles" ("Presidential Memorandum Regarding Fuel Efficiency Standards," May 21, 2010, www.whitehouse.gov), and on October 1, 2010, the Department of Transportation and the Environmental Protection Agency announced "Next Steps toward Tighter Tailpipe and Fuel Economy Standards for Passenger Cars and Trucks" (www.nhtsa.gov, October 1, 2010, accessed 10/1/10).
43. William Branigan, Juliet Eilperin, and Steven Mufson, "Obama Announces New Energy, Environmental Policies," *Washington Post,* January 26, 2009, www.washingtonpost.com, accessed 1/26/09.
44. *A New Era of Responsibility,* p. 21.
45. In addition, a report by the National Oceanic and Atmospheric Administration said that the administration kept its own worst-case estimates of the oil spill from the public, a charge the administration denied. See John M. Broder, "Report Slams

Administration for Underestimating Gulf Spill," *New York Times,* October 6, 2010, www.nytimes.com, accessed 10/7/10.

46. For interesting accounts of the BP incident used to write this section, see Dana Milbank, "Slimy Doings Weren't All at the Oil Well," *Washington Post*, May 26, 2010 (www.washingtonpost.com, accessed 5/27/10); Peter Baker, "Defending Spill Response, Obama Expresses Frustration," *New York Times*, May 27, 2010 (www.nytimes.com, accessed 5/27/10); Ian Urbina, "In Gulf, It Was Unclear Who Was in Charge of Rig," *New York Times*, June 5, 2010 (www.nytimes.com, accessed 6/7/10); Jackie Calmes and Helene Cooper, "BP to Suspend Dividend and Set Up Fund for Oil Spill Claims," *New York Times,* June 16, 2010 (www.nytimes.com, accessed 6/16/10); and David E. Sanger, "Twisting Arms at BP, Obama Sets Off a Debate on Tactics," *New York Times*, June 17, 2010 (www.nytimes.com, accessed 6/18/10).

47. Neil Irwin, "Geithner Plan Lacks Freshness and Clarity," *Washington Post,* February 11, 2009, www.washingtonpost.com, accessed 10/6/10.

48. See also the February 11, 2009, story in the *Times* by Stephen Labaton and Edmund L. Andrews where, on pp. 2-3, the argument is that Geithner wanted to placate the bankers (as opposed to the position taken by other Obama advisers) and he won out. Labaton and Andrews, "Geithner Said to Have Prevailed on the Bailout," *New York Times,* February 10, 2009, www.nytimes.com, accessed 10/6/10.

49. Associated Press, "White House Wants to Revise Compensation Part of the Stimulus," *New York Times,* February 16, 2009, www.nytimes.com, accessed 2/15/09.

50. Paul Krugman, "Banking on the Brink," *New York Times*, February 23, 2009, www.nytimes.com, accessed 10/6/10.

51. "Financial Regulation," *New York Times*, June 25, 2010, www.nytimes.com, accessed 6/27/10.

52. Binyamin Appelbaum, "On Finance Reform Bill, Lobbying Shifts to Regulations," *New York Times*, June 26, 2010, www.nytimes.com, accessed 6/27/10. See also Christine Hauser, "Banks Likely to Offset Impact of New Law, Analysts Say," *New York Times*, June 25, 2010, www.nytimes.com, accessed 6/27/10.

53. David E. Sanger, "In Week of Tests, Obama, Reasserts His Authority," June 25, 2010, www.nytimes.com, accessed 6/25/10.

54. Joel Achenbach, "The Audacity of Hope," *Washington Post*, January 27, 2010, www.washingtonpost.com, accessed 1/27/10.

55. See Jacobson's chapter in this volume.

56. Perry Bacon, Jr., "A Lame-Duck Session with Unexpected Victories," *Washington Post,* December 22, 2010, www.washingtonpost.com, accessed 12/22/10.

57. Jon Cohen, "Washington Post–ABC News Poll Finds Broad Bipartisan Support for Tax Package," *Washington Post,* December 13, 2010, www.washingtonpost.com, accessed 12/13/10. On the liberal reaction, see, for example, Paul Krugman, "Let's Not Make a Deal," *New York Times,* December 5, 2010, www.nytimes.com, accessed 12/6/10; and Perry Bacon, Jr., "Liberal Groups Blast Obama for Considering Tax Compromise," *Washington Post,* December 2, 2010, www.washingtonpost.com, accessed 12/2/10.

58. Peter Baker, "With New Tax Bill, a Turning Point for the President," *New York Times,* December 17, 2010, www.nytimes.com, accessed 12/17/10.

59. See the Singh chapter in this volume.

60. John Schwartz, "Obama Backs Off a Reversal on Secrets," *New York Times*, February 9, 2009, www.nytimes.com, accessed 10/6/10.

61. Charlie Savage, "Obama's War on Terror May Resemble Bush's in Some Areas," *New York Times*, February 17, 2009, www.nytimes.com, accessed 2/18/09.

62. William Glaberson, "Obama to Keep Tribunals; Stance Angers Some Backers," *New York Times*, May 16, 2009, www.nytimes.com, accessed 5/29/09.

63. See Peter Finn and Anne E. Kornblut, "Obama Creates Indefinite Detention System for Prisoners at Guantanamo Bay," *Washington Post,* March 8, 2011, www.washingtonpost.com, accessed 3/8/11.

64. See, especially, Peter Baker, "With Pledge to Troops and Iraqis, Obama Details Pullout," *New York Times*, February 27, 2009, www.nytimes.com, accessed 2/28/09.

65. David Stout and Brian Knowlton, "Gates Says Afghan Drawdown Timing Is Flexible," *New York Times*, December 4, 2009, www.nytimes.com, accessed 12/3/09.

66. Kirk Victor, "Letdown on the Left," *National Journal.com*, December 5, 2009, www.nationaljournal.com/magazine, accessed 9/29/10.

67. Bob Woodward, *Obama's Wars* (New York: Simon & Schuster, 2010). See also Bob Woodward, "Military Thwarted President Seeking Choice in Afghanistan, *Washington Post*, September 27, 2010, www.washingtonpost.com, accessed 9/27/10.

68. Savage, "Obama's War on Terror."

69. Ibid.

70. Charlie Savage, "Justice Department to Limit Use of State Secrets Privilege," *New York Times,* September 23, 2009, www.nytimes.com, accessed 9/23/09.

71. "An Incomplete State Secrets Fix," *New York Times,* September 29, 2009, www.nytimes.com, accessed 9/29/09. See also, a year later, "Shady Secrets," *New York Times*, September 29, 2010, www.nytimes.com, accessed 9/29/10. The *Times* argued about a request by the Obama administration asking a federal judge to dismiss a lawsuit because of the "so-called state secrets doctrine": "Everyone recognizes that there are secrets that must be protected, but the doctrine has been used to cover up illegal and embarrassing acts or to avoid needed public discussion of policies. . . . Despite President Obama's promises of reform in this area, the public still cannot reliably distinguish between legitimate and self-serving uses of the national security claims. Worse, some of the administration's claims clearly have fallen on the darker side of that line."

72. Rozell and Berman quoted in Michael D. Shear, "Government Openness Is Tested by Salahi Case," *Washington Post,* December 4, 2009, www.washingtonpost.com, accessed 12/7/09.

73. Charlie Savage and James Risen, "Federal Judge Finds N.S.A. Wiretaps Were Illegal," *New York Times,* March 31, 2010, www.nytimes.com, accessed 4/21/10.

74. James Risen and Charlie Savage, "Court Ruling on Wiretap Is a Challenge for Obama," *New York Times,* April 1, 2010, www.nytimes.com, accessed 4/2/10.

75. Howard Kurtz, "After Reporter's Subpoena, Critics Call Obama's Leak-Plugging Efforts Bush-like," *Washington Post,* April 30, 2010, www.washingtonpost.com, accessed 4/30/10.

76. Scott Shane, "Administration Takes a Hard Line against Leaks to Press," *New York Times,* June 11, 2010, www.nytimes.com, accessed 6/11/10.
77. Richard E. Neustadt, *Presidential Power* (New York: Free Press, 1990), p. 84.
78. A typical newspaper article in early 2010 was titled, "A Year Later, Where Did the Hopes for Obama Go?," Ann Gerhart, *Washington Post,* February 8, 2010, www.washing tonpost.com, accessed 2/8/10. On restored public support, see the article by Jon Cohen cited in note 57 above.
79. Jim Ruttenberg, "Bloggers and Unions Join Forces to Push Democrats," *New York Times,* February 26, 2009, www.nytimes.com, accessed 2/27/09.
80. David Brooks, "A Moderate Manifesto," *New York Times,* March 2, 2009, www.nytimes.com, accessed 3/3/09.
81. Robert Kuttner, quoted in Alan Brinkley, "This Is Our Moment," *New York Times,* January 16, 2009, www.nytimes.com, accessed 1/18/09.
82. In one of the most quoted statements of late 2010, an African American woman at a town-hall-style meeting with President Obama, said: "I'm exhausted of defending your administration. . . . I'm deeply disappointed where we are right now." She said that she had voted for him and thought that change would come to Washington, and then added, "I'm waiting, sir. I'm waiting. I don't feel it yet. . . . Is this my new reality?" Quoted in Michael D. Shear, "Disappointed Supporters Question Obama," *New York Times,* September 20, 2010, www.nytimes.com, accessed 9/20/10.
83. Charles M. Blow, "The Thrill Is Gone," *New York Times,* June 18, 2010, www.nytimes.com, accessed 6/18/10.
84. Newt Gingrich, "How America Became a 'Secular-Socialist Machine,'" *Washington Post,* April 23, 2010, www.washingtonpost.com, accessed 4/23/10.
85. Richard W. Stevenson, "The Muddled Selling of the President," *New York Times,* January 29, 2010, www.nytimes.com, accessed 2/23/10.
86. See Philip Rucker, "Incoming House GOP Chairmen Have a Long List of Issues to Investigate," *Washington Post,* January 4, 2011, www.washingtonpost.com, accessed 1/4/11. The story notes that Representative Darrell Issa (R-CA), the incoming chair of the House Oversight and Congressional Reform Committee had been particularly vociferous about the number and depth of the investigations he planned to undertake, and that he at one point went so far as to label the Obama administration as "one of the most corrupt."
87. Thomas E. Mann, "Books Closed on the 111th Congress, What to Expect in the 112th," Brookings Institution Up Front Blog, January 4, 2011, www.brookings.edu/Up_Front .aspx accessed 1/4/11.

CHAPTER 3

Strategic Assessments: Evaluating Opportunities and Strategies in the Obama Presidency

George C. Edwards III

PRESIDENTIAL POWER IS *NOT* THE POWER TO PERSUADE. Presidents cannot reshape the contours of the political landscape to pave the way for change by establishing an agenda and persuading the public, Congress, and others to support their policies. Instead, successful presidents *facilitate* change by recognizing opportunities in their environments and fashioning strategies and tactics to exploit them.[1]

These findings lead us to predict that governing strategies dependent on persuasion will fail. The Obama administration provides an excellent test for these predictions, because it adopted two governing strategies highly dependent on persuasion: "going public" and bipartisanship in Congress. This chapter analyzes the prospects of these strategies for governing adopted by the Obama White House.

First, however, we need to consider the nature of the president's agenda. The more ambitious the president's agenda, the more likely it will meet with intense criticism and political pushback. A White House strategy built on the assumption of persuading the public or members of Congress to support the president's programs can lead to an overly ambitious agenda that lacks the fundamental support it needs to weather the inevitable attacks from the opposition.

The Obama Agenda

In an article written days after the 2008 presidential election, Paul Light maintained that there was not room in government for the kind of breakthrough ideas that Obama had promised. Every Democratic president since Lyndon Johnson had sent fewer major proposals to Congress, just as every Republican president since

Richard Nixon had done the same. Thus, Light suggested that instead of presenting a massive agenda to Congress, the new president should start with a few tightly focused progressive initiatives that would whet the appetite for more. His best opportunity for a grand agenda was more likely to be in 2013 than in 2009.[2]

Obama had a different view. He proposed an agenda that confronted the era's most intractable problems, from a tattered financial system that helped fuel a deep recession to health care, education, and energy policies that had long defied meaningful reform. He persuaded Congress to spend more than three-quarters of a trillion dollars trying to jump-start the economy. On his own authority, he altered federal rules in areas ranging from stem cell research to the treatment of terrorism suspects. He launched efforts to help strapped homeowners refinance their mortgages, sweep "toxic assets" off bank balance sheets, and shore up consumer credit markets. He also set a timetable for ending the occupation of Iraq, increased the US presence in Afghanistan, and set about improving the American image in the world.

Given the policy environment he inherited, the president often declared that he did not have the luxury of addressing the financial crisis and issues such as health care, education, or the environment one at a time. "I'm not choosing to address these additional challenges just because I feel like it or because I'm a glutton for punishment," he told the Business Roundtable. "I'm doing so because they're fundamental to our economic growth and ensuring that we don't have more crises like this in the future."[3] He wanted a more sustained approach than patching the economy until the next bubble, like the technology bubble of the 1990s and the housing bubble of the 2000s.[4]

In Obama's view, it was impossible to deal with the economic crisis without fixing the banking system, because it was not possible to generate a recovery without liquid markets and access to capital. He insisted that the only way to build a strong economy that would truly last was to address underlying problems in American society like unaffordable health care, dependence on foreign oil, and under-performing schools. Reducing dependence on foreign oil required addressing climate change, which in turn required international cooperation and engaging the world with vigorous US diplomacy. His appointment of prominent White House "czars" with jurisdictions ranging across several departments reflected this syncretic outlook.

Moreover, the president had little patience for waiting to act. "There are those who say these plans are too ambitious, that we should be trying to do less, not more," he told a town hall meeting in Costa Mesa, California, on March 18, 2009. "Well, I say our challenges are too large to ignore." The next day in Los Angeles he proclaimed, "It would be nice if I could just pick and choose what problems to face, when to face them. So I could say, well, no, I don't want to deal with the war in Afghanistan right now; I'd prefer not having to deal with climate change right now.

And if you could just hold on, even though you don't have health care, just please wait, because I've got other things to do." Later, on *The Tonight Show with Jay Leno*, he repeated his standard response to critics who charged he was trying to do too much: "Listen, here's what I say. I say our challenges are too big to ignore."[5]

There was also an element of strategic pragmatism in the president's view. For example, Obama felt that health care was a once-in-a-lifetime struggle and a fight that could not wait. To have postponed it until 2010 would have meant trying to pass the bill in an election year. To have waited until 2011 would have risked taking on the battle with reduced majorities in the House and Senate.[6] Even when the administration began running into resistance to its health care plan in the summer of 2009 and key staff members pushed for a pared-back approach (to focus on expanding coverage for lower-income children and families and reforming the most objectionable practices of insurance companies), Obama persisted in his comprehensive approach.[7]

Obama's top strategists, including David Axelrod and Rahm Emanuel, repeatedly defended the administration's sweeping agenda by arguing that success breeds success, that each legislative victory would make the next one easier.[8] In other words, the White House believed success on one issue on the agenda would *create* further opportunities on additional policies.

There were some efforts to set priorities, of course. The White House and congressional Democrats deferred fights over tax policy, despite the impending expiration of many of the George W. Bush tax cuts. The White House also opposed a high-profile commission to investigate Bush administration interrogation practices and declined to engage in hot-button debates over gays in the military (until late 2010) or gun control (even then).[9] The administration also did not make immigration and union card check legislation priorities.[10]

Assessing Opportunities: Public Support

Public support is a key political resource, and modern presidents have typically sought public support for themselves and their policies that they could leverage to obtain backing for their proposals in Congress. It is natural for a new president, basking in the glow of an electoral victory, to focus on creating, rather than exploiting, opportunities for change. After all, if he convinced voters and party leaders to support his candidacy—and just won the biggest prize in American politics by doing so—why should he not be able to convince the public or members of Congress to support his policies? Thus, presidents may not focus on evaluating existing possibilities when they think they can create their own.

Barack Obama entered the presidency with an impressive record of political success, at the center of which were his rhetorical skills. In college, he concluded that words had the power to transform: "With the right words everything could

change—South Africa, the lives of ghetto kids just a few miles away, my own tenu-
ous place in the world."[11] It is no surprise, then, that Obama followed the pattern
of presidents seeking public support for themselves and their policies, in order to
leverage support for their proposals in Congress—especially since it was commonplace at the beginning of his term for commentators to suggest that the president
could exploit the capacity for social networking to reach people directly in a way
that television and radio could not and harness this potential to overcome obstacles
to legislative success.[12]

The Obama White House believes in the power of the presidential pulpit.
More importantly, it believes that the president is an irresistible persuader. According to the president's top counselor, David Axelrod, "I don't think there's been a
President since Kennedy whose ability to move issues and people through a speech
has been comparable."[13]

This faith in presidential persuasion underlay the administration's decision to
try to move a large agenda simultaneously and its response to political problems.
When times get tough, Obama goes public. In the campaign, he confronted the
issue of Rev. Jeremiah Wright's incendiary comments with an extended address on
race relations. When the White House encountered resistance to its stimulus program, the president held his first prime-time press conference. Rather than attempting to persuade individual members of Congress to support his record-setting fiscal
2010 budget, he traveled outside Washington, appearing at town hall meetings,
news conferences, and on late-night talk shows. When support for health care
reform was falling, the president delivered a prime-time televised address before a
joint session of Congress. And when the president made his decision to send 30,000
additional American troops to Afghanistan, he delivered a prime-time televised
address from West Point.

Such a strategy is common across recent presidencies. Yet it is a mistake for
presidents to assume they can lead the public. There is nothing in the historical
record to support such a belief. Research tracking the opinion leadership of Bill
Clinton and Ronald Reagan on a wide range of policies and efforts to defend themselves against scandal found that public opinion rarely moved in the president's
direction. On most of Clinton and Reagan's policy initiatives, pluralities, and often
majorities, of the public *opposed* the president. Moreover, movement in public
opinion was typically *against* the president.[14] Analyses of George W. Bush's and
Franklin D. Roosevelt's efforts to lead the public also found these presidents typically experienced frustration and failure.[15]

The dangers of overreach and debilitating political losses alert us that it is
critically important for presidents to assess accurately the potential for obtaining
public support. Moreover, the success of a strategy for governing depends on the
opportunities for it to succeed. Adopting strategies for governing that are prone to
failure waste rather than create opportunities.[16] Relying on going public to pressure

Congress when the public is unlikely to be responsive to the president's appeals is a recipe for failure.

There are two fundamental components of the opportunity for obtaining public support. First is the nature of public opinion at the time a president takes office. Does it support the direction in which the president would like to move? Is there a mandate from the voters in support of specific policies? Is there a broad public predisposition for government activism? Are opposition party identifiers open to supporting the president's initiatives? A second facet of the potential for public leadership focuses on the long run. What are the challenges to leading the public that every president faces?

I have analyzed these issues in detail in *On Deaf Ears*. In what follows I will explore the White House's view of the opportunities for change and then offer my own, quite different, evaluation. By analyzing the opportunity for obtaining public support for Obama's initiatives, it is possible to understand and predict the challenges President Obama faced in going public and the relative utility of this strategy for governing.

The View from the White House

Barack Obama is all about change. Calling for change was at the center of his campaign strategy, and he spoke tirelessly of fundamental reforms in health care, energy, the environment, and other policy areas. Once in office, the president and his aides embraced the view that the environment offered a rare opportunity for the changes they espoused. They reasoned that the crisis atmosphere would galvanize the country, perhaps even generating bipartisan support for the president's initiatives. Thus, they viewed the economic crisis as an opportunity, as a catalyst for action, rather than as a constraint. White House chief of staff Rahm Emanuel articulated this strategy most succinctly when he declared that one should "never let a serious crisis go to waste."[17] In other words, the new administration concluded that the economic crisis had heightened the desire for change that voters expressed in November, creating a once-in-a-generation opportunity for bold policy shifts.[18]

On the surface, it seemed reasonable to conclude that in a time of severe economic crisis that touched many aspects of everyday life such as housing, banking, and consumer credit, Americans were seeking reassurance from the White House and that the president would have both the public's ear and its good wishes. More importantly, Obama's team felt the recession had left public opinion malleable and highly responsive to bold leadership. Thus, even during the transition, the president-elect launched a full-scale marketing blitz to pass his massive stimulus package, including delivering a major speech at George Mason University.

The new president quite sensibly concluded that he had to promote economic recovery as his first order of business. Moreover, his proposal for recovery called for continuing the Bush administration's massive subsidies to keep the banking and automobile industries afloat, and adding a staggeringly expensive program to stimulate the economy. These expenditures and tax cuts produced by far the largest deficits in American history. In addition, passing them required the president to spend his political capital in the early days of his presidency, engaging in difficult legislative battles in which he could not attract bipartisan support. A politically costly battle over his budget followed directly, with similar legislative results.[19]

An alternative analysis of the policy environment might have viewed the economic crisis as a constraint. Obama could have justifiably argued that he would have to scale back his agenda, that the economy was in such a fragile state that he should focus all his attention on nursing it back to health as soon as possible. He also could have explained that, given the amount of money the government would be pouring into the economy, the country could not afford for the moment a costly overhaul of health care nor an ambitious initiative to combat global warming that included a controversial cap-and-trade system and energy taxes. Instead, he would work to overhaul the financial services industry, whose excesses triggered the crisis.

The White House was aware of the challenge it faced in dealing with the economy. According to senior adviser David Axelrod, "We came to office and immediately walked into a fiscal crisis, a financial crisis, and an economic crisis. It required some very difficult decisions, and it required everyone to spend some political capital."[20]

Nevertheless, the administration moved aggressively to propose the most ambitious domestic agenda since Lyndon Johnson's Great Society. Obama decided that he would convey the idea that the nation's problems, from the retreating economy to falling student test scores, were intertwined as he pressed for action on a host of fronts simultaneously.[21] The president often argued, as noted above, that the country had to address the cost and availability of health care and lessen its dependence on foreign oil before there could be a real economic recovery. From a policy analytic standpoint, the White House had a good case. Politics rarely defers to analysis, however.[22]

Even after the frustrations of his first year in office, President Obama declared in his State of the Union message in January 2010,

> From the day I took office, I've been told that addressing our larger challenges is too ambitious; such an effort would be too contentious. I've been told that our political system is too gridlocked, and that we should just put things on hold for a while.
>
> For those who make these claims, I have one simple question: How long should we wait? How long should America put its future on hold?[23]

After the Republican success in the 1994 elections, Bill Clinton felt that he needed to get ahead of the political passions of the moment and turned toward the center of the political spectrum with his triangulation strategy. Barack Obama had a different response to the setbacks of in his first year. He kept to his agenda, altering only its timing.[24]

The President's Mandate

New presidents traditionally claim a mandate from the people, because the most effective means of setting the terms of debate and overcoming opposition is the perception of an electoral mandate, an impression that the voters want to see the winner's programs implemented. Indeed, major changes in policy, as in 1933, 1965, and 1981, rarely occur in the absence of such perceptions.

Mandates can be powerful symbols in American politics. They accord added legitimacy and credibility to the newly elected president's proposals. Concerns for representation and political survival encourage members of Congress to support the president if they feel the people have spoken.[25] As a result, mandates change the premises of decision. Perceptions of a mandate in 1980, for example, placed a stigma on big government and exalted the unregulated marketplace and large defense budgets, providing Ronald Reagan a favorable strategic position for dealing with Congress.

Barack Obama won the presidency with nearly 53 percent of the popular vote, the first time a Northern Democrat had won a majority of the popular vote for president since Franklin D. Roosevelt's victory in 1944—and only the third time any Democrat had won a majority of the vote in those sixty-four years. Democrats won additional seats in both houses of Congress, and the historic nature of the election of the first black president generated an enormous amount of favorable press coverage. Further, the new president had emphasized change, not continuity, in his campaign and promised bold new initiatives.[26] Thus, it was easy for Democrats to overinterpret the new president's mandate for change.

Obama seemed to have a realistic interpretation of the nature of his victory, however, as we can see from his response to a question about his mandate in a press conference on November 25, 2008. "But I won 53 percent of the vote. That means 46 or 47 percent of the country voted for John McCain. And it's important, as I said on election night, that we enter into the new administration with a sense of humility and a recognition that wisdom is not the monopoly of any one party."[27]

The president-elect had it about right. An ABC News/*Washington Post* poll taken shortly before his inauguration found that although most people felt Obama had a mandate to work for major policy changes, 46 percent of the public felt he should compromise with Republicans in doing so.[28]

By inauguration day, however, the new president took a more expansive view:

Now, there are some who question the scale of our ambitions, who suggest that our system cannot tolerate too many big plans. Their memories are short, for they have forgotten what this country has already done, what free men and women can achieve when imagination is joined to common purpose, and necessity to courage. What the cynics fail to understand is that the ground has shifted beneath them, that the stale political arguments that have consumed us for so long no longer apply.[29]

Apparently, he had concluded that the contours of the political landscape had shifted in a way to expand the opportunities for major liberal change.

Support for Government Activism

Major expansions in public policy also require public support for, or at least toleration of, government activism in the form of new programs, increased spending, and additional taxes. It appears as though the White House concluded that Obama's victory indicated the electorate had turned in a more liberal direction and that the economic crisis had increased the public's demand for more government. Its allies agreed. "The center has moved," declared Robert Borosage, president of the liberal Institute for America's Future and co-director of the Campaign for America's Future.[30]

There was even some evidence from the right that times had changed. Republican Governor Arnold Schwarzenegger of California supported new federal spending on infrastructure and urged lawmakers to "get off of their rigid ideologies." Former Federal Reserve chairman Alan Greenspan revealed that the financial crisis caused him to reexamine his free market views. Martin Feldstein, a top economic adviser to Ronald Reagan, was advocating large increases in federal spending. George W. Bush himself had proposed a $700 billion bailout for financial institutions.[31]

There was reason for skepticism, however—if one was to look for it. The country's partisan balance had shifted more than its ideological balance. The broad repudiation of President George W. Bush propelled the Democrats to their widest advantage over Republicans in party identification in decades, but the public's ideological alignment did not change nearly as much. More Americans identified as conservatives than as liberals, for example (table 3.1). In both 2009 and 2010, 40 percent of Americans described their political views as conservative, and only 21 percent as liberal. Thirty-six and thirty-five percent, respectively, identified as moderates. The number of conservatives increased since 2008, reaching its highest level in the entire time series. The 21 percent calling themselves liberal was in line with findings throughout the decade. Equally significant, the number of moderates, potential supporters of Obama's agenda, was at its lowest point since the time series began in 1992 (when moderates were 43 percent of the public).

Despite the Democratic Party's political strength in representation in Congress, a significantly higher percentage of Americans in most states, even some solidly Democratic ones, called themselves conservative rather than liberal. No

TABLE 3.1   Trends in Ideological Identification

Year	% Conservative	% Moderate	% Liberal
1992	36	43	17
1993	39	40	18
1994	38	42	17
1995	36	39	16
1996	38	40	16
1997	37	40	19
1998	37	40	19
1999	38	40	19
2000	38	40	19
2001	38	40	20
2002	38	39	19
2003	38	40	20
2004	38	40	19
2005	38	39	20
2006	37	38	21
2007	37	37	22
2008	37	37	22
2009	40	36	21
2010	40	35	21

Source: Gallup Poll.

state in 2009 had a majority or even a plurality of people who called themselves liberal, with the conservative advantage ranging from one percentage point in Vermont, Hawaii, and Massachusetts to thirty-five percentage points in Alabama. (Washington, D.C., has a plurality of liberals, 36 percent.)[32]

We can also see the dominance of conservatism if we disaggregate opinion by political party. While 72 percent of Republicans in 2009 called themselves conservative, only 37 percent of Democrats identified as liberal. Thirty-nine percent of Democrats said they were moderates and another 22 percent saw themselves as conservative. Among Independents, 35 percent said they were conservative, and only 18 percent identified as liberal. Between 2008 and 2009, there was an increase of six points in the percentage of Independents calling themselves conservative.[33]

Ideological identification is not determinative, of course, and there is a well-known paradox of the incongruity between ideological identification and issue attitudes.[34] Scholars have long known that only a fraction of the public exhibits the requisite traits of an "ideologue."[35] Nevertheless, many more Americans are able to choose an ideological label and use it to guide their political judgments than in previous decades.[36] Scholars have found that ideological self-placements are influential determinants of vote choice,[37] issue attitudes,[38] and views toward government spending.[39]

There are other indicators of conservatism aside from ideological identification. For example, in December 2009, Pew found that Americans had become more conservative on abortion, gun control, and climate change.[40] Similarly, Gallup found that at the end of August 2009, 53 percent of Americans said the government should promote "traditional values," while 42 percent disagreed and believed the government should not favor any particular set of values. The previous year, Americans were divided down the middle, with 48 percent taking each position.[41] The shift in attitudes came primarily from Independents, whose views showed a dramatic turnaround, from a 55 percent to 37 percent split against government-promoted morality in 2008 to a 54 percent to 40 percent division in favor of it in 2009.[42]

The public also increased its traditional skepticism about expanding government's role. For example, in November 2008, 54 percent of the public said it was the responsibility of the federal government to make sure all Americans had health care coverage. A year later, this figure had decreased to 47 percent while 50 percent said it was not the government's responsibility. At the same time, there was an increase of twelve percentage points in the number of people rating health care coverage in the US as good or excellent.[43]

More broadly, when asked whether it preferred smaller government offering fewer public services or larger government offering more services, the public chose the former. Support for larger government was modest when Obama took office, and was down to 38 percent support a year later (see table 3.2). Meanwhile support for smaller government grew somewhat during his first two years in the White House.

TABLE 3.2   Support for Larger Government

Poll Dates	% Smaller Government, Fewer Services	% Larger Government, More Services	% No Opinion
October 29–November 1, 2007	50	44	5
June 12–15, 2008	50	45	5
January 13–16, 2009	53	43	4
June 18–21, 2009	54	41	4
January 12–15, 2010	58	38	4
April 22–25, 2010	56	40	4

Source: ABC News-*Washington Post* Poll.

Question: "Generally speaking, would you say you favor (smaller government with fewer services), or (larger government with more services)?"

The general state of the economy encouraged caution about bold innovation in public policy. With unemployment around 10 percent and a stock market plunge that threatened retirement savings, Americans started spending less, saving more,[44] and adopting a more measured approach to change. In March 2009, Gallup found that only 13 percent of Americans both approved of the government's expansion to address the economic crisis *and* wanted that expansion to be permanent. Another 39 percent favored the expansion but wanted it to be cut back once the crisis was resolved. A plurality—44 percent—of Americans opposed the expansion from the beginning.[45]

Overwhelming Republican opposition to government activism should surprise no one. But by July 2009, 66 percent of Independents thought Obama's proposals for addressing the country's major problems called for too much government spending and 60 percent said his agenda called for too much government expansion.[46] They supported fiscal discipline over economic stimulus by 56 percent to 41 percent.[47] By February 2010, 56 percent of the public preferred smaller government providing fewer services to 34 percent wanting bigger government providing more services.[48]

Another obstacle to change was paying for it, which is especially problematic in bad economic times. In August 2009, Gallup found that 68 percent of Americans expected their federal income taxes would be higher by the end of Barack Obama's first term as president. Nearly half of these people (35 percent) expected their taxes would be "a lot higher."[49] The rise in expectations that taxes would increase probably was a reflection on Obama's ambitious domestic agenda, which began with a $787 billion economic stimulus plan (the fact that a third of this came in the form of tax relief was poorly publicized) and then focused on a roughly $1 trillion health care reform bill. Although Obama regularly reiterated his pledge not to raise taxes on all but the wealthiest Americans, most Americans remained skeptical that the administration could pay for health care reform and its other programs without raising their taxes.

Americans were also markedly cynical about the amount of waste in federal spending. At the end of the summer of 2009, on average, Americans believed 50 cents of every tax dollar that went to the government in Washington, D.C., was wasted, an increase from 40 cents in 1979.[50]

The public's resistance to government activism should not be surprising. In their sweeping "macro" view of public opinion, Robert Erikson, Michael MacKuen, and James Stimson show that opinion always moves contrary to the president's position. They argue that a moderate public always gets too much liberalism from Democrats and too much conservatism from Republicans. Because public officials have policy beliefs as well as an interest in reelection, they are not likely to calibrate their policy stances exactly to match those of the public. Therefore, opinion movement is typically contrary to the ideological persuasion of presidents.

Liberal presidents produce movement in the conservative direction and conservatives generate public support for more liberal policies.[51]

Public Polarization

A primary reason for the difficulty of passing major changes in public policy is the challenge of obtaining support from the opposition party identifiers among the public. We know that partisan polarization reached record levels during the presidency of George W. Bush.[52] The election of Barack Obama did not diminish this polarization and presented an obstacle to the new president obtaining support from Republicans. We can start with the election results to understand better this context.

The 2008 Election

In 2008, party-line voting was 89.1 percent, the second highest level in the history of the American National Election Studies (ANES), which go back to 1952. This level was surpassed only by the 89.9 percent level in 2004. Moreover, Obama's electoral coalition contained the smallest share of opposite-party identifiers of any president elected since the advent of the ANES time series, just 4.4 percent.[53]

Republicans and Republican-leaning Independents not only did not support Obama. By Election Day, they perceived a huge ideological gulf between themselves and the new president and viewed him as an untrustworthy radical leftist with a socialist agenda. Forty-one percent of McCain voters judged Obama to be an "extreme liberal," further left than Republican voters had placed any previous Democratic candidate. Moreover, they placed him further to the left of their own ideologies than they had placed any previous Democratic candidate.[54]

Thus, the Republicans' campaign to brand Obama as a radical socialist[55] out of touch with American values resonated with many McCain voters. An African American candidate was also likely to exacerbate right-wing opposition,[56] as was his Ivy League education and somewhat detached manner. The fact that he spent part of his childhood in Muslim Indonesia and that his middle name was "Hussein" provided additional fodder for those willing or even eager to believe that he was outside the mainstream. Many Republican voters did not simply oppose Obama; they despised and feared him.

Jay Cost calculated both unweighted and weighted (where each state is factored according to its share of the nationwide popular vote) averages of Obama's share of the vote in each state plus the District of Columbia to calculate the standard deviation of votes. (The greater the standard deviation, the more the states varied around the average—meaning the more accentuated were their differences,

FIGURE 3.1   Polarized Voting

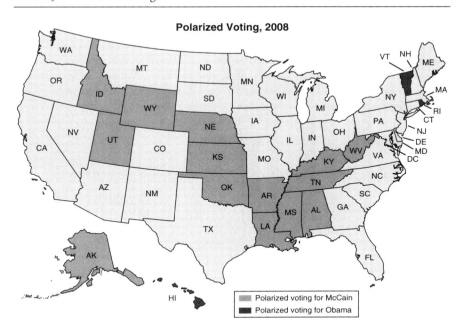

Polarized Voting, 2008

Polarized voting for McCain
Polarized voting for Obama

and thus the more polarization there was.) He found the highest level of partisan polarization in the past sixty years.[57]

Similarly, identifying the states that deviated from Obama's share of the nationwide vote (about 52.9 percent) by ten percentage points or more reveals that there were more "polarized" states than in any election in the past sixty years.[58] A few states (figure 3.1)—Vermont, Rhode Island, Hawaii, and the District of Columbia—were polarized in favor of Obama. Most of the polarized states, however, voted for Republican John McCain. The majority of these states form a belt stretching from West Virginia, Kentucky, and Tennessee through Alabama, Mississippi, Louisiana, and Arkansas over to Oklahoma, Kansas, and Nebraska. In addition, Wyoming, Idaho, Utah, and Alaska were strongly in the Republican camp. Never before had many of these states voted so heavily against a victorious Democrat.

In short, the electoral polarization of the Bush years persisted in the 2008 presidential election, indicating that it represented more than a reaction to George W. Bush (although he certainly exacerbated it).[59] The crucial point, however, is that Obama had his work cut out for him to reach the public in states that were turning increasingly red.

The polarization of the 2008 campaign and the nature of the opposition to Obama laid the groundwork for the intense aversion to Obama and his policies that appeared shortly after he took office. His initial actions of seeking the release of additional Troubled Asset Relief Program funds and promoting a historic economic stimulus bill confirmed to conservatives that he was indeed a left-wing radical who needed to be stopped at all costs and, along with the president's support of health care reform, fueled the emergence of the Tea Party movement.

Party and Ideological Divisions in the Public

The polarization evident in the 2008 election results did not end on Inauguration Day. Instead, it persisted in the underlying partisan and ideological divisions of the country. Indeed, there has been an increase in partisan-ideological polarization as Americans increasingly base their party loyalties on their ideological beliefs rather than on membership in social groups.[60]

When President Obama took office, he enjoyed a 68 percent approval level, the highest of any newly elected president since John F. Kennedy. For all of his hopes about bipartisanship, however, his early approval ratings were the most polarized of any president in the past four decades. By February 15, less than a month after Obama took office, only 30 percent of Republicans approved of his performance in office while 89 percent of Democrats and 63 percent of Independents approved.[61] The gap between Democratic and Republican approval had already reached fifty-nine percentage points—and thus far Obama has never again reached even 30 percent approval among Republicans. By the 100-day mark of his tenure, 92 percent of Democrats but only 28 percent of Republicans approved of his performance, a difference of sixty-four percentage points.[62]

The fact that the public had been polarized under his predecessor[63] was of little comfort to Obama. It merely showed the stability of the partisan divide and indicated the difficulty of reaching those identifying with the opposition party. Gallup reported that there was an average gap of sixty-five percentage points between Democrats' and Republicans' evaluations of the president in his first year, greatly exceeding the prior high of fifty-two percentage points for Bill Clinton.[64]

Moreover, ideological division reinforced partisan polarization. At the midpoint of the new president's first year in office, nearly half of Americans identified themselves as moderate or liberal white Democrats or conservative white Republicans, the poles of the political spectrum. Those in the middle, on the other hand, were a much smaller group. Only 6 percent of the public said they were conservative white Democrats, and only 11 percent moderate/liberal white Republicans.[65] Table 3.3 shows that in averaging its daily tracking polls over the July 1–August 17, 2009, period, Gallup found that the difference between white conservative

TABLE 3.3   Polarized Job Approval

Group	% Approval
All	56
White conservative Democrats	70
White moderate/liberal Democrats	88
White conservative Republicans	11
White moderate/liberal Republicans	32
White Independents	36
Blacks	94
Hispanics	74

Source: Gallup daily tracking polls, July 1–August 17, 2009.

Republicans and white moderate and liberal Democrats in evaluating the president's performance in office was seventy-seven percentage points.

We can also see the confounding influence of race in support for the president. While 94 percent of blacks, almost all of whom are Democrats, approved of Obama's handling of his job, only 11 percent of white conservative Republicans did so—an eighty-three percentage point difference. There is evidence that predispositions to opposing the president combined with the salience of race contributed to the acceptance of smearing labels such as Obama was Muslim or a socialist.[66] There is also reason to believe that negative stereotypes about blacks significantly eroded white support for the president.[67]

The Democratic political organization Democracy Corps concluded from its focus groups that those in the conservative GOP base believed that Obama "is ruthlessly advancing a secret agenda to bankrupt the United States and dramatically expand government control to an extent nothing short of socialism."[68] By June 2010, Democracy Corps found that 55 percent of the public found Obama to be "too liberal" and the same percentage thought "socialist" was a reasonably accurate way of describing him.[69] In July 2010, 41 percent of Republicans clung to the false belief that Obama was not born in this country.[70] A poll the next month found that 31 percent of Republicans thought he was a Muslim.[71] Another poll in the same month found that 52 percent of the Republican respondents said it was definitely (14 percent) or probably (38 percent) true that "Barack Obama sympathizes with the goals of Islamic fundamentalists who want to impose Islamic law around the world."[72] These views represented a profound sense of alienation.[73]

Contributing to this polarization was the insulation of the opposition. Sixty-three percent of Republicans and Republican leaners reported that they received most of their news from Fox News.[74] The president's initial actions were grist for commentators on the right, especially those on radio and cable television. They aggressively reinforced the fears of their audiences and encouraged active opposition to the White House.

Public Perspectives on Issues

As the Obama administration and Congress wrestled with how to fix the country's economic problems while at the same time dealing with the longer-term impact of those efforts, tensions between the two were inevitable. Differences in party and ideology inevitably result in different policy priorities and trade-offs between policies among the public. By June 2010, 63 percent of Democrats thought the government should do more to solve the country's problems, but only 13 percent of Republicans (and 32 percent of moderates) agreed.[75]

In mid-2009, Gallup reported that Republicans and Democrats viewed the economic issues facing the country today from substantially different perspectives (see table 3.4). Republicans were much more likely than Democrats to express worry about issues that represented *consequences* of attempting to fix economic

TABLE 3.4   Partisan Concerns about Economic Issues

Issue	% Concerned Republicans/ Leaners	% Concerned Democrats/ Leaners	Democrats minus Republicans Pct. Pts.
Increasing numbers of Americans without health care insurance	65	90	25
The rising unemployment rate	82	91	9
The increasing cost of health care	82	89	7
Decreasing pay and wages for the average worker	74	81	7
Increasing problems Americans have with personal debt and credit cards	75	74	−1
The increasing price of gas	79	76	−3
Increasing problems state governments have funding their budgets	84	79	−5
The increasing federal budget deficit	90	75	−15
Increasing state income taxes	78	59	−19
Increasing federal income taxes	86	62	−24
The federal government's increasing regulation of business and industry	78	40	−38
The federal government's expanding ownership of private corporations	82	42	−40

Source: Gallup poll, June 23–24, 2009.

Question: Please tell me whether you, personally, are worried about each of the following:

problems: the federal government's expanding ownership and regulation of private business and industry, increasing federal and state taxes, and the increasing federal budget deficit. Democrats, on the other hand, were much more likely to be worried about the societal problems that the increased spending and regulation were designed to address, including the increasing numbers of Americans without health insurance, and, to a lesser degree, about the rising unemployment rate, the increasing cost of health care, and decreasing pay and wages for the average worker.[76]

Another poll, conducted at the end of July 2009, also showed the differences between the parties on their priorities in making trade-offs between spending and reducing the budget deficit (see table 3.5). The biggest partisan difference—forty points—was over health care. Nearly three-quarters (72 percent) of Democrats saw spending more on health care as the priority, while 23 percent placed a higher priority on deficit reduction. By contrast, 63 percent of Republicans put deficit reduction ahead of increased health care spending, while 32 percent favored such spending over trimming the deficit. Just over half (54 percent) of Independents placed a higher priority on health care spending while 42 percent said deficit reduction was more important. Democrats stood apart from both Republicans and Independents in saying that stimulus spending was a higher priority than deficit

TABLE 3.5   Budget Trade-Offs by Party

| Higher Priority | % | | | Pct. Pts. |
	Republicans	Democrats	Independents	Dem. – Rep.
Spending more on health care	32	72	54	40
Reducing the budget deficit	63	23	42	−40
Spending more on education	43	69	56	26
Reducing the budget deficit	54	26	40	−28
Spending more on new energy technology	29	48	42	19
Reducing the budget deficit	67	43	53	−24
Spending more on economic recovery	43	68	47	25
Reducing the budget deficit	52	23	43	−29

Source: Pew Research Center for the People and the Press poll, July 22–26, 2009.

reduction. By a 68 percent to 23 percent margin, Democrats saw spending to help the economy recover as more important than reducing the deficit. By contrast, Independents were split about evenly (47 percent placed a higher priority on economic stimulus, 43 percent on deficit reduction), and a slim majority (52 percent) of Republicans saw deficit reduction as the bigger priority.

In March 2010, the public said it was more important to develop US energy supplies than to protect the environment by a 50 percent to 43 percent margin. Several weeks after the explosion of a BP oil rig in the Gulf of Mexico produced the biggest oil spill in American history, priorities shifted in favor of environmental protection, by a 55 percent to 39 percent margin. Support for the environmental protection option increased by fifteen percentage points among both Democrats and Independents. In contrast, Republicans' opinions did not change at all in response to the environmental disaster and continued to prioritize energy production over environmental protection by a 2-to-1 margin.[77]

Summing Up

Despite the historic and decisive nature of his election, Barack Obama did not enjoy an especially favorable environment for making major changes in public policy. The election results did not signal a mandate for change, an increased support for government activism, or an end to extreme partisan polarization. In addition, the long-term constraints on opinion change remained firmly in place.

Assessing Opportunities: Bipartisan Congressional Support

Every president needs support in Congress to pass his legislative proposals. We have seen that it is natural for a new president, having achieved electoral success, to focus on creating, rather than exploiting, opportunities for change. Thus, Obama lost no time to begin, as he put it in his inaugural address, "the work of remaking America."

As with leading the public, presidents may not focus on evaluating existing possibilities when they think they can create their own. Yet, for example, assuming success in reaching across the aisle to obtain bipartisan support is fraught with dangers. There is not a single systematic study that demonstrates that presidents can reliably move members of Congress, especially members of the opposition party, to support them.

The best evidence is that presidential persuasion is at the margins of congressional decision making. Even presidents who appeared to dominate Congress were actually facilitators rather than directors of change. They understood their own limitations and quite explicitly took advantage of opportunities in their environments. Working at the margins, they successfully guided legislation through

Congress. When these resources diminished, they reverted to the more typical stalemate that usually characterizes presidential–congressional relations.[78]

From the beginning, Barack Obama tried to strike a bipartisan pose. On the night of his election, he implored Democrats and Republicans alike, to "resist the temptation to fall back on the same partisanship and pettiness and immaturity that has poisoned our politics for so long." In his press conference on November 25, 2008, the president-elect declared, "It's important . . . that we enter into the new administration with a sense of humility and a recognition that wisdom is not the monopoly of any one party. In order for us to be effective . . . Republicans and Democrats are going to have to work together."[79]

Moreover, the president and his aides believed that a fair number of Republican lawmakers would rally behind the nation's first African American president at a time of crisis.[80] They saw his liberal programs drawing on Americans' desire for action and also counted on Obama's moderate, even conservative, temperament, to hurdle the ideological obstacles that had paralyzed Washington.[81]

Democratic activists agreed. "It is quite possible to see him as liberal and having an activist agenda, but being a type of leader who does not polarize partisans and finds ways of bringing people together to work on the things where they can find common ground," said Stanley B. Greenberg, a pollster in Bill Clinton's White House. "With this type of leader, the pent-up demand for action on the economy, health care and energy allows us to reach a series of big moments where many Republicans join the process and perhaps proposals pass with overwhelming majorities."[82]

The president made repeated and serious efforts to engage Republicans and win their support.[83] The question for us is whether there was any prospect of success in this effort.

The Prospect of Republican Support

A primary obstacle to passing major changes in public policy is the challenge of obtaining support from the opposition party. Such support can be critical in overcoming a Senate filibuster or effectively appealing to Independents in the public, who find bipartisanship reassuring. The *Washington Post* reported that the Obama legislative agenda was built around what some termed an "advancing tide" theory:

> Democrats would start with bills that targeted relatively narrow problems, such as expanding health care for low-income children, reforming Pentagon contracting practices and curbing abuses by credit-card companies. Republicans would see the victories stack up and would want to take credit alongside a popular president. As momentum built, larger bipartisan coalitions would form to tackle more ambitious initiatives.[84]

Just how realistic was the prospect of obtaining Republican support?

Perhaps the most important fact about Congress in 2009 was that polarization was at a historic high.[85] According to *Congressional Quarterly*, George W. Bush presided over the most polarized period at the Capitol since it began quantifying partisanship in the House and Senate in 1953. There had been a high percentage of party unity votes—those that pitted a majority of Republicans against a majority of Democrats—and an increasing propensity of individual lawmakers to vote with their fellow partisans.[86] Little changed in 2009, with extraordinarily high levels of party-line voting even in the first weeks of the Obama administration.[87] By the end of the year, 57 percent of the votes in Congress were party unity votes, just above the 56 percent average for the previous two decades.[88]

This polarization should not have been surprising. Republican constituencies send stalwart Republicans to Congress, whose job it is to oppose a Democratic president. Most of these senators and representatives were unlikely to be responsive to core Obama supporters. They knew their constituencies, and they knew Obama was unlikely to have much support in them. Thus, few of the Republicans' electoral constituencies showed any enthusiasm for health care reform. The partisan divisions that emerged in Congress on the health care issue were firmly rooted in district opinion and electoral politics.[89] Moreover, conservative Republicans were the group of political identifiers least likely to support compromising "to get things done."[90]

On the day before the House voted on the final version of the economic stimulus bill, the president took Aaron Schock, a freshman Republican member of Congress, aboard Air Force One to visit Illinois. Before an audience in Schock's district, Obama praised him as "a very talented young man" and expressed "great confidence in him to do the right thing for the people of Peoria." But when the representative stood on the House floor less than twenty-four hours later, his view of the right thing for the people of Peoria was to vote against the president. "They know that this bill is not stimulus," Schock said of his constituents. "They know that this bill will not do anything to create long-term, sustained economic growth."[91] Schock was typical of Republicans in early 2009, who viewed the stimulus debate as an opportunity to rededicate their divided, demoralized party around the ideas of big tax cuts and limited government spending.

In the 111th Congress (2009–2010), nearly half of the Republicans in both the House and Senate were elected from the eleven states of the Confederacy, plus Kentucky and Oklahoma. In each chamber, Southerners were a larger share of the Republican caucus than ever before. At the same time, Republicans held a smaller share of non-Southern seats in the House and Senate than at any other point in its history except during the early days of the New Deal.[92] The party's increasing identification with staunch Southern economic and social conservatism made it much more difficult for Obama to reach across the aisle. Southern

House Republicans, for instance, overwhelmingly opposed him, even on the handful of issues where he has made inroads among GOP legislators from other regions. Nearly one third of House Republicans from outside of the South supported expanding the State Children's Health Insurance Program, but only one tenth of Southern House Republicans did so. Likewise, just 5 percent of Southern House Republicans supported the bill expanding the national service program, compared with 22 percent of Republicans from other states.

The Republican Party's losses in swing areas since 2006 accelerated its homogenization. Few Republicans represented Democratic-leaning districts. As a result, far fewer congressional Republicans than Democrats had to worry about moderate public opinion. Fully thirty-one of the forty Republican senators serving in 2009 (thirty-one of forty-one in 2010), for example, were elected from the eighteen states that twice backed Bush and also opposed Obama. Five other senators represented states that voted for Bush twice and then supported Obama. Just six Republican senators were elected by states that voted Democratic in at least two of the past three presidential elections. One of these lawmakers, Arlen Specter of Pennsylvania, switched parties to become a Democrat.

Table 3.6 shows the impact of these constituency cross pressures on voting of Republican senators in 2009 and 2010. Most Republican senators represented reliably Republican states, and these senators voted in a considerably more conservative direction than their party colleagues from states that were more likely to support Democratic presidential candidates. At the time of the December 2010 vote to repeal "don't ask, don't tell," there were eleven Republican senators from states President Obama won in 2008. Of these, seven voted for repeal, three voted against, and one did not vote. On the other hand, only one of the thirty-one senators from states John McCain carried in 2008 voted for repeal.[93]

TABLE 3.6   Senate Republican Conservatism by Partisanship of State, 2009–2010

Number of Times States Voted Republican in 2000–2008 Presidential Elections	2009		2010	
	Number of Senators	Average Conservative Score*	Number of Senators	Average Conservative Score*
0	3	60	3	63
1	2	69	2	71
2	5	73	5	71
3	31	82	30	83

Source: Ronald Brownstein, "Serving behind Enemy Lines," *National Journal*, April 24, 2010; Ronald Brownstein, "Pulling Apart," *National Journal*, February 26, 2010.

* Calculated by *National Journal,* which ranks members along a conservative to liberal continuum.

In addition, Republican members of Congress faced strong pressure to oppose proposals of the other party. Senator Charles Grassley, the leader of the Senate Finance Committee's negotiations over health care reform, confronted whispers that he might lose his leadership position if he conceded too much to the other side. Iowa conservatives even threatened that Grassley could face a 2010 primary challenge if he backed committee chair Max Baucus's proposals. In a similar vein, the executive committee of the Charleston County, South Carolina, Republican Party censored Republican Senator Lindsey Graham because "U.S. Sen. Lindsey Graham in the name of bipartisanship continues to weaken the Republican brand and tarnish the ideals of freedom, rule of law, and fiscal conservatism."[94] Two months later another county party censored him for his stands on a range of policies, which it charged "debased" Republican beliefs.[95] When asked in 2010 if he would be as bipartisan if he were facing reelection that November, Graham replied, "The answer's probably no." Even a "maverick" like John McCain had to win his primary for renomination in Arizona and thus could not take bipartisan stances.[96]

In January 2010, 55 percent of Republicans and Republican leaners wanted Republican leaders in Congress, who were following a consistently conservative path, to move in a more conservative direction.[97] In perhaps the most extreme expression of this orientation, four months later the Utah Republican party denied longtime conservative Senator Robert Bennett its nomination for reelection. The previous month, Republican governor Charlie Crist had to leave his party and run for the Senate as an Independent in Florida because he was unlikely to win the Republican nomination against conservative Marco Rubio. A year earlier, Republican Senator Arlen Specter of Pennsylvania switched parties, believing there was little chance he could win a Republican primary against conservative Pat Toomey.

Similarly, House Republicans with any moderate leanings were more concerned about the pressures from the right than about potential fallout from opposing a popular president. The conservative Republican Study Committee—which included more than 100 of the 178 House Republicans—called for enforcing party unity on big issues and hinted at retribution against defectors. Conservatives also raised the prospect of primary challenges,[98] as they did in the 2009 race to fill the seat in New York State's twenty-third congressional district. Led by Sarah Palin and Dick Armey, conservatives forced the Republican candidate to withdraw from the race shortly before Election Day.

Compounding the pressure has been the development of partisan communications networks—led by liberal blogs and conservative talk radio—that relentlessly incite each party's base against the other. These constant fusillades help explain why presidents now face lopsided disapproval from the opposition party's voters more quickly than ever, a trend that discourages that party's legislators from working with the White House.

These centrifugal forces affect most the Republican Party. The right has more leverage to discipline legislators because, as we have seen, conservative voters constitute a larger share of the GOP coalition than liberals do of the Democratic Party. The right's partisan communications network is also more ferocious than the left's.

Given the broad influences of ideology and constituency, it is not surprising that scholars have shown that presidential leadership itself demarcates and deepens cleavages in Congress. The differences between the parties and the cohesion within them on floor votes are typically greater when the president takes a stand on issues. When the president adopts a position, members of his party have a stake in his success while opposition party members have a stake in the president's losing. Moreover, both parties take cues from the president that help define their policy views, especially when the lines of party cleavage are not clearly at stake or already well established.[99]

This dynamic of presidential leadership was likely to complicate further Obama's efforts to win Republican support. According to Republican representative Michael Castle of Delaware, the gulf between the parties had grown so wide that most Republicans simply refused to vote for any Democratic legislation. "We are just into a mode where there is a lot of Republican resistance to voting for anything the Democrats are for or the White House is for."[100]

Conclusion

It is difficult to decipher public opinion and to predict what forces may arise to influence it in the months ahead. It is even more difficult to predict public response to specific proposals, since candidates generally avoid delving into details on the campaign trail. Moreover, it is possible that presidential success at altering public policy will create a backlash against further change.

Nevertheless, it is critical that presidents carefully evaluate their opportunity structure regarding obtaining public support for their policies. If they do not ask the right question, they certainly will not arrive at the right answer. To answer the question requires, first, *not* assuming that opinion is malleable. Rejecting the *assumption* of opinion leadership leads one naturally to examine the nature of existing opinion. It also leads one to ask whether one can rely on going public to accomplish policy change.

Analyzing the opportunity structure of the Obama presidency reveals that the nature of a president's opportunity structure is dynamic. The new administration quite reasonably felt it had to devote its initial attention to the crisis in the economy before moving to the issues, such as health care reform, energy, and environmental protection, on which Obama had campaigned for the previous two years. Doing so cost vast sums of money, however, and required unparalleled government intervention in the economy. The scope of the response to the recession discouraged rather than encouraged demand for government services.

Despite voting for a presidential candidate espousing change, the public had not changed its basic skepticism of government or its resistance to paying for it. For some, these policies triggered serious anxiety about the future and were a catalyst for mobilization into intense opposition that manifested itself in both mass protests and hostile confrontations at meetings in congressional constituencies. In sum, by taking dramatic and sweeping action to stem the economy's slide, the president narrowed the prospects for change in other areas of public policy. Political analyst Charlie Cook termed the effort to pass a large agenda "a colossal miscalculation."[101]

What Obama and Democrats failed to realize [Cook said] was that the escalation of spending under Bush, the bailouts and the implementation of TARP, created a political environment that made significant climate change and health care reform ring up "no sale" in the minds of voters. It was too much for them to handle when all they [the public] wanted was a focus on job creation and the economy.[102]

It is not surprising that after a year of Obama's tenure, Americans said they preferred smaller government and fewer services to larger government with more services by 58 percent to 38 percent.[103]

The analysis of Barack Obama's opportunities for obtaining public support leads us to predict that he would have difficulty obtaining the public's backing for his initiatives—even allowing for his impressive public relations skills. In other words, a strategy of governing by "going public" was unlikely to be successful. And that is precisely what happened. With the exceptions of limits on executive pay, regulating the highly unpopular large financial institutions, strengthening food safety regulatory reform, and repealing "don't ask, don't tell," all of which the public had backed before Obama took office, there was no major Obama initiative that enjoyed widespread public support. In addition, identification with the Democratic Party declined substantially, as did evaluations of the party's ability to handle issues relative to that of the Republicans. These party assessments undermined the chances for Democratic success in the 2010 midterm elections, in which the Democrats lost sixty-three seats—and their majority—in the House and six seats in the Senate.[104]

The White House anticipated that it could attract bipartisan support from congressional Republicans. The foundations of this expectation were weak, however. Partisan polarization was at a historic high, and the Republican Party's locus in the economic and social conservatism of the South reinforced the disinclination of Republicans to offer support across the aisle. Indeed, the more homogeneous conservative ideology of Republican activists and the right's strident and ever-expanding communications network meant that Obama would face a vigorous partisan opposition with strong incentives not to cooperate with the White House.

The analysis of Barack Obama's opportunities for obtaining bipartisan support leads us to predict that he would have difficulty obtaining Republican backing for his most significant initiatives, and, thus, that bipartisanship would not be a useful strategy for governing. In fact, Republican support for the president's major initiatives was strikingly low. Indeed, it was usually nonexistent.[105]

If we ask the right questions, we can explain—and predict—the likely success of strategies for governing. Once we understand that presidents are unlikely to create opportunities for change, we naturally focus on whether presidents recognize and exploit opportunities that do exist.

In a rational world, strategies for governing should match the opportunities to be exploited. Barack Obama is only the latest in a long line of presidents who have not been able to transform the political landscape through their efforts at persuasion. When he succeeded in achieving major change, it was by mobilizing those *predisposed* to support him and driving legislation through Congress on a party-line vote. In other words, he succeeded by exploiting the opportunities provided by the large Democratic majorities in Congress. The president's failure to understand the nature of presidential power contributed to the Democrats' substantial defeat in the midterm elections and diminished his ability to govern in 2011–2012.

Notes

1. See George C. Edwards III, *The Strategic President: Persuasion and Opportunity in Presidential Leadership* (Princeton, NJ: Princeton University Press, 2009). For the claim that "presidential power is the power to persuade," see Richard Neustadt, *Presidential Power* (New York: Wiley, 1960).
2. Paul C. Light, "Less Room for Breakthrough Ideas," *Washington Post*, November 11, 2008.
3. White House Transcript, "Remarks by the President to the Business Roundtable," March 12, 2009. Accessible at http://www.whitehouse.gov/the-press-office/remarks-president-business-roundtable.
4. Peter Baker, "Obama Defends Agenda as More than Recession," *New York Times*, March 13, 2009.
5. Quoted in Helene Cooper, "Some Obama Enemies Are Made Totally of Straw," *New York Times*, May 24, 2009. See also Peter Baker, "The Limits of Rahmism," *New York Times Magazine*, March 14, 2010.
6. Dan Balz, "With New Priorities, Obama and Democrats Can Recover in 2010," *Washington Post*, December 27, 2009; Jonathan Alter, *The Promise: President Obama, Year One* (New York: Simon & Schuster, 2010), pp. 244, 246.

7. Baker, "The Limits of Rahmism"; Alter, *The Promise*, p. 395.

8. Michael D. Shear and Shailagh Murray, "President Is Set to 'Take the Baton': As Skepticism on Health Reform Mounts, He Will Intensify His Efforts," *Washington Post*, July 20, 2009. See also Baker, "The Limits of Rahmism"; and Scott Wilson, "Bruised by Stimulus Battle, Obama Changed His Approach to Washington," *Washington Post*, April 29, 2009.

9. Brian Friel, "Democrats Face Daunting Legislative Agenda," *National Journal Online*, May 9, 2009.

10. Jonathan Alter, *The Promise*, p. 9.

11. Barack Obama, *Dreams from My Father* (New York: Crown, 1995), p. 106.

12. See the Heith chapter in this volume.

13. Quoted in Ken Auletta, "Non-Stop News," *New Yorker*, January 25, 2010, p. 44.

14. George C. Edwards III, *On Deaf Ears: The Limits of the Bully Pulpit* (New Haven, CT: Yale University Press, 2003).

15. Edwards, *The Strategic President*, pp. 26-34; George C. Edwards III, *Governing by Campaigning: The Politics of the Bush Presidency*, 2nd ed. (New York: Longman, 2007).

16. See Edwards, *The Strategic President*, chaps. 2-3, 6.

17. Quoted in Dan Balz, "He Promised Change, But Is This Too Much, Too Soon?" *Washington Post*, July 26, 2009.

18. Shailagh Murray and Paul Kane, "Obama's Ambitious Agenda Will Test Congress," *Washington Post*, February 26, 2009.

19. See the Sinclair and Weatherford chapters in this volume for additional detail.

20. Ronald Brownstein and Alexis Simendinger, "The View from the West Wing," *National Journal*, January 16, 2010, p. 27.

21. Wilson, "Bruised by Stimulus Battle."

22. For example, White House communications director Anita Dunn concluded that the administration failed at selling health care reform as a central part of its economic message. Dan Balz, "For Obama, a Tough Year to Get the Message Out," *Washington Post*, January 10, 2010.

23. Barack Obama, State of the Union Address, January 27, 2010. Accessible at http://www.whitehouse.gov/the-press-office/remarks-president-state-union-address.

24. David E. Sanger, "Where Clinton Turned Right, Obama Plowed Ahead," *New York Times*, January 28, 2009.

25. George C. Edwards III, *At the Margins: Presidential Leadership of Congress* (New Haven, CT: Yale University Press, 1989), chap. 8; Lawrence J. Grossback, David A. M. Peterson, and James A. Stimson, *Mandate Politics* (New York: Cambridge University Press, 2006).

26. For more on the conditions that encourage perceptions of a mandate, see Edwards, *At the Margins*, chap. 8; and Grossback, Peterson, and Stimson, *Mandate Politics*, chap. 2.

27. Transcript of press conference on November 25, 2008.

28. ABC News/*Washington Post* poll, January 13-16, 2009.

29. Barack Obama, Inaugural Address, January 20, 2009, available at http://www.whitehouse.gov/blog/inaugural-address/ (accessed March 22, 2011).

30. Quoted in John Harwood, "'Partisan' Seeks a Prefix: Bi- or Post-" *New York Times*, December 7, 2008.

31. Harwood, "'Partisan' Seeks a Prefix."

32. Gallup Poll daily tracking polls, throughout 2009. The sample includes 291,152 US adults. The margin of sampling error for most states is ±2 percentage points, but is as high as ±5 percentage points for the District of Columbia.

33. Gallup Poll surveys conducted January–September 2009.

34. Shawn Treier and D. Sunshine Hillygus, "The Nature of Political Ideology in the Contemporary Electorate," *Public Opinion Quarterly* 73 (Winter 2009): 679-703; Christopher Ellis and James A. Stimson, "Symbolic Ideology in the American Electorate," *Electoral Studies* 28 (September 2009): 388-402; William G. Jacoby, "Policy Attitudes, Ideology, and Voting Behavior in the 2008 Election" (paper presented at the Annual Meeting of the American Political Science Association, 2009); James A. Stimson, *Tides of Consent: How Public Opinion Shapes American Politics* (New York: Cambridge University Press, 2004); Pamela J. Conover and Stanley Feldman, "The Origins and Meaning of Liberal/Conservative Identifications," *American Journal of Political Science* 25 (October 1981): 617-45; David O. Sears, Richard L. Lau, Tom R. Tyler, and Harris M. Allen, "Self-Interest vs. Symbolic Politics in Policy Attitudes and Presidential Voting," *American Political Science Review* 74 (September 1980): 670-84.

35. Philip E. Converse, "The Nature of Belief Systems in Mass Publics," in *Ideology and Discontent*, ed. David E. Apter (New York: Free Press, 1964), pp. 206-61.

36. Teresa E. Levitin and Warren E. Miller, "Ideological Interpretations of Presidential Elections," *American Political Science Review* 73 (September 1973): 751-71.

37. Robert Huckfeldt, Jeffrey Levine, William Morgan, and John Sprague, "Accessibility and the Political Utility of Partisan and Ideological Orientations," *American Journal of Political Science* 43 (July 1999): 888-911; Kathleen Knight, "Ideology in the 1980 Election: Ideological Sophistication Does Matter," *Journal of Politics* 47 (July 1985): 828-53; Levitin and Miller, "Ideological Interpretations of Presidential Elections"; James A. Stimson, "Belief Systems: Constraint, Complexity, and the 1972 Election," *American Journal of Political Science* 19 (July 1975): 393-417.

38. Paul Goren, Christopher M. Federico, and Miki Caul Kittilson, "Source Cues, Partisan Identities, and Political Value Expression," *American Journal of Political Science* 53 (October 2009): 805-20; Christopher M. Federico and Monica C. Schneider, "Political Expertise and the Use of Ideology: Moderating the Effects of Evaluative Motivation," *Public Opinion Quarterly* 71 (Summer 2007): 221-52; William G. Jacoby, "Value Choices and American Public Opinion," *American Journal of Political Science* 50 (July 2006): 706-23; Paul Goren, "Political Sophistication and Policy Reasoning: A Reconsideration," *American Journal of Political Science* 48 (July 2004): 462-78; Paul Goren, "Core Principles and Policy Reasoning in Mass Publics: A Test of Two Theories," *British Journal of Political Science* 31 (January 2001): 159-77; Huckfeldt, Levine, Morgan, and Sprague, "Accessibility and the Political Utility of Partisan and Ideological Orientations"; William G. Jacoby, "The Structure of Ideological Thinking in the American Electorate," *American Journal of Political Science* 39 (April 1995): 314-35;

William G. Jacoby, "Ideological Identification and Issue Attitudes," *American Journal of Political Science* 35 (January 1991): 178-205; Stanley Feldman, "Structure and Consistency in Public Opinion: The Role of Core Beliefs and Attitudes," *American Journal of Political Science* 32 (May 1988): 416-40; Sears et al., "Self-Interest vs. Symbolic Politics in Policy Attitudes and Presidential Voting."

39. Thomas J. Rudolph and Jillian Evans, "Political Trust, Ideology, and Public Support for Government Spending," *American Journal of Political Science* 49 (July 2005): 660-71; William G. Jacoby, "Issue Framing and Government Spending," *American Journal of Political Science* 44 (October 2000): 750-67; William G. Jacoby, "Public Attitudes toward Government Spending," *American Journal of Political Science* 38 (April 1994): 336-61.

40. Andrew Kohut, "Obama's 2010 Challenge: Wake Up Liberals, Calm Down Independents," Pew Research Center for the People and the Press, December 17, 2009.

41. The poll did not define the term "traditional values." Gallup found that when it disaggregated the results by party and ideology, they suggested that respondents understood traditional values to be those generally favored by the Republican Party.

42. Gallup poll, August 31–September 2, 2009.

43. Gallup polls, November 13–16, 2008, and November 5–8, 2009.

44. Phil Mattingly, "Debt Takes a Holiday," *CQ Weekly*, December 28, 2009, pp. 2934-41.

45. *USA Today*/Gallup polls of March 27–29, 2009.

46. Gallup poll, July 17–19, 2009.

47. *Washington Post*-ABC News poll, July 15–18, 2009.

48. *New York Times*/CBS News poll, February 5–10, 2010.

49. Gallup poll, August 6–9, 2009.

50. Gallup poll, August 31–September 2, 2009.

51. Robert S. Erikson, Michael B. MacKuen, and James A. Stimson, *The Macro Polity* (New York: Cambridge University Press, 2002), chap. 9.

52. See Gary C. Jacobson, *A Divider, Not a Uniter: George W. Bush and the American Public*, 3rd ed. (New York: Longman, 2010), and Jacobson's chapter in this volume.

53. If independent leaners are included as partisans, the figure rises to 8.0 percent; only John F. Kennedy attracted fewer (7.1 percent). These figures are from Gary C. Jacobson, "Barack Obama and the American Public: From Candidate to President" (paper delivered at the Conference on the Early Obama Presidency, Centre for the Study of Democracy, University of Westminster, London, May 14, 2010), pp. 6-7.

54. Ibid., pp. 7-11.

55. Kate Kenski, Bruce W. Hardy, and Kathleen Hall Jamieson, *The Obama Victory: How Media, Money, and Message Shaped the 2008 Election* (New York: Oxford University Press, 2010).

56. Spencer Piston, "How Explicit Racial Prejudice Hurt Obama in the 2008 Election," *Political Behavior* 32 (December 2010): 431-51; Michael Lewis-Back, Charles Tien, and Richard Nadeau, "Obama's Missed Landslide: A Racial Cost?" *PS: Political Science and Politics* 43 (January 2010): 69-76.

57. Jay Cost, "Electoral Polarization Continues under Obama," RealClearPolitics HorseRaceBlog, November 20, 2008.

58. Ibid.
59. See Jacobson, *A Divider, Not a Uniter.*
60. Alan I. Abramowitz, *The Disappearing Center* (New Haven, CT: Yale University Press, 2010).
61. Gallup Daily tracking averages for February 9–15, 2009.
62. Gallup Daily tracking averages for April 20–26, 2009.
63. Gary C. Jacobson, "The Bush Presidency and the American Electorate," *Presidential Studies Quarterly* 33 (December 2003): 701-29; Jeffrey M. Jones, "Bush Ratings Show Historical Levels of Polarization," *Gallup News Service,* June 4, 2004.
64. Jeffrey M. Jones, "Obama's Approval Most Polarized for First-Year President," Gallup poll, January 25, 2010; Jeffrey M. Jones, "Bush Ratings Show Historical Levels of Polarization," *Gallup News Service,* June 4, 2004.
65. Gallup Poll Daily tracking polls from July to mid-August 2009, including more than 47,000 interviews.
66. Spee Kosloff, Jeff Greenberg, Toni Schmader, Mark Dechesne, and David Weise, "Smearing the Opposition: Implicit and Explicit Stigmatization of the 2008 U.S. Presidential Candidates and the Current U.S. President," *Journal of Experimental Psychology* 139 (August 2010): 383-98.
67. Spencer Piston, "How Explicit Racial Prejudice Hurt Obama in the 2008 Election," *Political Behavior* 32 (December 2010): 431-51.
68. Charlie Cook, "Intensity Matters," *National Journal,* October 24, 2009.
69. Democracy Corps poll, June 19–22, 2010.
70. CNN poll conducted by Opinion Research Corporation, July 16–21, 2010. See also *Adam J. Berinsky Pollster.com, September* 13, 2010, www.pollster.com/blogs/poll_shows_false_obama_beliefs.php.
71. Pew Research Center for the People and the Press poll, July 21–August 5, 2010.
72. *Newsweek* poll, August 25–26, 2010.
73. As Gary Jacobson points out, some of the mistaken views about Obama were probably driven by opinions about Obama more generally. See "Legislative Success and Political Failure: The Public's Reaction to Barack Obama's Early Presidency," *Presidential Studies Quarterly* 41 (June 2011), pp. 229-30.
74. Pew Research Media Attitudes Survey, July 22–26, 2009.
75. Gallup poll, June 11–13, 2010.
76. Gallup poll, June 23–24, 2009.
77. Gallup poll, May 24–25, 2010.
78. Edwards, *The Strategic President,* chaps. 4-5; Edwards, *At the Margins,* chaps. 9-10; Jon R. Bond and Richard Fleisher, *The President in the Legislative Arena* (Chicago: University of Chicago Press, 1990), chap. 8; Richard Fleisher, Jon R. Bond, and B. Dan Wood, "Which Presidents Are Uncommonly Successful in Congress?," in *Presidential Leadership: The Vortex of Presidential Power,* ed. Bert Rockman and Richard W. Waterman (New York: Oxford University Press, 2007); Keith Krehbiel, *Pivotal Politics: A Theory of U.S. Lawmaking* (Chicago: University of Chicago Press, 1998), chaps. 7-8.
79. Transcript of press conference on November 25, 2008.
80. Wilson, "Bruised by Stimulus Battle."

81. Harwood, "'Partisan' Seeks a Prefix."

82. Quoted in Harwood, "'Partisan' Seeks a Prefix."

83. See George C. Edwards III, *Overreach: Leadership in the Obama Presidency* (Princeton, NJ: Princeton University Press, forthcoming), chap. 5, and also the Sinclair, Foreman, and Weatherford chapters in the present volume.

84. Shailagh Murray, Michael D. Shear, and Paul Kane, "2009 Democratic Agenda Severely Weakened by Republicans' United Opposition," *Washington Post*, January 24, 2010.

85. Nolan McCarty, Keith T. Poole, and Howard Rosenthal, *Polarized America: The Dance of Ideology and Unequal Riches* (Cambridge, MA: MIT Press, 2006).

86. Shawn Zeller, "Party Unity—Parties Dig In Deep on a Fractured Hill," *CQ Weekly*, December 15, 2008, pp. 3332-41.

87. John Cranford, "This Change Isn't Very Hopeful," *CQ Weekly*, February 17, 2009, p. 335.

88. Richard Rubin, "Party Unity: An Ever Thicker Dividing Line," *CQ Weekly*, January 11, 2010, p. 124.

89. Jacobson, "Barack Obama and the American Public," pp. 18-19.

90. See, for example, Gallup polls, December 4–7, 2010, and January 7–9, 2011; and Pew Research Center for the People and the Press poll, January 5–9, 2011.

91. Peter Baker, "Bipartisanship Isn't So Easy, Obama Sees," *New York Times*, February 13, 2009.

92. Ronald Brownstein, "For GOP, A Southern Exposure," *National Journal*, May 23, 2009.

93. Nate Silver, "Popularity of 'Don't Ask' Repeal May Have Drawn Republican Votes," *New York Times*, December 19, 2010.

94. Bruce Smith, "Graham Censured by Charleston County GOP," *The State*, November 12, 2009.

95. The Lexington County Republican Party, "Lexington County Party Passes Resolution of Censure for Lindsey Graham," accessed at www.lcrp-online.com/1.html.

96. Robert Draper, "Lindsey Graham, This Year's Maverick," *New York Times*, July 4, 2010.

97. Pew Research Center for the People and the Press poll, January 6–10, 2010.

98. Alan K. Ota, "GOP Moderates See Political Benefits in Opposing Obama's Economic Agenda," *CQ Today*, February 6, 2009.

99. Frances E. Lee, *Beyond Ideology: Politics, Principles, and Partisanship in the U.S. Senate* (Chicago: University of Chicago Press, 2009), chap. 4.

100. Quoted in Carl Hulse, "Legislative Hurdles in an Era of Conflict, Not Compromise," *New York Times*, June 19, 2010.

101. Charlie Cook, "Colossal Miscalculation on Health Care," *National Journal*, January 16, 2010.

102. Charlie Cook, "Too Much All At Once," *National Journal*, February 2, 2010.

103. *Washington Post*-ABC News poll, January 12–15, 2010.

104. See Edwards, *Overreach*, chap. 3.

105. See ibid., chap. 6.

CHAPTER 4

Political Forces on the Obama Presidency: From Elections to Governing

James E. Campbell

THE POLITICS OF THE PRESIDENCY, whether with respect to elections or to governing, are ultimately structured by the push and pull on presidents of two broad constituencies: the president's ideological and partisan base and moderate swing voters who support the president.[1] On one side are pressures pushing presidents to take more ideologically pure or extreme policy positions aimed at satisfying the party's base. On the other are forces pulling presidents to compromise toward the political center with the hope of pleasing pivotal swing voters who are generally more moderate in their policy preferences. Presidents who adopt more centrist policies risk satisfying moderates at the cost of displeasing their partisan base. On the other hand, presidents who advocate more ideologically ambitious policies risk pleasing their base at the expense of alienating supporters in the political center.[2]

Every president confronts the dilemma of how best to respond to the push of the base and the pull of the center. The names change throughout history and across parties, but the fundamental political tension is a constant. Neither the base nor the center can be ignored. The numbers do not allow it. Support from both is generally required in order to win elections and to govern effectively. Neither party's base alone, whether in the electorate or in the halls of Congress, is normally large enough to win elections or to pass legislation.[3]

Since neither the ideological base of a party nor its supporters in the center can be ignored—and since both have different demands—presidents must arrive at some balance between them. In no small part, the success of presidents in governing depends on their success in striking the right balance between governing to please their party's base and governing to please the political center. Like every presidency before his, this is the challenge for Obama's presidency. Its success in governing the nation, as well as the possibility of a second term, may hinge on how well the president strikes the right balance between appealing to his liberal base and simultaneously to his supporters in the political center.

Politics of the Base and Politics of the Center

The principal reason why a president's success in office depends on his ability to maintain the support of the president's electoral coalition (the combined partisan base and centrist supporters) is that this is also his governing coalition. Since political views are generally stable, a president should expect to receive most of his support while in office from the same quarters that supported him in his election. As a consequence, the success of a president in office depends to a great extent on his ability to maintain both the support of his base and the center. Just as the president's electoral success depended on maintaining his electoral coalition, his success in governing depends on maintaining the support of that same coalition. In effect, there is no bright line between the politics of governing and the politics of elections. In its most basic sense, the "permanent campaign" to maintain the president's constituency of supporters from election to office and on to the next election is fundamental to presidential politics.[4]

Though all presidents naturally emphasize the common views and unifying interests of their base and centrists and even those in the opposition, the views and interests of the base and the center are often not in accord. As a result, presidents are forced to make decisions that please one element of their constituency and not the other. The tension between the base and the center was expressed colorfully by former Vermont Governor and 2004 Democratic presidential hopeful Howard Dean when he sarcastically referred to his candidacy as coming out of "the Democratic wing of the Democratic Party," implying that moderate Democrats were not really Democrats. Conservative Republicans have similarly derided members of the more conciliatory or centrist wing of their party as "me too Republicans" or RINOs ("Republicans in Name Only").

The conflict between the base and the center is not one on which a president takes sides. Both have political leverage and presidents need support from both. Either wing of the coalition may withdraw its support if displeased by the president's policies. Centrist voters have a real option to vote for the opposing party in the next election and their representatives have the option to support the opposition party's legislative positions. While those in the base are unlikely to defect to the opposition, they may decide to sit out an election or withhold support for the president's program if they feel neglected. Differences in the turnout of partisans over the years have quite clearly affected the party vote divisions in both congressional and presidential elections.[5] As a result, presidents must work to maintain peace within their coalitions by simultaneously satisfying both base and centrist supporters as much as possible.

While neither the base nor moderates, as a practical matter, can get everything they want from a president, a central question for every president is whether he is able to steer a course between his base and the political center that holds their support for him. For President Obama, this led to the question: how could he best hold together the coalition of liberal Democrats and moderate swing voters who elected him in 2008? For analysts, the question is, how successful was he in doing this? The answer to the latter question may take us a long way toward understanding whether the public will regard the Obama presidency as a success, whether it provides him with support for his legislative agenda in the second half of his term and, ultimately, whether it confers a second term on him.

An Electoral Theory of Presidential Leadership

How should presidents attempt to balance the competing demands of their partisan base and their more centrist supporters? There is no one-size-fits-all presidential leadership of balancing these two constituencies.[6] Different presidents attempt to govern under different circumstances and with different amounts of support coming from their base and from centrists. The recognition of these differences, however, provides the basis for an electoral theory of presidential leadership.

The theory is grounded on three premises. The first is simply that presidents require political support in order to govern effectively. While there have been studies suggesting that presidential success in getting legislative support does not depend on approval by the public, this probably reflects the complications of varying lags and temporary fluctuations in levels of public support.[7] A thought experiment of extreme values suggests that there *must* be an association between public support and legislative support for presidents. Suppose a president's level of public support is complete. Everyone supports the president. It would be difficult to imagine a president with this much political capital not getting his way on just about everything. At the other extreme, suppose a president bereft of support. Would we seriously expect him to have any sway with Congress? Presidential success in governing depends on public support—not entirely, but substantially.[8]

The second premise of the theory is that presidents are most likely to find support in the same quarters that provided them support in their prior election. As public opinion studies since the 1940s have repeatedly demonstrated, there is a substantial inertia to opinions.[9] Attitudes, even if often inchoate and roughly measured, are generally stable. Neither support nor opposition is easily or frequently changed. Whatever caused citizens to support the president as a candidate should also cause them to support the president in office.

A third premise of the theory is that every supporter, whether from the base or in the center, is about equally valuable to a president's coalition and about equally deserving of the president's attention. Some claim that centrist supporters are more important in that they are more moveable.[10] However, though centrists may find it easier to drop their support for a president, they may also more easily return to the fold. In addition, centrist supporters are more replaceable. While some centrists may leave the president's coalition, others may join it. Once support is lost in the base, however, it is very difficult to restore. While centrists may move in and out of the president's coalition more freely, those in the base are more attentive to politics and watch their president more intently. While they are loyal, they also have high and often unrealistic expectations. They are not moved easily out of a president's coalition, but once they become disgruntled, their support is not easily regained. As a consequence, presidents need to nurture the support they receive from the base every bit as much as they need to attend to the preferences of supporters in the political center. The base cannot be taken for granted.

Though several other political considerations (including the appeal of the opposition party and the president's margin of victory) may come into play, and while the soundness of public policy as well as events may supersede politically calculated presidential decisions, all things being equal, the three premises identify an optimal presidential strategy for balancing responsiveness between the president's base and centrists. In general, from a political standpoint, *presidents should balance their overall leadership to their base and to the political center in proportion to the electoral support that they received from each.*

Another thought experiment taking presidential support levels to their extremes demonstrates the rationale for this. Suppose a president's base and centrists were far apart in their preferences and that all of the support that the president received in his election was drawn from his base. Having been elected by his base, it would be foolhardy to govern to the center. If centrists had provided no support in the election, they would not be especially likely to provide much support for the president's programs. Some centrists might move in his direction as a result of his newfound policy centrism, but this would likely be of marginal consequence. Meanwhile, the president's attention to centrists would earn him the wrath of his base. Having provided all of his support in the election, those in the base would have had every right to believe that they would be paid attention to when the candidate became president. Once they understood that they were being ignored, they would withdraw their support. A more politically astute president in this situation would tend to his base. These were the voters who elected him and who elected the representatives who would vote on his legislative program. Without them, he is without support.

The logic of the theory is the same if the president had been elected primarily by the support of centrists. It would be a political mistake for a president elected by centrists to govern to please the base. Having failed to support the president in the election, many in the base would only come around slowly and grudgingly to support the president. Centrists, on the other hand, would quite immediately feel abandoned and fooled by a candidate who appealed to their moderate views in order to get their votes and then acted as an ideologue once elected. In the end, the president would have lost the support he needed to govern.

The sensible political strategy of presidential leadership is for presidents to learn from their elections about who supports them and to try to satisfy the base and the center in proportion to the electoral support that each provided. In essence, as the old saying goes, presidents should "dance with the ones that brung them." Presidents who stray from the political balance between their base voters and swing voters that made their election possible do so at their own risk.

Values and Performance

Presidents receive electoral support for two fundamental reasons. Candidates are evaluated by some combination of what the public thinks of their values and of their performance—what candidates think should be done, and what incumbents have done. Perhaps the most prominent reference to the values–performance dimensions of evaluation in American politics came in the 1988 nomination acceptance speech by Democratic presidential candidate Michael Dukakis when he told his party's convention that "this election isn't about ideology. It's about competence."[11] In fact, though the emphasis on each may reflect the circumstances of the time, every election is about both.

The distinction between values and performance as a basis for supporting a candidate or a president is essentially the age-old distinction between policy and results. You may support or not support a president because of his positions, what he stands for (policy), or because of what he has accomplished or not accomplished (results). This distinction in the realm of economic voting is essentially the difference between prospective and retrospective voting.[12] Presidents can be supported for their policies (prospective) or for the condition of the economy during their term (retrospective). In essence, citizens rate presidents and presidential candidates more favorably to the extent that they share the same views about what government ought to be doing (using the preferred policies/values) and to the extent that they regard the president or candidate as successfully administering the office (effectively achieving the desired results/performance). For candidates who are not incumbents, the performance of the incumbent president affects how voters evaluate the candidates.[13]

While both supporters in the base and those in the center care about both values and performance, they differ in the emphasis that they place on them. With a strong commitment to their ideological perspectives, those in the base give greater weight to a president advancing their values (their preferred policies). Indeed, they even judge a president's performance through the lens of these values, giving a like-minded president the benefit of the doubt. Centrists, on the other hand, are less ideologically committed and care more about the performance of the administration. They demand results.

Just as elections provide guidance as to whether a president should govern to his base or the center, they also indicate whether a president should be more concerned about adhering to his party's principles (values) or ensuring that national conditions are satisfactory (performance). Certainly presidents want to do both, just as they want to please both their base and the center; but it is often necessary to prioritize and the reason for the president's election provides a clue to the politically healthiest priorities. Presidents who were elected primarily because of what they stood for should be less willing to compromise than presidents who were elected primarily because of their performance or the performance of their predecessor.[14] In short, *presidents should govern to respond to the nature of the reasons why they were elected in the first place.*

Essentially, every president has a mandate to some degree. The idea of a mandate has often been dismissed by political observers, but this dismissal is of an extreme idea of a mandate.[15] If a mandate is thought of as a set of specific directions from the public as to how a president should govern, then presidents seldom, if ever, are elected with a mandate. They are, however, elected for a general reason or a set of reasons. Elections are not randomly determined. In electing one candidate over another, voters are revealing what they want or do not want out of government. This should be regarded by leaders as their mandate—a general assignment from the electorate. Presidents are well advised to properly interpret what got them elected and to govern accordingly.

The Obama Presidency

With some theoretical guidelines in place, we can now turn to the Obama presidency. Based on what we know about the political landscape leading into the 2008 presidential election and his victory over his Republican rival John McCain, how should President Barack Obama have governed with respect to making a tradeoff between appealing to his liberal Democratic base and to his support among centrists? To what extent should he have geared his policy agenda to the liberal values of his party's base as opposed to the more moderate values and performance concerns of swing voters? Finally, has President Obama midway through his term followed the politically prudent and democratic course of presidential leadership to maintain his coalition?

The short answer to the last question is "no." In light of both the mix of the base and centrist votes in his column and the reasons for his victory in the 2008 presidential election, President Obama's prospects for a successful presidency would have been greater had he governed more to please the center than his base and had he focused his energies on performance issues, particularly with respect to getting the economy back on track. He was elected, in no small part, because of centrist support based on the unsatisfactory performance of his predecessor and the Wall Street Meltdown that sent the economy into a tailspin during September and October of 2008. These factors should have dominated the Obama presidency from the outset, but they did not. President Obama, instead, during the first two years of his presidency governed more to the values of his party's base and had little success in fostering a robust recovery. As a result, he lost much of the centrist support that got him elected and energized the opposition leading into the midterm elections. President Obama may have understood the gamble that he was taking in his governing decision, but the Democrats' loss of sixty-four seats and control of the House and the loss of six Senate seats in the 2010 midterm elections may have been more than he had bargained for. It was the biggest loss of House seats for either party in sixty-two years and put more Republicans in the House than in any election since 1946.[16] It was, in President Obama's own word, a "shellacking" that would greatly restrict and restrain him in the second half of this term.

Electoral Forces

There were three important and successive sets of conditions that ultimately determined the 2008 presidential election and affected the extent to which the liberal Democratic Party base or voters in the political center would provide the basis for Barack Obama's election and whether his election would reflect the appeal of his values or would reflect assessments of the performance of his predecessor and his party. The first set encompassed the long-term political predispositions of the voters. Americans in 2008 were highly polarized, very partisan, and quite evenly divided in their perspectives on politics. Normally, this would be an overriding consideration in the election, and though it was important, it was superseded by a second set of important conditions in the election: evaluations of the departing administration. Though America was nearly a 50-50 nation in its long-term political orientations, it was more like a "two-thirds to one-third" nation in its evaluation of the Bush presidency going into the 2008 election season.[17] Normally, this might have been the end of the story, but not in 2008. Retrospective evaluations of the Bush presidency meant only so much in an open seat contest with an unusually moderate Republican candidate in Arizona senator John McCain. In the end, both the balance of long-term political predispositions and the negative pre-campaign retrospective evaluations of President Bush's job performance were trumped by the third set of critical electoral forces: the financial crisis that became known as the Wall Street Meltdown. In mid-September of 2008, it sent the economy spiraling into

FIGURE 4.1   The Political Ideologies of Voters, 1972–2008

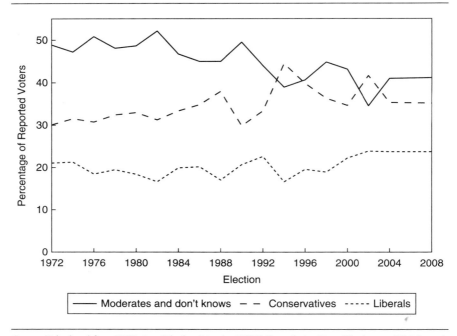

Source: Calculated from VCF0803 (ideology) in the ANES Cumulative Data File dataset. Weight variable VCF0009A was used. Note: The percentages are of reported voters. Those who would not classify themselves are grouped with the moderates. Conservatives include the slightly conservative, conservative, and extremely conservative. Liberals include the slightly liberal, liberal, and extremely liberal. ANES data were obtained from: http://www.electionstudies.org/.

a deep recession, the worst economic crisis since the Great Depression of the 1930s, and sent Democratic presidential candidate Barack Obama to the White House.

A Polarized and Partisan Nation. The electorate that Barack Obama and John McCain faced in their 2008 election was highly polarized. It had been so for many years, but became even more so in the early 1990s.[18] Figure 4.1 presents the percentages of reported voters in the American National Election Study (ANES) who were moderates, conservatives, and liberals. Both self-described moderates and those who said that they did not know how to classify themselves ideologically are counted as moderates. Conservatives include those who declared themselves slightly conservative, conservative, or extremely conservative. Liberals also include the equivalent three degrees of commitment to the liberal label. The data series begins in 1972, the first year that ANES asked the ideology question.

The figure indicates a rise in the number of conservatives and liberals and a decline in non-ideological moderates. According to ANES data, about half of all voters were moderates in the 1970s and 1980s. Their numbers declined in the late 1980s and 1990s. Since 1990, compared to those with a definite ideological perspective, moderates have been a minority of voters in every election. Moderates now typically comprise about 40 percent of the electorate. The number of conservatives since 1994 has rivaled and on occasion exceeded the number of moderates (including "don't knows"). In 2008, 35 percent of voters called themselves conservatives(37 percent in Gallup data). And while the percentage of self-identified liberals has increased slightly since the 1970s, they remain less than a quarter of all voters (22 percent in Gallup data). The electorate is unmistakably center-right.

The 2008 electorate was also highly partisan and evenly divided. Figure 4.2 presents a plot of the distribution of party identification among voters in elections since 1952. The ANES data have been adjusted to bring them into line with actual turnout rates and vote choice divisions.[19] The figure indicates that the large party identification advantage that Democrats held over Republicans largely disappeared in the 1980s. Since 1984, the gap between Democrats and Republicans has bumped around between near-parity and a slight Democratic edge. The small differences from election to election reflect the political climate of the particular elections. In good years for Republicans (1984, 1988, 2004), there was virtually no gap. In good years for the Democrats (1992, 1996, and 2008), Democrats had an edge. Some of this may be the political climate temporarily pulling people into the party or pulling partisans to the polls, but the operative word is "temporarily." For all intents and purposes, partisanship as a long-term disposition in the American electorate has seen Democrats and Republicans at a nearly equal division since the mid-1980s.

Partisanship in the American electorate is not only evenly divided, it is intensely divided. Nearly 38 percent of voters in the 2008 election indicated a strong identification with either the Democratic or the Republican Party. In the short period of partisan dealignment in the 1970s, fewer than 30 percent of voters indicated an allegiance this strong. One important reason for the strength of partisanship is the ideological polarization that undergirds it.

What are the implications of a polarized partisan electorate near parity (say that three times fast!) for the potential of building a winning presidential coalition out of each party's base and from the political center? First, polarization makes it more difficult for presidents to assemble and maintain their coalitions. It is easier to please voters with a smaller range of views than voters whose perspectives are more diverse. Second, polarization affects the composition of coalitions. It increases the potential number of votes in both parties that might be drawn from their base of supporters. By the same token, with fewer moderates in the electorate, centrists

FIGURE 4.2   Party Identifications of Voters, 1952–2008

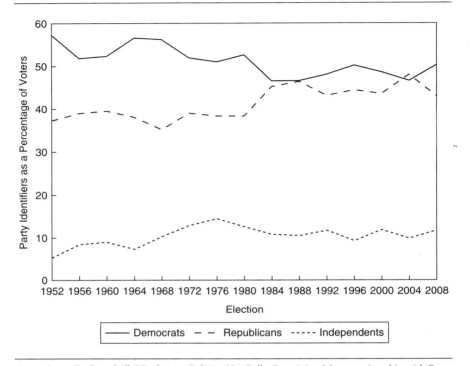

Source: James E. Campbell, "Explaining Politics, Not Polls: Examining Macropartisanship with Recalibrated NES Data," *Public Opinion Quarterly* 74, 4 (October 2010): 616-42. ANES data were obtained from: http://www.electionstudies.org/. The data have been corrected to reflect the actual divisions of voters and nonvoters and the partisan division of the presidential vote. Note: Leaners are counted as partisans.

are likely to make up less of a president's coalition than they did in the past. Still, the percentage of the electorate in the middle is a large pool of votes that is likely to be a significant component of any winning coalition.

The implications of the polarization and partisan parity of the electorate, while important to both parties, are not the same for each party. There is more potential for Republicans to draw from their base than there is for Democrats to draw from theirs. There are two reasons for this. First, as figure 4.1 showed, conservatives continue to outnumber liberals by twelve to fifteen percentage points. Second, the realignment of partisans in the 1980s increased Republican ranks, and these new Republicans were particularly likely to be conservatives.

According to ANES data in 2008, while there are roughly the same number of strong Democrats and strong Republicans (about 19 percent with corrected data each averaged over 2004 and 2008), strong Republicans were almost twice as likely to be conservatives as strong Democrats were to be liberals. Among strong Democrats, 45 percent claimed to be liberals. Among strong Republicans, 85 percent claimed to be conservatives. Even with the general increase in polarization, the potential for drawing support out of their base is greater for Republicans than it is for Democrats.

Retrospective Evaluations of President Bush.   As important as polarization and reinvigorated partisanship were to setting the context for the 2008 election, they were no match in importance to the widespread frustration with the performance of the Bush presidency. When President Bush was reelected in 2004, his approval rating stood at 51 percent. For the first half of 2005, his approval rating averaged 49 percent. Though not strong, these were respectable ratings, but they would head steadily downward throughout his second term.

One issue after another took its toll on President Bush's support. As the Iraq and Afghanistan wars dragged on, support dropped. Then there was Hurricane Katrina and the mishandling of the relief and reconstruction efforts. Support among independents and Republicans eroded. Then the administration advocated a comprehensive immigration reform that was anathema to the conservative Republican base. With unrelenting criticism from conservative media pundits, support among Republicans dropped from nearly 90 percent to only 70 percent.

Table 4.1 presents the average Gallup approval ratings for Bush at various periods of his second term among all respondents and for each of the party identification groups. Bush was reelected with substantial support of his base, some support from independents, and negligible support from Democrats. From early 2005 to early 2008, his approval ratings dropped eighteen percentage points to only 31 percent. By historical standards (where approval averages 49 percent), this signaled widespread dissatisfaction with his performance. Most Democrats in 2005 had already rejected him on both values and performance grounds. By early 2008, most independents and many Republicans had lost confidence in the administration, and this was where things stood as late as mid-September. Between 2005 and mid-September of 2008, President Bush's approval dropped about fifteen points among independents and twenty points among Republicans.

Nonetheless, despite the poor grades that President Bush had been given, the presidential race was remarkably close through mid-September. Since 1948, in the seven elections in which a president had an approval rating of over 50 percent in July's Gallup poll, the in-party presidential candidate had a lead over his opponent

TABLE 4.1   Approval Ratings for President Bush, 2005 to 2008

Time Period	Overall	Democrats	Independents	Republicans
2005, January to June (21 polls)	49	17	41	89
2008, January to June (15 polls)	31 (−18)	7 (−10)	24 (−17)	69 (−20)
2008, June to mid-September (6 polls)	32 (+1)	5 (−2)	27 (+3)	70 (+1)
2008, late-September to Election Day (6 polls)	27 (−5)	5 (0)	21 (−6)	61 (−9)

Source: Computed from Gallup Poll data available at http://www.gallup.com/poll/116500/Presidential-Approval-Ratings-George-Bush.aspx (accessed March 25, 2011).

Note: The percentage point change from the earlier period is in parentheses.

in the preference polls at Labor Day. At the other end of the spectrum, each of the six in-party candidates who ran when their party's president had ratings of 45 percent or less trailed their opponent at Labor Day.

The race in 2008, however, was different. Despite President Bush's approval ratings of just over 30 percent in July (tied for the lowest since 1948), McCain held a lead over Obama at Labor Day (52.7% to 47.3%). In fact, considering the baggage of President Bush's basement dwelling approval ratings, the race had been surprisingly close through much of August, and McCain came out of the conventions with a poll lead that lasted until mid-September. The average of Gallup's pre-convention polls (August 1 to 24) had the race at 51.3 percent Obama to 48.7 percent McCain, a gap of less than three points. With the higher propensity of registered Republicans to turn out to vote and the closing of the gap in the ten days before the conventions (50.6 Obama to 49.4 McCain), the race going into the conventions was a toss-up. Despite Iraq, a sluggish economy, an unpopular president, and all the elements of the Democratic year, McCain was still quite clearly in the game and Obama had not "sealed the deal."

An important reason for the race being competitive until mid-September was that the Democrats' advantage on performance grounds, reflecting the poor approval numbers for President Bush, was offset by the Republicans' advantage on values grounds. As noted above, the nation is center-right ideologically. McCain was a center-right candidate (too centrist for many conservatives) and Obama had a liberal record (decidedly not center-right).[29] Northern liberal Democrats have not had much electoral success in national elections since the late 1960s. Five have run and five have lost: Humphrey in 1968, McGovern in 1972, Mondale in 1984, Dukakis in 1988, and Kerry in 2004. Polls in 2008 also indicated that Obama's ideological perspective was not an asset. An October Gallup poll indicated that 29 percent of respondents regarded Obama as "very liberal" while only 16 percent found McCain to be "very conservative." ANES data indicate that more voters placed themselves closer on the ideological scale to McCain (47%) than to Obama (40%). In the exit polls, 42 percent of voters considered Obama to be "too liberal" and 89 percent of them voted for McCain.[21] Of the 30 percent of voters in the exit polls saying that the candidate quality that mattered to them most was whether the candidate "shares my values," McCain beat Obama by two-to-one (65% to 32%). With values considerations on McCain's side of the scale and performance considerations on Obama's side, the election was on course to be narrowly decided—but then all hell broke loose. The campaign and the economy collapsed with the financial crisis.

The Wall Street Meltdown.   In mid-September, the 2008 presidential campaign was derailed by the unforeseen economic crisis. It was unforeseen not only by political leaders in both parties, but even by economic forecasters just weeks before the collapse. In mid-August of 2008, the Federal Reserve Bank of Philadelphia released a survey of forty-seven prominent economic forecasters who predicted a third-quarter real GDP growth rate of 1.2 percent, a sluggish economy, but certainly not one in recession.[22] Despite the fact that this forecast was made midway through the quarter being forecast and the meltdown occurred only in the last month of the quarter, the actual GDP growth rate for the quarter according to the Bureau of Economic Analysis was *negative* 4.0 percent, more than five points lower than the forecast made *during* the quarter![23]

The initial signs of the brewing crisis began in early September when the government seized control of Fannie Mae and Freddie Mac, the two government-sponsored mortgage institutions. In the next several weeks, Lehman Brothers declared bankruptcy, Bank of America bought a distressed Merrill Lynch, the government bailed out insurance giant AIG, the FDIC seized Washington Mutual, and President Bush proposed and Congress passed the $700 billion Bipartisan Emergency Economic Stabilization Act. From September 8 to October 9, the stock market lost a quarter of its value (a 25 percent drop in the Dow Jones index and a 28 percent drop in the Standard and Poor's index). Though the economy had been sluggish, the meltdown deepened and prolonged the worst economic downturn since the Great Depression of the 1930s.

The meltdown had an immediate impact on public opinion about the economy, about President Bush's performance, and about the race between McCain and Obama. A *USA Today* and Gallup poll in late September asked respondents how they would describe "the current situation." Forty percent said that it was "the biggest financial crisis in [their] lifetime." Another 24 percent said that it was "a crisis but not the worst in [their] lifetime." The percentage rating economic conditions as poor (the lowest rating) jumped from 46 percent in August and early September to 68 percent in October.[24]

The political fallout was clear. Despite President Bush's low approval ratings going into the election and the polarization of the electorate, his ratings sank even lower after the meltdown. They dropped from an average of 32 percent in mid summer and early fall polls to just 27 percent from late September to Election Day. As Frank Newport and his colleagues at Gallup observed, the meltdown was "the turning point in the campaign."[25] Senator McCain's preference poll numbers dropped from 51 percent to 45 percent in the three weeks between September 14 and October 6. The polls in the remaining four weeks bounced around a bit without much real change. The election had been decided in Obama's favor.

On Election Day 2008, the exit polls confirmed as much. They indicated that 71 percent of voters disapproved of how President Bush had performed his job as president and Barack Obama received about two-thirds of their votes. An overwhelming majority of voters, 63 percent, said that the economy was the most important issue facing the nation. This was more than six times the number who said that the Iraq War was the most important issue and seven times the number who said health care was. Of the 81 percent of voters who said that they were worried that the economic crisis would hurt their families, 58 percent voted for Obama. Only 40 percent voted for McCain.

The standoff for some voters between regarding Republicans positively on values and negatively on performance was settled. Enough was enough. There were the wars in Iraq and Afghanistan, the Katrina fiasco, the ballooning deficits, the illegal immigration quagmire, and now the financial institution meltdown. Each took its toll on Republican support, but for a critical number, the meltdown was the proverbial straw that broke the camel's back.[26] It was one crisis too many. On performance grounds, voters turned to Obama and the Democrats.

The Base and the Center in Perspective

President Obama was elected because of voter dissatisfaction with his predecessor's performance in office, particularly the inability to prevent the financial meltdown that sent the economy into a tailspin. He was not elected because a center-right electorate embraced his liberal perspective of change in public policies. This suggests that President Obama's election may have depended more on the support of pragmatic centrists than the idealistic liberals of his base, but we now turn to the direct evidence of this. To what degree did President Obama's winning coalition depend on support from his liberal base and to what degree did it depend on

FIGURE 4.3   The President's Base and Non-Base Vote, 1972-2008

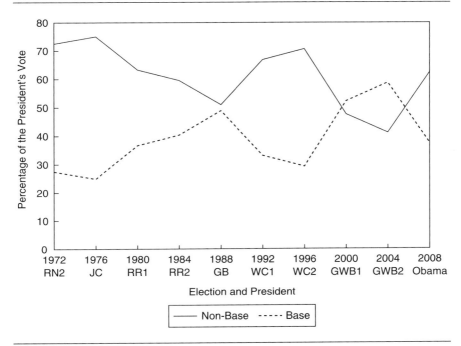

Source: Calculated from variables VCF0803 (ideology) and VCF0705 (presidential vote) in the ANES Cumulative Data File dataset. Weight variable VCF0009A was used. ANES data were obtained from: http://www.electionstudies.org/. Note: The base vote consists of party identifiers claiming an ideological perspective consistent with the president's party (e.g., liberal Democrats for a Democratic president, conservative Republicans for a Republican president). The non-base vote consists of moderates, don't knows, and those with ideological views opposite of those of the president. Both percentages are of reported voters for the president.

centrists? How does the mix of President Obama's coalition compare to those of previous presidents? How much emphasis should President Obama have placed on promoting liberal policies to please his party's base as opposed to policies that were effective from the standpoint of satisfying the concerns of those in the political mainstream?

Figure 4.3 displays the mix of base and centrist support in the ten presidential elections since 1972. The percentages of support from both groups were calculated from ANES data. The analysis begins with the 1972 election, since that is the first in which ANES respondents were asked about their ideological disposition. Voters in the president's base are defined as those identifying with the president's party who also are ideologically disposed to that party (conservative Republicans and liberal Democrats), and voted for their party's winning presidential candidate.[27] Moderates in the president's coalition are those who voted for the president and were either self-described moderates or did not know their ideological disposition. The inclusion of those failing to claim an ideological perspective may cause an over-count of centrists, since there are undoubtedly some who have conservative or liberal perspectives on politics but just are unfamiliar with the labels. However, it is probably safe to assume that most who are unaware of ideological labels are also not very ideological. Finally, there is always a small, but nontrivial, number of voters who vote for the winning presidential candidate but hold ideological views that are opposite those associated with the president's base—self-described conservatives who vote for a Democratic president and self-described liberals who vote for a Republican president. These voters are counted with the centrists since they are clearly not in the president's base. They were certainly centrist enough that they opted to vote for the candidate from the opposing perspective rather than their own or not voting at all.

As the figure indicates, the coalition that elected President Obama in 2008 drew more support from centrists than from the liberal base of the Democratic Party. Of Obama's total popular vote, 62 percent came from moderates (and some conservatives) and 38 percent came from his liberal base. A separate examination of the exit polls in 2008 indicates precisely the same mix of 38 percent of the Obama vote from his liberal base and 62 percent from moderates and a few conservatives.

Putting these numbers into the perspective of past presidencies, there appear to have been three general compositions of presidential coalitions. First are those of presidents who depended heavily on centrist support (two-thirds or more of their support from centrists). This would include the pre-polarization presidencies of Richard Nixon in 1972 and Jimmy Carter in 1976 as well as Bill Clinton in both 1992 and 1996. A second group of presidents are those who relied more on votes from the center than from the base, but whose division of support was not lopsided. This would include Reagan's coalitions in 1980 and 1984. Finally, there are the coalitions that were evenly balanced between the base and the center or in which the base predominated. In this group are George H. W. Bush in 1988 and George W. Bush's coalitions in both 2000 and 2004.

Of all the previous presidents examined, President Obama's mix of base and centrist votes most resembles that of President Reagan's in 1980. Both relied quite a bit on the votes of centrists in their elections, but the ratio of base to centrist votes in both cases was less than two to one. It is certainly in contrast to the coalition of his predecessor. Unlike President Obama, President George W. Bush received more of his vote from his base than from the center.

This analysis indicates that President Obama owed his election substantially to the votes of centrists. Though President Obama's victory surely owed much to the support from and enthusiasm of the base, its votes were not as important as the support he received from those in the political center. Combining this finding with the analysis of the issues that determined the 2008 election (reactions to the Wall Street Meltdown) and the political implications for politically sensitive governing are clear: President Obama should have given a much higher priority in governing to pleasing centrists on the matters of performance that they were most concerned about than to the more value-based issues of concern to his liberal Democratic base. Of course, presidents may gamble that they can do both—or that they can tend to the base and that those policies will eventually be appreciated by centrists (Reagan in 1980)—but there is often a price to be paid for a gamble of this sort. And in the 2010 midterm, Democrats paid that price.

From Elections to Governing

The composition of his electoral coalition and the circumstances under which he was elected in 2008 should have caused President Obama to govern to the center and to make setting the economy on a path of sustained growth his highest priority. This was not, however, the course he followed. President Obama's priorities in governing were more consistent with those of his liberal base than the political center. The left got a number of big items on its "wish list," including a national health care law, a large stimulus package of domestic spending and targeted tax cuts, and the appointments of two liberal Supreme Court justices in Sonia Soto-mayor and Elena Kagan.[28] In contrast, moderates were disappointed on policy grounds, but even more so on performance grounds. Midway through Obama's term, the economy had yet to recover from the recession. Moreover, a large major-ity of Americans did not think that real recovery was imminent or that the admin-istration's policies to that point had been helpful.

Not Enough for the Left

Though President Obama was more attentive to those in his base than to his centrist supporters, the base was not altogether pleased midway through the term. As one might expect from the polarization of political views as well as from the unrealistic expectations generated by the rock-star-like idolization of Obama as a candidate (dubbed "Obamamania"), there were inevitable disappointments on the left. They did not get everything that they wanted (and some might not have been satisfied with anything less than everything). Though President Obama pushed a historic national health care bill through Congress, he backed off on supporting the "public option" health care reform favored by the most liberal ele-ments of his party. Though he ran as the antiwar candidate, albeit accepting the Afghanistan war as a necessary war, to the displeasure of the very liberal elements of his coalition, he continued to prosecute both the Iraq and Afghanistan wars. (In the case of the Iraq war, this was as much a concession to reality as to centrists, since that war had taken a positive turn in the last year of the Bush presidency.) While the administration made plans to close the terrorist detention camp at Guantanamo Bay, a measure advocated by many on the left, the prison remained in operation two years into Obama's presidency. The "don't ask, don't tell" policy regarding gays in the military, a policy opposed by those on the left, was not an early priority (though it was repealed after the midterm). The "card check" bill, also known as the "Employee Free Choice Act," was the chief priority of labor unions, but failed to make legislative headway. Though he made an effort in its behalf, efforts to pass the left's environmental and energy "cap and trade" proposal were stalled in the Senate. There were undoubtedly other areas of disappointment, as well, for Obama's liberal supporters.

Policy Disapproval from the Center

Though the left had some disappointments, centrists suffered many more. These were of two sorts. First, the administration pursued a number of policies that were not popular with political moderates. Most notable of these was health care reform. A *USA Today* and Gallup poll in late August of 2010 indicated that 39 percent approved of the health care overhaul, but 56 percent disapproved of it. A CBS News and *New York Times* poll in mid-September similarly found 37 percent approval of the health care law, 49 percent disapproval, and 14 percent unsure.[29] The Kaiser Health Tracking Poll in November 2010 found that 49 percent of Americans wanted to repeal all or part of the new health care law and only 40 percent wanted to keep or expand it.[30] Some angry with the law, to be sure, felt it was not expansive enough. But the bottom line is that the single greatest legislative achievement of the Obama administration upset many more Americans than it pleased and this included many centrists who had made Obama's election possible. One analysis estimated that Democrats lost between two and three percentage points of the national congressional vote because of health care reform.[31]

Other administration policies also met with centrist disapproval. In an effort to reinvigorate the economy and speed up the recovery, the administration and congressional Democrats enacted an $800 billion stimulus package. This contributed to a ballooning of the federal deficit and was seen by many Americans as ineffective and misguided. An ABC News and *Washington Post* poll in early October of 2010 reported that 68 percent of respondents considered this spending as "mostly wasted."[32] The exit polls of 2010 found that 31 percent of voters thought that the stimulus plan made "no difference" and that another 34 percent thought it had "hurt the economy." Only 32 percent said that they thought the stimulus had "helped the economy."[33]

Other policies and actions, generally falling under the heading of policies that were widely perceived as left-leaning, rankled centrists (e.g., the Justice Department's legal challenge to Arizona's law targeting illegal immigration.) They also had the effect of energizing a disparate conservative opposition of various stripes, from the traditional to the emerging Tea Party movement. Overall, the exit polls of 2010 indicated that 53 percent of voters thought that President Obama's policies would "hurt the country" and only 43 percent thought they would "help the country."

Disappointment with Performance

The second set of centrist disappointments—which likely have had larger political repercussions—dealt with performance. The mandate that President Obama should have carried away from the election of 2008 was that voters expected him to govern more effectively than his predecessor, whether with respect to the economy, to environmental disasters, or to any other issue. Government should work. Midway through his term, many moderates were not convinced that things had gotten any better on this score. Neither President Obama's handling of the economy, nor of the BP oil drilling catastrophe in the Gulf of Mexico, inspired confidence in his leadership.[34]

The basis for Obama's victory over McCain, the turning point in the 2008 election, was the Wall Street Meltdown. The meltdown greatly deepened the recession into which the economy was slipping. The severity of the recession saw the real gross domestic product (GDP) shrink in four consecutive quarters beginning in the third quarter of 2008. Barack Obama was elected to turn this around. Despite the fact that the National Bureau of Economic Research declared the recession over in June 2009, roughly five months into Obama's term, most Americans did not believe this—or felt that the recovery was so anemic as to be equivalent to a continuing recession.

As the Obama presidency moved toward the half way point of its term, there was a broad consensus that the economy remained very weak. Notwithstanding NBER's announcement of the recession's end, 74 percent of those surveyed in late September of 2010 said that they thought that the economy was still in recession. There were good reasons to think this. As the 2010 midterm election approached, the economy had not grown for three consecutive quarters at even a weak 2 percent growth rate in two and a half years. As of November 2010, the nation had suffered its eighteenth straight month with unemployment rates of at least 9.4 percent. This was the longest number of consecutive months of 9.4 percent or higher unemployment rates since the Bureau of Labor Statistics started reporting monthly unemployment rates in 1948.[35] As of this writing in January 2011, that figure stands at twenty months and counting.

When Barack Obama won the presidency in 2008, his mandate was clear: revive the economy. The yardstick for determining whether this was done was the number of Americans deeply worried about the economy. In the exit polls of 2008, 93 percent said that the economy was "not so good" or "poor" and 63 percent said that the economy was the nation's most important problem. No other problem was mentioned by more than 10 percent of respondents. Two years into the Obama presidency, 90 percent indicated that the economy was "not so good" or "poor" and still 63 percent said the economy remained the most important problem facing the nation. More simply put: mission not accomplished.

President Obama's approval rating in the Gallup Poll dropped from an average of 63 percent in the first three months of his presidency to an average of 45 percent in October through the first week of November in 2010. Having governed more to the base than to the center, but having left some in the base disappointed—and having fallen well short of expectations with respect to the performance of the economy—Obama's approval rating dropped twelve points among liberals and twenty points among both moderates and conservatives.

A Crisis Is a Terrible Thing to Waste

Why did President Obama give priority to the policy goals of his base rather than his centrist supporters when he had greater support from the centrists than from his base? And why did the administration fail in its attempt to put the economy on the track to a robust recovery? There are a number of plausible answers to these questions. Some claim that the inherited recession was so severe that no policy could have turned the economy around by the midterm. While there might be some merit to this, and while the public's patience for results is certainly short, the administration raised expectations of a quicker recovery than it could deliver and many in the public doubted that the administration's economic policies were helping matters.

It could also be argued that the polarization of the parties has made governing to the base the only legislatively viable approach to governing. Because of the extent of polarization, the prospects for bipartisanship are greatly reduced from what they once were.[36] Liberal Democrats insist on having things their way and conservative Republicans are similarly unwilling to compromise.[37] Even as liberally oriented as the first half of President Obama's term appeared to be, there were a significant number of very liberal Democrats who felt short-changed by President Obama's policies.

While these are plausible explanations, two others should also be considered. The first of these concerns the failure of the administration, at least at the outset, to get the economy up on its feet. It may be the case that the administration did what it thought was appropriate to reinvigorate the economy, but that these were ineffective or counterproductive policies that had the unintended effect of prolong-ing the recession and delaying and dampening the recovery. A number of stimulus programs, from the huge stimulus package itself to programs regarding first time home-buying, home weatherization, "cash for clunkers," and other programs, may have had the effect of simply time-shifting economic activity. The policies gave incentives for undertaking economic activity sooner rather than later, but this may have depressed economic activity in the later period. Other policies such as those that delayed foreclosures and extended unemployment benefits may have simply stretched out the pain of the recession.

Related to the polarization explanation for the administration's attentiveness to the liberal base is an explanation suggested by a comment made by President Obama's first chief of staff, Rahm Emanuel. Alluding to the Wall Street Meltdown and the deepening recession in which the new administration took office, Emanuel told an interviewer that "You never want a serious crisis to go to waste."[38] In essence, a crisis gives a president a virtual blank check. Policies that would have little pros-pect in normal times are plausible in times of crisis when everyone is inclined to support the president. Add large Democratic Party majorities in both the House and the Senate and decades of frustration for liberal Democrats in promoting a national health care plan, and the opportunity to push the health care plan through Congress may have been simply too tempting to resist. Though the large Demo-cratic congressional majorities had little to do with the public's support for a national health care plan, they could be used to pass the plan and they were.

It is true that President Obama's unfulfilled mandate of restoring the economy's health and his pursuit of a policy agenda more to the liking of the liberal base than centrist supporters exacted a huge political price for Democrats in the 2010 midterm elections. It is worth remembering, however, that Presidents Reagan and Clinton both gambled on policies that appealed more to their bases than to cen-trists after their 1980 and 1992 elections. They also inherited economic problems from their predecessors and their parties sustained significant midterm seat losses. Two years later, both were reelected—President Reagan in a landslide, President Clinton by a healthy margin. As the experience of these presidents suggests, a great deal can happen between a midterm and the next presidential election. While the nation is polarized and the parties are invigorated and near parity, President Obama's prospects for reelection in 2012 would seem to once again depend on what centrists think of the in-party's performance in office.

The Post-Midterm Obama Presidency

Two developments in the aftermath of the 2010 midterm offered early clues about the politics of the second half of President Obama's term. First, after years of decry-ing the Bush tax cuts of 2001 as a shameless give away to the very wealthy, and pledging not to renew the tax cuts for those making over $250,000 a year, President Obama relented in the face of the incoming Republican House. In the lame-duck session of the outgoing Congress, Obama reached a compromise with Republicans to extend the Bush income and estate tax cuts for two years along with extending unemployment benefits, a number of stimulus targeted cuts, and adding a one-year cut in the payroll tax to stimulate employment.[39] Despite the president's taking the lead in putting the deal together, many liberal members of his base opposed the measure because the cuts included those at the highest income levels. While 139 Democrats in the House voted with the President, 112 opposed him. Republicans, on the other hand, more cohesively supported the tax cut renewal package (138 to 36).

The second development shedding light on post-midterm politics were reactions to the tragic attempted assassination of Democratic Representative Gabrielle Giffords in Tucson, Arizona, in early 2011. The shooting killed six (including a nine-year-old girl), wounded thirteen, and left the congresswoman clinging to life. The massacre set off a political firestorm. A number on the left leveled accusations that the gunman had been motivated by the vitriolic rhetoric of conservative commentators and politicians. Conservatives defended themselves, responding that the charges from the left were baseless, reprehensible attempts to politically exploit the tragedy. In his speech at the University of Arizona, President Obama took the high ground, observing that the gunman was mentally deranged and that the tragedy had nothing to do with politics. He then urged greater civility in political discussion, not because it had engendered the shooting, but because "only a more civil and honest public discourse can help us face up to our challenges as a nation, in a way that would make [those lost in the tragedy] proud." Praise for the speech came from both ends of the political spectrum.

These two developments in the first weeks of the second half of President Obama's term suggest two features likely to shape the politics of the next two years: a recalcitrant, frustrated, and ill-tempered liberal base and a Democratic president ready to or forced to reach out to the political center and even to the right. First, the 2010 midterm election left a depleted Democratic congressional caucus, but also one that was more liberal. Those members and their supporters had seen their expectations raised to great heights and (with apologies to Dylan Thomas) they will "not go gentle into that good night."[40] Dealing with the tempestuous impulses of the liberal base is likely to be a big concern for President Obama in the second half of his term.

The second insight from these developments is that President Obama may make greater use of one of the most important advantages available to presidents: the ability to seize the high ground. In both the tax compromise and in the tragedy in Tucson, President Obama had the opportunity to be a uniter and he seized it. He was seen as welcoming bipartisanship on the tax cut compromise and transcending partisanship in his speech in Tucson. The latter was the unifying silver lining to the dark cloud of every national tragedy, but the former was a unifying event of political origins, the Republican victory in the midterm.

The most effective tone of politics (particularly with those in the political center) is always that which appears least politically partisan. That President Obama now has little choice but to reach toward the political center may draw disenchanted moderates back into the fold. It is more than a little ironic, given his earlier choices, that this could ultimately prove to be to his benefit in 2012.

Notes

1. The president's base includes those individuals who are most ideologically attuned to the president and his political party. It should be recognized that the categories of base and center simplify, perhaps oversimplify, the degrees of ideological commitments. There are those in the base who are somewhat inclined to the ideology of the president and his party and there are those who are fanatical in that commitment. By the same token, there is a range of commitments among centrist supporters from those who have views that are just a shade less ideological than those in the base to those who are verging on support for the opposition party.

2. This, in essence, is the classic tension of representation. On the one hand, popular government demands representatives who act as delegates to reflect the popular will. On the other, as Edmund Burke put the case so well centuries ago, representatives owe the public their good judgment and this quite likely reflects the views of fellow partisans. For an early empirical assessment of orientation of legislators see John C. Wahlke, Heinz Eulau, William Buchanon, and LeRoy C. Ferguson, *The Legislative System: Explorations in Legislative Behavior* (New York: Wiley, 1962). The push and pull of the center and the party base has also been studied in political campaigns. See Benjamin I. Page, *Choices and Echoes in Presidential Elections: Rational Man and Electoral Democracy* (Chicago: University of Chicago Press, 1978).

3. Control of the legislative process by the base not only requires party control of both chambers of Congress, but control of them by the party's base and a sixty-seat majority in the Senate by the party's base to invoke cloture on filibusters. This rarely, if ever, occurs.

4. Contrary to the progressive-era view of politics still held by many, there is and should be no "bright line" separation between the politics of elections and governing. From a theoretical standpoint, electoral politics and governing should not be divorced from one another in a representative democracy. A government that rests on the will of the people, expressed in an election, should govern with that will in mind. More practically, the political divisions evident in elections do not disappear once the votes are counted and those who supported (or opposed) the president in the election are likely

to support (or oppose) him in his attempt to govern. Presidents would be naive to ignore this and negligent not to try to keep their supportive coalition intact.

5. My previous research documents these partisan turnout effects. See *The Presidential Pulse of Congressional Elections*, 2nd ed. (Lexington, KY: University Press of Kentucky, 1997), pp. 174-87, and *The American Campaign: U.S. Presidential Campaigns and the National Vote*, 2nd ed. (College Station, TX: Texas A&M University Press, 2008), pp. 84-86. There are some high-profile cases of centrist coalitions in which the president's legislative base voted against him. Perhaps the most well-known of these is the passage of the North American Free Trade Agreement under President Clinton. This was passed with the votes of moderate Democrats and Republicans. Liberal Democrats, aligned with labor unions, generally opposed the measure. President George W. Bush's immigration plan in 2007 also lost the support of his party's base. Finally, President Obama's base "took a walk" on the compromise reached after the 2010 midterm on renewing the Bush tax cuts.

6. Most studies have treated the issue as though all presidents respond and should respond to their partisan base and to the center in the same way. See B. Dan Wood, *The Myth of Presidential Representation* (New York: Cambridge University Press, 2009).

7. George C. Edwards III, *At the Margins: Presidential Leadership of Congress* (New Haven, CT: Yale University Press, 1989); and see Edwards's chapter in this volume.

8. Richard E. Neustadt, *Presidential Power: The Politics of Leadership from FDR to Carter* (New York: John Wiley and Sons, 1980) pp. 64-73.

9. Paul F. Lazarsfeld, Bernard Berelson, and Hazel Gaudet, *The People's Choice*, 3rd ed. (New York: Columbia University Press, 1968).

10. Anthony Downs, *An Economic Theory of Democracy* (New York: Harper & Row, 1957). Downs's theory hypothesized that centrists, especially the median voter, would have the greatest leverage in the process. This greatly underestimated the ability and willingness of stubborn members of the base to withdraw their support if they feel they are being taken for granted. The real option of those in the base acting as "political amateurs" and "taking a walk" if displeased gives them leverage over their party.

11. Michael Dukakis, "1988 Nomination Acceptance Speech," Democratic National Convention, Atlanta, Georgia, July 21, 1988. The American Presidency Project's Document Archive: http://www.presidency.ucsb.edu/ws/index.php?pid=25961#axzz1HeFUdT68 (accessed March 25, 2011).

12. Retrospective voting essentially refers to voting based on evaluations of past performance of those in office. There is an extensive literature on retrospective voting. See Walter Lippmann, *The Phantom Public* (New York: Harcourt, Brace, 1925); Morris P. Fiorina, *Retrospective Voting in American National Elections* (New Haven, CT: Yale University Press, 1981); and James E. Campbell, Bryan J. Dettrey, and Hongxing Yin, "The Theory of Conditional Retrospective Voting: Does the Presidential Record Matter Less in Open Seat Elections?" *Journal of Politics* 72, 4 (2010): 1083-95.

13. An in-party candidate's evaluation rises and falls with the performance of the incumbent president. Similarly, the fortunes of out-party candidates rise on bad ratings of the incumbent's performance and fall when the incumbent performs well.

14. If the president is of the same party as his predecessor, then he may have been elected because of the positive performance of that predecessor. If the president is of the opposite party, he may have been elected because of the poor performance of his predecessor.

15. Robert A. Dahl, "Myth of the Presidential Mandate," *Political Science Quarterly* 105, 3 (Autumn, 1990): 355-72. For a defense of the idea of presidential mandates, see Patricia Heidotting Conley, *Presidential Mandates: How Elections Shape the National Agenda* (Chicago: University of Chicago Press, 2001).

16. James E. Campbell, "The Midterm Landslide of 2010: A Triple Wave Election," *The Forum* 8, 4, article 3 (December 2010).

17. The average of four Gallup polls from late July to early September 2008 indicated a 32 percent approval rating for President Bush. The data were obtained from the Gallup website: http://www.gallup.com/poll/116500/Presidential-Approval-Ratings-George-Bush.aspx.

18. Alan Abramowitz, *The Disappearing Center* (New Haven, CT, Yale University Press, 2010). For a contrasting view, see Morris P. Fiorina, Samuel J. Abrams, and Jeremy C. Pope, *Culture War? The Myth of a Polarized America*, 2nd ed. (New York: Pearson Longman, 2004); and Paul DiMaggio, John Evans, and Bethany Bryson, "Have American Social Attitudes Become More Polarized?" *American Journal of Sociology* 102, 3 (1996): 690-755.

19. James E. Campbell, "Explaining Politics, Not Polls: Examining Macropartisanship with Recalibrated NES Data," *Public Opinion Quarterly* 74, 4 (October 2010): 616-42.

20. The Senate voting records for McCain and Obama document their ideological positions. Combining the liberal Americans for Democratic Action roll call scores with the American Conservative Union roll call scores (flipped to make them comparable) for 2006 and 2007, McCain had a rating of 24 percent liberal. He was almost perfectly positioned between a 50 percent moderate score and a perfectly consistent conservative score. Obama, on the other hand, voted 95 percent of the time in the liberal direction.

21. CNN, "Election 2008: Exit Polls," http://www.cnn.com/ELECTION/2008/results/polls/#val=USP00p1 (accessed March 25, 2011). It is interesting to note that the exit poll in 2008 did not even ask about McCain's position on the issues as being too liberal or too conservative. This might be interpreted as the ultimate testimony to McCain's centrism.

22. Survey of Professional Forecasters, Third Quarter 2008, Release Date: August 12, 2008. Released by the Research Department of the Federal Reserve Bank of Philadelphia, http://www.philadelphiafed.org/research-and-data/real-time-center/survey-of-professional-forecasters/2008/survq308.cfm (accessed March 25, 2011).

23. Bureau of Economic Analysis. National Economic Accounts, Gross Domestic Product, Percent Change from Preceding Period, http://bea.gov/national/index.htm#gdp (accessed March 29, 2011).

24. The consumer confidence ratings are from Gallup at http://www.gallup.com/poll/1609/Consumer-Views-Economy.aspx. Respondents are asked, "How would you rate economic conditions—as excellent, good, only fair, or poor?" The ratings are averages of three polls in August and early September and two polls in October.

25. Frank Newport, Jeffrey M. Jones, Lydia Saad, Alec M. Gallup, and Fred L. Israel, *Winning the White House 2008: The Gallup Poll, Public Opinion, and the Presidency* (New York: Checkmark Books, 2009), p. 584.
26. The performance-based loss of support for President Bush is also supported by Arthur Lupia's analysis that showed that "Bush voters' decisions not to vote or to support Obama were a sufficient condition for Obama's victory." Arthur Lupia, "Did Bush Voters Cause Obama's Victory?" *PS: Political Science and Politics* 43, 2 (April 2010): 239-41.
27. Respondents who said that they "leaned" toward the Democratic or Republican Party are classified as partisans rather than independents. As Bruce Keith and his colleagues concluded, these "independent leaners" in nearly every important respect are like other partisans and unlike independents who do not indicate a leaning. See Bruce E. Keith, David B. Magleby, Candice J. Nelson, Elizabeth Orr, Mark C. Westlye, and Raymond E. Wolfinger, *The Myth of the Independent Voter* (Berkeley: University of California Press, 1992).
28. For a contrasting view, see the Aberbach chapter in this volume.
29. Jeffrey M. Stonecash, "The 2010 Elections: Party Pursuits, Voter Perceptions, and the Chancy Game of Politics," *The Forum* 8, 4, article 11 (December 2010). Stonecash cites a Gallup poll from September 11–13, 2009, that finds that only 37 percent of all Americans and 34 percent of political independents thought that "the government should be primarily responsible for making sure that all Americans have health insurance."
30. Robert P. Saldin, "Healthcare Reform: A Prescription for a 2010 Republican Landslide?" *The Forum* 8, 4, article 10 (December 2010): 8.
31. Costas Pangopoulos, "The Dynamics of Voter Preferences in the 2010 Congressional Midterm Elections," *The Forum* 8, 4, article 9 (December 2010): 7.
32. *Washington Post*-ABC News poll, http://www.washingtonpost.com/wp-srv/politics/polls/postpoll_10052010.html (accessed March 25, 2011). The question is item 27 in the report of survey results.
33. CNN Politics, Election Center, "Full National House Exit Polls," http://www.cnn.com/ELECTION/2010/results/polls/#val=USH00p3 (accessed March 25, 2011).
34. Three separate polls conducted between late June and mid-July by Fox News, by CNN and Opinion Research, and by ABC and the *Washington Post* indicated that approval of President Obama's handling of the BP oil spill ranged between 41 and 45 percent and that disapproval stood at 52 or 53 percent. See PollingReport.com on Energy at http://www.pollingreport.com/energy.htm (accessed March 25, 2011).
35. Bureau of Labor Statistics, Databases, Tables and Calculators by Subject, Unemployment Rates, http://data.bls.gov/PDQ/servlet/SurveyOutputServlet (accessed January 8, 2011).
36. David Mayhew, *Divided We Govern*, 2nd ed. (New Haven, CT: Yale University Press, 2005).
37. See the Sinclair chapter in this volume.
38. Jack Rosenthal, On Language, "A Terrible Thing to Waste," *The New York Times*, August 2, 2009. Accessed at http://www.nytimes.com/2009/08/02/magazine/02FOB-onlanguage-t.html on March 29, 2011. As Rosenthal observes, the sentiment expressed

by Emanuel did not originate with him. Rosenthal attributes the more pithy original version of this observation, "a crisis is a terrible thing to waste," to Stanford economist Paul Romer.

39. The compromise left the highest tax rate at 35 percent. Without the compromise all income tax rates would have increased and the highest rate would have jumped to 39.6 percent.

40. From Dylan Thomas, "Do Not Go Gentle into That Good Night" (1940). See http://oldpoetry.com/opoem/show/2906-Dylan-Thomas-Do-Not-Go-Gentle-Into-That-Good-Night (accessed March 29, 2011). From their perspective, the liberal base is likely to, as the poem concludes, "Rage, rage against the dying of the light."

CHAPTER 5

Polarization, Public Opinion, and the Presidency: The Obama and Anti-Obama Coalitions

Gary C. Jacobson

BARACK OBAMA'S VICTORY IN 2008 sparked a brief moment of postelection euphoria during which most Americans celebrated the passing of the George W. Bush administration and the historically remarkable election of an African American president. Democratic partisans had particular reason to celebrate, as their party won enlarged majorities in the Senate and House of Representatives as well as the White House. But if they imagined that these victories, along with the damage the Bush presidency had inflicted on the Republican Party,[1] would usher in an era of durable Democratic majorities, the first two years of the Obama administration have proven thoroughly disillusioning. Despite important victories on his main legislative initiatives—the economic stimulus, health care reform, and financial regulation packages—Obama's approval ratings drifted below 50 percent during his second year in office (see figure 5.1) and his party suffered a decisive defeat in the 2010 midterm elections that cost it control of the House and reduced its Senate majority by six seats, to fifty-three. The evenly balanced, sharply polarized party alignments characteristic of the previous two administrations also reemerged with a vengeance. Congressional Republicans voted with near unanimity against Obama's signal initiatives, and the extraordinarily wide partisan differences in presidential approval typical of George W. Bush's final five years in office reappeared under Obama (see figure 5.2). Although this partisan divide has yet to reach the record levels inspired by Bush, it has become wider than under any president other than Bush.

The public's overall assessment of Obama's performance has been in part a conventional response to national conditions. Obama took office during the worst

FIGURE 5.1   Barack Obama's Job Approval Ratings

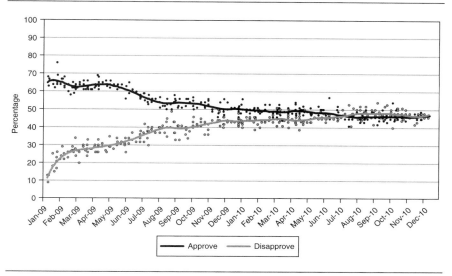

Sources: 299 ABC News/*Washington Post,* CBS News/*New York Times,* CNN, CNBC, NBC News/*Wall Street Journal,* AP-Ipsos, *Newsweek,* Gallup, Ipsos, *Los Angeles Times, Time,* Bloomberg, Marist, and Pew surveys.

economic crisis since the Great Depression, and the economic recovery has been painfully slow, with stubbornly high unemployment depressing consumption and growth. He also inherited two troublesome wars. While the drawdown of US troops from Iraq continued on schedule, Obama's escalation of US involvement in Afghanistan has inevitably led to higher casualties, greater pessimism, and declining public support for continuing the war. Nor could Obama avoid the fallout from public frustration with the April 2010 BP oil spill in the Gulf of Mexico, a disaster for which neither the federal government nor the oil industry had an effective solution for nearly three months. Yet it remains puzzling why major victories on legislation—aimed directly at the economic crisis and its causes and fulfilling his popular campaign promise to reform a health care system—did so little to stem the spreading public dissatisfaction with Obama's performance. Not only did he fail to persuade most Americans that these achievements had or would eventually benefit them, but his actions provoked intense hostility from a substantial faction of those Americans who opposed them, reactions that seemed far out of proportion to the provocation.

In this chapter, I argue that the public's response to the Obama is not merely a consequence of national conditions and his political agenda, but also arises from deeper and more fundamental divisions within the American polity. These predate

FIGURE 5.2   Approval of Obama's Performance, by Party

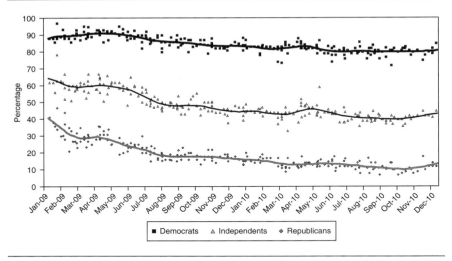

Sources: 216 ABC News/*Washington Post,* CBS News/*New York Times,* CNN, NBC News/*Wall Street Journal, Newsweek,* Gallup, and Pew surveys.

Obama but have been exposed in their rawest form by his presidency. I begin with a brief discussion of the party coalitions that supported and opposed his election in 2008 and that now applaud or pan his performance in office. Next I explore in some depth the attitudes and beliefs of his harshest critics, exemplified by the "Tea Party" movement's activists and sympathizers. I then consider the public's general response to actions dealing economic crisis, the health care system, and the wars in Iraq and Afghanistan. I finish by analyzing how reactions to Obama shaped electoral politics in the 2010 midterm elections.

The Party Coalitions

During his first two years in the White House, Barack Obama faced relentless Republican opposition while trying to hold together fractious Democratic majorities in the House and Senate. Considering how the mass bases of the Democratic and Republican parties have evolved over the past four decades, this circumstance is scarcely surprising. The ideological sorting among partisans since the 1970s[2] has left both parties' coalitions on average further from the center, but its consequences have been asymmetrical. As figure 5.3 illustrates, the Republican coalition, predominantly conservative from the start, has grown substantially more so; in the most recent decade, a majority (52 percent) of Republicans have categorized themselves

FIGURE 5.3   Ideology of Republican Identifiers, by Decade

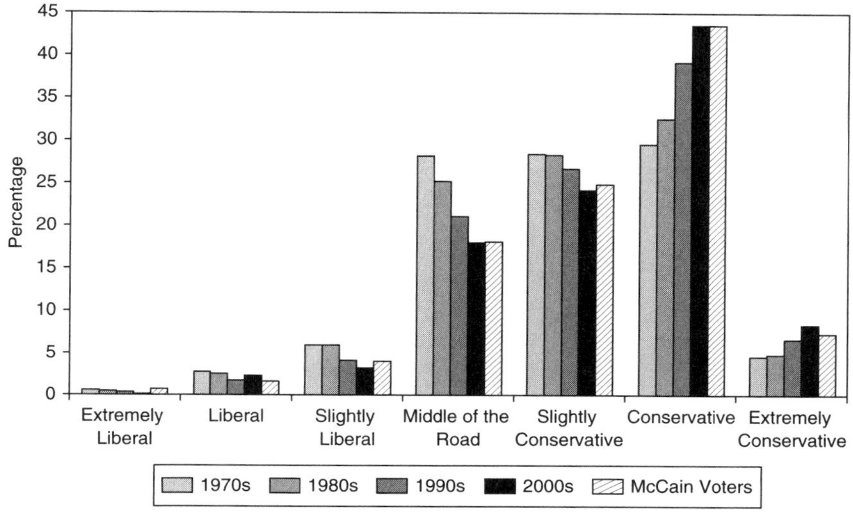

Sources: American National Election Studies.

as conservative or extremely conservative, up from 34 percent in the 1970s. The proportion placing themselves somewhere right of center has grown from 63 percent to 76 percent; only 6 percent now place themselves left of center (down from 11 percent in the 1970s) and only 18 percent in the middle category (down from 28 percent).³ In short, over the past four decades, the ideological center of gravity of the Republican coalition has shifted gradually but decisively to the right.

Ordinary Democrats have also moved away from the center in the opposite direction (see figure 5.4), although not nearly as far as Republicans, and, more important, at the popular level, the Democratic Party remains a broad center-left coalition in which self-identified liberals are still a minority. The proportion of Democrats placing themselves at the two most liberal points on the scale has grown from 20 percent to 29 percent over this period, and the proportion locating left of center has grown from 36 percent to 48 percent. The share of Democrats locating right of center has fallen six points but remains at 18 percent; the modal location of Democratic identifiers continues to be "middle of the road" (35%).

The ideological composition of the party coalitions at the time of Obama's election carried two important implications for his administration. First, congressional Republicans were unlikely to find much benefit in cooperating with him. Their conservative core never warmed to Obama during the campaign⁴ and liked

FIGURE 5.4   Ideology of Democratic Identifiers, by Decade

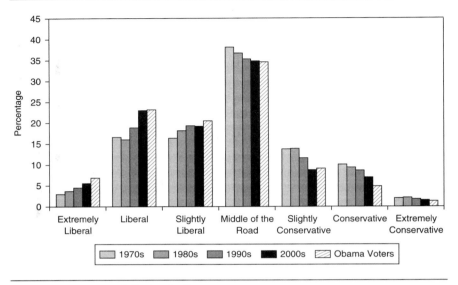

Source: American National Election Studies.

him even less once his agenda was on the table.[5] Second, Obama (and Democratic leaders in Congress) would find it difficult to satisfy their party's ideologically diverse coalition. Democrats cannot win and hold majorities without appealing to moderates as well as liberals, because there are simply not enough liberals.[6] But the Democratic coalition's diversity meant that one faction or another would regard Obama's policies as too liberal or too conservative no matter what direction they took, leaving his approvers somewhat more lukewarm in their assessments of his performance than his disapprovers.[7]

Finally, notice that the distribution of Obama and McCain voters on the liberal-conservative scale in 2008 matches the distributions for their respective party coalitions in the 2000s quite closely. Indeed, each candidate's electoral coalition was basically his party's coalition. At 89.3 percent, party-line voting in the 2008 presidential election was surpassed only by 2004's 89.8 percent in the entire American National Election Studies (ANES) series going back to 1952. Moreover, Obama's electoral coalition contained the smallest share of opposite-party identifiers of any president elected since the advent of the ANES time series, just 4.4 percent.[8] Obama won despite having very little crossover appeal by inspiring unusually high turnout among Democrats, particularly African Americans and younger voters, and by winning a majority of independents, most of whom

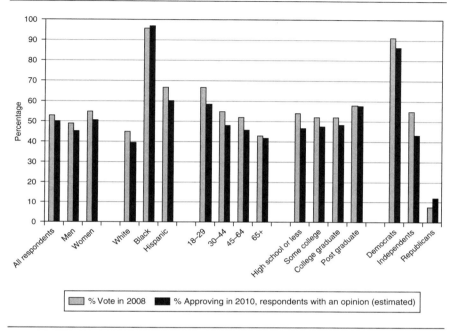

Source: See note 10.

were thoroughly dissatisfied with the Bush administration. Obama also benefited from a significant decline in Republican Party identification during Bush's second term.[9]

By November of his second year in office, Obama's supporting coalition (those who said they approved of his job performance) looked remarkably like his electoral coalition, slightly diminished. Obama won 52.9 percent of the votes cast for president in November 2008. His average approval rating among respondents expressing an opinion in seventy polls taken during the first ten months of 2010 was 50.8 percent. Figure 5.5 displays the average vote for Obama as reported in three major national election surveys of 2008 and the average approval level in Gallup polls taken during 2010, broken down by a common set of demographic categories.[10] The average difference between a demographic group's approval in 2010 and vote in 2008 is about three percentage points. Notice in particular that the unusually steep age gradient evident in the 2008 vote, with Obama doing best in the youngest cohort and worst in the oldest, persisted in 2010, with Obama's approval rating averaging seventeen points higher among respondents aged eighteen through twenty-nine than among those over sixty-five. Obama also retained his appeal to the highly educated.

The Tea Party Movement

The continuity in popular reactions to Obama from the 2008 campaigns through the first two years of his presidency extends beyond these simple demographic and partisan patterns. It is also evident in the intensity of the opposition he has aroused and in the bizarre notions circulating among some of his detractors, most prominently among activists in the Tea Party movement, an assortment of populist conservatives and libertarians, not a few of whom display in classic form the "paranoid style in American politics."[11] To the more unhinged of these self-proclaimed "patriots," Obama is not merely an objectionable liberal Democrat, but a tyrant (of the Nazi, fascist, communist, socialist, monarchist, or racist variety, depending on the critic)[12] intent on subjecting Americans to, variously, socialism, communism, fascism, concentration camps, or control by the United Nations, Interpol, international bankers, the Council on Foreign Relations or the Trilateral Commission.[13] It is important to emphasize that far from all Tea Party adherents (12–18 percent of the public) or sympathizers (about a third of the public[14]) entertain such notions. But they are nearly unanimous in their hostility toward Obama and belief that his policies are moving the country toward socialism.[15]

This slice of Tea Party sympathizers join the sizable fraction of mainstream Republicans who say that Obama is not even a native-born American and thus ineligible to be president. An April 2010 CBS News/*New York Times* poll found 32 percent of Republicans and 30 percent of Tea Party activists saying Obama was foreign born, with only 41 percent saying he was born in the United States.[16] A similar proportion of Republicans (31 percent in an August 2010 Pew survey) also said they thought Obama was a Muslim, more than said (correctly) that he is a Christian (27 percent).[17] A *Time* survey taken the same month found an even more remarkable 46 percent of Republicans expressing this misconception; among the 60 percent of Republicans calling themselves conservatives, 57 percent said Obama was a Muslim, with only 14 percent saying he was a Christian. Ninety-five percent of Republicans who thought Obama was a Muslim disapproved of his job performance, with only 2 percent approving.[18]

Conservative voices on talk radio, Fox News, and the Internet have encouraged the Tea Party movement in its bitterly anti-Obama stance, sticking to a successful business model in which outraged opposition, unconstrained by any fetish for accuracy, is the stock in trade. Glenn Beck, a demagogic conspiracy theorist with the rant of a street-corner crank, became a star performer on Fox, with a nightly audience of millions.[19] According to the April 2010 CBS News/

New York Times survey, Fox News is the preferred news source for 63 percent of the Tea Party supporters, and 59 percent of them view Glenn Beck favorably (the equivalent figures for the general public are 23 and 18 percent, respectively).[20]

Like the coalitions approving and disapproving of Obama's performance in 2010, the Tea Party movement's roots can be found in the 2008 campaigns. Tea Party activists display the same inchoate anger at Obama first observed at campaign rallies for John McCain and Sarah Palin.[21] The Republican campaign had sought to offset a toxic political environment by portraying Obama as a sixties-style radical plotting to turn the United States into a socialist country.[22] Although the campaign failed to win the election, it did succeed in shaping Obama's image among people who did not vote for him. A large proportion of voters on the losing side in 2008— the vast majority of them Republicans or independents leaning Republican—had by election day come to regard Obama as the McCain-Palin campaign had portrayed him: as an untrustworthy leftist radical with a socialist agenda.[23] There was also a racial element in attitudes toward Obama; Herbert Weisberg and Christopher Devine found an unusually strong relationship between the racial resentment scale and the presidential choice in 2008, with the racially resentful much less likely to vote for Obama.[24]

Obama's victory naturally rattled those people who regarded him as an unreconstructed leftist radical, as foreign-born and thus ineligible to be president, as a secret Muslim, or through racist spectacles. One tangible reaction was a sharp increase in the purchase of guns and ammunition;[25] requests to the FBI for background checks (required for new gun purchases) were 29 percent higher in the year following Obama's election than in the year preceding it.[26] Although Obama took pains during the campaign to pledge support for Second Amendment rights— Democrats have long since learned that gun control is a losing issue in some important swing states, even in the face of such tragedies as the Tucson shooting in January 2011—a majority of gun owners came to believe that he would try to ban gun sales during his presidency.[27]

Authoritarianism

How did a politician accurately characterized by a moderately conservative columnist as a "center-left pragmatic reformer" advocating "a moderately activist government constrained by a sense of tradeoffs"[28] provoke such extraordinary reactions? Marc Hetherington and Jonathan Weiler's research offers some useful guidance here. They argue that an important component of the sorting that has left Democratic and Republican identifiers increasingly distinct in their political views has occurred along what they term "the authoritarian divide," with "both the average Democratic identifier . . . becoming less authoritarian and the average Republican identifier . . . becoming somewhat more so."[29]

The term "authoritarian" carries a lot of baggage, and Hetherington and Weiler adopt it basically for want of anything better. Yet as their and other recent work has shown, "authoritarianism" labels a measurable, stable individual predisposition that is a significant predictor of political beliefs and attitudes.[30] Because authoritarianism is supposed to explain political attitudes, it cannot be measured by responses to questions about politics. Rather, it is measured by an index of responses to a set of questions about which of a pair of attributes the respondent thinks is preferable in children: independence or respect for elders, curiosity or good manners, obedience or self-reliance, and being considerate or being well behaved.[31] Typically, people at the high end of the authoritarianism scale, so measured, tend to desire order and fear disorder, to dislike ambiguity, and to be uncomfortable with difference and thus averse to a wide range of groups outside of their own. They tend to prefer force to diplomacy in dealing with foreign threats, to be more fearful of terrorism, and to be more inclined to expressions of "superpatrotism." They tend to hold authority (of texts such as the Bible or the Constitution, read literally, as well as of "legitimate" leaders) in high regard, but "nothing aggravates authoritarians more than feeling that leaders are unworthy of their trust."[32] They also display "a tendency to rigid thinking and an unwillingness or inability to process new information that might challenge such thinking."[33]

People low in authoritarianism, in contrast, tend to be more tolerant of ambiguity and more comfortable with difference, to prefer nuanced to black-and-white thinking, to have a stronger "accuracy motivation" and "need for cognition," and to emphasize the value of personal autonomy over social conformity.[34] They are also inclined to prefer diplomacy to force and to be less fearful of terrorist threats.

As Hetherington and Weiler point out, many (though not all) of the issues that have come to divide the two parties line up on the authoritarian/nonauthoritarian dimension. These include: treatment of minorities, gay rights, women's rights, multiculturalism, immigration, the Bush administration's policies after the terrorist attacks of September 11 (especially regarding the Iraq War, the treatment of captured terrorists, and civil liberties), and the use of force in foreign affairs more generally. Party positions on these issues have made the Democratic Party more attractive to people lower on the authoritarianism scale and the Republican Party more attractive to those higher on it. Moreover, the theory posits that a person's location on the scale reflects fundamental beliefs and basic ways of absorbing and processing information. Thus, sorting along this dimension has increasingly left Democrats and Republicans in separate cognitive and moral worlds. "Differences in policy preferences on some of the key issues go far beyond disagreements over policy choices and even ideology, to conflict about core self-understandings of what it means to be a good person and to the basis of a good society."[35]

From this perspective, it becomes easier to understand why Barack Obama has provoked such strong reactions from so many of his opponents.[36] His combination of background, personality, and political style are almost perfectly designed to antagonize people at the high end of the authoritarian scale. An African American (his father a Kenyan, his mother a white American) carrying a foreign-sounding name with "Hussein" in its middle, Obama also has an Ivy League education, a detached manner, and a nuanced, cerebral approach to political questions. As a child he lived for several years in predominantly Muslim Indonesia. He began his political career as a community organizer on Chicago's South Side and maintained links with local black activists and leaders, some with fairly radical views, including his long time minister, Rev. Jeremiah Wright. Thus to someone high on the authoritarian scale, Obama would be not merely on the wrong side of political issues, but his race, upbringing, mentality, associations, and presumed values would place him outside the boundaries of what is acceptable in an American leader. The eagerness of his opponents to say that he was not born in the United States and thus not even eligible to be president reflects this kind of thinking, as does the belief that he is a secret Muslim.

Although no studies to date have included both the authoritarianism battery and questions about Tea Party sympathies, the beliefs and attitudes expressed by the movement's supporters and opponents appear to line up along the authoritarian dimension. Table 5.1 displays the distribution of opinions about the Tea Party movement, broken down by party, ideology, and the 2008 vote from a May 2010 NBC News/*Wall Street Journal* survey. Overall, supporters and opponents are evenly balanced in the population, but with stark partisan differences. Republicans

TABLE 5.1   Opinions of the Tea Party Movement (%)

	Very Positive	Somewhat Positive	Neutral	Somewhat Negative	Very Negative
All Respondents	17	15	37	11	20
Republicans (39%)	33	24	34	6	3
Independents (17%)	12	15	48	11	14
Democrats (45%)	4	6	37	15	38
Very liberal (8%)	2	5	37	8	47
Somewhat liberal (14%)	5	6	33	18	38
Moderate (38%)	6	15	43	12	23
Somewhat conservative (22%)	22	19	41	11	7
Very conservative (18%)	46	18	27	2	4
Voted for Obama (49%)	2	3	37	18	40
Voted for McCain (40%)	36	25	32	5	3
Voted for someone else (7%)	32	25	39	2	1

Source: NBC News/*Wall Street Journal* poll, May 6–10, 2010.

view the movement positively by a ratio of about 6:1; Democrats view it negatively by about 5:1; independents are evenly divided (nearly half are neutral).[37] The more conservative the respondent, the more likely a positive opinion of the Tea Party; the more liberal the respondent, the more likely a negative opinion. A large majority of McCain voters but very few Obama voters expressed favorable views of the Tea Party. This survey also found only 8 percent of Tea Party sympathizers reporting a vote for Obama in 2008, compared with 89 percent of those holding negative views of the Tea Party. In this and other surveys, Tea Party activists and sympathizers tend to be overwhelmingly white, conservative, and Republican or independent leaning Republican (83 to 88 percent, depending on the survey).

Some Tea Party enthusiasts express disdain for the Republican establishment (a stance that had intriguing effects in the 2010 primaries), but most fit seamlessly into the party's conservative core, holding attitudes and opinions similar to those of other Republicans, only with more thorough conservative orthodoxy.[38] This is evident from the data in table 5.2. Partisanship divides respondents on all of these questions, with the Republican and Democratic distributions of opinion on average more than forty points apart. But attitudes toward the Tea Party movement differentiate respondents sharply as well. I focus here on Republican identifiers because my main goal is to understand why Obama has provoked such intense hostility among the opposition, but similar gradients of opinion across degrees of sympathy for the Tea Party movement appear among independents and Democrats as well.

Table 5.2 shows that the more positive the opinion of the Tea Party movement, the more likely Republicans are to disapprove of Obama's performance, to oppose his health care package, to consider his economic stimulus package a failure, to dislike him personally, and to consider him dishonest, indifferent to the average American, and a servant of large corporations. The differences are quite large, averaging twenty-eight points between Republicans with very positive and merely neutral views of the Tea Party. Responses to this set of questions show that, even within the Republican coalition, opinions of the Tea Party movement and opinions of Obama and his policies are strongly and negatively related.

Responses to an additional six questions reported in table 5.2 suggest that attitudes toward the Tea Party movement map onto the authoritarianism dimension. The more positively Republicans view the movement, the more likely they are to hold views expected of people at the high end of the authoritarianism scale: to support Arizona's controversial immigration law, to worry about a terrorist attack, to support ethnic profiling to combat terrorism, to be willing to use military force to prevent Iran from acquiring nuclear arms, and to oppose gays in the military. This is not simply a manifestation of greater conservatism among Tea Party sympathizers; assessments of the movement have a substantial and statistically significant effect on responses to all of the questions in table 5.2 even when self-reported

TABLE 5.2 Opinions of the Tea Party Movement and Other Political Attitudes (%)

| | Republicans | | | | | | |
| | Opinion of the Tea Party Movement | | | | | Independents | Democrats |
	Very Positive	Somewhat Positive	Neutral	Negative	All		
Disapprove of Obama's performance[c]	96	87	72	45	81	51	13
Oppose Obama's health care reforms[c]	92	91	72	47	81	38	14
Believe Obama's economic stimulus will not help[c]	89	70	55	49	69	47	18
Dislike Obama personally[c]	71	57	43	35	55	19	8
Rate Obama "very poor" on being "honest and straightforward"[d]	70	52	37	33	53	19	4
Rate Obama "very poor" on being "compassionate enough to understand average people"[d]	60	33	16	20	37	16	4
Believe Obama serves interests of large corporations, not those of average people[c]	65	52	57	25	56	39	20
Support Arizona immigration law[c]	92	96	73	66	83	61	48
Very/Fairly worried about terrorist attack[c]	80	60	62	56	67	55	51
Approve of ethnic profiling to combat terrorism[c]	82	78	65	75	74	46	35
Support use force if necessary to destroy Iran's ability to make nuclear weapon[b]	70	64	68	42	64	41	43
Oppose gays in the military[e]	53	45	29	40	40	17	19
Believe global warming given too much attention[a]	82	59	43	54	63	27	10

[a] January, 2010, NBC News/Wall Street Journal poll.

[b] March, 2010, NBC News/Wall Street Journal poll.

[c] May, 2010, NBC News/Wall Street Journal poll.

[d] June, 2010, NBC News/Wall Street Journal poll.

[e] February, 2010, Pew Research Center for the People and the Press poll.

location on the liberal–conservative scale is taken into account.[39] About two-thirds of all Tea Party supporters deny that global warming is occurring or is a threat.[40] Although this rejection of the strong scientific consensus[41] that human activities are warming up the planet has become Republican orthodoxy, Tea Party sympathizers are much more likely than other Republicans to think the issue has received too much attention. Tea Party supporters are also about twice as likely as other Americans to say that "too much has been made of the problems facing black people" in recent years (52 percent take this position).[42]

In short, Tea Party sympathizers tend to view the political world in ways consistent with a location at the high end of the authoritarianism scale (again, keeping in mind the contentiousness of this term). In their own minds, the Tea Partiers' central objection to Obama is his push to expand the federal government's authority in direct violation of the Constitution. But Stenner's conjecture that "whether or not authoritarians will get behind government intervention should depend crucially on who will be doing the governing" seems prescient.[43] In historical context (consider the New Deal and Great Society) or cross-national comparison (consider other affluent democracies), Obama's policies hardly seem radical. What makes them so threatening to the Tea Party conservatives is the perception that the government is in hands of a leader and, by extension, party outside the circle of "real Americans." Three-quarters of the Tea Party supporters think Obama does not share "the values most Americans try to live by."[44] When one activist was reminded of the contradiction between his demand for both a smaller government and at the same time more action to prevent job losses or Medicare cuts, he responded, "If you don't trust the mindset or the value system of the people running the system, you can't even look at the facts anymore."[45] It is no coincidence, then, that the Tea Party movement's banner objective is to "take back our country."[46]

The Economic Crisis

The deep hostility of the Tea Partiers and other conservative Republicans would have been a relatively minor annoyance for Obama were it not for the much broader discontent generated by the economic crisis he inherited but has had only limited success in overcoming. The crisis—really, crises—began with the onset of the housing price deflation in late 2006 that eventually left millions of Americans with negative equity in their homes and rendered billions of dollars in subprime mortgages worthless. By the summer of 2008, financial institutions heavily invested in mortgage-backed bonds were on the brink of collapse. The credit markets froze, hammering the stock market and eventually plunging the economy into a deep recession with massive job losses, particularly in manufacturing and construction. Millions of Americans saw their homes, jobs, and much of their wealth and retirement savings disappear.

The Bush administration responded in September 2008 with a bipartisan plan, strongly supported by Obama, to shore up the financial system (and eventually Chrysler and General Motors) with a $700 billion rescue package, the Troubled Assets Relief Program (TARP), giving the federal government unprecedented authority over the financial sector. TARP was not at all popular. Propping up the very institutions whose greed and recklessness had created the crises proved a tough sell. Most Democrats thought it would mainly benefit Wall Street, not ordinary Americans.[47] Republicans objected to its cost and the expanded government role in economy.[48]

TARP seems to have worked as planned. It stabilized the financial sector and is projected to end up costing taxpayers a small fraction of the $700 billion authorized.[49] The stock market also rebounded smartly and by the end of 2010 the S&P 500 was up 86 percent from its March 2009 low. But success has not made it any more popular. With jobs still scarce and millions of homeowners still underwater on their mortgages, the revival of the banks and Wall Street firms (along with handsome bonuses for their executives) was not only galling, but fed suspicions that big business and big government had colluded to stick ordinary Americans with the bill for elite greed and ineptitude. Notwithstanding a broad consensus among economists that failure to rescue the banks would have been much more devastating for jobs, housing, and small businesses, the costs appeared to outweigh the benefits to much of the public. People who had lost their jobs, businesses, and homes did not see the bailout as benefiting them; people who had kept them because the economic contraction hadn't been even more severe could see no direct evidence that TARP had anything to do with their good fortune. An April 2010 Pew survey found that only 42 percent of Americans believed the "loans to troubled banks" prevented "a more severe crisis," while 49 percent did not; asked in the October 2010 *Newsweek* poll if the bank bailout had been good or bad for the country, 26 percent of respondents said "good," 63 percent, "bad."[50]

Although TARP was a product of the Bush administration, by July 2010, more Americans thought it was Obama's bill (47%) than Bush's (34%).[51] Most congressional Republicans who supported it had done so reluctantly.[52] Once their party no longer shared responsibility for governing, they were free to disown the unpopular bailout. When Obama turned to dealing with the deep recession sparked by the banking crisis, partisan lines on economic policy were already firmly drawn. His $787 billion stimulus package—a combination of tax cuts, expanded unemployment and other social welfare benefits, and spending on infrastructure, energy development, education, and health care—passed in February 2009 with no Republican votes in the House and only three in the Senate.

As with the bank bailout, the benefits of the stimulus package for ordinary Americans were at best ambiguous. It may have increased economic growth by as much as 4.5 percent and saved as many as 3.3 million jobs, as the Congressional Budget Office concluded,[53] but the unemployment rate was higher in November

2010 (9.8 percent) than it had been when the bill was passed (8.2 percent). Only 35 percent of respondents to a July 2010 Pew survey thought the stimulus had helped "keep unemployment from getting even worse," including only 49 percent of the Democrats. Asked a more general question about who had been helped by the "federal government's economic policies since the recession began in 2008," respondents ranked the beneficiaries (helped "a great deal" or "a fair amount") this way: large banks and financial institutions, 74 percent; large corporations, 70 percent; wealthy people, 57 percent; poor people, 31 percent; middle-class people, 27 percent; and small businesses, 23 percent.[54] The administration's argument that the economic contraction and unemployment rates would have been much worse without its actions evidently did little to mollify people continuing to face bleak economic realities. Obama's approval rating on the economy was on average about five points lower than his overall rating throughout the first ten months of 2010.

Health Care Reform

Obama's pledge to overhaul the health care system, providing affordable health care to all, had been popular during the 2008 campaign. Asked "Do you favor or oppose the U. S. government guaranteeing health insurance for all citizens, even if it means raising taxes?" about 62 percent of respondents to the 2008 Cooperative Congressional Election Study supported the idea, although partisans were far apart, with 89 percent of Democrats, 62 percent of independents, but only 23 percent of Republicans in favor (table 5.3).[55] The partisan gap remained a year later, when the

TABLE 5.3   Partisan Opinion on Health Care Reform, 2008 and 2009 (%)

	Democrats	Republicans	Independents
2008 CCES: Do you favor government guaranteeing health insurance for all citizens, even if it means raising taxes?	89	23	62
2009 CCES: We'd like to know how you would have voted on the Comprehensive Health Reform Act: Requires all Americans to obtain health insurance. Allows people to keep current provider. Sets up national health insurance option for those without coverage. Paid for with tax increases on those making more than $280,000 a year.	82	23	44
Difference	−7	0	−18

Source: 2008 and 2009 Cooperative Congressional Election Studies.

FIGURE 5.6   Support for Obama's Health Care Reform Proposal
Among Respondents With an Opinion

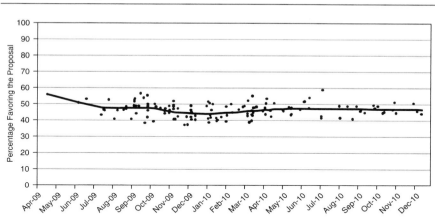

Source: 140 ABC/*Washington Post,* CBS News/*New York Times,* CNN, Gallup, Ipsos, Marist, NBC News/*Wall Street Journal,* Pew Research Center for the People an the Press, Bloomberg, NPR, AP-GfK, Kaiser/PSRA, *National Journal,* and Quinnipiac polls.

2009 CCES asked respondents if they would have voted for the actual bill as passed by the House in November of that year, but overall support, at 53 percent, was considerably lower. Independents showed the most noticeable drop in support, a crucial change. While the legislation was under consideration and after its final passage in March 2010, overall public support for the extraordinarily complicated legislative package was fairly evenly divided (figure 5.6), but with majorities of those with an opinion usually opposed (some because they did not think it went far enough). Partisan views did not change appreciably over months that the legislation was working its way through Congress and afterward, so table 5.4 simply displays the averages. Republicans remained overwhelmingly opposed to the legislation throughout, Democrats predominantly but somewhat less lopsidedly in favor of it. The notable lack of enthusiasm for the proposal among independents is the main reason support generally falls below 50 percent (of respondents with an opinion) in figure 5.6.

A review of the extensive polling data on the health care issue suggests an explanation for the bill's low support among independents. Although Americans tended to express fairly strong views, pro or con, on the legislation adopted in March 2010, opinions on its most important elements range from solidly in favor to solidly opposed. Predictably, majorities tended to like its benefits but dislike its costs. Thus, for example, most people favored requiring insurance companies to

TABLE 5.4   Support for Obama's Health Care Reform Proposal,
July 2009–December 2010 (%)

	Democrats	Republicans	Independents
Favor	70	13	36
Oppose	18	80	52
Not sure	12	7	12

Source: Average of 70 ABC/ Washington Post, CBS News/ New York Times, CNN, Gallup, Ipsos, Marist, NBC News/ Wall Street Journal, Pew Research Center for the People and the Press, and Quinnipiac polls.

cover pre-existing conditions and to continue to cover people who become sick; providing subsidies so that poor families can buy insurance; and requiring employers to provide health insurance to workers. The idea of universal coverage also generally won majority support. But majorities also tended to oppose the components necessary to pay for these features: taxing the most generous health care policies (the so-called Cadillac policies); limiting some Medicare reimbursements; and requiring everyone to buy health insurance (so that the risk pool is large enough) and enforcing this requirement through fines.[56] In addition, most people did not see the whole package of changes as improving their own health care coverage, even if they believed it would improve the health care delivery system more generally.

However, the most important reservation, at least among people not reflexively opposed to any government involvement, was that whatever its virtues, the legislation would cost too much, leading to tax increases and adding to the national debt. And it was the prevalence of these reservations among independents that seems to have turned a majority of them against the bill. Observe, for example, their responses to questions regarding the legislation's financial effects in the Quinnipiac poll taken just before the legislation passed (table 5.5). The independents' opinions on these questions are much closer to those of Republicans than to those of Democrats. Obama thus generally succeeded in persuading his own partisans that the legislation was a good thing (some of them, of course, wanted reform to go further, with a government insurance program to compete with private providers or even a Canadian-style single-payer system), but lost most independents on this issue. Obama "went public" on the issue several times, but his efforts to increase overall public support for his health care proposals were not successful, an outcome consistent with a skeptical view of the "bully pulpit's" alleged potency.[57]

The health care debate contributed to a more general loss of support for Obama among independents, which was the most significant change in his public

TABLE 5.5   Opinions on Costs of Obama's Health Care Reform Package (%)

	Democrats	Republicans	Independents
Proposed changes in the system:			
Are too expensive	27	82	62
Will increase my health care costs	27	81	60
Will increase the taxes I pay	51	93	77
Will increase the federal budget deficit	52	90	74
Will hurt the quality of my health care	10	68	46
Will help the quality of my health care	36	3	12
Will not be worth the cost	25	93	74

Source: "Obama Gets Small Bounce from Health Care Win, Quinnipiac University National Poll Finds; Net Disapproval Drops 9 Points," at http://www.quinnipiac.edu/x1295.xml?ReleaseID=1437 (accessed March 27, 2010).

standing since the election. Obama had won a majority of independent voters in 2008,[58] but as figure 5.2 indicates, his approval rating among independents has typically fallen below 50 percent since August of 2009. Among independents and all respondents alike, the relationship between opinions on health care reform and evaluations of Obama's performance has been extraordinarily strong (with the causal arrow no doubt running in both directions); on average during 2010, about 90 percent of Republicans, 89 percent of Democrats, 82 percent of independents, and 89 percent of all respondents offered consistent opinions on Obama and his health care reforms, approving of both or disapproving of both.[59] Remarkably, opinions of Obama and his health care proposals were even more tightly linked than were opinions of George W. Bush and the Iraq War.[60]

Partisan divisions in public opinion on Obama's health care reform proposals were both a cause and a consequence of the congressional Republicans' resolute opposition to changes in the health care system that, as its Democratic defenders were fond of pointing out, looked very much like those Republican presidential aspirant Mitt Romney had pushed through when he was governor of Massachusetts and that Republicans had proposed as alternatives to Bill Clinton's plan in 1993. The anger and energy manifested by the Tea Party movement—most prominently in helping elect Republican Scott Brown in January 2010 to the late Edward Kennedy's Senate seat in Massachusetts on a platform opposing Obama's health care plan—resolved any doubts among Republican leaders that unrestrained opposition to the president's agenda on health care and other matters was their best strategy for retaking control of Congress. In the health care debates, Republican leaders even adopted some of the Tea Party's apocalyptic rhetoric in denouncing the legislation: House minority leader John

Boehner called the struggle over the final vote "Armageddon" because the bill would "ruin our country."[61] His Republican colleague, Devin Nunes of California, declared that with this "Soviet"-inspired bill, Democrats "will finally lay the cornerstone of their socialist utopia on the backs of the American people."[62] A promise to repeal the bill featured prominently in most 2010 Republican congressional campaigns and topped the agenda of the new Republican House majority in 2011.

Obama's Wars

Popular disaffection with the Iraq War and the party and president behind it contributed crucially to Barack Obama's nomination and election.[63] On assuming office, he proceeded to fulfill his campaign promise to wind down the Iraq War and redirect forces to fighting the resurgent Taliban in Afghanistan. Both moves enjoyed broad public backing. Partisan divisions on his conduct of foreign policy have been much smaller than on domestic policy (table 5.6), no doubt because his policies toward both have pleased Republicans as much (Iraq) or more (Afghanistan) than Democrats. Republicans have had little reason to object to his policy of drawing down forces in Iraq because it follows the path laid out by the Bush administration and is consistent with their assessment of Bush's "surge" of 2007–2008 as a great success. Democrats were happy with a trajectory that would finally extract the US from a war most of them now consider a monumental mistake, although enough Democrats prefer a hastier departure to account for their comparatively tepid approval ratings in this domain.[64]

Obama's Afghan policies left partisans internally conflicted. For example, Republicans' support for the December 2009 decision to commit another 30,000 US troops to the fight averaged 70 percent in polls taken in the months after it was announced, thirty-three points higher than their approval of his handling of the Afghan war, while Democrats' approval of the escalation averaged 49 percent, fourteen points lower than their approval of his handling of the war.[65] Thus many Republicans approved of the president's most important decisions regarding Afghanistan but not his handling of the war, while many Democrats approved of his handling of the war but not his decisions, a nice illustration of reflexive partisan bias in responses to the approval questions. In neither case, however, did opinions on Obama's performance in this domain (or regarding Iraq) have an appreciable effect on his overall approval ratings. As the entries in table 5.6 show, Republican approval of Obama's overall job performance averaged twenty points lower than their approval of his handling of Afghanistan and Iraq, while Obama's overall approval among Democrats averaged fifteen points higher than his ratings on the wars. In sharp contrast to evaluations of Bush, then, overall assessments of

TABLE 5.6   Approval of Obama's Job Performance,
by Party and Domain, January–December 2010

	All Respondents (%)	Democrats (%)	Republicans (%)	Independents (%)	Percentage- Point Partisan Difference
Overall (103)	48	81	13	43	68
Economy (36)	43	73	12	37	61
Health care (20)	40	70	10	34	60
Afghanistan (23)	48	62	33	45	29
Iraq (10)	50	70	33	44	37

Note: The number of surveys averaged is in parentheses.

Sources: ABC News/*Washington Post*, CBS News/*New York Times*, NBC News/*Wall Street Journal*, Gallup, Quinnipiac, CNN, Fox News, Pew, Ipsos, *Newsweek*, Marist, and Franklin and Marshall polls.

Obama have so far reflected reactions to his domestic rather than his foreign policies, a consequence of both his agenda and the economic crisis he inherited. If the war in Afghanistan drags on without an end in sight, however, this could change.

Conclusions: The 2010 Midterm Elections and After

Barack Obama's election to the American presidency was a remarkable historical event, but not all Americans were ready for it or happy with the results. Public reactions to the first two years of his presidency strongly echoed the divisions that emerged during the 2008 campaign. Those predisposed to think of him as a radical leftist—mainly Republicans, but now joined by some conservative independents—took his economic stimulus and health care initiatives as cases in point. Their intense opposition shaped the strategies of Republicans congressional leaders, who sought to ride right-wing populist anger to victory at the polls in 2010. His Democratic supporters, meanwhile, suffered inevitable disappointments with the compromises needed to enact his domestic agenda and with the continuing military involvements in Iraq and Afghanistan. More important, they, like many of the more moderate independents, were also unhappy about the slow pace of the economic recovery and worried about the rising national debt. The economy was obviously Obama's and the Democrats' biggest problem going into the fall of 2010. Although as late as August 2010, Americans were still twice as likely to blame Bush as to blame Obama for the recession,[66] Obama nonetheless received poor ratings on his handling of the economy (table 5.6), which a large majority of Americans saw as the most important issue in the 2010 election (62 percent, according to the 2010 exit poll).

In combination with a weak economic recovery and lingering near double-digit unemployment, the configuration of public opinion regarding Obama and his policies created serious problems for Democrats in the 2010 midterm elections. Although the country as a whole was quite evenly divided about Obama, his disapprovers tended to be more adamant in their views and more motivated to vote than his approvers.[67] This was the reverse of 2006 and 2008, when antipathy to Bush and the Iraq War were powerful motivators for Democrats. Moreover, Obama's success in 2008 was driven by unusually high turnout among black voters, his large majorities among younger voters, and majority support among independents, with positive spillover effects for Democratic congressional candidates.[68] Young and minority voters tend to be less committed to voting and thus more likely than other voters to drop out of the electorate at the midterm, while voters over sixty-five, who held the most negative opinions of Obama, tend to be the most reliable midterm participants. And as we have seen, independents were more likely than not to disapprove of Obama's performance. Thus the electorate appearing at the polls in 2010 was considerably more favorable to the Republicans than were the electorates in 2006 and 2008.

Democrats faced yet another problem in 2010. Presidents have a powerful effect on popular attitudes toward their parties; one of George W. Bush's signal contributions to Obama's victory in 2008 was the damage done to the Republican Party image during his second term.[69] At the time Obama took over, the Democratic Party was regarded much more positively than was the Republican Party (figure 5.7). As the share of Americans with positive opinions of Obama declined, so did the share with positive opinions of his party.[70] Meanwhile, the Republican Party's image improved, and the net effect was to shrink the Democrats' initial twenty-three-point advantage on this measure to basically nothing by the end of 2010. Marginal changes in mass party identification also track presidential approval quite closely;[71] with Bush's exit and Obama's approval ratings falling into the middling range, the gains Democrats made in party identification during Bush's second term have been completely erased, at least according to the Gallup party identification series (figure 5.8).

The effects of these developments registered powerfully in the 2010 midterm. Republicans picked up a net of sixty-three House seats, winning their largest majority, 242-193, since 1946. They also picked up six Senate seats and would have won two or three more had unusually eccentric or ideologically extreme Tea Party favorites not won Republican nominations in Delaware, Nevada, and Colorado. The Democrats' reduced 53-47 majority in the Senate leaves them vulnerable in 2012, when they will have to defend twenty-three seats to the Republicans' ten.

FIGURE 5.7   Positive Opinions of Barack Obama and the Parties

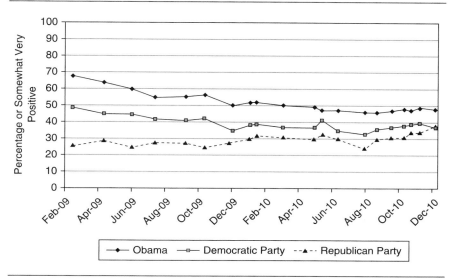

Source: NBC News/*Wall Street Journal* polls.

FIGURE 5.8   Party Identification, 2001–2010

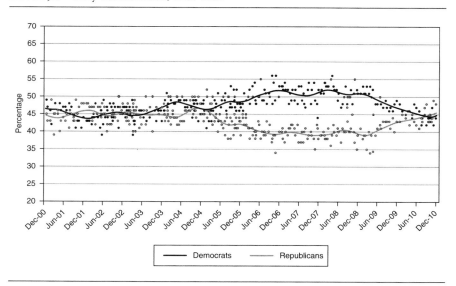

Note: Independent leaners are included as partisans.

Source: 293 Gallup polls.

As expected, turnout among younger and African American voters was down, but the Democrats' biggest problem was loss of support among independent voters. According to the exit polls, party-line voting remained very high in 2010. Self-identified Democrats voted almost as loyally for their party's candidates in 2010 (92%) as they had in the 2006 midterm (93%); Republicans voted a bit more loyally (95% compared to 91% in 2006). But independent voters applied the decisive blow; having favored Democratic House candidates 57-39 in 2006 and 51-43 in 2008, independents favored the Republican candidates 56-37 in 2010, and this reversal was the primary source of the Republicans' historic victory.

The Republican takeover of the House and gains in the Senate put Obama on the political defensive for the remaining two years of his current term. With Republicans vowing to repeal (or at least de fund) his signature health care reforms and roll back financial and environmental regulations, Obama faces the political equivalent of trench warfare just to keep his legacy from being undone. Intensified partisan conflict seems inevitable, not only because the Republicans' principal objective, openly articulated by Senate minority leader Mitch McConnell, is to make Obama a one-term president,[72] but also because the parties in the new Congress are even more ideologically polarized than in the last one. The departing House Democrats were, on average, much more moderate than those remaining, so the party's ideological center of gravity will move further left. More than half of the new Republican members identify with the Tea Party faction and so will pull their party to the right.[73] Obama's fate in 2012 will be shaped in part by how the American people, most of whom claim to detest partisan conflict, react to the spectacle; Obama should benefit if he can continue to position himself as the voice of reasoned compromise as effectively as he did during the productive post-election lame-duck session of the 111th Congress. Indeed, as 2011 dawned his approval ratings had tracked back above 50 percent in most polls. But his political fortunes will be shaped even more powerfully by the realities of the economy, international terrorism, and developments in Afghanistan, Iraq, Iran, and other global trouble spots.

Notes

1. Gary C. Jacobson, "The Effects of the George W. Bush Presidency on Partisan Attitudes," *Presidential Studies Quarterly* 39 (June 2009): 172–209.
2. Joseph Bufumi and Robert Y. Shapiro, "A New Partisan Voter," *Journal of Politics* 71 (January 2009): 1-24; Alan I. Abramowitz, *The Disappearing Center: Engaged Citizens, Polarization, and American Democracy* (New Haven, CT: Yale University Press, 2010); Matthew Levendusky, *The Partisan Sort: How Liberals Became*

      Democrats and Conservatives Became Republicans (Chicago: University of Chicago Press, 2010); Gary C. Jacobson, *A Divider, Not a Uniter: George W. Bush and the American People,* 2nd ed. (New York: Pearson Longman, 2011).

3. This analysis excludes partisan leaners; if they are included, the only differences are that 74 percent locate themselves right of center and 20 percent in the middle. Decades are defined by redistricting cycles, for example, the 1980s cover 1982–1990. The 2000s include 2002, 2004, and 2008; there was no ANES study in 2006. Respondents who could not place themselves on the scale are excluded; if they are placed in the middle category, the same trends emerge. Over this period, the proportion of Americans not placing themselves fell from 22 percent to 15 percent among Republicans and from 31 percent to 26 percent among Democrats.

4. Republicans in the 2008 ANES who identified themselves as "conservative" or "extremely conservative" rated Obama at a chilly 36° on the 100-point feeling thermometer, compared with 53° among other Republicans and 78° among all other respondents.

5. Even during the first three months of the Obama administration, nearly three-quarters of Gallup poll respondents who identified themselves as conservative Republicans (about two-thirds of all Republicans in the Gallup surveys) disapproved of Obama's performance; during 2010, an average of only 7 percent of this faction have approved of his performance (based on forty-six surveys taken between January and mid-November 2010; available through the Roper Center, University of Connecticut).

6. On average since 2008, Gallup has found about 40 percent of Americans calling themselves conservatives, 21 percent calling themselves liberals; see Lynda Saad, "In 2010, Conservatives Still Outnumber Moderates, Liberals," Gallup News Service, June 25, 2010; 44 percent of respondents in the 2008 ANES survey placed themselves right of center, only 27 percent left of center, on the seven-point liberal-conservative scale.

7. For example, in the nine ABC News/*Washington Post* poll taken in the first ten months of 2010, 80 percent of the disapprovers disapproved of Obama's performance strongly, compared with 56 percent of the approvers who approved strongly; at http://www .washingtonpost.com/wp-srv/politics/polls/postpoll_10302010.html?sid=ST201010 3100110 (accessed November 15, 2010).

8. If independent leaners are included as partisans, the figure rises to 8.0 percent; only John F. Kennedy (6.4 percent) and Bill Clinton in 1992 (7.9 percent) attracted fewer. See the Campbell chapter in this volume for a somewhat different interpretation.

9. Jacobson, "Effects of the Bush Presidency"; Gary C. Jacobson, "George W. Bush, the Iraq War, and the Election of Barack Obama," *Presidential Studies Quarterly* 40 (June 2010): 207–24.

10. Election data are from the National Exit Poll, the 2008 American National Election Study, and the 2008 Cooperative Congressional Election Survey; the Gallup averages include only respondents expressing an opinion, averaging about 93 percent of respondents; unfortunately, Gallup does not report the share expressing no opinion (or disapproval) in its published demographic breakdowns, so these are estimates calculated by

assuming that the proportion of respondents without opinions is the same across demographic categories, which is certainly not true but unlikely to produce significant distortions here. Gallup data are the weekly averages reported from Gallup's daily surveys reported at http://www.gallup.com/poll/124922/Presidential-Approval-Center .aspx (accessed December 31, 2010).

11. Richard Hofstadter, "The Paranoid Style in American Politics," *Harper's Magazine* (November 1964): 77–86.

12. Google "Obama" in conjunction with any of these labels to see how routinely they are used—and defended—on the Internet.

13. David Barstow, "Tea Party Lights Fuse for Rebellion on Right," *New York Times,* February 16, 2010.

14. In nineteen surveys taken between January and October 2010, between 18 and 41 percent said they had a favorable view of the Tea Party movement (average, 32 percent), and from 12 to 50 percent had an unfavorable view of it (average, also 32 percent); the rest were uncertain or did not know enough about it to have an opinion; from NBC News/*Wall Street Journal,* CBS News/*New York Times,* Quinnipiac, Fox News, AP-GfK, and ABC News/*Washington Post* polls available at http://www.pollingreport .com/politics.htm (accessed November 7, 2010).

15. Only 7 percent of Tea Party supporters in the April 5–12 CBS News/*New York Times* poll approved of Obama's performance; 88 percent disapproved, and 92 percent said his policies were leading the country toward socialism; see "Tea Party Movement: What They Think," at http://www.cbsnews.com/htdocs/pdf/poll_tea_party_041410 .pdf (accessed April 15, 2010).

16. "Polls: 'Birther' Myth Persists among Tea Partiers, All Americans," at http://www .cbsnews.com/8301-503544_162-20002539-503544.html?tag=contentMain;contentBo dy (accessed April 15, 2020); the February ABC News/*Washington Post* poll found 31 percent of Republicans and a like proportion of Tea Party sympathizers believing Obama was not US born; see http://abcnews.go.com/PollingUnit/poll-half-birthers-call-suspicion-approve-obama/story?id=10576748&page=2; asked in a July, 2010, survey if Obama was born in the US, only 23 percent of CNN's Republican Respondents said "definitely," 34 percent said "probably," 27 percent said "probably not," and 14 percent said "definitely not." The respective percentages for Democrats were 64, 21, 7, and 8; results at http://i2.cdn.turner.com/cnn/2010/images/08/04/rel10k1a.pdf (accessed August 4, 2010).

17. "Growing Number of Americans Say Obama Is Muslim," Pew Survey Report, August 19, 2010, at http://people-press.org/report/645/ (accessed August 23, 2010).

18. Eleven percent of Democrats and 17 percent of independents also thought he was a Muslim; *Time Magazine*/Abt SRBI Poll: Religion, August 16–17, 2010, available from the Roper Center, University of Connecticut; secondary analysis by the author.

19. For a sample of Beck's flights of rhetoric, see http://politicalhumor.about.com/ library/bl-glenn-beck-quotes.htm (accessed March 24, 2010); by one count reported in July, 2010, since Obama's inauguration, Beck transcripts included "202 mentions of Nazis or Nazism, . . . 147 mentions of Hitler, 193 mentions of fascism or fascist, and another 24 bonus mentions of Joseph Goebbels. Most of these were directed in some

form at Obama—as were a majority of the 802 mentions of socialist or socialism"; see Dana Milibank, "The Tea Party Makes Trouble with a Capital T," *Washington Post,* July 18, 2010.

20. "Tea Party Movement: What They Think."
21. Ed Henry and Ed Hornick, "Rage Rising on the McCain Campaign Trial," CNN, October 11, 2008, at http://www.cnn.com/2008/POLITICS/10/10/mccain.crowd/ (accessed July 8, 2010); Jake Tapper, "Another Man Yells 'Kill Him!' about Obama at Palin Rally," ABC News, October 14, 2008, at http://blogs.abcnews.com/political punch/2008/10/another-man-yel.html (accessed July 8, 2010).
22. Scott Conroy, "Palin: Obama's Plan Is 'Experiment with Socialism,'" CBS News, October 19, 2008, at http://www.cbsnews.com/8301-503443_162-4532388.html (accessed June 21, 2010); Bob Drogan and Mark Barabak, "McCain Says Obama Wants Socialism," *Los Angeles Times,* October 19, 2008; Alex Johnson, "McCain Hammers Obama on Ayers Ties," MSNBC, October 23, 2008, at http://www.msnbc.msn.com/ id/27343688/ (accessed March 20, 2010); Kate Kenski, Bruce W. Hardy, and Kathleen Hall Jamieson, *The Obama Victory: How Media, Money, and Message Shaped the 2008 Election* (New York: Oxford University Press, 2010).
23. Gary C. Jacobson, "Obama and the Polarized Public," in *Obama in Office: The First Two Years,* ed. James A. Thurber (Boulder, CO: Paradigm Publishers, 2011), 19–40.
24. Herbert F. Weisberg and Christopher J. Devine, "Racial Attitude Effects on Voting in the 2008 Presidential Election: Examining the Unconventional Factors Shaping Vote Choice in a Most Unconventional Election," presented at the Mershon Conference on the Transformative Election of 2008, Columbus, Ohio, October 1-4, 2009. The vote for Obama among respondents in the quintiles ranging from least to most racially resentful was 91 percent, 66 percent, 50 percent, 39 percent, and 20 percent; the least racially resentful respondents rated Obama 55 degrees warmer on the ANES's 100-point feeling thermometer scale than the most racially resentful respondents; if party identification and ideology are controlled, an estimated difference of 32 degrees remains between the respondents at the highest and lowest points on the scale. The scale is described in Donald R. Kinder and Lynn M. Sanders, *Divided by Color* (Chicago: University of Chicago Press, 1996), chap. 3.
25. Chris McGreal, "Americans Stick to Their Guns as Firearms Sales Surge," *The Guardian,* April 13, 2009.
26. Calculated from data at http://www.fbi.gov/hq/cjisd/nics/Total%20NICS%20 Background%20Checks.htm (accessed March 26, 2010).
27. Frank Newport, "Many Gun Owners Think Obama Will Try to Ban Gun Sales," Gallup News Service, October 20, 2009.
28. David Brooks, "Getting Obama Right," *New York Times,* March 12, 2010.
29. Marc J. Hetherington and Jonathan D. Weiler, *Authoritarianism and Polarization in American Politics* (New York: Cambridge University Press, 2009), 6–7.
30. Karen Stenner, *The Authoritarian Dynamic* (New York: Cambridge University Press, 2005); Stanley Feldman and Karen Stenner, "Perceived Threat and Authoritarianism," *Political Psychology* 18 (December 1997): 741–770.

31. Except for the third pair, the more authoritarian response is the second one; the index sums the responses to these questions.

32. Stenner, *Authoritarian Dynamic*, 178-179.

33. Hetherington and Weiler, *Authoritarianism and Polarization*, 41.

34. Ibid., 43-47.

35. Ibid., 11.

36. It also helps explain why so many Democrats developed extremely negative opinions of George W. Bush.

37. Independents who say they lean toward one of the parties are treated as partisans in this analysis because their views are indistinguishable from those of other identifiers of that party.

38. Frank Newport, "Tea Party Supporters Overlap Republican Base," Gallup News Service, July 2, 2009.

39. This is true for Democrats and independents as well, and the Tea Party variable has a significant effect on the responses to these questions of all survey respondents even when party identification and ideology are controlled.

40. "Tea Party Movement: What They Think," report of CBS News/*New York Times* poll, April 5-12, 2010, at http://www.cbsnews.com/htdocs/pdf/poll_tea_party_041410.pdf (accessed April 15, 2010).

41. William R. L. Anderegga, James W. Prall, Jacob Harold, and Stephen H. Schneider, "Expert Credibility in Climate Change," *Proceedings of the National Academy of Sciences of the United States*, April 9, 2010.

42. "Tea Party Movement: What They Think."

43. Stenner, *Authoritarian Dynamic*, 179.

44. "Tea Party Movement: What They Think."

45. Kate Zernike, "With No Jobs, Plenty of Time to Tea Party," *New York Times*, March 27, 2010.

46. See, for example, "What Does Take Back Our Country Mean to You?" Tea Party Blogs, at http://teapartypatriots.org/BlogPostView.aspx?id=09c08c91-528c-41d6-91ca-3896dd378c7a (accessed July 23, 2010).

47. In a CBS News/*New York Times* poll taken September 27–30, 2008, 56 percent of Democrats said they thought the bill would benefit "mostly just a few big investors and people who work on Wall Street," while only 37 percent thought it would help "homeowners and people throughout the country." Republicans were split, 48 percent to 46 percent on this question. Most Democrats wanted the government to provide financial help to homeowners (75%), while only 43 percent of Republican agreed.

48. A month after the bill passed, only 32 percent of respondents to the October 19–22 CBS News/*New York Times* poll approved of the bailout, with Republicans only slightly more supportive (35%) than Democrats (31%).

49. See the Weatherford chapter in this volume. The most recent estimate is that TARP's final cost to the treasury will be about $50 billion—a modest price if it helped avoid a replay of the 1930s; see Ronald D. Orol, "Treasury: Total Cost of TARP Will Be $50 Billion," *Marketwatch*, October 5, 2010, at http://www.marketwatch.com/story/treasury-total-cost-of-tarp-will-be-50-billion-2010-10-05-164330 (accessed November 7, 2010).

50. Partisans were not particularly far apart on either question; the breakdown on the Pew survey for Democrats was 54-37, for independents, 37-58, for Republicans, 35-56; see "Pessimistic Public Doubts Effectiveness of Stimulus, TARP," Pew report, April 28, 2010, at http://people-press.org (accessed April 28, 2010); on the second, the respective breakdowns were 39-48, 26-64, and 13-79; at http://pollingreport.com/business.htm (accessed November 7, 2010).

51. Pew Center for the People and the Press poll, July 1-5, 2010.

52. In the House the Democrats split 172-63 for the bill, Republicans 91-108 against. The respective partisan votes in the Senate split 39-3 and 34-15.

53. The CBO estimated that the stimulus bill increased the number of full-time-equivalent jobs by between 1.7 million to 3.3 million and the GDP by from 1.7 to 4.5 percent, compared to what would have occurred without the stimulus; see Congressional Budget Office, "Estimated Impact of the American Recovery and Reinvestment Act on Employment and Economic Output from October 2009 through December 2009," CBO Report, August 2010, at http://www.cbo.gov/ftpdocs/117xx/doc11706/08-24-ARRA.pdf (accessed August 25, 2010).

54. "Gov't Economic Policies Seen as Boon for Banks and Big Business, Not Middle Class or Poor," Pew Survey Report, July 19, 2010, at http://people-press.org/report/637 (accessed July 26, 2010).

55. See Stephen Ansolabehere, Cooperative Congressional Election Survey, 2008: Common Content [Computer File] Release 1: February 2, 2009, Cambridge, MA: MIT [producer]; Stephen Ansolabehere, "Guide to the 2008 Cooperative Congressional Elections Survey," Harvard University, draft of February 9. The 2009 CCES was conducted in November and December using the same methodology as the 2008 CCES; the module used in the analyses reported here included 6,000 interviews. I am obliged to Steve Ansolabehere for providing access to this study. For comparison, the 2008 ANES asked respondents if they favored or opposed "the U.S. government paying for all necessary medical care for all Americans." Fifty-one percent said they favored the idea, 37 percent opposed it, and 12 percent said they neither favored nor opposed it. Among partisans, 70 percent of Democrats, 56 percent of independents, and 22 percent of Republicans favored the idea.

56. See the extensive compilation of survey questions and responses at http://www.pollingreport.com/health.htm (accessed April 4, 2010).

57. George C. Edwards III, *The Strategic President: Persuasion and Opportunity in Presidential Leadership* (Princeton: Princeton University Press, 2009); and see the Edwards chapter in this volume.

58. In the CCES survey, 52 percent of independents favored Obama, 44 percent McCain; in the ANES survey, 56 percent of independents favored Obama, 40 percent McCain; in the national exit poll, it was 52 percent Obama, 42 percent McCain.

59. From averages of nine Gallup, CNN, and NBC News/*Wall Street Journal* polls taken in 2010 and available for secondary analysis.

60. Gary C. Jacobson, "George W. Bush, Polarization, and the War in Iraq," in *The George W. Bush Legacy*, ed. Colin Campbell, Bert A. Rockman, and Andrew Rudalevige (Washington, DC: CQ Press, 2008), 81.

61. "Boehner: It's 'Armageddon,' Health Care Bill Will 'Ruin our Country,'" The Speaker's Lobby, Fox News, March 20, 2010, at http://congress.blogs.foxnews.com/2010/03/20/boehner-its-armageddon-health-care-bill-will-ruin-our-country/comment-page-3/?action=late-new (accessed April 2, 2010).

62. Speech on the House floor, March 21, 2010, video available at http://vodpod.com/watch/3280104-devin-nunes-health-care-the-ghost-of-communism-a-socialist-utopia (accessed April 10, 2010).

63. Gary C. Jacobson, "The 2008 Presidential and Congressional Elections: Anti-Bush Referendum and Prospects for the Democratic Majority," *Political Science Quarterly* 124 (Spring 2009): 1–30; Jacobson, "Election of Barack Obama."

64. Gary C. Jacobson, "A Tale of Two Wars: Public Opinion on the U.S. Military Interventions in Afghanistan and Iraq," *Presidential Studies Quarterly* 40 (December 2010): 585–610.

65. Ibid., 603–604.

66. On average in the ten surveys that asked the question in 2010, 56 percent blamed Bush, 25 percent blamed Obama; results from ABC News/Washington Post, NPR, Fox News, Democracy Corps, NBC News/*Wall Street Journal, Time Magazine*/Abt SRBI, and Quinnipiac polls reported at the Roper Center's *iPoll* facility at http://webapps.ropercenter.uconn.edu (accessed October 10, 2010).

67. For example, in the three ABC News/*Washington Post* polls taken during the first quarter of 2010, 75 percent of respondents who disapproved of Obama's performance said they disapproved strongly, compared 59 percent of approvers who said they approved strongly; the comparable figures for disapprovers and approvers of his handling of health care were 84 percent and 60 percent, respectively. In six Gallup Polls taken in May and June, an average of 42 percent of Republicans but only 25 percent of Democrats said they were very enthusiastic about voting for Congress this year; at http://www.gallup.com/poll/127439/Election-2010-Key-Indicators.aspx (accessed June 23, 2010).

68. Jacobson, "2008 Presidential and Congressional Elections."

69. Jacobson, "Effects of the Bush Presidency."

70. Positive opinions of Obama drop twenty points, from 68 percent to 48 percent across these surveys; positive views of the Democratic Party drop twelve points, from 49 percent to 37 percent; the two series are correlated at .88 The relationship between opinions of Obama and the Republican Party is considerably weaker, with a correlation of −.49.

71. Jacobson, "Effects of the Bush Presidency."

72. "GOP Leader's Top Goal: Make Obama 1-Term President," MSNBC, November 4, 2010, at http://www.msnbc.msn.com/id/40007802/ns/politics-decision_2010/ (accessed December 29, 2010).

73. Gary C. Jacobson, "The Republican Resurgence in 2010," *Political Science Quarterly* 126 (Spring 2011): 27–52.

CHAPTER 6

Obama and the Public Presidency: What Got You Here Won't Get You There

Diane J. Heith

> It's always nice to get out of Washington—at least for a little bit—and to come to places like this. The climate is nicer. So is the conversation sometimes [*Laughter*]. So I am looking forward to taking your questions and hearing about your concerns.
>
> —*President Barack Obama, Los Angeles, California, March* 19, 2009

PRESIDENT OBAMA'S WRY observation about the ways of Washington highlights an important presidential leadership strategy: getting out of town. By "going public," in Samuel Kernell's phrase, presidents seek ways to go above and get around Washington insiders by establishing a direct relationship with the electorate.[1] The White House's "permanent campaign" noted in the 1980s, expressed through the Reagan White House's use of addresses to the nation, travel around the nation, reliance on public opinion polls, and management of the media, has only grown and solidified under Reagan's successors.[2]

This development reflects technological changes and an increasingly hard-to-reach, fragmented public. But the institutionalization of the permanent campaign also reflects the fact that winning presidential candidates led effective campaigns, in terms of strategy, organization, and communications. Thus incoming presidents are not randomly selected in terms of their skills at and reliance on "going public": they are good at it. On the other hand, as all presidents come to learn, governing is not the same as campaigning. Campaigning depends on persuasive efforts but also, as Hugh Heclo observes, "is geared to one unambiguous decision point in time. . . . [and] is necessarily adversarial."[3] In contrast, governing is continuous and often requires coalition building and compromise.

More than most campaigns, Obama's 2008 effort raised great expectations for the potential of presidential communications as part of presidential leadership. Based on his performance as a candidate, the Obama presidency was thought to herald the dawn of the new "Great Communicator." Perceptions during the campaign, and the post mortems afterward, all touted Obama's oratory skill and his use of old and new media to dominate. By the end of his second year in office, however, headlines trumpeted the failure of the Obama administration to communicate effectively. A Google search of "Obama failed communicator" revealed close to two million hits both from the blogosphere and traditional news outlets, like the *Washington Post* and *New York Times*. Obama's own analysis after the 2010 midterms was that "I neglected some things that matter a lot to people and rightly so . . . [such as] making sure that the policy decisions that I made were fully debated with the American people and that I was getting out of Washington and spending more time shaping public opinion and being in a conversation with the American people about why I was making the choices I was making."[4] A senior White House aide, while praising the administration's substantive achievements, was more scathing. "They need to fire people," the aide told a reporter. "In politics and communications, this White House has been terrible."[5]

There are multiple explanations for the dramatic pendulum swing from grandiose expectations to labels of failure. The existence of such a lofty beginning perch itself relates to the perceptions of communications failure. Clearly, having reached oratorical and campaign success not witnessed in twenty years left the new president nowhere to go but down. Yet there is more to the story than the failure to live up to heightened expectations: this explains some of the fall from grace, but not all. Ironically, Obama's implementation of his successful campaign communication strategy (effective organization, a strategic use of new media, and a minimizing of old media) had a detrimental effect on his influence on the public as president. Using the campaign as a model, the Obama administration expanded the capacity of White House communications efforts to lead directly. Through its use of new media, and new outlets of the "old" media, the Obama administration attempted to employ the last component of campaign strategy that had eluded previous administrations as it sought to diminish the media's capability to filter presidential messages. The Obama communications strategy represents the culmination of the "campaigning to govern" strategy, institutionalized. However, the net result in the short term was, ironically, a *loss* of control over the narrative as the press became significantly more confrontational over the first two years, after continued exposure to the Obama communications strategy.

A New Model for a Successful Campaign

The Obama campaign brought to fruition what many had been waiting for as the Internet expanded: a marriage between old and new media tools and strategies. Television, radio, and newspapers represent the old; newspapers have been the mechanism by which presidents communicate with the public for two hundred years. Independent press critique of the president is over one hundred years old.[6] The Internet is the new technology offering multiple avenues for political interaction: from old media offering a web presence, to the independent blogosphere, to the web pages of candidates, campaigns, and governing institutions. Traditional campaign communications strategies include advertising in critical markets, interviews with key media outlets, and quick responsiveness to media coverage of the candidate and his or her opponents. Obama's new media strategy added a web presence that enabled increased connectivity between voters and candidates, to enhance outreach, fundraising, volunteer coordination, and strategic responsiveness.

Massive fundraising totals allowed Obama to employ television advertising in an unprecedented way in expensive media markets, saturating airtime.[7] The campaign also employed the "war room" tactics popularized by the 1992 Clinton campaign with immediate responses to news stories and candidate charges.[8] More significantly, the Obama team won the contest to define the terms of debate: the Obama message of hope and change dominated discussion of the campaign. Thus, the Obama campaign successfully defined the frame ("change") employed by the media and the other candidates.

If the Obama team had simply excelled at old media, they might still have triumphed over John McCain. However, if the Obama team had not employed a vastly superior web-based communications strategy, they might not have had the chance to do so, given the hugely competitive Democratic nomination race. The Obama web presence was head and shoulders above his competitors' on either the Democratic or Republican side. Obama's web page was much more sophisticated, allowing users to use the site the way they were used to using the web generally: to buy, to donate, to join in, to be social and to gather information.[9] In addition, the campaign created an impressive e-mail database used to contact and update potential voters through texting and e-mail. The field of candidates never caught up to Obama's web and e-mail efforts, although the Clinton campaign came closest.[10]

Its sophisticated web presence coupled with the massive sums of money to buy TV and web advertising allowed the Obama campaign to bypass the gatekeeping feature of the traditional media. Early in 2007, the mainstream press anointed Hillary Clinton the presumptive Democratic nominee due to her party insider status and fundraising capabilities. Traditionally, upstart campaigns like Obama's would have withered in the face of the invisible primary: little or bad media coverage leads to lack of fundraising, and lack of fundraising produces little or bad media coverage. Money and media coverage traditionally went hand in hand as shortcuts for the punditocracy's assessments of viability. The Obama campaign's use of the Internet to fundraise and reach voters in primary states short-circuited the media's ability to declare the candidate unviable and thus limit the public's access to the candidate. The campaign's presence on Facebook, MySpace, and other social networking sites also allowed the Obama campaign to broaden its reach beyond the typical TV and newspaper audiences. Thus, the Obama campaign was never dependent on favorable press coverage, although it typically received it.[11]

The Obama campaign received generally positive press coverage for reasons derived from the campaign as well as the psychology of the press. The first reason was simple: the campaign was effective, and initially successful. The press typically rewards unexpected outcomes—recall Bill Clinton's second-place finish in the New Hampshire primary in 1992—and Obama's surprise victory in the Iowa caucus yielded overwhelmingly positive coverage (and negative press coverage for his opponents). The Obama campaign organization was effective; there were few negative indicators and thus few reports of infighting, errors, or other problems, which faltering campaigns frequently receive. By contrast, the Clinton campaign was disastrously divided. An e-mail from Washington insider Robert Bennett released by the *Atlantic* magazine hints at the tone of both campaign and subsequent coverage. "This circular firing squad that is occurring is unattractive, unprofessional, unconscionable, and unacceptable," pled Bennett. "After this campaign is over there will be plenty of time to . . . blame or claim credit."[12] But the blame game continued, and the campaign was over sooner than Bennett hoped.

In addition, since press coverage expands toward new information, Obama's personal characteristics produced favorable press coverage. He was relatively new on the political scene; he was younger than his opponents; he was African American, with a compelling life story; and he was a product of the same liberal elite that had produced many members of the mainstream press corps. Each of those traits were often portrayed as flaws by his opponents, but they were interesting to the press. The upside of the press preference for the new, unusual, and competent was relatively positive press coverage during the campaign. The downside did not emerge until approximately six months into the Obama administration—when the press rejected being managed, Obama-style.

White House Communications Strategy 2.0

The purpose of a campaign communications strategy is obvious: to get more voters to the polls and voting for you than for your opponent on Election Day. The purpose of a White House communications strategy has far less focus. Moreover, the differences between the two underscore the differences between campaigning and governing. In office, the presidents seeks to communicate not with voters per se, but with those Richard Neustadt termed "his five constituencies: Congress, executive officialdom, partisans, citizens at large and those abroad."[13] The media is the primary conduit for the information to partisans, citizens, the world at large, and even members of Congress. Even when the president speaks directly via national speeches, the media provides commentary and interpretation, particularly now in what Jeffrey Cohen has termed the "post-broadcast age."[14] In a widely discussed 2010 op-ed, the venerable journalist and former host of ABC's *Nightline*, Ted Koppel, summed up the "narrowcasting" or targeted news and opinion business model produced in the post-broadcast age with a lament:

> Broadcast news has been outflanked and will soon be overtaken by scores of other media options. The need for clear, objective reporting in a world of rising religious fundamentalism, economic interdependence and global ecological problems is probably greater than it has ever been. But we are no longer a national audience receiving news from a handful of trusted gatekeepers; we're now a million or more clusters of consumers, harvesting information from like-minded providers.[15]

Even at the best of times, the unavoidable relationship between the president and the media is codependent and often contentious.[16] In a representative democracy, citizens require information from the government, information the government does not always wish to share. The president seeks to communicate unfettered and unfiltered to control information regarding his policy agenda, but also to achieve reelection. The press naturally rejects the role of mere conduit, preferring to assert its preferred (and more self-satisfying) "watchdog" role as guardians of democracy and check on government. These competing goals (not to mention those that arise from the business demands of the media) produce the tension and the strategy inherent in the presidential efforts to go public.

The Obama White House used a two-pronged communications strategy: old and new. The traditional approach continued the use of a White House Office of Communications, as well as a press secretary. This office followed the script provided by presidents in the post-Watergate media age: it aimed to manage the media by engaging it, and to manage the public by polling it.

The second prong of the strategy, however, challenged the traditional relationship between the president and the press and aimed to forge a new relationship with the public. The Obama White House added their new media savvy and public connectivity to the traditional public outreach structure and expanded it. This aggregated approach lives in both the new and old White House structure as part of the Office of Public Engagement (formerly the Office of Public Liaison, which dealt primarily with interest groups) and the Office of Communications. The overlap and merging of the outreach to ordinary citizens, interest groups, and the media challenged and changed the traditional communications institutions by allowing an exponential increase in the opportunities to pursue the campaign tactic of bypassing the press from the White House. Predictably, these efforts damaged the presidential relationship with the press and consequently his press coverage.

Traditional White House Communications—with a Twist

Staffing the White House is a critical component of a presidential transition because it is a significant component of a successful presidency.[17] Like many of the White House staff units, the Office of Communications (OC) must facilitate presidential decision making. However, few of the other boxes of the organization chart have an explicit public component. While the OC seeks to manage the president's message, it must work with the press. Like cabinet secretaries who can "go native" and be "captured" by their departments, this life on the border causes an inherent tension within a communications staff that must balance the goals of the president with the demands from the press.

Staffing.   The Obama White House organization chart revealed a lot about its methods and motivations. At its heart was a traditional hierarchy with the White House and Executive Office of the President (EOP) staff reporting to a chief of staff, first Rahm Emmanuel and then William Daley. The subunits within the Office of Communication, though, were reworked to reflect the administration's efforts to bring their successful campaign tactics to the White House: Communications, Media Affairs, New Media, Research, and Speechwriting. Interestingly, President Obama's first press secretary's office was a separate entity from the Office of Communications. It also provided equal rank for the press secretary and the director of communications within the White House hierarchy. This may have been an effort to establish Robert Gibbs and his office as a reflective voice of the president rather than a component of the president's media management efforts. Alternatively, it might have reflected the desire to shore up the known "messy management" practices of Gibbs.[18] Most likely, the status reflected the longstanding working relationship between Obama and Gibbs.

Obama's second press secretary marked a change along all these dimensions. Although Jay Carney was widely respected within the press corps, and not new to the administration—he had served as Vice President Biden's spokesperson—he lacked a personal relationship with Obama. A reorganization pushed by new chief of staff Daley, consequently, placed the new press secretary under the director of the Office of Communications.

The demands of the offices that serve the president, the people, and the press take a toll on its staffers. In his first term, Obama employed two press secretaries (Gibbs and Carney) and three different directors of the Office of Communications (Ellen Moran, who lasted only three months due to a poor fit with the duality of the position; Anita Dunn, who served as the interim replacement; and then Dan Pfeiffer).

The hierarchy also reveals a new entity, the Office of Public Engagement and Intergovernmental Affairs (OPE), formerly the Office of Public Liaison. The OPE aimed to reflect President Obama's stated desire for a more open government. "Our commitment to openness means more than simply informing the American people about how decisions are made," Obama said on the White House website the day after his inauguration. "It means recognizing that government does not have all the answers, and that public officials need to draw on what citizens know."[19] The importance of OPE was emphasized by the president's choice to head it: Valerie Jarrett. Jarrett has been one of the president's most senior and trusted advisers, with him from his early days in Chicago. It is important to note here that the organizational separation between Communications and OPE has a substantive significance. Although previous administrations desired to go around the mainstream press, the opportunity to do so only existed using other press avenues. The George W. Bush administration paid pundits, like conservative political commentator Armstrong Williams (to defend No Child Left Behind), and routinely produced prepackaged news videos in support of administration policies, but did so as part of the traditional communications structure.[20] By contrast, the Obama White House distinguished immediately between outreach *through* the press, and outreach *around* it, and created separate offices using that distinction.

Tactics to Manage the Press.   Outreach to the press and outreach via the press takes various forms, most of which have been employed by White Houses for decades. Presidents give speeches, nationally and locally; they give interviews, on and off the record, as do their staff; they give press conferences; and they employ a press secretary to regularly, even routinely, disseminate information.[21] Here the Obama White House followed the traditional script, as well as the adjustments made by his predecessor to adapt to the post-broadcast media era.[22]

President Obama gave seven national addresses in his first two years; Presidents Clinton and Bush each gave eleven. National speeches serve multiple purposes: to signal legislative goals, to reveal new policy goals, or to respond to an event or crises. Obama gave three major addresses on foreign policy, for instance, detailing his foreign policy approach to Middle East policy (in Cairo), the War in Iraq (at West Point), and upon accepting his unexpected Nobel Peace Prize (in Oslo). Having discussed economic recovery in February 2009, he also gave other major addresses that attempted to seize control of the agenda, first on health care and then on energy, both in response to outside stimuli (the declining support for health care; and, in 2010, the BP oil spill in the Gulf of Mexico, which was his first address from the Oval Office and also his first poorly received set piece speech). National speeches used to be the easiest way for the president to reach a large percentage of the nation. In 1981, when Ronald Reagan delivered his proposals for economic recovery before Congress, some three-fifths of Americans watched it.[23] In contrast, though it was broadcast on ten channels, far fewer watched Obama's parallel February 2009 speech on economic recovery.

That fragmentation of the national audience meant that the president and his staff sought out other ways to be present in the public sphere. The president's staff performed on the Sunday morning talk shows with regularity. The president himself was available individually quite consistently, averaging one interview by an American news organization every two weeks.[24] However, President Obama did not give frequent press conferences with the press corps at the White House. As table 6.1 reveals, rather surprisingly, President Obama held only slightly more press conferences then did George W. Bush—*not* considered a great communicator— over the equivalent period, and far fewer than Bill Clinton. While Clinton gave approximately one solo press conference a month, both Obama and Bush averaged less than one every two months. On the whole, then, President Obama has been as inaccessible as George W. Bush was with the national media.

The distance with the traditional press is hardly surprising given the distance established by the campaign. A *New York Times Magazine* article during the transition

TABLE 6.1   Presidential Press Conferences

President	Total in First Two Years (including foreign dignitaries)	Total in First Two Years (not including foreign dignitaries)
Obama	46	12
Bush	39	7
Clinton	83	21

Data provided by the American Presidency Project, gathered by John Woolley and Gerhard Peters, University of California, Santa Barbara http://www.presidency.ucsb.edu/ws/.

period in 2008 highlighted the delight of the Obama insiders when they rejected traditional press-candidate relations. "In part because we were in Chicago and in part because of our approach, we did not do 'cocktail party' interviews," said Dan Pfeiffer, the campaign's communications director, who ultimately became communications director at the White House. "These are interviews that you agree to because you were always bumping into the reporter at cocktail parties, and they keep asking for the candidate's time. We would laugh every time our opponents would do them."[25] The campaign believed it did not need to develop inside-the-Beltway techniques to win. Indeed, "the campaign bragged that Obama never even visited with the editorial board of the *Washington Post*—a decision that would have been unheard of for any serious candidate in a previous presidential cycle."[26] Consequently, the Obama White House had only truncated relationships with the national media to build on once ensconced in the White House.

To be sure, the experiences of earlier presidents like Ronald Reagan and even George W. Bush suggest that presidents do not necessarily require cozy press relations to accomplish their goals. The primary strategic component of outreach via the press stems from the effort of the White House to control discussion in the political sphere by controlling the dissemination of information. Consider the example of the Reagan administration, which set the standard for news management via implementation of a seven-point approach, as described by political scientist Lori Cox Han: it sought to "plan ahead, stay on the offensive, control the flow of information, limit reporters' access to Reagan, talk about the issues the White House wants to talk about, speak in one voice, and repeat the same message many times."[27] The "line of the day," which the Reagan White House decided via its morning meeting that the White House and administration would highlight during the course of a day, was the logical culmination of this approach.[28] Han notes that Reagan's strategy tempered aggressive press management of the Washington press corps with wide availability to the local press and effective understanding of the visual needs of television.[29] As a result, Reagan received relatively positive press coverage despite his relatively poor relationship with the Washington press corps.

George W. Bush's administration followed the Reagan model, altering the strategy for the changed media context. Bush's White House, under Karl Rove's direction, was relentlessly disciplined in following the line of the day as well as the Bush policy doctrines. There were few leaks. However, the Bush communications team sometimes took the Reagan view of the visual too far, culminating in embarrassing episodes such as the president's appearance under a "Mission Accomplished" banner on the deck of an aircraft carrier six years before combat troops would leave Iraq.

The disciplined lack of information created a press corps dependent on the White House for information. More significantly, the White House was also able to manipulate the rules between staffers and reporters regarding on-the-record and off-the-record information. The upper hand granted by the stingy flow of information enabled top staffers to hide the White House agenda in plain sight, including the release of an undercover CIA agent's name. Nor did the press aggressively question the administration regarding the need for war in Iraq in 2003. All of this may have been bad for the public, but it was seen internally as a "win" for the president.[30]

As president-elect, Obama appeared to believe he could manage the press, at least to some extent. "It will be easier to replicate the leak-free environment of the campaign 'once we get into the building,' meaning the White House," the president noted. But he added: "This is Washington. . . . So I'm sure it will not be perfect."[31] Consequently, the Obama administration followed the Reagan and Bush playbook on managing the DC press through consistency and conformity across departments and issues. In the first six months of the administration, the White House easily achieved at least issue conformity, as the floundering economy was the primary story across media outlets. Staffers appearing on television or in the press practiced line-of-the-day consistency. The White House also reached out to outside-the-Beltway local and specialized press. In particular, the African American media received significantly more access than ever before; Obama gave his first interview as president-elect to *Ebony* magazine.[32]

However, the Obama White House was less successful in achieving universal adoption of its preferred "frame" of the economic issue: that the president was in charge, working hard; that it will be tough, but things will get better. Some of the conflict with this frame stemmed from the reality on the ground; no spin could alter the devastating economic numbers or the state of the Big Three automakers. The withdrawal of Tom Daschle as nominee for secretary of health and human services and Bill Richardson as secretary of commerce respectively, and the vacancies at the undersecretary levels in the Department of Treasury, also undermined the president's efforts to project confidence and competence. The president's high approval rating in the first six months, over 60 percent, served as a counterweight to these missteps. But that ballast fell away as his ratings dipped lower, dropping below 50 percent by August 2009.

The Obama administration's efforts to control the depiction of their work were affected not only by the dire economic circumstances in his first two years but also, as noted above, by rapid changes to the media environment. Ronald Reagan had the comparative luxury of a relatively narrow media sphere.[33] The Reagan communications staff dealt with the national press, local press, and specialty press. CNN was in its infancy, so ABC, NBC, and CBS ruled network news and the airwaves. By contrast, the Obama administration had to attempt to manage the incredible proliferation within those extant layers but also a wide-open electronic arena and blogosphere.[34] It also confronted a changed media style that included a vocal and often partisan punditry. With the number of voices in the old media environment multiplied, control, consistency, and conformity became elusive goals.

The Polling Apparatus.   A core component of the post-Watergate efforts to manage communication and thus lead the public rested on the development and institutionalization of the White House public opinion apparatus. Any successful public relations strategy rests on knowledge of the target audience and feedback from that audience. Following Madison Avenue's lead in selling products to America, White Houses since Nixon created a mechanism to sell the president and his policies effectively.[35]

The polling apparatus represents the heart of the permanent campaign because of its "presidency-centered" rather than "party-centered" approach to politics.[36] A presidency-centered approach requires a means to explain the "why" and the "how" of support for the president and his policies, without relying on the party as political shorthand or for support. Voters become linked to the person, not the party.

Previous presidents tried mightily to hide their attention to public opinion polling, fearing the appearance of "finger in the wind" followership.[37] President Obama, though, has been startlingly frank about his attention to public opinion, even if dismissive of it. In his public comments, President Obama comfortably references White House public opinion polling, though he does not bring it up often (it amounts to less than 1 percent of his rhetoric).[38] As he noted in February 2010, talking about health care reform,

> Now, I—you heard me at the State of the Union—I didn't take this on because it was good politics. I love how the pundits on these cable shows, they all announce, "Oh, boy, this was really tough politically for the President." Well, I've got my own pollsters; I know—[*laughter*]—I knew this was hard. I knew seven Presidents had failed. I knew seven Congresses hadn't gotten it done. You don't think I got warnings, "Don't try to take this on"? [*laughter*] I got those back in December of last year.[39]

Structurally, the Obama White House polling operation resembles the Obama campaign operation.[40] According to Ben Smith of *Politico*, President Obama's polling operation "combines elements of the Clinton and Bush models. He is polling more than Bush—a bit less than once a week."[41]

Likewise, the Obama White House appears to use the polling apparatus in the ways established by his predecessors.[42] Since 1969, the White House has used public opinion polls to track their electoral coalition as well as to craft speech language that resonates with the public.[43] Again, President Obama publicly highlighted aspects of the operation most presidents chose to hide. In a day-long meeting between Democrats and Republicans at the White House on health care reform, toward the end of that marathon process he told the assembled legislators that

> I hear from constituents in every one of your districts and every one of your States. And what's interesting is, actually, when you poll people about the individual elements in each of these bills, they're all for them. So you ask them, do you want to prohibit preexisting conditions? Yes, I'm for that. Do you want to make sure that everybody can get basic coverage that's affordable? Yes, I'm for that. Do you want to make sure that insurance companies can't take advantage of you and that you've got the ability, as Ron said, to fire an insurance company that's not doing a good job and hire one that is—but also, that you've got some basic consumer protections? Yes, we like that.[44]

Further, presidents have long known that terminology—"crafted talk"—matters. Just as the Reagan White House famously changed the name of their satellite weapons protection system from the Strategic Defense Initiative (SDI) to "Star Wars" after polling demonstrated vastly increased public support under the latter name,[45] the press reported evidence of similar behavior from the Obama administration. Smith wrote that

> Elements of Obama's approach bear the hallmarks of message testing, like the introduction of the words "recovery" and "reinvestment" to rebrand the "stimulus" package, and aides said the polling has focused almost entirely on selling policy, not on measuring the president's personal appeal. A source familiar with the data said a central insight of more recent polling had been that Americans see no distinction between the budget and the popular spending measures that preceded it, and that the key to selling the budget has been to portray it as part of the "recovery" measures.[46]

However, in language eerily similar to previous White House officials, former press secretary Robert Gibbs argued, "Not unlike news organizations, we poll public attitudes about where the economy is. . . . We're not polling to see what should be in an economic-recovery plan."[47]

Thus, on the surface, Obama's communications approach reflects the institutionalization of the need of the White House to communicate through the press to the public. Like its predecessors, the Obama White House established the means to disseminate information to national and local media through controlled accessibility. They also employed a means to manage the targeting and construction of messages. However, it is the combination of Obama's views about openness with the application of new technology that fundamentally changed the institutional capacity and capability of the White House to exercise public leadership.

New Media Approaches

On January 20, 2009, the George W. Bush White House home page disappeared, replaced by the Obama web page. The new site had the same address—http://www .whitehouse.gov—but it was significantly different. Borrowing from the campaign, the Obama White House website offered interested individuals multiple mechanisms to gather information and contact the administration, from email to RSS feeds. A regular feature entitled "White House Week" provided a carefully edited view of the week for web viewers. In addition, the White House continued Obama's campaign presence on YouTube, Facebook, MySpace, Flickr, LinkedIn, and iTunes. On iTunes, the White House offered podcasts and features with the appearances and speeches of the president, vice president, first lady, and second lady, as well as other notables, like Supreme Court Justice Elena Kagan as a nominee. They also included other little insider pieces—for instance, "All the President's Pens," where a staffer displays Obama's pens and the production made over signing a bill into law. These fluff pieces used to be the purview of the media for filler material. Now they provide another way to connect with a constituency.

On Facebook, the White House also has an array of appearances, but alongside the videos are participatory opportunities, as "friends" of the administration can comment on each offering, as well as offer a "thumbs up" or "thumbs down" response. On a given day in the fall of 2010, the video posts ranged from "What Wall Street Reform Means for You" to "Drumline in the White House" to "President Obama's Surprise Lunch Stop in Savannah." As the midterm elections approached, the White House used their Facebook "Wall" to link to the White House web page comment on the battle with John Boehner over tax cuts. The post received over 500 comments. The White House has over 152,000 friends on MySpace and more than 930,000 on Facebook. On LinkedIn, the professional networking site, the White House is connected to more than 72,000 members. The White House also joined the Twitter-verse. The White House has over 2,100,000 followers and has offered over 2,300 tweets about current political events.[48] Individual staffers, like Press Secretary Gibbs and his deputies, also created their own Twitter accounts and have followers of their own.

More than any of the other new media sites, YouTube represents the best opportunity for the White House to go filter-less and be its own conduit to citizens. Prior presidents were wholly dependent on networks and radio to air presidential speeches, and on newspapers to reprint the text of a speech. However, those efforts always came with a cost—external commentary. No message went unfiltered, in contrast to the campaign where candidates (provided they had the money to do so) could use advertising to avoid the media. On YouTube, the White House created a new "President Barack Obama" channel as a place to post video of his appearances. The administration made the traditional weekly radio address a video address posted each Saturday, and used their page to post video from ongoing events, for instance the Deepwater Horizon Oil Spill, and the administration's response to them. If individuals wanted to see what the White House and the president were doing on a daily basis, they could find out without waiting till 6:30pm EST, or even turning from their computer to their TV. Moreover, viewers could find videos of specific interest and watch them in their entirety without reporter voice-overs.

This is not a passive enterprise; interested viewers must seek out the White House offerings. But many have. Since January 20, 2009, when the Obama White House "joined" YouTube, there have been almost 6,500,000 views of its channel and over 45,000,000 individual videos watched. The channel also has over 133,000 regular subscribers, individuals who want a consistent stream of White House information.[49]

This expansive approach to information dissemination spread beyond the White House to the executive branch departments. During the campaign, Obama and top staff blogged regularly; the White House communications staff continues that practice. Of more interest and utility is the blogging by members of the executive branch. Almost all of the departments—even the Office of Management and Budget—have a relatively highly placed political appointee, often multiple individuals, blogging regularly. The Department of Health and Human Services offers blogs for each sector of the services they provide, including Medicare, Medicaid, HIV/AIDS Programs, and the Office of Disabilities. The departments vary in the depth and development of their open.gov efforts; however, there is a clear commitment to conversing with experts and ordinary citizens on specific topics. The State Department's blog (called the DipNote) baldly states the rationale for open.gov: "Blogs.state.gov offers the public an alternative source to mainstream media for U.S. foreign policy information. This blog offers the opportunity for participants to discuss important foreign policy issues with senior Department officials."[50] The blog does not receive as many daily comments or response posts as the White House Facebook page, but it receives enough to be the source of citizen questions for the State Department's online chat series, "Conversations with America," where "the State Department's senior leadership hold discussions live, online, with government officials and leaders of prominent non-governmental organizations."[51]

The connection between the public and the departments is clearer in departments that have direct effect on individuals via statutory or regulatory policy, such as Health and Human Services or Education. Those web pages have multiple blogs that receive a larger response rate, although still far behind a typical day on the White House Facebook page. These departments also present far more postings from individuals not employed in the department, like Peggy Bertrand, a physics teacher who was one of the winners of the Presidential Award for Excellence in Mathematics and Science Teaching. Ms. Bertrand posted about her move from private-sector industry to become a teacher.

Thus, the Obama White House, and the wider executive branch, made a commitment to new media, to interactivity, and to interconnectivity with the public. On the surface, these efforts appear to invite more dialogue, more participation, sending the message that the Obama administration is listening and that governing is a two-way street between citizens and leaders. There is, however, a difference between listening and hearing; is it not yet clear that the White House is responsive to the views of online participants. Ultimately, the White House public efforts are not just in service of connectivity; the effort is part of a larger program to equate government with competence and relevance.

The organizational adoption of new media into the White House mimics the creation of the White House polling operation. Starting with Nixon in 1968, candidates attributed their victory to their clever use of such technology, and brought the use of polls and their pollsters to the White House.[52] Similarly, President Obama staffed his White House with campaign staffers fully cognizant of the edge produced by the use of new media. However, the polling apparatus simply offered presidents a better way to do what they were already doing. A White House polling operation provided a scientifically rigorous means to make political decisions regarding timing, language, appeal, and even policy choices. The data provided the White House a more sophisticated means to understand their audience (as well as various congressional constituents), but the information did not fundamentally change the mode of communication. Polling made White House communications better, and made it possible to manipulate media or congressional frames. Nevertheless, the communications effort remained situated behind a media filter.

By contrast, the online presence of the Obama White House was meant to enable the president to truly evade the press corps. When prior administrations wanted to get outside the media filter, they merely meant avoiding the Washington press corps in favor of other types of press—as when President Bush appeared on the cover of *Runner's World*. President Obama's communications approach includes reaching other forms of traditional media, including the black press, women's magazines, and other specialty outlets. However, a concerted, daily presence on the Internet is wholly different and potentially rewrites the rules of engagement between the president, the press, and the public. The shift occurring within White House communications is not the desire to reach the masses without a filter; it is the capacity to do so.

Prior to the Obama administration, the White House did have a web presence; in fact, the Clinton White House created www.whitehouse.gov in 1994. However, the Clinton and subsequent Bush White House web pages contained less content than the Obama page and offered no links to social networking media. Of course much of that media did not exist during the Clinton administration; however, the Bush administration, after 2004, affirmatively decided not to connect. At a 2010 conference, David Almacy, the Bush White House's internet director from 2005 to 2007, discussed that decision at length. As he recounted, Facebook approached the White House soon after its launch, but the White House dismissed the infant site as a place for college students. Almacy argued that since the White House page received seven million views, at that time hosting a profile on a college-based site was perceived as less "impactful."[53] George W. Bush's first Facebook page (and Twitter account) did not appear until 2010 in commercial support of his memoir, *Decision Points*. Thus, in the Bush years, the technological limitations stemming from content management and archival document rules limited where the site *could* connect, but the mindset of the administration also limited where they *would* connect.

The Obama administration made a fundamentally different choice, driven in part by the impact of sites that have grown dramatically in just a few years. It is worth noting that the Obama web presence on the most highly trafficked websites means the president's message is not limited to arenas devoted simply to news. In addition, the social aspect of many of these sites allows for a virtual marketplace and exchange of ideas. On Facebook for example, users who post a comment on the White House wall can have that posting on their wall, thus sharing their own ideas, plus the Obama content, with their "friends" on the site.

To recap, then: presidential candidates learn on the campaign trail effective mechanisms that reach enough voters to win office. Innovations on the campaign trail in this arena invariably end up in the White House as part of efforts to increase capacity. Public opinion polling and those skilled in its use have become omnipresent in the White House and have been considered a pillar of campaigning to govern.[54] However, until the Obama administration, the presidency has been limited in its capacity to adopt the most powerful aspect of campaigning: setting the agenda, defining the issues by appealing directly to the voters via advertising. Via open.gov, social networking, and YouTube, President Obama increased the capacity of the White House to communicate directly with the people. Of greatest significance is the capacity for growth and the extension of the White House message or "brand." Prior to 2004 and the growth of social networking and the blogosphere, the mainstream press decided what presidential efforts were worth public attention; the media framed presidential efforts to explain the presidential policy agenda. The media also characterized the legitimacy of political battles (and participants' positions therein) by the focus and frame of news stories. This was possible because of the press's gatekeeping function. But the presidential presence on the web preempts the ability to control access to information. The media cannot critique, fact check, or comment on all the online areas where presidential outreach occurs—especially where that outreach is direct (via direct email), and/or targeted (to sympathetic audiences).

The Costs of the Obama Communications Strategy

Yet the outreach strategy proved to be rather less successful than this summary suggests.

For one thing, it was expensive. According to the organization Accuracy in Media, the Obama White House spent approximately $80,000 a week on old and new media, including public opinion polling and maintaining their website and its links.[55] For another, it was hard to measure its results. Communicating directly with the public during the campaign, and certainly at its endpoint, has a currency of sorts: candidates see the evidence of televised or online advertising in tracking polls, and most crucially at the ballot box. For President Obama, replacing candidate Obama, it was not clear that increased communicative capacity could be quantified as easily.

As figure 6.1 demonstrates, despite all the subscribers and "hits" noted above, and while spending more than $4 million a year, Obama's approval rating declined over twenty percentage points while Democrats took a "shellacking" in the 2010

FIGURE 6.1   President Obama's Approval Rating in the First Two Years

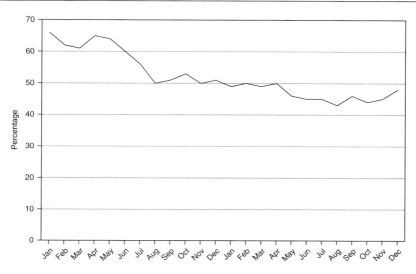

Source: Gallup Polling Center, www.gallup.com

midterm elections.[56] Seemingly all this effort should produce better poll numbers for the president, or at least better press coverage.[57] So what happened?

The presidency, to some extent, is all about leadership without tools—the enlargement of expectations without a comparative increase in organization or power. Increases in presidential capacity aim to produce increased opportunities, even absent new grants of power. The increased use of executive orders and signing statements, for instance, are components of a "unilateral" presidency precisely because of the increased power the tools provide at Congress's expense.[58]

But the presidents' various Washington partners have resources of their own.[59] White House efforts to go around, over, and above the press angered the press corps. That is nothing new; all modern presidents complain about their treatment by the press while the press corps whines about access and manipulation.[60] However, in the short term, the costs resulting from the choices made by the president to continue his direct public leadership approach appear to outweigh the benefits.

Media Coverage of the Obama Presidency

President Obama entered office with a 67 percent approval rating, according to Gallup.[61] He also entered office known for the skillful use of rhetoric and the skillful employment of new media. Thus, the campaign raised the bar considerably higher than for most incoming presidents. This did not take into account the fact that the new president would inherit two wars and the Great Recession; it was inevitable that Obama's honeymoon with the press would end. Nevertheless, the press reaction to the presidential communication effort to bypass the press seemingly exacerbated the traditional downturn toward negative coverage of the president.

The *New York Times* provides a fascinating elucidation of the shift in press coverage over the president's first two years. Depending on who is asked, the *Times* stands either as the nation's newspaper of record or as a bastion of the liberal press. As the paper of record, the newspaper is neutral in ideology, albeit subject to the shifting mores of the press, which currently include a preference for providing subjective, game-oriented, softer news, rather than objective information.[62] As a bastion of liberalism, the newspaper would be more favorable to the president and his policies, meaning it would be slower to criticize the administration.[63] In either case, a shift in tone from this newspaper would serve as a useful lens for examining the evolution of press coverage within the mainstream press as a whole.

The *Times*'s coverage of President Obama on the surface appears to track with his approval rating. The press and presidential approval ratings are inexorably intertwined with events as they unfold in a classic chicken-and-egg scenario: the numbers fall and press coverage worsens, while at the same time press coverage worsens and the approval rating dips. Bad news leads to bad ratings, and vice versa.

A Republican strategist quoted early in Obama's term predicted the pattern: "I think Obama can count on a very long honeymoon. . . . I think he's got about six months, which is about five and a half months longer than usual."[64] Indeed, Obama received favorable to neutral coverage based on favorable to neutral language in the first six months of his administration. As figure 6.1 demonstrates, President Obama's rating dipped under 60 percent for the first time in June 2009 and dipped under 50 percent at the end of August 2009. The ten-point drop, which articulates a switch from majority support to partisan division, corresponds to the language employed by the *Times* during this period. Moreover, the subsequent language employed in the coverage between September 2009 and September 2010 was dramatically different.

From the beginning, the *Times* took note of efforts to circumvent press interpretation of the president's message. Three days after the inauguration, they marked the first time the White House provided a photo of an event (the redo of the president's oath of office, muffed by Chief Justice John Roberts) rather than to allow media photographers to cover it. On January 26, the *Times* noted that Obama's "YouTube presidency" allowed for bypassing the mainstream news media.[65] Yet no overt disapproval or condemnation of these White House practices appeared. In the first six months, the *Times* was more inclined to blame the other members of the media for the administration's choices. When the paper observed Obama's preference for sticking to a script and using a teleprompter, the article speculated it was an effort to avoid becoming the subject of endless media commentary over a verbal gaffe.[66] The newspaper chronicled the feverish partisan pitch of commentary on the cable channels, likening the coverage to campaign coverage without a campaign.[67] And the *Times* approvingly noted the boon for the African American press corps, as its reporters received new entrée into the world previously occupied only by Washington media insiders (like the *Times* itself). Thus, in the first six months the *Times* consciously or unconsciously supported the president's view: that the twenty-four-hour news cycle is a problem requiring management strategies.

Moreover, during that time period, the *Times* presented the president's initial accessibility as an asset, a refreshing break from the detachment of the Bush administration. As the summer of 2009 devolved into contentious town halls over health care and the financial bailout program, though, the paper's presentation of the president's effectiveness became more ambivalent. During June and July, its focus was on his overexposure. In a four-day span in July, the president "gave 'exclusive' interviews to Jim Lehrer of PBS, Katie Couric of CBS and Meredith Vieira of NBC. He gave two interviews to *The Washington Post* on one day, one to the editorial page editor and one to news reporters. He held a conference call with bloggers. His hour-long session in the East Room on Wednesday night was his second news conference of the day. And on Thursday, he invited Terry Moran of ABC to spend the day with him for a 'Nightline' special."[68] The *Times* referred to the president's accessibility as an "all-the-time carpet bombing of the news media." By September, another *Times* headline read "Obama the Omnipresent" and asked the question, "How much Obama is too much Obama?" Recall that just months earlier, the complaint had been instead the unwillingness of the media to let go of the campaign saturation approach.[69]

The real problem, media outlets began to suggest, was not communication strategy—where to speak, or how often to speak—but the president's very skill as a communicator. The president's rhetorical talents were no longer news; instead, his inability to achieve results despite possession of such a stellar skill set became news. By the end of Obama's first year, the *Times*'s news stories combined oversaturation, the president's dipping approval numbers, and the public confusion over the scope and content of the health care bill, in announcing the disappearance of Obama's "oratorical touch." The *Times* claimed that "pushing polices requires more explanation than inspiration."[70] This view reflected Senator McCain's campaign charge that Obama represented the triumph of celebrity over substance—a charge the press and the public rejected during the campaign, in the wake of the Lehman Brothers collapse (and McCain's own poor reaction).[71]

The nadir of the coverage of the president's communications, perhaps, came in the aftermath of the loss of Ted Kennedy's Democratic senate seat in Massachusetts to Republican Scott Brown after Kennedy's death. The headlines and the language again shifted tone to stress Obama's need to rebound and rebuild: "Obama Trying to Turn Around His Presidency," "White House Eager to Project Image of Competence," "The Muddled Selling of the President," read a sampling.[72]

Accompanying these stories of the president's failures were the failures of his staff, notably the impolitic, if accurate, "Sixteen Words of Infamy" spoken by Press Secretary Gibbs regarding the Democrats' chances in the midterm elections.[73] Another example of what the *Times* called "media catnip" during the summer of 2010 was the firing of Department of Agriculture staffer Shirley Sherrod in a rushed reaction to an erroneous charge of racism. The *Times* presented the cases as failures of administration exacerbated by failures of communication, and by media ferocity.

Thus, the *Times* continued the tangential story regarding the changing state of the media and its effect on the presidency through 2010, and used that lens to structure its coverage of the president. In contrast, the White House implicitly rejected the media lens, as they resisted abandoning their view, which originated with the campaign. As Dan Pfeiffer, the White House communications director, noted, "Elite opinion still matters. . . . [but] on any given day, a blogger, a local reporter or someone on Facebook or Twitter can be as influential."[74] Pfeiffer may have been right about the trees while wrong about the forest. Between summer 2009 and fall 2010, the White House lost control of the narrative. But perhaps more significantly, they had done so despite real efforts to invest in their belief in the increased democratization of the political sphere.

Yet in politics, it is sometimes better to have low expectations. President Obama's press coverage improved significantly in the wake of a significant political setback: the loss of the Democratic majority in the House of Representatives in the 2010 midterm election. After the elections, which were cast as a repudiation of the president's agenda, Obama successfully negotiated and signed a new tax relief law, the repeal of the "Don't Ask, Don't Tell" ban on gays serving in the military, and a new food safety law, while achieving the ratification of the Strategic Arms Reduction (START) treaty. The news coverage of Obama's performance in the lame-duck congressional session trumpeted his skill in responding to a tough political situation, particularly with his own party.

The positive press coverage was buoyed in early 2011 by a "rally-round-the-flag" moment. On January 8, a gunman shot Tucson Congresswoman Gabrielle Giffords, critically wounding her. Fourteen others were wounded, and six were killed.

The shooting brought renewed attention to the vitriolic political environment that often referenced violent war and gun rhetoric. President Obama's speech at the memorial, which was televised live, might have reset the president's relationship with the public and the press. Almost thirty-one million watched the president speak, and most—press, partisans, and pundits alike—widely praised his performance. Obama received high marks for his handling of the shooting, and his job approval rating surged after his speech. By mid-January, 54 percent of Americans approved Obama's job performance, the highest since April 2010; 78 percent approved of his handling of the shooting, including 71 percent of Republicans.[75] The news coverage invoked a return to vintage Obama; as Helene Cooper and Jeff Zeleny wrote, "It was one of the more powerful addresses that Mr. Obama has delivered as president, harnessing the emotion generated by the shock and loss from Saturday's shootings."[76]

Conclusions

Presidential communications serve democratic purposes and political ends. Representation and accountability require an exchange of information. Reelection requires a retrospective view of performance. From the president's perspective, controlling the flow of information, the tone of information, and the access to information is the most effective way to attempt to control the reaction to presidential activity. As a result, the White House communications structure is a key component of presidential leadership.

The media environment faced by President Obama presented an inherent challenge to traditional approaches to public leadership, challenges which his predecessors (with the partial exception of George W. Bush) did not face. With a cacophonous coupling of old and new media, President Obama faced an exponential increase in the number of voices in the political system. A president can naturally cut through the clamor by virtue of his stature in the political system—the "bully pulpit" still stands—but it has become much more difficult to control the background noise.

To use an online term, President Obama's communications strategy reflects acceptance of the "cloud" of information and ideas, rather than a hierarchical exchange of ideas between elites and the mass public. The White House took advantage of the democratization of ideas and access promoted by the Internet, and planted the president within the cloud. The White House continues to participate in the traditional media–president battle to frame and prime the agenda and subsequent policymaking, but appears to relish opportunities to avoid what once was a powerful gatekeeper. Indeed, the first peek at his 2011 State of the Union address was leaked not to reporters but by a video link e-mailed to his campaign list, once again "prioritizing his outside-the-Beltway backers over the capital's political class."[77]

As with Obama's policymaking efforts, though, such fundamental change has come with heavy short-term costs. The president's communication strategy increased the capacity to reach the public without the filter of media coverage; but it did nothing to eliminate the cacophony of competing voices. It is unclear whether this outreach positively influenced presidential approval, or indeed whether it reinvented direct communications (rather than just moving it to a different platform). And in fact, it could be argued that the effort to go directly to the people dilutes the power of the presidential pulpit. It remains to be seen whether the criticism accurately reflects some newfound inability to lead or sell, or is simply a repudiation of the new pathway to public leadership.

While the new critiques of the Obama's communications skills surely relate in part to the policy choices made in response to an almost catastrophic economic situation, the intensity of the criticism undoubtedly reflects a view that he should have done more, and better, in explanation and education of the public. "We have not done a good job of saying what our message is, a simple message of what we stand for or what we're trying to do," one senior aide said. Obama seemed to accept this himself, noting after the 2010 midterms, "A couple of great communicators, Ronald Reagan and Bill Clinton, were standing at this podium two years into their presidency getting very similar questions because the economy wasn't working the way it needed to be and there were a whole range of factors that made people concerned that maybe the party in power wasn't listening to them."[78] Both Reagan and Clinton, of course, won reelection. It will remain for the 2012 campaign to determine how significant the direct public outreach efforts were in shaping actual—rather than virtual—support.

Notes

1. Samuel Kernell, *Going Public: New Strategies of Presidential Leadership*, 4th ed. (Washington, DC: CQ Press, 2007).

2. Sydney Blumenthal, *The Permanent Campaign: Inside the World of Elite Political Operatives* (New York: Beacon Press, 1980).

3. Hugh Heclo, "Campaigning and Governing: A Conspectus," in *The Permanent Campaign and Its Future*, ed. Norman Ornstein and Thomas Mann (Washington, DC: Brookings, 2000), 12.

4. Exchange with Reporters aboard Air Force One, November 14, 2010, John Woolley and Gerhardt Peters, eds., *The American Presidency Project*, http://www.presidency.ucsb.edu/ws/index.php?pid=88733&st=&st1=.

5. Quoted in Richard Wolffe, *Revival: The Struggle for Survival inside the Obama White House* (New York: Crown Books, 2010), 274.

6. Richard Rubin, *Press, Party, and Presidency* (New York: W.W. Norton, 1981).

7. Kate Kenski, Bruce Hardy, and Kathleen Hall Jamieson, *The Obama Victory: How Media, Money, and Message Shaped the 2008 Election* (New York: Oxford University Press, 2010).

8. Kenski et al., *The Obama Victory*; William Crotty, ed., *Winning the Presidency 2008* (Boulder, CO: Paradigm, 2009).

9. Diane Heith, "The Virtual Party Campaign: Connecting with Constituents in a Multimedia Age," in *From Votes to Victory: Winning and Governing the White House in the Twenty-First Century*, ed. Meena Bose (College Station: Texas A&M University Press, 2011).

10. Heith, "Virtual Party Campaign."

11. Diana Owen, "The Campaign and the Media," in *The American Elections of 2008*, ed. Janet Box-Steffensmeier and Stephen Schier (Lanham, MD: Rowman & Littlefield, 2009).

12. Robert Barnett e-mail to Clinton and senior staff, March 6, 2008, posted on the *Atlantic Monthly* website. Available at http://www.theatlantic.com/politics/archive/2008/11/robert-barnett-email-to-clinton-and-senior-staff-march-6-2008/37967 (accessed March 25, 2011).

13. Richard E. Neustadt, *Presidential Power and the Modern Presidents: The Politics of Leadership from Roosevelt to Reagan*, rev. ed. (New York: Free Press, 1990), p. 8.

14. Jeffrey E. Cohen, *The Presidency in the Era of 24-Hour News* (Princeton, NJ: Princeton University Press, 2008).

15. Ted Koppel, "Olbermann, O'Reilly and the Death of Real News," *Washington Post*, November 11, 2010.

16. Lori Cox Han, *Governing from Center Stage: White House Communication Strategies during the Television Age of Politics* (Cresskill, NJ: Hampton Press, 2001); Martha Kumar, *Managing the President's Message: The White House Communications Operation* (Baltimore: Johns Hopkins University Press, 2007); Doris Graber, *Mass Media and American Politics*, 8th ed. (Washington, DC: CQ Press, 2010).

17. Karen Hult and Charles Walcott, *Empowering the White House: Governance under Nixon, Ford, and Carter* (Lawrence: University Press of Kansas, 2004).

18. Mark Leibovic, "Between Obama and the Press," *New York Times*, December 17, 2008. Available at http://www.nytimes.com/2008/12/21/magazine/21Gibbs-t.html?_r=1&ref=robert_gibbs.

19. President Obama, January 21, 2009, http://www.whitehouse.gov/administration/eop/ope.

20. Jacob Weisberg, "Beyond Spin: The Propaganda Presidency of George W. Bush," December 7, 2005, available at http://www.slate.com/id/2131768/.

21. Kumar, *Managing the President's Message*.

22. Cohen, *Presidency in the Era of 24-Hour News*; Jeffrey E. Cohen, *Going Local: Presidential Leadership in the Post-Broadcast Age* (New York: Cambridge University Press, 2010).

23. Martin Wattenberg, "The Presidential Media Environment in the Age of Obama," in *Obama: Year One*, ed. Thomas R. Dye et al. (New York: Longman, 2009).

24. He also spoke with the international press corps. See the American Presidency Project, John Woolley and Gerhard Peters, http://www.presidency.ucsb.edu/ws/.

25. Leibovic, "Between Obama and the Press."

26. Ibid.

27. Han, *Governing from Center Stage*, 181.

28. Ibid.

29. Ibid., 182-183.

30. W. Lance Bennett, Regina Lawrence, and Steven Livingston, *When the Press Fails: Political Power and the News Media from Iraq to Katrina* (Chicago: University of Chicago Press, 2007).

31. Leibovic, "Between Obama and the Press."

32. Rachel Swarns, "With Obama in White House, Flush Times for the Nation's Black New Media," *New York Times*, March 28, 2009; and see http://www.ebonyjet.com/Templates/DetailsView.aspx?id=10738.

33. Cohen, *Presidency in the Era of 24-Hour News*.

34. Cohen, *Going Local*.

35. Lawrence Jacobs and Robert Shapiro, "The Rise of Presidential Polling: The Nixon White House in Historical Perspective," *Public Opinion Quarterly* 59 (Summer 1995): 163-195; Jacobs and Shapiro, *Politicians Don't Pander: Political Manipulation and the Loss of Democratic Responsiveness* (Chicago: University of Chicago Press, 2000); Robert Eisinger, *The Evolution of Presidential Polling* (New York: Cambridge University, 2003); Diane Heith, *Polling to Govern: Public Opinion and Presidential Leadership* (Stanford: Stanford University Press, 2004); Kathryn Dunn Tenpas, *Presidents as Candidates: Inside the White House for the Presidential Campaign* (New York: Garland, 1997).

36. Heith, *Polling to Govern*; and see Sidney Milkis, "The President and the Parties," in Michael Nelson, ed., *The Presidency and the Political System*, 9th ed. (Washington, DC: CQ Press, 2009).

37. Eisinger, *Evolution of Presidential Polling*; Heith, *Polling to Govern*.

38. The American Presidency Project, John Woolley and Gerhard Peters, eds., http://www.presidency.ucsb.edu/ws/index.php.

39. Remarks at a Democratic National Committee Fundraiser and a Question-and-Answer Session, February 4, 2010, The American Presidency Project, John Woolley and Gerhard Peters, eds., http://www.presidency.ucsb.edu/ws/index.php.

40. The Obama design is typical of his predecessors' efforts. Since the institutionalization of the White House polling operation in the 1960s, most administrations mimicked their campaign operations in design and usage of polls. The George H. Bush White House is an exception, as it actually distanced itself from campaigning; it spent less money and employed fewer consultants and staffers than other administrations (see Heith, *Polling to Govern*).

41. Ben Smith, "Meet Obama's Pollsters," April 3, 2009, http://www.politico.com/news/stories/0409/20852.html.

42. See Heith, *Polling to Govern.*

43. Heith, *Polling to Govern*; Jacobs and Shapiro, *Politicians Don't Pander.*

44. Remarks in a Discussion on Insurance Coverage at a Bipartisan Meeting on Health Care Reform, February 25, 2010, The American Presidency Project, John Woolley and Gerhard Peters, eds., http://www.presidency.ucsb.edu/ws/index.php.

45. Heith, *Polling to Govern*, 54.

46. Smith, "Meet Obama's Pollsters."

47. Mark Blumenthal, "News Flash: Obama Using Polling Data," January 9, 2009, available at http://www.pollster.com/blogs/news_flash_obama_using_polling.php; for a broader view of this topic, see Jacobs and Shapiro, *Politicians Don't Pander.*

48. All figures are as of March 25, 2011.

49. As of March 25, 2011.

50. http://blogs.state.gov/index.php/site/about.

51. http://blogs.state.gov/index.php/site/entry/qddr_discussion_cwa.

52. Heith, *Polling to Govern.*

53. http://thenextweb.com/us/2010/04/20/political-start-slow-whitehousegov/.

54. Tenpas, *Presidents as Candidates*; Heith, *Polling to Govern.*

55. K. Daniel Glover, "The Cost of Controlling the Press," Accuracy in Media, July 7, 2009, available at http://www.aim.org/aim-column/the-cost-of-controlling-the-press/. It is important to note that this spending is in line with previous administrations' efforts on communication and public opinion polling.

56. Heith, *Polling to Govern*; Eisinger, *Evolution of Presidential Polling*; Tenpas, *Presidents as Candidates.*

57. Shoon Murray and Peter Howard, "Variations in White House Polling Operations: Carter to Clinton," *Public Opinion Quarterly* 66 (2002): 527-558; Kathryn Dunn Tenpas and James A. McCann, "Testing the Permanence of the Permanent Campaign: An Analysis of Presidential Polling Expenditures, 1977–2002," *Public Opinion Quarterly* 71, 3 (2007): 349-366.

58. Andrew Rudalevige, "The Presidency and Unilateral Power," in Michael Nelson, ed., *The Presidency and the Political System*, 9th ed. (Washington, DC: CQ Press, 2009); David Lewis and Terry Moe, "The Presidency and the Bureaucracy," ibid.

59. This of course is a key tenet of Neustadt's 1990 classic *Presidential Power.*

60. Thomas Patterson, *Out of Order* (New York: Knopf, 1994).

61. Gallup's Presidential Job Approval Center, available at http://www.gallup.com/poll/124922/Presidential-Job-Approval-Center.aspx.

62. Thomas Patterson, "Doing Well and Doing Good: How Soft News and Critical Journalism are Shrinking the News Audience and Weakening Democracy," *Political Communication*, 2000; Matthew Baum, "Sex, Lies and War: How Soft News Brings Foreign Policy to the Inattentive Public," *Political Communication*, 2002.

63. Although all presidents argue they receive critical coverage from the press.

64. Adam Nagourney, "Obama Embarks on His Honeymoon. The Question: How Long Will It Last?," *New York Times*, January 21, 2009.

65. Jim Rutenberg and Adam Nagourney, "Melding Obama's Web to a YouTube Presidency," *New York Times,* January 26, 2009.

66. Peter Baker, "President Sticks to the Script, With a Little Help," *New York Times,* March 6, 2009.

67. David Carr, "Cable News Stokes Political Fever," *New York Times,* March 30, 2009.

68. Peter Baker, "White House Memo: Obama Complains about the News Cycle but Dominates It, Worrying Some," *New York Times,* July 24, 2009.

69. Mark Leibovich, "Obama the Omnipresent," *New York Times,* September 18, 2009; Baker, "President Sticks to the Script."

70. Peter Baker, "The Words That Once Soared," *New York Times,* November 8, 2009.

71. James Campbell, "The Exceptional Election of 2008: Performance, Values, and Crisis," *Presidential Studies Quarterly* 40 (June 2010): 225-246.

72. Peter Baker, "Obama Trying to Turn Around His Presidency," January 20, 2010; Mark Landler and Helene Cooper, "White House Eager to Project Image of Competence," January 21, 2010; Richard Stevenson, "The Muddled Selling of the President," January 30, 2010 (all from the *New York Times*).

73. On NBC's *Meet the Press*, Gibbs was asked if Democrats could lose the House in the fall midterm elections. "There's no doubt there are enough seats in play that could cause Republicans to gain control," Gibbs answered. See Peter Baker, "Sixteen Words of Infamy," *New York Times,* July 18, 2010.

74. Adam Nagourney, "Does It Matter If Obama Loses the Pundits?" *New York Times,* June 19, 2010.

75. http://www.nydailynews.com/news/politics/2011/01/18/2011-01-18_president_obamas_approval_rating_surges_in_polls_following_tucson_arizona_shooti.html?r=news.

76. Helene Cooper and Jeff Zeleny, "Obama Calls for a New Era of Civility in U.S. Politics," *New York Times,* January 12, 2011.

77. See Glen Thrush, "Obama Previews SOTU Job Pitch," *Politico*, January 22, 2011, available at http://dyn.politico.com/printstory.cfm?uuid=4A3A14C3-928E-496F-AFB0-E2F442374D36.

78. Aide quoted in Wolffe, *Revival*, 115; Obama from presidential news conference of November 3, 2010, John Woolley and Gerhardt Peters editors, The American Presidency Project, http://www.presidency.ucsb.edu/ws/index.php?pid=88668. And see similar critiques quoted in Peter Baker, "What Does He Do Now?," *New York Times Magazine,* October 17, 2010, 44-45.

CHAPTER 7

The Privileges of Access:
Interest Groups and the White House

Lawrence R. Jacobs

AS THE EXECUTIVE BRANCH and office of the presidency swelled and exercised more power, pressure groups formed or expanded to sway administration policy—to better serve their ends or to blunt initiatives that threatened their interests. Alert to constraints and opportunities in their environment, presidents came to recognize interest groups as organizations with the potential to rally support of valued constituencies and to serve as a kind of political infantry to press home their agenda in a recalcitrant congress.

Changing political needs prompted successive presidents to reorganize their institution to serve their interest to track the views of organized associations and to rally them in support of administration initiatives. How presidents manage their relations with organized groups is a source of ongoing study. Research on presidents has devoted particular attention to the expansion of White House staff responsibility from serving as "interest group liaisons" that connect with influential Washington stakeholders to performing "public liaison" functions that target politically important constituents in the general electorate or within the political parties, even if they lack significant organizational might or pull in the White House.[1]

Less attention has been devoted, though, to the influence of interest groups on the White House, and how these dynamics interact with organizational changes, including the emergence of the public liaison. The capacity for presidential policy initiative has been blunted by the over-time "thickening" of pressure groups in Washington and by their "individualization"—that is, their proliferation in number and diversity.[2] When presidents seek to change government operations and established policy, they often run into a phalanx of organized groups that are sophisticated in seeking to undermine their proposals in Congress, the courts, and public opinion. If administration policies do survive the stakeholder onslaught, these groups turn adeptly to utilize the process of implementation and its additional opportunities for delay and obstruction. Strategic and well-organized groups have a well-stocked arsenal to tame White House aspirations that threaten them: they are skilled at reframing what presidents present as "leadership" as "costs" that hurt stakeholder groups and constituencies (including those that the administration counts as its supporters), and may activate counter-mobilization through legislative lobbying, well-honed advertising campaigns, and contributions to political opponents in the next election. One study of Ronald Reagan's bold efforts to scale back or terminate government programs in the early 1980s found a decidedly uneven result after interest groups rallied to use Congress and later the courts to counteract many of the president's initiatives.[3] This pattern might be described as the "interest group presidency."

There is, though, a puzzle. How are the inside-Washington dynamics of elite jostling reconciled with the increasingly public face that modern presidents have presented over the past half century? Even as presidents have continued to engage in deal-making behind closed doors, they have also increasingly relied on appealing over the heads of legislators and others in Washington to build public support for themselves and their policies.

This "public presidency" has been interpreted as introducing a plebiscitary form of government that relies on the support of the mass public and the president's supplication to the majority, reversing the efforts of the Constitution's framers to replace populist demagoguery with "republican" governance, anchored in elite deliberation and balanced institutional participation.[4] The responsiveness of presidents to the public would appear to be facilitated by the White House's expanding outreach to diverse interests and groups and, specifically, by its establishment of the Office of Public Liaison (OPL), which started in fragmented forms under Richard Nixon and grew under successive administrations into Obama's Office of Public Engagement (OPE).[5] These expansions in the president's openness to organized interests seem to confirm Arthur Bentley's prescient (1908) optimism that multiple avenues of institutional access foster government responsiveness—"If interest groups . . . are checked in their course through Congress, they will find their way through the presidency."[6] The visible additions of the OPL and then OPE would seem to open up another access point to the president.

While the public presidency and the increasingly visible public liaison operations created the appearance of popular control, actual White House decision making is characterized by the tiered access and influence of interest groups. Presidents do reach out—at times in quite visible ways—to a broad array of groups. Still, not all interests are represented, and presidents do not treat equally those that are. The result is a tiering of access and influence: The White House's visible public liaison operations intentionally communicate openness and a commitment to listening to valued electoral constituencies without conceding critical policy issues; meanwhile, private and largely invisible high-level meetings focus on accommodating narrowly based, particularistic, and resource-laden lobbies that are decisive for passing legislation. A differentiated pattern results: access to the White House varies, from highly public events for broad swaths of voters, who reap few policy concessions, to private deals or accommodations for narrowly based special interests or their institutional supporters (in Congress, the administration, or other authoritative governmental bodies), who trade their support or quiescence in legislative battles in exchange for favorable presidential proposals. As Bentley observed with regard to agricultural politics, "The president was the legislative organ, through which *the great group interest* functioned."[7] What Bentley did not witness was the presidency's development of an institutional showcase of its outreach to the public—one that concealed private access where possible, or legitimized it when it became public (by making it possible to point to efforts to listen to a broad array of voices.)

In short, the form of the interest group presidency has diversified to include a highly public façade, but the effect remains biased to favor the organized and better established. The broadening scope of government and the penetration of well-organized interest groups into the executive branch has, paradoxically, ceded back to private interests' control over those new government resources and authorities. The consequence is semiautonomous and largely unaccountable power by alliances of lobbyists with their supporters in the White House and in Congress.[8] From afar, it is not hard to be confused by the seemingly contradictory developmental patterns of the public presidency (including its visible outreach to organized groups) and the interest group presidency. The appearance of openness and responsiveness exists alongside the privileged access and influence of interest groups, not as an accident but as a front, intended to sustain the myth of the public presidency as the dependable reservoir of democratic responsiveness.

The first two years of the presidency of Barack Obama presented a striking pattern of interest group penetration behind the façade of public engagement. A historic surge of government activity followed the sharp economic downturn that swept Obama and super-sized Democratic congressional majorities into positions of power and created a palpable mandate for change that staggered established interests. The Democratic advantage in unified party control of the lawmaking branches stemmed from the size of their congressional majorities (enough to overcome the Senate filibuster after Al Franken was seated in July 2009) as well as those majorities' broad ideological compatibility. Although liberals fumed when moderate and conservative members of Congress compromised bolder reform of health care and finance, the partisan and ideological convergence was extensive and made possible the most sweeping economic and social welfare legislation in more than a generation.

But far from representing the demise of the interest group presidency, the initial Obama presidency confirms its resilience—even in a period of extensive and landmark legislation that rivals the New Deal and Great Society. Indeed, established interests exercised persistent, wide-ranging, and quite effective influence in securing compromises and suffocating the most threatening proposals, preventing them from making it into law or even from getting a sustained hearing in Congress or the country.

The persistence of interest group influence even in a period of landmark reform stems from several factors. One was the decision of Obama and his Democratic allies to seek historic landmark changes to established policy areas that were densely populated with interest groups, many of which were organized not only in Washington but in states and some cities as well, mirroring America's federal system. Those groups were well equipped to generate public unease about disruptions, to mobilize organizational allies in order to maintain existing authority and benefits, and to avoid new costs. By comparison, many of Franklin Roosevelt's social welfare and economic initiatives charted new policy terrain that lacked the thickly layered and often federated pressure groups and voting constituencies that confronted Obama. The organized vigilance and resistance to Obama's reforms took a number of potent forms—fanning public unease, intense lobbying of legislators and administration officials, and the use of real and threatened campaign contributions to Republicans, in order to intimidate and unseat Democrats in November 2010. The Obama White House and congressional Democratic leaders engaged in sustained negotiations with interest groups or reached accommodations to quell concerns within congressional Democratic ranks, the administration, and authoritative government institutions like the Federal Reserve. These insider deals impacted the administration's initial proposals, as well as its later compromises. In addition to agreeing to a host of concessions, Democratic leaders rejected the most threatening reforms of health care and finance—elimination of private health insurance in favor of a national public option and the nationalization or liquidation of banks—even though party activists supported the proposals. These "pre-decision" allowances resulted from active lobbying and from the tendency of certain key administration officials to share the same mindsets as the targeted stakeholders—in part, perhaps, because they were their past and likely future employers.

The nature and extent of pressure group influence on Obama's policy did vary in part with the nature of interest organization and unity. Where interest groups were intensely opposed to reform and acted as a bloc or close to it, Democrats made extensive concessions: on finance reform, regulations and new watchdog agencies were watered down. But when interest groups splintered—as when medical providers and suppliers supported reform while the insurance industry opposed it—reforms were more extensive and far reaching in recasting the health care financing and delivery.

The Obama administration's approach to interest groups rests on a striking contradiction: it engaged in extensive bargaining and accommodations with interest groups while it publicly promoted its commitment to broad public engagement and to departing from the storied Washington practice of deal-making. The White House's "public liaison" office did reach out to large numbers of groups and individuals, but there is little or no evidence that this significantly influenced policy. Indeed, it appears to have been an elaborately drawn façade designed to shield insider trading of the political sort. While the form of White House organization changed under Obama, the interest group presidency continued to function and indeed accelerated to facilitate legislative breakthroughs.

The remainder of this chapter traces the Obama presidency's interest group strategy of melding public engagement with privatized negotiations and accommodations with well-organized stakeholders who possessed the potential to block or delay administration priorities. It begins by tracing the historic development of the White House's public performance of reaching out to Americans up through the changes made by the Obama White House (including its use of the Internet—what we might call the "webinizing" of White House communications and relations). The White House's public liaison function was visibly advertised but was not generally a major influence on the formulation of the president's policy. The second section uses Obama's major reforms of health care and finance to explore low-visibility White House negotiations and accommodation with interest groups. The visibility and impact of White House interactions with interest groups varied based on their influence in Congress and effectiveness in blocking the president's agenda: influential groups enjoyed low salience attention from the White House while others received visible attention but no sustained role in policymaking.

Liaisoning in Public

The president must work with others. There are few—if any—activities of substance on which the president can act completely alone. Passing new laws requires support in Congress and the backing of the interests and individuals that legislators listen to. Even national security actions require not only the military but also a host of supporting actors—from members of Congress who acquiesce and provide funding, to businesses that equip the military and are relied on in other ways.

At one point, the president could rely on a hyper-social and connected aide to keep in touch with key players in Washington and around the country. Even as the White House grew and the responsibility for connecting with organized groups was shared among staff, it was not routinized up through the presidency of Lyndon Johnson—requests for meetings and information were handled on an ad hoc basis or individual staff members became lead contacts with certain key groups.

Those days are long gone. The president's need to work with others has fueled a thoroughgoing reorganization of the White House to create offices and staff positions that cast a veritable spider web over Washington and key partners around the country, connecting the president to a wide array of institutions, organizations, and individuals.

Much of the White House's outreach is out of public view. The president has a stable of staffers who meticulously track the views of individual members of Congress toward specific bills—especially those that the president has proposed and supports. The reports from the congressional liaison office are privately held by the White House.

The White House's institutionalized relations with diffuse groups and the broader public are different—they are highly public. Indeed, their mission is to advertise the White House's accessibility for the strategic purpose of reassuring groups and key political constituencies that their views are being heard and seeking to rally them to support the president's agenda.[9]

Visibility is the first of two features of public liaison; the second is its connection to policy formulation. This is perhaps the most important of the two, given that the White House's public liaison operation reaches out to organized groups and key constituents to solicit their views with the ostensible purpose of incorporating the feedback into making policy. As we will see, this feedback effect is generally quite weak.

Taking the White House Public

Beginning in earnest with Richard Nixon, the White House devoted a set of staff with the explicit responsibility of reaching out to organized groups and key constituents, and created routinized mechanisms for sustaining these connections and linking them to the president's policy priorities and political needs. Until the Obama administration, this new component of the White House was named the Office of Public Liaison (OPL).

Over time, the White House organized itself to appoint staffers who were recognized as the "inside" contact for key interests and voting blocs, creating two-way communications. On the one hand, external groups had an "in" with the White House, which would solicit and track their views and signal their status as politically important. One staffer reported that "we never turned anybody down when they requested a meeting," and OPL privately shared with key group representatives relevant new policies before they became public, to build good will— "you get a lot of help from people by recognizing what their own system rewards [so they are] the first to know . . . [and] can call [their boss] . . . before he hears it on the news."[10] In addition to creating a point of mutually beneficial access for organized interests, the OPL also cultivated relations with major demographic groups (women, blacks, Hispanics, and others) and key parts of the president's electoral support. "The strategies we developed," one OPL staffer explained, were "based on trying to keep the [voting] coalition together."[11] This helped not only with election battles but also with disseminating the administration's talking points and with trying to mobilize support for key initiatives. Both Carter and Reagan used OPL to build support for their budgets prior to their State of the Union Addresses; George W. Bush relied on it to build coalitions to support his legislation to reduce taxes.

On the other hand, OPL was also a transmission line into the White House to collect information on the agendas and concerns of organized groups and key constituents and to serve as an early warning system of potential problems. When groups representing gays and lesbians prepared to denounce Clinton after his retreat on their status in the military, OPL's contacts with these groups gave the White House an early warning and allowed the president's staff to head off a public battle.

The result was a highly articulated organization that publicly courted organized groups and constituents as well as invited communications from them. Its reach was wide and consistent. Business and organized labor have consistently been enveloped within the White House's public liaison effort, but OPL expanded to incorporate other discrete groups and constituents as they wielded power in the ballot box or in Congress—women, consumers, Hispanics, African Americans, youth, seniors, veterans, religious and faith organizations, and, in recent years, gays and lesbians.

The Public Liaison under Obama

Obama continued the White House's public liaison functions and expanded them by creating the Office of Public Engagement (OPE) to host public meetings and (according to president's video message on OPE's web page, shortly after his inauguration) to "tak[e] the administration beyond the beltway and mak[e] the White House more accessible to all Americans."[12] The president's launch of health reform in spring 2009 was spearheaded in part by a series of events organized by OPE, including a roundtable discussion between Health and Human Services secretary Kathleen Sebelius and female small business owners. OPE events enabled the White House to reach out to interest groups (such as advocates for women entrepreneurs and for gays and lesbians) and politically important components of the president's coalition. The White House initially calculated that it could transfer the support for Obama during the election campaign to the health reform campaign by giving its backers the opportunity to "ask questions and share ideas with some of the Administration's leading experts" (as one OPE post put it).[13] OPE events seemed not only to promise a means for rallying allies but also to address the uncertainties and concerns of others (such as small businesses).

The White House's public liaison operations were expanded by Obama in two notable respects. First, Obama widened the visibility of the White House's outreach not only to organized groups but also to the general public in order to serve (according to a press release) as the "front door to the White House through which ordinary Americans can participate and inform the work of the President." The Office of Public Engagement, Obama explained in a video, will "engage as many Americans as possible . . . through meetings and conversations with groups and individuals held in Washington and across the country."[14]

In an implicit acknowledgment of its promotional objectives, the White House hired a prominent television actor—Kal Penn, who was Dr. Lawrence Kutner on the popular series "House" —to serve as associate director of OPE with responsibility for connecting with young people, the arts, and Asian Americans.

Obama's OPE orchestrated a series of events in the Eisenhower Executive Office Building and, occasionally, with the president to profile his administration's intent to hear from everyday Americans and politically important electoral clusters. Within several months of the inauguration, OPE's events were attracting 450 people a week to the White House.[15] It actively convened meetings to reach out to key electoral clusters that extended beyond the major established stakeholder groups to include youth, women, minorities (blacks, Hispanics, Asians, and Native Americans), gays and lesbians, small business owners, and others. OPE reached out to young CEOs to augment its ties with major national business organizations. It regularly interacted with progressives to coordinate messages and strategies to win passage of health reform, to achieve confirmation of Supreme Court nominees, and to advance other areas of shared concern.[16]

OPE's outreach focused not only on electoral clusters but also on policy areas—such as health care and financial reform—that cut across these discrete subgroups. The consistent message was to present OPE as the White House's "open front door" to fulfill Obama's "goal of making government inclusive, transparent, accountable and responsible" by facilitating "direct dialogue [with] the American public [including 'new voices']."[17]

During the administration's drive to enact finance reform, OPE orchestrated events to play up its engagement with, for instance, African American business leaders and a commitment to boosting financial literary. It reached out to female small business owners impacted by high medical care costs during its struggle to pass health reform and then hawked its payoff to beneficiaries, including women who had previously been denied coverage or charged exorbitant rates by private insurers because of a previous medical condition or being of childbearing age or struggling with infertility. On issues of concern to gays and lesbians (such as granting new rights of hospital visitation), OPE created a mechanism both to rally their support and to mollify religiously affiliated hospitals.[18]

The second significant change by the Obama White House was to capitalize (though incompletely) on the Internet for communications and mobilization of support—the "webinizing" of the White House noted above. Although the White House started to take advantage of the Internet during the 2004 and 2006 elections, the presidential election of 2008 was a breakthrough year. Hillary Clinton announced her campaign via the web. All the major campaigns had staff skilled in using information and digital technology. The Obama campaign, though, was the most sophisticated and effective, using the Internet as a kind of "force multiplier"—leveraging the effort of a relatively few campaign staff into an army of tens of thousands of fundraisers, event organizers, and precinct volunteers who were contacting and turning out voters in communities around the country.[19] Obama's March 2008 speech on race drew over 5 million views on YouTube. His staff skillfully used the web to create networks of supporters who linked together to create videos, to identify and persuade potential Obama voters, and to form neighborhood organizations to work for the candidate and turn out the vote.[20]

The sophistication of the Obama campaign's use of the Internet created heightened expectation that the White House's operations would be reshaped. Soon after his inauguration, the president promised in an online video that the Office of Public Engagement "will have a strong on line presence, including blogs, postings from OPE staff, and other interactive elements." For the first time, the White House created blogs, with OPE staff providing overviews of meetings and events.[21]

Despite the Obama White House's new steps in using the Internet, however, its efforts fell far short of the 2008 campaign and the expectations created by the president's promise to substantially rely on the web to reach out to Americans and to bring them into the White House. The White House and OPE primarily used the web as an electronic bulletin board to disseminate information that promoted its agenda and to deliver politically crafted messages.

The broader potential of the Internet to lower the barriers to engagement and therefore to stimulate citizen participation and engagement, which Obama's campaign tapped into, has been largely missed. OPE, for instance, does not use the Internet to inform citizens of meetings and networking opportunities. Its invitation to sign up for e-mail alerts, which could be a first step to fostering networks, is a dead-end operation—it produces no follow-up apart from a "Thank You."

Political and institutional barriers prevented breakthroughs in information technology and the Internet from transforming White House operations. Although the Obama administration (more than any of its predecessors) appreciated the potential to webinize the White House, the new capacities to distribute and make use of information and networking technology were not simply technical challenges.[22] Whatever benefits candidate Obama reaped from the technological breakthroughs were recalculated based on the political and institutional interests and vulnerability of President Obama.

The inherent features of the Internet—decentralization, quick and around-the-clock decision making about messages and meetings, and the self-initiative of Internet networking—were all assets to a campaign that was both devoted to a single objective (winning the most votes on Election Day) and stretched thin in seeking to build an organization across the country. Once in the Oval Office, however, the strengths of Internet mobilization posed political liabilities—diminished control and the inevitability of statements or actions that would threaten delicate White House efforts to balance coalitions and bargains. Decentralization and unmonitored decisions around-the-clock about messaging and events worked during a sprawling campaign but risked the president's political capital by alienating coalition partners or potential partners. In addition, White House websites became a target of political opponents (such as when the site posted initially flawed tallying of stimulus funding) or became a visible platform for criticizing the president, which the traditional media covered as indications of public unease or opposition to his policies. Even apart from the White House's Internet operations, the administration was acutely aware of its general challenge to impose a system of control on its former campaign staff. To take but one example, one new administration staffer—Yosi Sergant, who helped produce the campaign's famous "hope" poster—took the initiative for what seemed to him to be a great idea (recruiting artists, as he had done during the campaign, to create work supporting Obama); inadvertently, he exposed the White House to withering criticism from Fox News host Glenn Beck for using public dollars for political purposes.[23]

In short, the hungering to exploit the Obama campaign's success in using the Internet as a "force multiplier" was overtaken by political imperatives. The president and his senior aides were willing to sacrifice the advantages of webinizing the White House in order to protect his professional reputation, advance their primary strategic interests, and allocate their scarce political and institutional resources in order to maximize the president's influence on Congress and Washington policymaking.

The Snare of Public Input—Little Policy Impact

As the White House's public liaison operators were waving the flag of accessibility and outreach, administration officials were playing a different game behind closed doors. Feedback and input were solicited, but rarely impacted policy.[24] In the four decades of the public liaison office, what stand out are the exceptions to the general pattern of insulation. Carter's public liaison operation, for instance, sought to counter congressional resistance to the president's budget by attempting to convey the views of organized groups to key budget officials, in the hope that this would build congressional support—responding to organized groups, one study observed, was believed to be "critical to success in selling the projects; groups wanted to be in on the take-off as well as the landing of legislation."[25]

More commonly, however, White Houses pursued a simple political strategy of "listening"—signaling respect and openness, even as influence over policy remained closely held and shielded from public input. Despite Carter's dabbling with responsiveness to increase support for his budget, his public liaison generally focused on its primary mission—enlisting organized groups to support the administration's already formulated policy agenda, such as ratification of the Panama Canal Treaty.

Obama has continued to deploy the public liaison "listen to co-opt" strategy. At the outset of his administration in 2009, Obama introduced OPE as "increasing [the public's] meaningful engagement with the federal government" and "allow[ing] ordinary Americans to offer their stories and ideas regarding issues that concern them and share their views on important topics."[26] Meanwhile, no sustained effort was put in place to convert the ballyhooed "engagement" into actual policy. Translation: We will listen without acting.

Although public liaison outreach and policy formulation were largely disconnected within the White House, various administrations did their best to encourage groups and valued constituents to assume that the two (listening and policy influence) were synonymous. Several administrations strategically appointed senior advisers with close contacts with the president in charge of the public liaison operation. Karl Rove ran it (for George W. Bush), as does Valerie Jarrett (President Obama's close friend and adviser). These assignments invited the natural assumption by organized groups and constituents that input to OPL and OPE "mattered," even though the actual operation of public liaison rarely interacted with White House offices devoted to designing policy and was often run on a day-to-day basis by a lower-level assistant. The Obama White House may have been a bit more direct in inviting the assumption that "listening" and policymaking were linked: the president explicitly linked the OPE's "direct dialogue" with "ensuring that everyone can participate and inform the work of the President."[27]

Private and Powerful Interest Group Bargaining

The White House's institutionalized relationships with interest groups is often described in general and undifferentiated terms. For instance, Joseph Pika describes the "persistent, clearly identified White House staff specialization" that is "dedicated to working with interest groups," adding that future presidents "will need to establish a way to oversee interest group relationships."[28] There are two tendencies in this characterization that obscure the White House's relations with interest groups. First, it suggests that OPL takes responsibility for mediating the White House's contacts with interest groups. Second, interest groups are treated as a general category rather than as differentiated within that category based on power relations—on their economic and organizational resources and influence in Washington and especially in Congress.

The White House tiers access to interest groups based on power. OPL is its visible face: it ostentatiously encourages communications with the large number of groups and constituents that are politically valued for providing support or refraining from active opposition, but which lack the organizational and financial resources of large organizations of businesses, labor, and consumers. Yet, as noted, it rarely delivers access to policy formulation. By contrast, the president's most senior policymakers (the chief of staff and other top White House aides, or senior department officials) quietly accommodate powerful interest groups or reach out to them to include them in private policy decisions and perhaps strike bargains with them.

The Obama presidency pursued a consistent interest group strategy. Indeed, Obama's demonstrable focus on engaging everyday citizens as a candidate and as president puts into relief his differentiated strategy toward interest groups and more diffuse clusters in his electoral coalition. The strategy flowed from a hard-headed calculation about the imbalance in American political organization and its devastating impact on the reformist agenda of the previous Democratic president, Bill Clinton. The biggest beneficiaries of Democratic reforms tended to be diffuse and poorly organized: the uninsured, underemployed, minorities, and youth often do not accurately recognize their "interests" in public policy debates and are rarely organized or represented by well-equipped associations.[29] By contrast, stakeholders in existing consumer, business, and government policies are well organized and often vigilant in defending their interests. Obama and his senior staff were acutely aware of the disjuncture between their reformist policy goals and the organizational imbalance in Washington, as well as of the politically lethal consequences of this disjuncture on Clinton's agenda, especially during the opportune period of unified government in 1993 and 1994.

Obama's political learning from Clinton's failures led to a two-pronged strategy for handling the potently organized stakeholders and the diffuse beneficiary groups. Drawing on the modern presidency's evolving public liaison capacities, the Obama White House simultaneously sought to project an open administration free of Washington insider dealing and, incongruously, to engage in sustained negotiations with stakeholders to blunt their opposition or split their coalitions by striking deals with particular groups. Past research on the public liaison operations concentrated on the outreach component described above; but it neglected the private sustained negotiations with stakeholders that impacted administration policy.

Two of Obama's highest priorities were health care and financial reform. On both, he made significant accommodations or explicit deals with stakeholders. We discuss these in greater depth below.

Landmark Health Reform and Momentous Concessions

Soon after his inauguration in January 2009, Barack Obama made a momentous decision behind closed doors—to stake his presidency on passing health care reform. His senior advisers, including his chief of staff, Rahm Emanuel, counseled against it as posing enormous political risks that could cripple his presidency; they warned of divisions within the Democratic Party, the strong likelihood that most Republicans and perhaps all of them would unify against it, and the real possibility that Obama's efforts would be crushed by the well-funded united front of stakeholders who had successfully defeated President Bill Clinton's attempts at health reform fifteen years earlier. The president overruled his aides, out of the conviction that his commitments during the campaign had locked him into such a path and that reform was necessary to control the health care costs that were drowning both businesses and state and federal government budgets. He also believed that he could change the political equation in his favor by striking a high-stakes bargain with the stakeholders in the health care industry.

While the White House's public liaison operations appeared to invite input from groups and valued electoral clusters, other parts of the staff conducted secretive deal-making with powerful interests capable of defeating or allowing the legislation to pass. Like generals who prepare for war by studying the last battle, Obama and his senior aides carefully analyzed why Clinton's effort to reform health care had failed in 1994. One of their conclusions was that organized interests with tangible stakes in the existing system would be far more motivated and better equipped than the broad swath of Americans who would eventually benefit by gaining wider access to insurance and medical care. Patients without insurance or medical care were confused about their stake in reform and lacked the clout and resources to loudly and effectively counteract organized interests in the battle for influence in Congress.[30]

The "real" action was being conducted by the president's chief of staff, who worked with a small number of senior congressional Democrats (especially, taking the congressional lead on health reform, the Senate Finance Committee and its chair Max Baucus) to strike bargains behind closed doors. Their objective was to "keep powerful groups at the table [and] . . . prevent them from allying against [Obama] as they did against Clinton." Along with other administration officials, the White House's political guru, David Axelrod, made it clear that accommodations with stakeholders were the price of "get[ting] things done within the system as it is."[31] There was "no chance at winning the necessary sixty votes in the Senate if interest groups were against you," explained a White House aide.[32] An aide to a senior congressional Democrat closely involved in the outreach elaborated in a private interview that negotiations were used to "keep every stakeholder in discussion to keep talking" and to prevent or even delay them from attacking the bill. Although liberals criticized the deal-making when it eventually became public, the inside players discounted their critiques as "underestimat[ing] the strategic value of . . . alliances in . . . being able to keep [the reform] thing going." Indeed, the staff of liberal icon Ted Kennedy also participated in the outreach to the stakeholders to forestall an early and sustained "massed attack" and to "keep them at the table" in order to "road test ideas," detect fault lines, and convey the "sense of being listened to," as possible compromises were devised.[33]

The president's senior advisers quietly engaged in bare-knuckled instrumental bargaining for active stakeholder support (or at least agreement to withhold their vocal opposition) in exchange for a new lease on life for private providers, suppliers, and insurers, along with new revenue and exemptions worth billions of dollars. Emanuel and Baucus and their aides negotiated on the basis of "how much the stakeholders stood to gain."[34] For the lead representatives of health care providers, the White House traded on the $171 billion hospitals stood to gain and the $228 billion of new payments for doctors to win their support for legislation and agreement to accept lower reimbursement rates. The accommodation with the established representative of doctors (the American Medical Association [AMA]) was particularly striking, as it had been the implacable foe of national health insurance reform for nearly a century, including its opposition to the enactment of Medicare in 1965, when it threatened to go on strike and refuse to treat ill patients.

The White House also spearheaded the accommodation with major drug companies and its powerful lobbying group known as PhRMA (for Pharmaceutical Research and Manufacturers of America; pronounced "Farma").

PhRMA agreed to charge lower drug prices and pay fees that amounted to $85 billion over ten years, as well as pump $100 million in advertising and other efforts to pass reform.[35] In exchange, the representatives of the major pharmaceutical companies would receive tens of billions of dollars in new customer prescriptions as well as protections against new competition from makers of cheaper generic drugs and importation of cheaper medications from other countries (a deal which overturned an Obama campaign promise).

The AARP, which represents Americans aged fifty and over and boasts 40 million members, won an expansion of Medicare's prescription drug benefit to cover the so-called "doughnut hole"—the gap between $2,700 when coverage stopped (as of 2009) and $6,154 when it kicked in again. As legislation took shape and improved various Medicare benefits, including the gap in prescription coverage, AARP became a stalwart supporter of the bills that were introduced and eventually passed in the House and Senate.

The White House's negotiations also delayed the opposition of private health insurers. Beginning soon after inauguration, the president's top aides conducted extensive private negotiations with insurers and their lobbyist arm, America's Health Insurance Plans (AHIP), highlighting their benefits from having 32 million new customers. AHIP's president and CEO, Karen Ignagni, participated in the president's health care summit in March 2009 and declared "our commitment to play, to contribute, and to help pass health-care reform this year."[36] Ignagni also signed onto a letter to Obama offering to reduce insurance prices/costs voluntarily. The negotiations also led the Senate Finance Committee in the early fall of 2009 to reject what insurers most intensely opposed—a national public option—and to adopt forty-eight amendments that responded to insurance industry complaints, provoking Senator Rockefeller to quip that "the insurance industry is not running this markup but it is running certain people in this markup."[37] But new government regulations and the prospects for future restrictions did prompt insurers to openly oppose reform in October 2009.

While the White House's negotiations with insurers ultimately broke down, they delayed the onslaught of harsh ads and negative lobbying in Congress until the endgame—avoiding the early and intense campaign that Clinton's reform faced. Certain organized groups—particularly those representing business—were unalterably opposed to health reform and the White House did not engage them in serious negotiations because of the weak prospects for reaching a deal or delaying their public opposition. The Chamber of Commerce devoted millions to running negative ads, and the National Federation of Independent Businesses, which presents itself as the voice of small businesses, channeled the opposition of employers who do not offer insurance to their employees.

The health care stakeholders enjoyed privileged access to the president and his chief of staff and were privately granted substantial concessions. Although these deals were condemned by conservatives and by liberals as unfair and corrupt, they effectively split the anti-reform coalition that blocked Clinton's campaign and was a critical factor in the passage of health reform. Obama and his allies never faced the full force of all-out, unified opposition. Looking back at the deal-making and its impact in passing legislation, a senior aide to Senator Ted Kennedy bluntly concluded that "without a shadow of doubt the accommodations were necessary."[38]

As deals with stakeholders were struck (or attempted), important groups of the broad public lacked similarly organized and influential brokers. The organized groups representing them did not get the same access as the pressure groups for insurers and pharmaceutical companies. Organizations representing the uninsured and lower-income individuals, for instance, bitterly complained about "giveaways" to the medical industry; a large and diffuse group of taxpayers similarly complained to pollsters, though their voice was not present at the West Wing bargaining table.

Accommodative Reform: Landmark Finance Legislation

With populist anger at Wall Street unabated as the Obama term wore on, the White House orchestrated a symphony of visible public displays to portray the administration as serving the people in the face of venal lobbyists. Obama barnstormed the country during the first half of 2010 touting himself (as he did on May 20) as an uncompromising fighter for the "American people" who was rebuffing "the financial industry [that] has repeatedly tried to end this reform [and water it down] with hordes of lobbyists and millions of dollars in ads." In Racine, Wisconsin, on June 30, Obama portrayed himself as stiff-arming the special interests to serve the "men and women who have been out of work for months at a time [who] . . . expect their leaders in Washington to do whatever it takes to make sure a crisis like this doesn't happen again." He triumphantly signed the Dodd-Frank Wall Street Reform and Consumer Protection Act on July 21 as a victory for reformers who "look[ed] out for the public interests" and defeated the "furious lobbying of an array of powerful interest groups."[39]

While it is true that finance reform was passed over the intense opposition of the financial sector and its allies, it is also the case that the Obama White House consistently accommodated financial interests out of the public eye.

Unlike health reform, where the Oval Office set broad objectives and then deferred to Congress to design the law, the White House and, especially, the Treasury Department led by Secretary Timothy Geithner, took the lead in formulating the Wall Street package and setting many of the parameters adopted by the House (and its Financial Services chair Barney Frank) and the Senate (and its Banking Committee chair Christopher Dodd). With both committees granted unusual deference within Congress, the White House's decisions had particular impact on Frank, who adopted much of its package, and on Dodd, who worked closely with the administration and especially the Treasury Department in ironing out details and fending off unwanted amendments.[40]

As in health reform, the administration realistically sized up the organizational imbalance in the fight for health reform; they may well have appreciated that the finance lobby was even better funded than its health industry counterparts, as well as more unified and more focused in impacting Washington and the Obama administration.[41] Representing US and global financial interests, the American Bankers' Association, the US Chamber of Commerce, and others outspent all other sectors of the economy—including health and energy—in lobbying Washington over the past dozen years ($4 billion). In just the first three months of 2010 as reform moved through Congress, it racked up $592 million.[42] In addition to greasing the legislative wheels, financial interests contributed more to Obama than to his Republican rival in the 2008 presidential race. Obama enjoyed tighter connections to financiers than had past Democratic presidents—a striking contrast with President Franklin Delano Roosevelt, for example, who was less constrained in unleashing paint-peeling attacks on Wall Street.

Facing off against these well-appointed financial interests and their webs of contacts were outmatched pro-reform organizations (like organized labor). The pro-reform groups lacked comparable financial and lobbying resources. Making matters worse, they were overstretched; the most significant pro-reform groups had dissipated their already meager resources to support reform of health care and other Obama initiatives.

In addition to wielding an enormous edge in organizational resources, the interest groups resisting finance reform enjoyed several other advantages. First, key decision-makers in the administration had close ties with Wall Street or had actually worked in finance and may well expect to return to it in the future. The careers of the administration's key figures on finance reform were "interwoven" in the "Wall Street–Washington Corridor"—from Rahm Emanuel and Lawrence Summers in the White House to Secretary Geithner and his top aides in Treasury.[43] The flow of personnel between Wall Street and the White House created what former International Monetary Fund chief economist Simon Johnson called "channels of influence" that allowed "easy access of leading financiers to the highest U.S. government officials." While the finance industry could access the top of the Obama administration through mere phone calls (rather than the hearings and petitions available to others), direct arm-twisting was often not necessary because administration officials had already internalized the expectations of finance and therefore could anticipate their interests and likely reactions to reform proposals. As economics Nobel prize winner Joseph Stiglitz explained, the "mindsets" of government officials who worked on Wall Street were "shaped by [the] people [they] associate with [so they came] to think that what's good for Wall Street is good for America."[44] Put simply, concrete and observable lobbying and negotiations of the sort seen in the White House's handling of health reform were not as necessary on finance reform, because the industry was represented within the administration—or, more precisely, *was* the administration in certain respects.

One of the vivid displays of the government's concession to finance was its resistance to establishing an independent consumer financial protection agency that would have watched out for consumers. A consumer agency, advocated for by Harvard law professor Elizabeth Warren as early as 2007, had been proposed and defeated in the past, even though Canada had, to good effect, adopted something like it about a decade earlier. But Summers and Geithner blocked the administration from initially proposing it, reflecting the vociferous opposition in finance and the battle to protect bureaucratic turf in Washington. Warren lashed out at the opposition within the administration, charging at a Senate Finance hearing in September 2009 that the "problem starts with Treasury." Because of persistent pressure from Congress and consumer groups, however, a watered-down consumer agency—the Bureau of Consumer Financial Protection—was enacted. But Treasury and the Federal Reserve were able to contain its effectiveness by housing it within the Federal Reserve and imposing constraints (such as establishing a board to oversee the bureau, with the power to put a "stay" on its actions). On another front, the administration initially proposed weak regulations of credit-rating agencies—a key source of the financial crisis. Congress stepped in to attempt to strengthen the rules for credit-rating agencies but the administration used the conference committee to cripple important parts of the new requirements.[45]

Beyond these visible concessions, the Obama administration accommodated the financial industry by adopting an approach to reform—as the president explained at the bill signing—that was geared to restoring and maintaining the "financial industry [as] central to our nation's ability to grow, to prosper, to compete and to innovate." This approach reflected a "mindset" that the finance industry was essentially healthy with the exception of a discrete set of faulty (but remediable) rules, rule-keepers, and rogue operators who relied on "tricks and . . . traps," as Obama put it.[46] Meanwhile, independent economists and analysts who investigated the financial system complained that Obama and his aides failed to appreciate that the existing model of finance was "busted" and needed a "radical rethink." Stiglitz harshly criticized the administration's overly deferential approach to finance reform for "muddl[ing] through" and resorting to policies with "deeply obvious flaws."[47] Stiglitz and other prominent economists urged a restructuring that was anathema to the finance industry—breaking up big banks, heavily regulating derivatives, and controlling the securitization of mortgages that precipitated the crisis in 2007. Within the Obama administration, these proposals were brushed aside as inconceivable.

The Two Faces of the White House

The organization of the White House has dramatically changed over time. On the most basic level, the size of the staff long ago outgrew the White House itself and the nearby Eisenhower Executive Office Building, spilling over into additional large office buildings. The growth in size has been accompanied by specialization— the proliferation of a large number of differentiated offices and staff who assume finely prescribed roles and responsibilities for domestic and foreign policy.

Organizational innovation should not be confused, however, with the metrics of power. The specialization of staff to "engage" the broader public has proceeded quite independently of the process of formulating presidential policy, which is driven by the struggle for institutional position within the administration and the pressure of privileged private interests that wield leverage in Congress, in legislative districts, and in the court of public opinion.

The Obama presidency has adopted an approach to interest groups that is strikingly incongruous. On the one hand, it has accentuated the White House's public liaison operation to highlight its commitment to "making the White House more accessible to all Americans" and "inform[ing] the work of the President." On the other hand, the balance of power among organized groups remains a driving force in policy development, generating lucrative deals and accommodations. The Obama presidency is characterized by the simulation of organizational openness, even as it grants stakeholders privileged access: it publicly trumpeted its open outreach while it also continued to conduct a quiet process of highly consequential negotiations and accommodations with powerful organized groups.

The seeming mismatch of promoting openness while practicing insider dealmaking is particularly striking for a president who professes a devotion to remaking Washington's ways. But, in truth, the contradiction also reflects the historically evolving structure of American politics. The populist backlash against Washington that Obama rode to victory in 2008 and continues to pursue is driven by a deep political distrust among Americans and the electoral significance of weary independents and fickle partisans who are prone to sit out elections. Meanwhile, the Obama White House's acceptance of the durable insider access of stakeholders was a clear-eyed acknowledgment that the policy areas it targeted were densely populated by well-organized groups that could both readily mobilize its members and intimidate legislators (including members of the president's party) by activating angry constituents and directing campaign contributions to a challenger (or threatening to).

The privileged access of well-organized stakeholders in the Obama administration has its unique coloring, but it fits into a long-standing pattern. Even presidencies that pursued landmark reforms have had to contend with the power matrix in Washington. Their reward was to enact pioneering legislation. But, inevitably, such success required concessions and accommodations to the well organized. That much has not changed.

Notes

1. See, e.g., Mark Peterson, "The Presidency and Organized Interests: White House Patterns of Interest Group Liaison," *American Political Science Review* 86 (September 1992).
2. Stephen Skowronek, *The Politics Presidents Make: Leadership from John Adams to Bill Clinton* (Cambridge, MA: Harvard University Press, 1994); Samuel Kernell, *Going Public: New Strategies of Presidential Leadership*, 3rd ed. (Washington, DC: Congressional Quarterly, 1997).
3. Robert Stein and Kenneth Bickers, *Perpetuating the Pork Barrel: Policy Subsystems and American Democracy* (New York: Cambridge University Press, 1995).
4. Jeffrey Tulis, *The Rhetorical Presidency* (Princeton, NJ: Princeton University Press, 1987).
5. Joseph Pika, "The White House Office of Public Liaison," The White House Transition Project, 2009, http://whitehousetransitionproject.org/resources/briefing/WHTP-2009-03-Public%20Liaison.pdf, accessed April 30, 2011; Peterson, "The Presidency and Organized Interests."
6. Arthur Bentley, *The Process of Government: A Study of Social Pressures* (Chicago: University of Chicago Press, 1908), 351.
7. Ibid., 351, emphasis in original.
8. Theodore Lowi, *The End of Liberalism: The Second Republic of the United States*, 2nd ed. (New York: Norton, 1979); Lowi, *The Personal President: Power Invested, Promise Unfulfilled* (Ithaca, NY: Cornell University Press, 1985).
9. Pika, "White House Office of Public Liaison"; Peterson, "The Presidency and Organized Interests"; and see the Heith chapter in this volume.
10. Quoted in Pika, "White House Office of Public Liaison," 19.
11. Quoted ibid., 20.
12. http://www.whitehouse.gov/administration/eop/ope.
13. Ibid.
14. Ibid.
15. Michael Fletcher, "High Powered and Low Key: Washington Observes the Influence of Obama Adviser Valerie Jarrett," *Washington Post*, March 15, 2009.

16. Annie Gowen, "His Business Is Bonding," *Washington Post*, January 4, 2010; Michael Shear, "How Obama Brought Big Change with a Small Step: Visitation Is an Example of How President Manages to Sidestep Major Battles," *Washington Post*, April 18, 2010.

17. White House website, "About the Office of Public Engagement," http://www.white house.gov/administration/eop/ope , accessed April 11, 2011.

18. Gowen, "Business Is Bonding"; Shear, "Big Change with a Small Step."

19. John Heilemann and Mark Halperin, *Game Change* (New York: Harper, 2010).

20. Virginia Heffernan, "Clicking and Choosing: The Election According to YouTube," *New York Times Magazine*, November 16, 2008, 22-23.

21. See the Heith chapter in this volume for more detail.

22. Bruce Bimber, "The Internet and Citizen Communication with Government," *Political Communication* 16 (1999): 409-28; Julianne Mahler and Priscilla Regan, "Crafting the Message: Controlling Content on Agency Web Sites," *Government Information Quarterly* 24 (July 2007): 505-521.

23. Garance Franke-Ruta and Michael Fletcher, "Obama Campaign's Yosi Sergant Quits," *Washington Post*, September 25, 2009.

24. Pika, "White House Office of Public Liaison."

25. Ibid., 5.

26. http://www.whitehouse.gov/administration/eop/ope.

27. White House website, "About the Office of Public Engagement."

28. Pika, "White House Office of Public Liaison," 1-2.

29. Suzanne Mettler, *The Submerged State* (Chicago: University of Chicago Press, 2011).

30. This discussion is based on Lawrence Jacobs and Theda Skocpol, *Health Care Reform and American Politics: What Everyone Needs to Know* (New York: Oxford University Press, 2010).

31. Peter Baker, "The Limits of Rahmism," *New York Times Magazine*, March 8, 2010.

32. Interview with executive branch official on January 5, 2010.

33. Jackie Calmes, "A Policy Debate and Its Lesson: Clinton's Defeat Sways Obama's Tactics," *New York Times*, September 6, 2009.

34. Jacobs and Skocpol, "Health Care Reform," 70-75.

35. Reed Abelson, "In Health Care Reform, Boons for Hospitals and Drug Makers," *New York Times*, March 22, 2010.

36. Ceci Connolly, "Ex-Foes of Health Care Reform Emerge as Supporters," *Washington Post*, March 6, 2009.

37. Senator John D. Rockefeller IV during a Senate Finance Committee hearing, September 24, 2009.

38. Interview with congressional official on January 5, 2010.

39. http://www.whitehouse.gov/the-press-office/remarks-president-wall-street-reform-0; http://www.whitehouse.gov/the-press-office/remarks-president-a-town-hall-meeting-economy-racine-wisconsin; http://www.whitehouse.gov/the-press-office/remarks-president-signing-dodd-frank-wall-street-reform-and-consumer-protection-act.

40. Daniel Carpenter, "The Contest of Lobbies and Disciplines: Financial Politics and Regulatory Reform in the Obama Administration," in *Reaching for a New Deal:*

Ambitious Governance, Economic Meltdown, and Polarized Politics in Obama's First Two Years, ed. T. Skocpol and L. Jacobs (New York: Russell Sage Foundation, 2011).

41. See the Weatherford chapter in this volume.
42. Carpenter, "The Contest of Lobbies and Disciplines."
43. Jo Becker and Gretchen Morgenson, "Geithner, Member and Overseer of the Finance Club," *New York Times,* April 27, 2009; Morgenson and Louise Story, "Testy Conflict with Goldman Helped Push A.I.G. to Edge," *New York Times,* February 7, 2010.
44. Quoted in Becker and Morgenson, "Geithner, Member and Overseer."
45. Carpenter, "The Contest of Lobbies and Disciplines."
46. White House transcripts of president's speeches and remarks, http://www.whitehouse.gov/briefing-room/speeches-and-remarks.
47. Quoted in Becker and Morgenson, "Geithner, Member and Overseer"; Philip Augar, *Chasing Alpha: How Reckless Growth and Unchecked Ambition Ruined the City's Golden Decade* (London: Bodley Head, 2009); and see Joseph Stiglitz, *Free Fall: America, Free Markets, and the Sinking of the World Economy* (New York: Norton, 2010).

CHAPTER 8

Rivals, or a Team? Staffing and Issue Management in the Obama Administration

Andrew Rudalevige

TO THE DISMAY OF THEIR AUTHORS, serious books rarely become integral to presidential discourse. But nearly fifty years after Richard E. Neustadt's *Presidential Power* was glimpsed in John F. Kennedy's suitcoat pocket, Doris Kearns Goodwin's *Team of Rivals* shot to like prominence during Barack Obama's run for the White House.[1] In May 2008, Obama called Goodwin's take on Abraham Lincoln's cabinet "a wonderful book," and endorsed the management style it described as what "has to be the approach that one takes, whether it's vice president or cabinet, whoever."[2] Indeed, when asked by CBS's Katie Couric what book (besides the Bible) Obama would find most useful in the Oval Office, he named *Team of Rivals*: "It's a remarkable study in leadership."[3]

Obama's praise sprung from Goodwin's depiction of Lincoln as a master of manipulating advisers to obtain the expertise he needed, willing to overlook past enmities to build a talent-laden administration in a time of crisis. In constructing his first cabinet, Lincoln selected four rivals from the 1860 presidential campaign, all more politically prominent than he. Obama, of course, also came both from Illinois and from virtually nowhere electorally, to defeat a variety of more-experienced rivals for his party's nomination and ultimately the presidency. The analogy of New York senator William Seward in 1860 to New York senator Hillary Clinton in 2008 was especially irresistible.

Historians were quick to point out that Lincoln's experience with his "team" was not so consistently positive as Goodwin suggested.[4] It hardly mattered. "'Team of Rivals' has become a term of art here," a senior Obama staffer on the transition told *Newsweek*.[5] The phrase served as shorthand for a model of open and inclusive staffing

[handwritten margin note: Obama is different from Bush in his selection of appointees]

and governance. It encompassed Obama's stated willingness to open his advising channels to all comers, including political actors who disagreed with or even disliked him. "My attitude is that whoever is the best person for the job is the person I want," Obama noted. This stance had the additional benefit of marking out a useful campaign contrast with the purported "bubble" that protected President George W. Bush from any advice that did not conform to his pre-existing views.

Senator Clinton, like Senator Seward before her, would become secretary of state. But as the Obama administration took shape—and as it was reorganized in 2011 in partial reaction to its midterm "shellacking"—the prominence of the "team of rivals" metaphor in those early days begged at least two questions. First, was institutionalizing such a staff model really a good idea? That a "team of rivals" would provide the positive effects Obama (and the press) assumed received little scrutiny. We might ask more broadly: how should an administration be structured, in order to provide the optimum flow of timely advice, without overload? Second, did President Obama follow such a strategy? No matter what academics recommend, a president's staff structure must stand up under the pressures of day-to-day politics—public, bureaucratic, and personal.

This chapter traces staff and issue management in the first part of the Obama administration with an eye toward these questions. To do so it builds on the literature of the "institutional presidency" that traces the way the flow of information through a staff institution matters for the type and quality of advice received by the chief executive. This literature holds that a wide diversity of viewpoints must be provided through the advising process. It suggests that a competitive model—most commonly discussed as a feature of Franklin Roosevelt's management style—is one way to achieve this.

To this extent, then, utilizing a "team of rivals" does have theoretic and empirical support. Still, few presidents have used a competitive model for any length of time; and in the end, despite the drive of the president personally for more and better information, the organization of the Obama administration only partly reflected its tenets. Indeed, in the national security area, by mid-2011 observers feared the outcome was the opposite: a "corps of consensus."[6] This divergence reflects the president's own preferences, the institutional stickiness of what has become the hierarchical "standard model" of presidential staffing—and the real costs, despite the benefits, of such an approach in the modern presidency.

Organizing for Information

George W. Bush, who would title his own memoir *Decision Points*, contended that the most important questions for a future president were "How do you intend to make decisions? . . . How do you decide?"[7] Decision making is at the very heart of the office.

While the presidency has always served as a focal point for choice, the growth of the American state—in Depression, war, globalization, and regulatory enthusiasm—has greatly expanded both the size of the executive branch and the range of decisions its chief must make. Further, the issues demanding presidential judgment rarely have an obvious right answer: they are controversial, large in scale and in impact, and embody both substantive trade-offs and competing values.[8] How presidents make those decisions is thus shaped by what they know, or think they know, at the time of decision. Neustadt argued that presidential power itself rests on what, when, and how much a president can get "into his mind. His first essential need is for information."[9]

Information, in turn—at least in the modern presidency—is a function of staffing. The primary job of presidential staff is to help the president understand the alternatives available in a given policy arena and calculate the expected consequences of selecting any given alternative—"A good White House staff can give a President that crucial margin of time, analysis and judgment that makes an unmanageable problem more manageable," wrote Kennedy adviser Theodore Sorensen.[10]

We know that organizational variation can have important real-world impacts when presidents get differential information, even within the same administration. The textbook example compares two of Kennedy's decisions involving Cuba. The 1961 Bay of Pigs invasion showed a president making a series of poor choices at least in part because he failed to create a staffing structure that would give him full understanding of the plan's parameters and (very poor) prospects. The 1962 Cuban missile crisis, by contrast, showed how the same president could enhance the information available to him by deft use of staff and non-staff resources, and thus improve his odds of a successful outcome. Others have held up the differences in staffing between the first and second terms of Ronald Reagan, or the (good) Eisenhower and (bad) Johnson decision-making processes with regard to American military involvement in Vietnam. The aim is for the president to "enhance his capacity to test reality," a major study on the latter topic argues: "A well-devised advisory system—one geared to the incumbent's style and needs—will aid the president's process of choice, and . . . poorly devised systems will lead him astray."[11]

The management issues involved in devising such a system have grown greatly over time. From the 1939 authorization of six administrative assistants, the White House staff, broadly defined, rose to just over 1,500 members in 2011.[12] That mass of people is a great presidential resource, but it can also be insulating. An assistant to Lyndon Johnson, Harry McPherson, warned of "the danger of bias or omission" that results from presidents' inevitable reliance on information received "through the filter of other men's convictions."[13] It is important to reduce the sea of information at the bottom of any hierarchical pyramid to a puddle at the top. But different hierarchies will bring different kinds of problems and alternatives to the president's attention. Some issues will never make it to the president. Others will, but with

- large staff can be beneficial in the dif. resources / perspectives it provides

- can be detrimentally 'insulating' as well

certain options weeded out, as each level of staff review simplifies what passes upwards. The choices made along the way will matter for the choices the president in turn can make.

How to construct the "filter," then? Scholars have most often categorized presidential efforts in this regard into a structural trinity: as formalistic, collegial, and competitive.[14] All are hierarchical, of course, in that the president has no equal in the White House; but a formalistic model is more so, in that it posits a single chief of staff and a set of substantively specific offices that report to the president through that chief. Competitive and collegial models (the difference is really in the way staffers are utilized) place the president at the center of a network of advisers—as the hub of a wheel, fed by various spokes—with fewer levels and less staff specialization.

Any such framework is, of course, too simple: presidents utilize multiple formal and informal channels of information, and these vary not only across administrations but within them. They may even vary within a single issue area, over time. However, for present purposes, especially since the "team of rivals" approach is clearly closest to the "competitive" model in outlook, building on this typology provides a useful lens for examining different management strategies. Further, as Charles Walcott and Karen Hult have pointed out, at least in terms of formal organization, since the 1970s a sequence of presidents have utilized a very similar template for their White House staff—basically a formalistic framework so institutionalized as to have become the "standard model."[15]

In a perfect world, presidents would receive comprehensive advice that covers a wide range of options; that encompasses diverse assumptions about possible outcomes; and that incorporates relevant practical policy and political contexts. The advice should provide perspectives that challenge presidential preconceptions, since value judgments can lead to prejudgments that cut off deliberation. And it should be timely, available to the president when he needs to draw on it.[16]

But the world is rarely perfect, and often these positive attributes come into direct conflict. A broad search for options, for instance, clearly makes timeliness more difficult. Each of the three organizational templates noted above prioritizes some aspect of advising; thus each has advantages, but also drawbacks. The formalistic model above requires a hierarchical division of labor where staff are assigned a well-defined substantive jurisdiction (for instance, national security) and follow a clear chain of command (through, for instance, the National Security Council [NSC] staff, the assistant to the president for national security, and the office of the chief of staff). Such a system emphasizes systematic, well "staffed-out" analysis. A wide range of issues can be tracked and advisory accountability is clear. On the other hand, such a system can insulate the president from much of the disputation over policy decisions. Because information moves from the bottom up, the issues that arise are not necessarily defined by the president, nor can he guarantee he is receiving all relevant advice. Staff members, given unique authority over a given substantive area, may refuse to share information about their bailiwick or become advocates rather than analysts.

Staffing Prescriptions

If each model brings trade-offs with it, what should presidents do? The "institutional presidency" literature makes some strong and sometimes counterintuitive suggestions for presidents seeking good advice.[17]

For instance, presidents often seek to install personal loyalists across the executive branch as a means of enforcing their own—as opposed to bureaucratic—policy preferences.[18] As one George W. Bush staffer put it, this involves the president trying to "implant his DNA throughout the government."[19]

This strategy, often called "politicization," has real use in enhancing organizational responsiveness. It is particularly useful if the focus is on bureaucratic *output* (as was in fact largely the case for Reagan and Bush II). But such a setup has shortcomings when considering *input*, that is, when building a system designed to formulate new policy options and outcomes. Responsiveness and substantive expertise are both good things for presidents, but they are rarely found in the same staffer.[20] And cloning presidential DNA merely makes sure, as in nature, that new information will not be added to the advisory gene pool.

Instead, presidents are better off with a range of subordinates who do *not* mirror their preferences. A wide mix of opinions, backgrounds, and assumptions *(in favor of a diverse bureaucracy)* sprinkled throughout the advising process helps give contrary advice serious consideration. This can be reinforced by providing for an "honest broker" in a coordinating role, who makes sure that the president receives a fair accounting of all views.[21]

Still, elevating expert over loyal views potentially leaves presidents vulnerable. Presidents, however smart or sure of themselves, are hardly expert on every topic—and may not even know what they need to ask. They may not be aware if expert conventional wisdom has eliminated key options from the menu they receive. So a careful choice of personnel cannot be the only answer: it matters too how they are arrayed, and how the president uses them.

Thus we turn from *people* to *process*. In November 2008, former presidential staffer Tom Korologos told incoming Obama aides that "the Cabinet should exhaust all the options and disputes before they rise to the president. . . . Intramural conflicts," he opined, are "the trash of government."[22]

But structuring the flow of information through an advisory institution is in fact all about conflict—because different institutions influence *which* conflicts reach the president's attention. Processes that rely on consensus building may lead directly to what Irving Janis termed "groupthink."[23] If presidents are protected

politicization may also lead to groupthink

from internal argument, they may wind up unalerted to key issues whose resolution has been preempted by lower-level officials. Thus they need to be careful to sift at least some of Korologos's trash before it is discarded. George W. Bush, for example, discovered the divide that had opened between the White House and the Justice Department over his anti-terror domestic wiretap program only when the Justice staff threatened mass resignation.

Guarding against being thus blindsided means presidents should provide for another form of variance in staff preferences by ensuring that different *types* of expertise (policy, political, etc.) are brought to bear on any given problem. Compartmentalized channels of advice may not produce the key information about how different problems connect across policy areas, or how politics and policy interact, factors which can have large if usually unintended consequences for outcomes. Thus, narrow subject-matter specialists should be assigned to issues as just one part of a wider decision stream. Further, presidents are likely to get better information about policy matters when they have effective monitoring mechanisms that allow spot-checks on lower-level decision making, outside "reality checks" to people on the ground that go around the hierarchy.[24]

A related, reinforcing strategy is to duplicate staff jurisdictions: to create multiple channels of comparable information. Doing so can improve the quality of the information received by creating a market of sorts, allowing the president to cross-check one flow of advice against another and determine a clear standard for assessing different staffers' preferences and biases. This "parallel processing"[25] is a key part of the "competitive model" of presidential staff management noted earlier.

Franklin Roosevelt is one of the few presidents to practice this systematically. As described by Matthew Dickinson, "FDR violated traditional administrative canons by assigning overlapping staff duties, utilizing duplicate communications channels, and mixing the lines of authority connecting him with his advisers," to great effect.[26] Others have followed FDR's lead for discrete periods. Nixon domestic adviser John Ehrlichman tells of a situation when Nixon asked him to become involved in defense matters so as to give the president an "outsider's view" on the situation.[27] And after the disastrous 1994 elections, a chastened Bill Clinton sought new advice from a cadre of consultants and staffers willing to work quietly behind the backs of other advisers. One initiative developed by this group was dubbed the "immaculate conception" when the president presented it, seemingly arrived fully formed from nowhere.[28]

Ronald Reagan's first-term "troika" provided a different model. There is little to suggest that Reagan intentionally set up a competitive system; in 1985 he rather casually dismantled it. But when in his first term his three top generalist aides held equal rank, they did not divide up issues so much as work on them simultaneously. Since each was wary of the others, all sought to make sure they could give input throughout the decision process. One of their colleagues argued that "in the incessant jockeying for power, creative juices often ran strong and they added immensely to the quality of [Reagan's] stewardship." Reagan was served far better in his first term in this regard than in his second, when new chief of staff Don Regan sought to install a far more structured hierarchy.[29]

Roosevelt did the coordinating himself; Reagan delegated it. In both cases, though, policy advising invited competition and review by generalists more attuned than specialists to the widest range of presidential goals and needs.

Summary

In short, there is some agreement in favor of a presidential strategy of what Richard Rose felicitously called "institutionalizing distrust" of any single point of view. Perhaps Alexander Hamilton phrased it even better, more than 220 years ago: "The oftener the measure is brought under examination, the greater the diversity in the situations of those who are to examine it, the less must be the danger of those errors which flow from want of due deliberation, or of those missteps which proceed from the contagion of some common passion or interest."[30]

How does this compare to a "team of rivals" approach? It is worth remembering that Goodwin's description of Lincoln's cabinet is set in an era without a White House staff to duplicate cabinet members' (or other staffers') jurisdictions. Still, given that the nineteenth-century cabinet was more apt to be made up of generalists and to meet as a single body, discussing issues that were in each other's department or cut across departmental boundaries, there are parallels. Lincoln, too, was certainly proactive in working through but also around and behind the backs of his cabinet members, as he felt best.[31] The idea of expanding the information available to the president by bringing together multiple views potentially hostile to each other (thus "rivals" in one sense) and to the president's own views (through bringing in his own political opponents, thus "rivals" in a second sense) does seem to be what Obama himself meant in invoking the phrase. In December 2008, for instance, he asserted that "I'm a strong believer in strong personalities and strong opinions—I think that's how the best decisions are made."[32]

If this describes the strategy accurately, it matches up fairly well with the prescriptions above. But it shares their costs as well as their benefits. Such a model forces a wealth of information to the president and ensures that he maintains final control over decisions. However, that control costs him his time and managerial effort, and does not make for quick decision making. The higher up the hierarchy the competition is installed, the harder it is to coordinate the various streams: this places yet more burden on those at the top, normally the president himself. Nor do staff themselves tend to like competitive models, and thus, implementing them runs the risk of building a backbiting culture in the White House.

Which of these trade-offs did the Obama administration choose as it unfolded? It is to this question we turn next.

The Obama Administration in Practice

The 2008–2009 transition received initially high marks for its discipline and outreach, aided by unprecedented cooperation from the outgoing Bush administration. Democratic party veteran Harrison Wellford called Obama's transition squad "the most mature, moderate, sensible I've ever seen."[33] Still, while early, high-profile appointments earned broad kudos, a series of nominees with various financial or disclosure difficulties earned the administration some bad press, and cost the president some high-profile personnel. The most notable withdrawal was former Senate majority leader Tom Daschle, nominated as secretary of health and human services. (When asked early on what had surprised him most, since taking office, Obama answered, tongue only partly in cheek, "The number of people who don't pay their taxes.")[34]

Opening Moves

Consistent with the Lincoln template, Obama appointed several of his former presidential rivals to key positions. Delaware senator Joseph Biden was Obama's choice to become vice president. As noted earlier, his chief opponent in 2008, Hillary Clinton, became secretary of state. Another former candidate, New Mexico governor and former cabinet secretary Bill Richardson (who endorsed Obama, irking the Clinton family) was Obama's choice to lead the Department of Commerce, though Richardson ultimately withdrew his name.

Obama also selected several Republicans for critical positions. In an important statement of wartime continuity, Bush defense secretary Robert Gates was asked to remain in office. Utah governor Jon Huntsman was named ambassador to China. Longtime Illinois Republican congressman Ray LaHood became transportation secretary. And after Richardson withdrew, Obama named Senator Judd Gregg (R-NH) to the Commerce slot. But Gregg, after agreeing to serve ("this is not a time for partisanship. . . . This is a time to govern and govern well"),[35] soon also demurred, saying he could not support enough of Obama's agenda to accept a position in his administration.[36]

One face new to the public, though not to the financial community, was installed at Treasury: Timothy Geithner, head of the New York Federal Reserve Bank and thus already enmeshed in the minutiae of the banking crisis.[37] Otherwise the cabinet was rounded out with a familiar mix of former Democratic administration officials (Clinton deputy attorney general Eric Holder took over the top spot at Justice), elected officials, and state-level technocrats, such as new

Secretary of Education Arne Duncan, the "CEO" of the Chicago public schools. One intriguing choice in terms of substantive talent was Steven Chu, a Nobel-winning physicist and director of the Lawrence Berkeley National Laboratory, at the helm of Energy.

As usual, a westerner (Sen. Ken Salazar of Colorado) took over at Interior, while a midwesterner (Governor Tom Vilsack of Iowa) took the helm of Agriculture. Governor Janet Napolitano of Arizona became the first female secretary of Homeland Security. Indeed, the cabinet was impressively diverse in terms of gender, race, and geography. Of the twenty-one individuals with cabinet rank in the Obama administration as of mid-2009, seven were women. The total included four African Americans, including Holder and EPA administrator Lisa Jackson; three Asian Americans, including Chu and Veterans secretary Eric Shinseki; and two Latino/as, Salazar and Labor secretary Hilda Solis. Seven of the twenty-one came from the Northeast (including District of Columbia "lifers"); five came from the West, five from the Midwest, and four from the South or Southwest. All this was consistent with recent administrations in seeking to create a cabinet that, as Bill Clinton put it, "looks like America."[38] Indeed, while the definition of diversity has certainly broadened, balancing it is hardly a new phenomenon. In searching for a new attorney general, for example, Abraham Lincoln himself observed that "I must find a Southern man. I suppose if the twelve Apostles were to be chosen nowadays the shrieks of locality would have to be heeded."[39] A different "shriek" came from Obama's campaign commitments to limit the role of lobbyists in his administration, discussed below.

Just as these sorts of political imperatives are potentially constraining, so the "deep structure" of the Executive Office of the President (EOP) tends to live on from administration to administration.[40] The development of the institutional presidency is one of accretion but rarely of deletion. Often there is good reason for that: presidents find new staff units useful in traversing the interstices between the White House and Capitol Hill, the bureaucracy, and the public. There was no National Security Council staff until the 1940s, no presidential office of congressional relations until the 1950s, no office of communications until the 1960s. But once created, each of these staffs became indispensable to successive administrations, either functionally or politically (as they developed their own constituencies, with their own expectations for presidential interaction; for example, George W. Bush had hoped to eliminate the Office of Intergovernmental Affairs, but changed his mind after protests from state and local officials).

In an early organizational chart drafted for candidate Obama, a dozen senior staff reported directly to the president. Obama rejected that model in favor of one labeled "collaborative hierarchy," which in its allocation of power to a chief of staff strongly emphasized hierarchy over collaboration.[41] With this, his White House slotted comfortably into the "standard model" noted above. This included the chief of staff's office complete with two deputies (for policy and internal management), a staff secretary to manage paper flow, a series of policy councils (domestic, national security, economic), and an array of offices and officers for communications and outreach (to Congress, to other government entities, to interest groups, to the press and public). The new administration thus was structurally similar to its immediate predecessor, more so than its rhetoric suggested. Obama even kept in place Bush's controversial Office of Faith-Based and Community Initiatives (OFCI), albeit re-branded as the Office of Faith-Based and Neighborhood Partnerships. He also changed the name of the longstanding Office of Public Liaison to the Office of Public Engagement (OPE), subsuming the intergovernmental affairs role and emphasizing interaction between the White House and members of the public.[42] There were new arrivals to the EOP, as well. The Council on Women and Girls, created by executive order in March 2009, fell under OPE's purview. And a series of coordinating offices—staffed by what were inevitably dubbed presidential "czars," as discussed below—were established to handle crosscutting policy issues such as environmental affairs, the financial bailouts, and the war in Afghanistan. The EOP staff was far more diverse in racial and ethnic terms than in previous presidencies. The variance in worldview this provokes is hard to calculate, but should not be underestimated. On the other hand, there were numerous attitudinal commonalities across the ranks of Obama's new staffers, especially given their prov-enance and consistently high-powered academic backgrounds that hinted at the Vietnam-era reliance on the "best and the brightest."[43]

The Obama administration also followed past practice—certainly that of his immediate predecessor—in centralizing authority in those White House staffers, as opposed to the cabinet. Obama certainly said all the right things to his cabinet appointees. "This is an extraordinary collection of talent, and you inspire great confidence in me," he told them the day after his inauguration.[44] But, consistent with past lessons—not least from the Clinton administration, which took so long in making its cabinet appointments that it had to rush to staff the EOP—Obama put great emphasis on White House staff resources, and he was faster than any recent president in naming his top forty aides and defining their roles.[45] Any delays in personnel selection were in the wider bureaucracy: at various subcabinet levels hundreds of vacancies remained well past the "first 100 days" marker of Obama's term. Those holes in staffing arguably underpowered the administration in terms of expertise even as they empowered the White House vis-à-vis the departments. That was not always helpful to the administration, as the later floundering of the Interior Department over the BP spill suggested.

The most dramatic notice of Obama's intentions for the White House, per-haps, was his choice for chief of staff. Former Clinton staffer and House whip Rahm Emanuel was a proudly profane political animal, with a combative persona described as "larger than life" as early as his elementary school days.[46] "Like some

Brazilian soccer star, the chief of staff went by one name in staff conversations," one reporter observed, as "Rahm" became "pseudo-prime minister, uber-press secretary, and strategist in chief."[47] Though from Chicago, Emanuel did not have close ties to Obama prior to his appointment, having stuck with the Clintons during the primary process. But Obama appreciated both Emanuel's deep knowledge of White House and congressional operations and his immense store of energy. If Emanuel was the temperamental antithesis of his "no drama" boss, that was the point; as Dwight Eisenhower argued, the role of chief of staff was to serve as the president's personal "son of a bitch," and that was a role "Rahm-bo" delighted in.[48]

Emanuel was one of what the *Financial Times* dubbed the "Fearsome Foursome," a small and often dominant inner circle.[49] Another was David Axelrod, chief strategist for Obama's campaign; Axelrod, not Emanuel, scored the coveted broom-closet's worth of desk space closest to the Oval Office.[50] Longtime friend and high-powered lawyer Valerie Jarrett took over OPE; campaign spokesman Robert Gibbs became press secretary. Obama's Senate chief of staff, Pete Rouse, along with Axelrod and Jarrett, was named not only an assistant to the president (the highest-ranking designation on the staff) but was distinguished in the hierarchy by also serving as "senior advisor."

Obama, with a very limited background in national security affairs, chose an experienced team to him advise him in this area—but one not particularly close to him personally. He made a full-court press to convince Bush appointee Robert Gates to stay on as Defense secretary, and Gates became increasingly important to his decision making over time.[51] Obama asked James L. Jones, Jr., a Marine general who had retired after forty years of service (and had thirty years of professional and personal ties to Obama's 2008 opponent John McCain), to become his assistant for national security, and retired admiral Dennis Blair to serve as director of national intelligence (DNI). At CIA—putatively but not practically under the purview of the DNI—Obama did choose as director someone from outside the defense/intelligence establishment, former congressman and Clinton chief of staff Leon Panetta. John Brennan, whose longtime service at the CIA and support for Bush-era intelligence activities alarmed some of Obama's political allies, moved to the White House rather than face confirmation hearings; he became deputy director of the NSC and the president's top counterterrorism adviser. General Douglas Lute was kept on from the Bush administration as "war czar" within the White House.[52]

The economic advisory staff was placed on a par with the national security staff, given the ongoing recession and financial crisis—indeed, Obama announced immediately after taking office that he would receive a daily economic briefing as an analogue to the threat briefing already in place. Former Harvard president and Treasury secretary Larry Summers became chair of the National Economic

Council, in charge of providing that briefing, which was attended by principals such as Treasury's Geithner, budget director Peter Orszag, Council of Economic Advisers (CEA) chair Christina Romer, and Domestic Policy Council chair Melody Barnes. CEA member Austan Goolsbee, White House economist Jared Bernstein (a Biden staffer, on paper at least), and longtime Washington economics hand and former Federal Reserve chair Paul Volcker were also important players, not least as part of a new Economic Recovery Advisory Board.[53] In August 2009, Obama chose to reappoint Federal Reserve chair Ben Bernanke, originally elevated by George W. Bush, to a second term beginning in early 2010.

As noted above, Obama also put in place a number of aides who were assigned primary responsibility for a specific policy area. Since many issues are both hugely complex and also cut across a variety of departmental jurisdictions, these appointments aimed to create a "go to" staffer backed with presidential authority, transcending organizational lines in order to keep relevant agencies working together. Carol Browner, who had headed the EPA under Bill Clinton, came into the White House to serve as "Energy Coordinator," for issues regarding energy and climate change (Obama had originally hoped to recruit Al Gore to this slot). Nancy-Ann DeParle was named to head a White House Office on Health Reform. There was also an "ethics czar" and others tasked with coordinating such issues as urban affairs, "green jobs," domestic violence, "Recovery for Auto Communities and Workers," and consumer protection in the financial services arena. Similarly, in foreign policy Obama named a series of high-profile subject-specific envoys such as Lute; Richard Holbrooke, who became the president's special adviser on Pakistan and Afghanistan; George Mitchell, focusing on the Middle East; Dennis Ross on Iran; and Stephen Bosworth on North Korea. Later Elizabeth Warren was added to manage implementation of the new Financial Consumer Protection Bureau.[54]

These staffers were immediately dubbed "czars," accused by the president's political adversaries (and some of his legislative allies) of exercising unaccountable, unchecked power. Fox News's Glenn Beck seized on the issue to charge that Obama had created a thirty-plus person "iceberg" on which the Constitution would run aground. Clearly some of those placed in the White House would have faced difficult confirmation processes in the Senate. But Beck's list included such statutorily created, and Senate-confirmed, positions as director of national intelligence; more neutral sources suggested the number of staffers in this category who were appointed directly by Obama without legislative approval (and thus able to evade testifying before Congress) was closer to eight.[55] Nor was the practice particularly new—the term "czar" had arisen during Franklin Roosevelt's administration, and presidents such as Dwight Eisenhower, Richard Nixon, and especially George W. Bush had frequently utilized the tactic as a managerial mechanism. Along those lines it is worth noting that the health care "czarship" was originally intended for

Tom Daschle, who would also have served as secretary of health and human services.[56] Though this experiment never got off the ground, even without it the czar system suggested a clear pattern of White House influence over the cabinet.

Another czar of sorts, though one with multiple crowns, was the vice president. Joe Biden entered office in the wake of perhaps the most influential VP in American history, Richard Cheney. Few expected Biden to match Cheney's advisory role, which Biden himself argued during the campaign had been "dangerous."[57] It seemed more likely he would be sidelined or supervised into silence—as indeed he was, during the campaign—given his career-long proclivity toward unedited pronouncement. In stark contrast to Cheney, Biden was not generally consulted on administration appointments; nor was he as craftily effective a bureaucratic operator as his predecessor. (One profile called Biden a "gifted expostulator and an indifferent schemer.")[58] But while the vice presidential staff were shy of influence if judged by the imposing bar set by Cheney aides such as Lewis Libby or David Addington, a half dozen of them retained the "dual hats" pioneered by Cheney to ensure the integration of his staff with the president's own. Former Al Gore aide Ron Klain, for instance, was named assistant to the president as well as chief of staff to the VP. The National Security Council staff was told that it reported to the president *and* to the vice president.

Biden himself became an increasingly trusted voice in the West Wing, especially on foreign policy matters. Given his long experience with the president's advisers (in many cases longer than the president's own), he was a useful intermediary when they squabbled. In June 2009 he became Obama's point person in Iraq, to assure the splintered government there of high-level US commitment despite ongoing troop withdrawals, and was soon deeply involved in the administration's review of its policy in Afghanistan. He also became immersed in the implementation of the 2009 stimulus law, charged with ensuring that it avoided undercutting public confidence through "fraud and stupidity."[59] (This, perhaps, was an even more intractable assignment than Iraq.)

Matching the Model

Given Obama's relatively short career in electoral politics, he could have relatively few long-term loyalists. Further, on entering office the president issued an executive order regulating the "revolving door" between government and lobbies with interests before the government. Registered lobbyists could not seek employment in an executive branch office they had recently lobbied; and appointees were required to certify that, for two years after joining his administration, they would avoid participating in issues relating to former clients or even substantive areas in which they had lobbied for two years previous.[60]

Some twenty individuals, most notably the new deputy secretary of defense, were granted waivers from this rule.[61] But while each exception proved politically embarrassing, given the scope of the original pledge, they represented a small fraction of the jobs that needed to be filled. In rounding out his administration, then, Obama turned to ready-made pools of potential Democratic appointees: past administrations, academia, and the liberal think tank community. Of those appointed to positions requiring Senate confirmation, according to the *Washington Post*'s "Head Count" feature, the most common attributes were some connection to the Clinton administration—about a quarter of the total—or to Harvard University, though of course frequently these overlapped. More than fifty people returned from electoral exile spent in the offices of the Center for American Progress, founded by Clinton chief of staff John Podesta.[62] Perhaps as notable was the influx of aides from the Democratic side of Capitol Hill. Emanuel, of course, left a House seat to become chief of staff; Rouse had worked for Obama, Tom Daschle, and Dick Durbin (D-IL); domestic aide Barnes had served as Senator Ted Kennedy's (D-MA) counsel; deputy chief of staff Jim Messina was an aide to Senator Max Baucus (D-MT); the Office of Management and Budget's (OMB) Orszag came from the Congressional Budget Office and his deputy from the House Appropriations Committee staff; and legislative affairs chief Phil Schiliro spent more than two decades working for Representative Henry Waxman (D-CA). Other lawmakers also saw their staff alumni well-represented in EOP positions.[63]

All this made for an odd version of politicization. Those on the left, who claimed Obama as their own (it was not clear whether he claimed them, in turn), were generally unhappy with his appointments: "Cries of 'betrayal,' 'sellout,' and 'Clintonian copycat' fill the air," wrote one liberal blogger. The Democratic faithful were eager to return to power, sensing a new "Camelot" in the making, but neither the army of Clinton veterans nor the legislative staff moving to their new digs northwest up Pennsylvania Avenue could be termed true Obama replicants, spreading his DNA across the executive branch. Obama argued that all "share[d] a core vision."[64]

But what was it? In his inaugural, Obama steered a careful middle course away from the ideological extremes encapsulated in endless debate over the size and scope of government. "The stale political arguments that have consumed us for so long no longer apply," he claimed, hopefully: "The question we ask today is not whether our government is too big or too small, but whether it works."[65]

The frequent calls on the president to "take a stand"—that is, to be more harshly partisan—thus misread his philosophy of governance. But if pragmatism as a means to good government has real appeal, as a mechanism for bureaucratic control its very reliance on contingency makes its day-to-day guidance ambiguous. The lowest-ranking civil servant never doubted "what would Reagan do?", but it was hard to say the same for Obama. Richard Wolffe, in his snapshot of the Obama inner circle as of spring 2010, distinguished between a cadre of "revivalists" committed to "the transformational spirit of Change" and rival "survivalists" more willing to compromise with the realities of Washington policymaking.[66] The balance was delicate but ultimately came down on the side of realism (or cynicism, from the "revivalist" point of view). Partly this was a question of having to deliver results, and the related reliance on legislation to achieve them.

Indeed, early policy was seen through the prism of the legislative process—the reason Obama wanted to center so much legislative experience in the White House, but also a vantage that reinforced itself as a result of that decision. This was clearly limiting in some ways with regard to being proactive on behalf of presidential preferences ("when Harry Reid and Nancy Pelosi's decision making drives your strategy, it's just hard," one White House aide noted).[67] It also meant that in low-salience areas congressional preferences in the bureaucracy went unchallenged by administrative attention—until those areas were no longer low salience. The Minerals Management Service, for instance, was dramatically reorganized—but not until the horse was out of the barn (or, rather, the oil was out of the well).

However, consistent with the discussion above, it also meant that generalist political perspectives had pride of place in the White House. And, more than most presidents, Obama relied on advisers without portfolio within the White House, especially Axelrod and Jarrett. While Jarrett formally headed the OPE, she was not tied to that assignment in any serious way day to day, and grew in authority as the term wore on.[68] High-level staff without specific "line" responsibility normally become lost in the West Wing, their power quickly diffused by lack of purpose. But the tight links Axelrod and Jarrett shared with Obama and with others close to him (e.g., Michelle Obama) prevented their marginalization.[69]

All this made for a large "team" and at least the prospect of rivalry. There was friction between State and the envoys, between the DNI and the CIA, between the czars and the departments. Most obvious was the "dysfunctional" relationship between the various persons and institutions with responsibility for dealing with economics and fiscal policy.[70] The flow of information funneled through Larry Summers, the director of the National Economic Council (NEC); but Summers, by his own admission, was an advocate, not a neutral coordinator. He loved the give and take of argument, and he liked to win those arguments. "He isn't an honest broker. He litigates things until he wins," one colleague complained. (Another suggested he was "much better at telling you why you're stupid than creating a system that can produce usable policy solutions.")[71]

The process showed both the pros and cons of a competitive process. On the plus side, it resulted in a wide-ranging discussion and potential policy options, giving the president a plethora of choices. However, decisions took a long time to make; and the sheer number of high-ranking advisers present in the White House, combined with Summers's strong opinions in the coordinating role, meant that the true role of adjudicating debates could fall only to the president. While this appealed to his professorial instincts—Obama happily dove into the minutiae of policy debates[72]—it carried potentially unsustainable costs, in terms of time and cognitive pressures. Those costs rose when views were "settled" too early or when Obama himself found the system failing to generate sufficient information. "Get me some other people's opinions on this," he had to tell Emanuel after one meeting on financial markets regulation: "I want more than what's in this room."[73]

Similar points arose in the 2009 review of the war in Afghanistan. Obama, unfamiliar with military culture, made a point of seeking out information;[74] while he generally worked through the chain of command, not seeking direct material from the field, Obama did utilize aides like Lute, Jones, and the vice-chair of the Joint Chiefs of Staff, Marine general James Cartwright, to provide a reality check on Pentagon assumptions. It became clear, too, that there were multiple lines of access to the president through which national security advice was transmitted—not only through the national security adviser but around him, through NSC and political aides with closer relationships to the president.[75]

Soon after taking office, Obama had approved an increase of 21,000 troops, following up his campaign's emphasis on Afghanistan as a "war of necessity," in contrast to Iraq. This was to be reviewed in a year, in March 2010, but by September 2009 the uniformed military began publicly suggesting that as many as 85,000 additional troops would be needed to achieve American goals. Obama put in motion a long process of examining his options and the broader context they fit in, asking direct questions about those goals ("defeat"? or merely "degrade"?), opportunity costs (were other interests being overlooked, because of focus on the war?), the realities of counterinsurgency, Afghan corruption, and the passive-aggressive role of Pakistan.[76] Some, including the vice president, thought a counterterrorism strategy light on troops and heavy on covert action was the only plausible direction. But it became clear that the military's clear preference was for 40,000 additional troops (the 85,000 was floated, in the memo style made famous by Henry Kissinger, to make the preferred option seem more reasonable). Despite increasingly aggressive efforts to get the Pentagon to provide an array of possible policy choices, a November 2009 meeting featured a rare scolding from the president. "You have essentially given me one option," he told his military advisers. "It's unacceptable."[77] Obama would wind up not only drafting his own compromise, but putting it in writing, a six-page "terms sheet" that specified his preferred goals, timelines, and benchmarks. It provided for 30,000 additional troops, but with a more limited mission under a specified schedule for the beginning of disengagement. Still, the widest range of alternatives had probably never received a full airing; the long discussion, however thoughtful, wound up constrained by the parameters set by its original assumptions.

These processes, then, usefully expose several functions of presidential decision making. One is the need to match personnel with their place in the structure, so that key options are not edited out en route to the president. In both the economic and military cases, the president had to seek out additional alternatives on his own initiative. In the May 2011 decision to risk a raid into Pakistani territory to find and kill Osama bin Laden, the unique vantage of the presidency—and the uncertainties and burdens it brings to decision-making—was on full display. And in other lower-priority areas, where the president had not invested much personal time before the fact (as with oil permitting), he ran the risk of being blindsided by events. This reflects, in part, the potential hazard of reliance on the assumptions and advice of specialist advisers.

[margin note: potential hazard of reliance upon advisors]

Interestingly, in announcing his December 2009 Afghanistan decision, Obama quoted not Dwight Eisenhower the general but Eisenhower the peacetime manager. "Each [national security] proposal must be weighed in the light of a broader consideration," he noted, "the need to maintain balance in and among national programs." If foreign and domestic policy issues are part of the same problem stream for presidents, that implies no less a balancing act is needed in the vantages provided within the advising process as well.

Midterm Shifts

The calibration of that balance began to shift as the term wore on. The Obama cabinet remained very stable over the first two years of the administration; all the original department heads remained in place as of early 2011, with even Defense Secretary Gates having overstayed his original promise to the president to serve just one year. Instead, as the midterm elections approached, it was the EOP economic team that began to crumble. Orszag left OMB, eventually to join Citibank, in the summer of 2010; soon thereafter Summers and Romer announced their departures from NEC and CEA, respectively, to return to their tenured posts at Harvard and Berkeley.

This quiet exodus was made louder when DNI Dennis Blair was eased out of office and national security adviser James Jones retired. More dramatic still was the decision of Rahm Emanuel to resign as chief of staff in the wake of Chicago mayor Richard Daley's surprise announcement that he would not run for reelection in 2011. Emanuel departed on October 1, 2010, to succeed Daley, leaving Pete Rouse as the interim chief of staff.

The "shellacking" of the midterms themselves led to what one Obama aide called "soul searching" and renewed attention to a staff reorganization the president had already set in motion under Rouse's direction.[78] In late 2010 and early 2011, turnover began in earnest. David Axelrod returned to Chicago to begin to plan for the 2012 campaign; Robert Gibbs stepped down as press secretary; and both deputy chiefs of staff, plus the vice president's chief of staff, left the White House, too. Gates announced a summer 2011 departure date, and deputy secretary of state James Steinberg returned to academia.

None of this served to push "a reset button," as one close observer put it.[79] On the whole, the changes occurred gradually, with few recriminations. Blair, and perhaps Jones and Summers, left before they were pushed; Blair, in particular, suffered from the inchoate nature of the DNI post (and the president's decision to back the CIA when Blair attempted to assert his statutory authority over that agency). The departure of White House counsel Greg Craig, on the wrong side of Emanuel and hurt by White House infighting over the policy and politics of closing the Guantanamo Bay detention facility, was perhaps the most contentious of the high-profile personnel shifts.[80]

But certainly the president's choices of successors in all these areas signaled both continuity and low-key moderation. Obama's personal and campaign lawyer, Bob Bauer, replaced Craig. Jones was succeeded by his deputy, Tom Donilon; CEA member and 2008 campaign adviser Austan Goolsbee became the council's chair. The political affairs staff moved to the Democratic National Committee and to the new 2012 headquarters in Chicago; as Axelrod moved west, in a tag team of sorts, his 2008 campaign colleague David Plouffe came to Washington in his stead. Leon Panetta moved from CIA to succeed Gates at the Pentagon.

A series of old Clinton hands also moved back into the White House, in some cases reprising old roles. Jack Lew, OMB director from 1998 to early 2001, returned to that post in late 2010 from the State Department. Gene Sperling, who had directed the NEC in Clinton's second term, succeeded Summers after a spell as a counselor in the Treasury. Bruce Reed, another domestic staffer in the Clinton years, became Biden's chief of staff. And, as Rouse moved back to his quiet "fixer" role in early 2011, JPMorgan Chase executive and former Clinton commerce secretary William Daley became chief of staff. Daley re-consolidated the communications and press operations, and announced a Biden aide, former reporter Jay Carney, as press secretary.[81]

All this signaled renewed attention to economic policy, and to soliciting a better relationship with the business community (even as revolutions erupted in the Middle East and North Africa in the spring of 2011, Obama maintained a public schedule devoted to economic recovery and energy independence). It also elevated people with experience working with divided government, a newly compelling necessity in the 112th Congress. And if it downsized campaign expertise within the West Wing, it hardly meant the new White House was apolitical—merely that its political emphasis was on showing a president rising above the electoral fray.

This was of course the original Obama "brand," and it fed into the broader emphasis on a shift to centrist, more calming, and perhaps more centralized management. Rouse (often termed "the fixer") and Daley were certainly more polished figures than Emanuel, though at the same time less likely to spur new ideas through bludgeoning their colleagues into inspired creativity. Daley was noted for "his crisp suits and management style to match" and as a skilled negotiator who (one former colleague said) would bring "order to the house."[82] Thus scholar David Rothkopf's comment about the elevation of Donilon might serve more generally in assessing the midterm shift: "With Jones, at least you had the illusion of a man of great stature in this important job. We've gotten rid of that and said, no, what we want is Donilon. He's going to make the trains run on time. He's a super-staffer."[83]

But punctual trains might be the key to the remainder of the administration. As Obama took office, after all, he was expected to prompt profound change—but his campaign was built around an odd amalgam of inspirational competence rather than a specific policy agenda. He came into office not selling an agenda but still devising one.

This changed, however, with the passage of the large legislative centerpieces of the 111th Congress (and even with the failure to pass other things, like climate change legislation). If the original staff was selected to give Obama leverage in Congress, the post-midterm "super-staff" model places more emphasis on operations and implementation. "It's fair to say the next phase is going to be less about legislative action than it is about managing the change that we've brought [about]," Axelrod noted. As the president himself put it, "even if we don't lose a seat in the Senate and we don't lose a seat in the House. . . . there's going to be a lot of work in this administration just doing things right and making sure that new laws are stood up in the ways they're intended."[84]

Such a focus on unilateral action is increasingly important, given the boom in rule-making prompted by the large, complex statutes passed during 2009–2010. It is hardly foolproof—witness the president's failure to close the detainee camp at Guantanamo Bay after issuing an executive order to set that in motion the first week of his presidency. (A later executive order effectively waved the white flag, restructuring but reviving the military tribunal system at Guantanamo.) Still, it provides a potential mechanism—for instance, by using regulation to evade legislative gridlock, or by using recess appointments to evade the need for Senate confirmation—for gaining policy traction in the absence of congressional cooperation.[85] And it suggests a different model of issue management. It implies more emphasis on unity and less on diversity, more on administrative strategy and less on legislative gain. In fact, it suggests less emphasis on rivalry—and more on teamwork.

Conclusion

The trade-offs of the "team of rivals" staffing model had become clear by the time the 112th Congress was seated in early 2011. In the abstract, the idea of generating information by confrontation, as endorsed by candidate Obama, is appealing. And in fact, it fits quite neatly the staffing strategies endorsed by scholarship stressing an active and sometimes competitively driven search for advice.

On the other hand, that scholarship also emphasizes that such strategies tend to require a lot of the president. If taken too far, the constant channeling of controversy to the Oval Office might prevent the staffing system from its most crucial function: ameliorating presidential ignorance while preventing presidential overload.

The parameters of Obama's style of issue management in practice highlight both the positive and negative sides of the strategy. The administration, as it took shape, did provide advisory responsibility to a wide range of policy vantages. It relied on generalists, from the cadre of senior advisers to the czars, for organized coordination of specialized policy lines as they made their way to the president. Obama himself actively sought out information, both from aides and from the media—the transition debate over whether he would be able to keep his Blackberry (and thus pierce the presidential "bubble," at least virtually) was more than symbolic.[86] He reached, sometimes aggressively, for competing views.

On the other hand, the system was rarely compatible with quick decision making, which sometimes (as in the Afghanistan review process, and later with regard to Libya) led to political sniping at the president's "dithering." Further, it required the president to invest a good deal of his personal management resources—time and attention—in monitoring and coordination. That Obama had to reach out to force more views to the table means they were not being generated by the structure of the system. With a small circle of advisers ascendant in practice if not on paper, the Obama White House's match to a full "competitive" model seemed at best incomplete.

Yet that is understandable given political realities. Appointments could not completely reflect an Obama ideology—partly because his emphasis on pragmatic compromise outweighed any clear policy preferences—but also because the hunger for representation by groups largely ignored during the previous administration, and the desire to provide reassurance to other groups and observers, could not be denied. The latter, for example, meant continuity in the national security arena, soothing and often substantively valid, but hardly resonant of "Change."

In organizing itself, the White House also had to deal with another fact of life for modern presidents: the media environment. The twenty-four-hour news cycle and the concomitant hunger of cable and Internet outlets for new news, of any level of seriousness, combined with bitter partisan polarization, combined with social networking technology, means that internal arguments (not to mention simple mistakes) will be globally distributed within hours. Thirty years ago the first Reagan team provided the administration with the creative conflict a "team of rivals" can provide—but also provided the public with backbiting internecine battles played out in the press. In the modern media context, it is harder for that to occur without casting doubt on the fitness of the president himself. The efforts of the Obama administration to tighten ranks—even to prosecute leaks—suggested this was an issue on the president's mind.

An additional constraint was precedent and the fact of an ongoing staff template bequeathed from administration to administration. The continued ascendance of the "standard model" of staffing that has developed since the

Nixon administration provides a premade list of job titles and functions which are rarely rethought by incoming presidents. It has survived by helping presidents create a counter-bureaucracy to aid in their efforts to control the executive branch and connect to Washington and the wider world. But the "swelling of the presidency," as Thomas Cronin put it, brings with it its own managerial costs; the structural stickiness of the EOP threatens to shape presidents and their advisory patterns as much as it is shaped by them.[87]

To be sure, President Obama made some important efforts to evade the official advisory architecture. His decision-making process—on issues ranging from the economy to the Libyan intervention to the mission to kill Osama bin Laden—could certainly be contentious. Still, overall that process relied more heavily than advertised on a small, tight-knit group; and that circle "shrank rather than expanded" over time.[88] That seemed likely to continue with the departure of Gates and the September 2011 expiry of JCS chief Mike Mullen's term.

Yet this divergence from the "team of rivals" model seems consistent with the president's own preferences and temperament. Obama was famously self-reliant and hardly insecure in his own cognitive abilities; some found him oddly introverted for such a public figure and stellar communicator. Intriguingly, an October 2010 profile noted Obama's frustration with advisory "friction." It quoted an aide as saying Obama was "a little frustrated with the internal dysfunction. He doesn't like confrontation."[89] That in itself would make it unlikely that a "team of rivals" model would have lasting staying power in the Obama administration.

Any advising system, of course, must mesh with the president's own style and personality; the rational "professor-in-chief" can hardly have liked the dramatic conflict engendered by aides who could be less than reasonable in seeking to win his ear. And as noted above, the political dynamics driving the White House reorganization in late 2010 and 2011 seemed to favor consolidation, not conflict. The future success of Obama's issue management, then, rests on whether he will continue to force his advisers to get him the information he needs, when he needs it, for deliberation and decision. After all, as Obama himself noted somewhat wistfully after the 2010 midterms, "When you're in this place, it is hard not to seem removed."[90] The president might do well to recall one of Napoleon's maxims: that a leader has the right to be beaten—but never to be surprised.

Notes

1. Richard E. Neustadt, *Presidential Power* (New York: Wiley, 1960); Doris Kearns Goodwin, *Team of Rivals: The Political Genius of Abraham Lincoln* (New York: Simon & Schuster, 2005).

2. As reported on ABC News's campaign blog of May 22, 2008, "Obama Proposes 'Team of Rivals' Cabinet." See http://blogs.abcnews.com/politicalpunch/2008/05/obama-proposes.html [accessed April 7, 2011]. See, too, Andrew Sullivan, "Obama-Clinton, A Hate-Filled Dream Ticket," *Sunday Times* of London, May 4, 2008.

3. Katie Couric, "Candidates on White House Reading," CBS Evening News, January 29, 2008, available at http://www.cbsnews.com/stories/2008/01/29/eveningnews/main3767057.shtml [accessed April 7, 2011]; see also Evan Thomas, "Obama Looks to Lincoln," *Newsweek*, November 15, 2008, available at http://www.newsweek.com/2008/11/14/obama-s-lincoln.html [accessed April 7, 2011].

4. See, for example, Matthew Pinsker, "Lincoln and the Myth of *Team of Rivals*," *Los Angeles Times*, November 18, 2008.

5. Quoted in Thomas, "Obama Looks to Lincoln."

6. David E. Sanger and Thom Shanker, "Obama Is Set to Redo Team on War Policy," *New York Times*, April 7, 2011.

7. George W. Bush, *Decision Points* (New York: Crown, 2010); Alexis Simendinger, "Bush's 'Aha!' Moments," *National Journal* (July 23, 2005), 2358; and see, more broadly, Andrew Rudalevige, "'The Decider': Issue Management in the Bush Presidency," in Colin Campbell, Bert A. Rockman, and Andrew Rudalevige, eds., *The George W. Bush Legacy* (Washington, DC: CQ Press, 2008).

8. Michael Barzelay and Colin Campbell, *Preparing for the Future: Strategic Planning in the U.S. Air Force* (Washington, DC: Brookings Institution, 2003), 111.

9. Neustadt, *Presidential Power*, 128.

10. Theodore Sorensen, *Decision Making in the White House* (New York: Columbia University Press, 1963), 71. More broadly see Norman Thomas, "Presidential Advice and Information: Policy and Program Formulation," *Law and Contemporary Problems* 35 (1970): 540-572.

11. John P. Burke and Fred I. Greenstein, with Larry Berman and Richard Immerman, *How Presidents View Reality: Decisions on Vietnam, 1954 and 1965* (New York: Russell Sage Foundation, 1989), 292-293.

12. This figure is derived from the Appendix to the fiscal year 2011 budget released by the Office of Management and Budget. It does not include maintenance and residential staff, nor those who work for the Office of the US Trade Representative, a cabinet-level agency with operational functions that happens to be located in the EOP. For a complete accounting, see Bradley Patterson, *To Serve the President: Continuity and Innovation in the White House Staff*, paperback ed. (Washington, DC: Brookings Institution Press, 2010). Patterson counts 135 separate offices comprising the "whole White House" (p. 4).

13. Harry McPherson, *A Political Education: A Washington Memoir* (Boston: Houghton Mifflin, 1988), 292.

14. Richard Tanner Johnson, *Managing the White House* (New York: Harper and Row, 1974); Roger Porter, *Presidential Decision Making* (New York: Cambridge University Press, 1980); Burke et al., *How Presidents Test Reality*, 274.

15. Charles Walcott and Karen Hult, "White House Structure and Decision Making: Elaborating the Standard Model," *Presidential Studies Quarterly* 35 (June 2005): 303-318.

16. Alexander L. George, *Presidential Decisionmaking in Foreign Policy: The Effective Use of Information and Advice* (Boulder, CO: Westview Press, 1980), 23; Doris A. Graber, *The Power of Communication: Managing Information in Public Organizations* (Washington, DC: CQ Press, 2003), ch. 6; Bryan D. Jones, *Politics and the Architecture of Choice*

(Chicago: University of Chicago Press, 2001), 44; Harold L. Wilensky, *Organizational Intelligence: Knowledge and Policy in Government and Industry* (New York: Basic Books, 1967), viii.

17. This section is drawn from the longer discussion, and references, contained in Andrew Rudalevige, "The Structure of Leadership: Presidents, Hierarchies, and Information Flow," *Presidential Studies Quarterly* (June 2005): 333-360. See also Rudalevige, "'Therefore, Get Wisdom': What Should the President Know, and How Can He Know It?," *Governance* 22 (April 2009): 177-187.

18. Terry Moe, "The Politicized Presidency," in John Chubb and Paul Peterson, eds., *New Directions in American Politics* (Washington, DC: Brookings Institution Press, 1985); David E. Lewis, *The Politics of Presidential Appointments: Political Control and Bureaucratic Performance* (Princeton, NJ: Princeton University Press, 2008).

19. Mike Allen, "Bush to Change Economic Team," *Washington Post*, November 29, 2004, A1.

20. On this point see especially Lewis, *Politics of Presidential Appointments*; Lewis, "Testing Pendleton's Premise: Do Political Appointees Make Worse Bureaucrats?" *Journal of Politics* 69 (2007):1073-1088.

21. The role of the "honest broker" is discussed at length in Porter, *Presidential Decision Making*, and in John P. Burke, *Honest Broker? The National Security Advisor and Presidential Decision Making* (College Station: Texas A&M Press, 2009), 3-11.

22. Tom Korologos, "The White House: An Operating Manual," *Washington Post*, November 23, 2008.

23. Irving Janis, *Groupthink*, 2nd ed. (Boston: Houghton Mifflin, 1982); Paul A. Kowert, *Groupthink or Deadlock: When Do Leaders Learn from Their Advisors?* (Albany: State University of New York Press, 2002).

24. President Clinton, for instance, used his many "Friends of Bill" as extra eyes or brains to provide outside views, just as Kennedy had been known for his proclivity to call on bureaucrats at all levels of the organizational chart in search of unfiltered information about an issue.

25. Herbert Simon, *Administrative Behavior*, 4th ed. (New York: Simon & Schuster, 1997), 241.

26. Matthew J. Dickinson, *Bitter Harvest: FDR, Presidential Power, and the Growth of the Presidential Branch* (New York: Cambridge University Press, 1997), 4, and see 228-231.

27. John Ehrlichman, *Witness to Power* (New York: Simon & Schuster, 1982), 95.

28. Robert Schlesinger, *White House Ghosts: Presidents and Their Speechwriters from FDR to George W. Bush* (New York: Simon & Schuster, 2008), 424.

29. The aide quoted is David Gergen, in a 1985 memo to Regan: see Rudalevige, "The Structure of Leadership," 352. Among other problems, Regan was unable to gain jurisdiction over national security advising, a lack of supervision blamed by the Tower Commission for the Iran-CONTRA scandal.

30. Richard Rose, "Organizing Issues In and Organizing Problems Out," in James P. Pfiffner, ed., *The Managerial Presidency* (Pacific Grove, CA: Brooks/Cole, 1991); Hamilton, *Federalist #73*.

31. See Eliot Cohen, *Supreme Command: Soldiers, Statesmen, and Leadership in Wartime* (New York: Free Press, 2002).

32. Quoted in Liz Sidoti, "Obama Taps Clinton, Gates for US 'New Dawn' Abroad," *Associated Press On line,* December 1, 2008.

33. Quoted in Jonathan Alter, *The Promise: President Obama, Year One* (New York: Simon & Schuster, 2010), 66.

34. Quoted in Peter Baker, "The Education of a President: What Does He Do Now?," *New York Times Magazine,* October 17, 2010, 46.

35. "Remarks by the President and Senator Judd Gregg at Announcement of Commerce Secretary," Office of the White House Press Secretary, February 3, 2009.

36. Ultimately former governor Gary Locke (D-WA) became Commerce secretary. Locke became ambassador to China in 2011, succeeding Huntsman, when the latter resigned in order to seek the Republican nomination for the presidency in 2012.

37. Obama was forced to utilize more political capital on this appointment than he intended, when Geithner proved to have underpaid federal taxes in past years while working for the World Bank. Getting Geithner approved meant that Daschle's appointment, which foundered on somewhat similar issues, had to be abandoned.

38. See the Aberbach chapter in this volume; Clinton quoted in Gwen Ifill, "Three Women Are Said to be Candidates for Cabinet Posts," *New York Times,* December 7, 1992, A1. See more broadly Andrew Rudalevige, "The President and the Cabinet," in Michael Nelson, ed., *The Presidency and the Political System,* 8th ed. (Washington, DC: CQ Press, 2005).

39. Quoted in Goodwin, *Team of Rivals,* 675.

40. Hugh Heclo, "The Changing Presidential Office," in Pfiffner, ed., *The Managerial Presidency;* and see John Burke, "The Institutional Presidency," in Michael Nelson, ed., *The Presidency and the Political System,* 9th ed. (Washington, DC: CQ Press, 2009).

41. Alter, *The Promise,* 20.

42. On OFCI, see Executive Order 13498, dated February 5, 2009. On OPE, see the Heith chapter in this volume.

43. See Robert Draper, "The Ultimate Obama Insider," *New York Times Magazine,* July 26, 2009; David Halberstam, *The Best and the Brightest,* paperback reprint (New York: Ballantine Books, 1993).

44. "Remarks by the President in Welcoming Senior Staff and Cabinet Secretaries to the White House," Office of the White House Press Secretary, January 21, 2009.

45. Paul C. Light, "Obama and the Federal Bureaucracy," in Thomas Dye et al., *Obama: Year One* (New York: Longman, 2010).

46. Ryan Lizza, "The Gatekeeper: Rahm Emanuel on the Job," *New Yorker,* March 2, 2009.

47. Richard Wolffe, *Revival: The Struggle for Survival inside the Obama White House* (New York: Crown, 2010), 97.

48. Stephen Hess, *Organizing the Presidency,* 3rd ed. (Washington, DC: Brookings Institution Press, 2002), 57; in fact, Emanuel had a nameplate on his desk proclaiming his role as "Undersecretary for Go [Expletive] Yourself." See Mike Dorning, "Rahm Emanuel: President's Chief of Staff Has Lost None of His Drive," *Chicago Tribune,* April 26, 2009.

49. Edward Luce, "A Fearsome Foursome," *Financial Times*, February 3, 2010.

50. Jeff Zeleny, "President's Political Protector Is Ever Close at Hand," *New York Times,* March 9, 2009.

51. Alter, *The Promise*, 48; Bob Woodward, *Obama's Wars* (New York: Simon & Schuster, 2010), 289-290.

52. Peter Baker, "A Wartime Chief's Steep Learning Curve," *New York Times*, August 29, 2010, A1; Woodward, *Obama's Wars*, 40.

53. This board was replaced by a new Council on Jobs and Competitiveness chaired by General Electric CEO Jeffrey Immelt in January 2011; see Executive Order 13564, dated January 20, 2011.

54. Warren was named as a special assistant to the president and special adviser to the Treasury secretary, an odd pairing designed to avoid the need to obtain her own confirmation in the Senate as head of the new agency. See the Aberbach chapter in this volume.

55. Beck, "List of Obama's Czars," August 21, 2009, available at http://www.glennbeck .com/content/articles/article/198/29391/ [accessed April 7, 2011]; but see also Fact-Check.org's parsing of this list, entitled "Czar Search," September 25, 2009, available at http://www.factcheck.org/2009/09/czar-search/ [accessed April 7, 2011]. Warren, named in September 2010, would be a ninth.

56. Peri Arnold, *Making the Managerial Presidency* (Princeton, NJ: Princeton University Press, 1986). Even without Daschle, the health "czar" position was contentious enough that funding for it, along with three others, was cut out of the fiscal 2011 budget when it was finally passed in April 2011.

57. See, e.g., Monica Langley, "After Jabs at Cheney, Biden Pursues an Activist Role," *Wall Street Journal*, January 30, 2009.

58. James Traub, "After Cheney," *New York Times Magazine*, November 29, 2009, MM34.

59. Wolffe, *Revival*, 164. See also Traub, "After Cheney"; Woodward, *Obama's Wars*.

60. Executive Order 13490, dated January 21, 2009.

61. See "Obama Says Lobbyists Have Been Excluded from Policy-Making Jobs," *PolitiFact.com*, January 27, 2010, available at http://www.politifact.com/truth-o-meter/ statements/2010/jan/27/barack-obama/obama-says-lobbyists-have-been-excluded-policy-mak/ [accessed April 7, 2011].

62. See the statistics and interactive worksheet online at http://projects.washingtonpost .com/2009/federal-appointments/by-status/ [accessed April 7, 2011]. See also Alter, *The Promise*, 47.

63. White House website; Brian Friel and Kerry Young, "A Trying Relationship," *CQ Weekly*, September 13, 2010, 2076-2079.

64. Jack Rothman, "Appointments and Disappointments: Sizing up Obama's New Cabinet," *Huffington Post*, December 9, 2008 (available at http://www.huffingtonpost.com/ jack-rothman/appointments-and-disappoi_b_149671.html [accessed April 7, 2011]; Alter, *The Promise*, 57, 66.

65. "Inaugural Address," January 20, 2009, available at http://www.whitehouse.gov/blog/ inaugural-address/ [accessed April 7, 2011].

66. Wolffe, *Revival*, 94-95.

67. Wolffe, *Revival*, 109.

68. Draper, "Ultimate Insider"; Dana Milbank, "Valerie Jarrett: The Real Center of Obama's Inner Circle," *Washington Post*, September 29, 2010, A21; Christi Parsons, "The President's Right-Hand Woman," *Chicago Tribune*, February 19, 2011. Rouse called Jarrett's role during the campaign "sort of outside and free-floating," and at least in the early days of the administration this continued within the more formal confines of the White House. Indeed, day to day the OPE is not understaffed: besides Jarrett's chief of staff, there is a separate director for the Office of Public Engagement (plus two deputy directors, plus an astonishing nine associate directors) and another director for the Office for Intergovernmental Affairs (plus two deputy and three associate directors).

69. Draper, "Ultimate Insider"; Milbank, "Real Center."

70. Jackie Calmes, "Obama's Economic Circle Keeps Tensions Simmering," *New York Times*, June 8, 2009; Wolffe, *Revival*, ch. 4; Peter Baker, "The White House Looks for Work," *New York Times Magazine*, January 23, 2011, 36-45.

71. Quoted in Wolffe, *Revival*, 170, and Baker, "White House Looks for Work," 41, respectively.

72. Neil King, Jr., and Jonathan Weisman, "A President as Micromanager: How Much Detail Is Enough?" *Wall Street Journal*, August 12, 2009.

73. Quoted in King and Weisman, "President as Micromanager." For other examples see Wolffe, *Revival*, 170-176; Baker, "White House Looks for Work."

74. Baker, "Steep Learning Curve," A10.

75. Woodward, *Obama's Wars*, 138.

76. A good discussion is in Woodward, *Obama's Wars*, 167-169.

77. Quoted in Woodward, *Obama's Wars*, 278-279. See, too, Bob Woodward, "Military Thwarted President Seeking Choice in Afghanistan," *Washington Post*, September 27, 2010, A6; there Obama is quoted as complaining that the Pentagon were "really cooking this thing in the direction they wanted."

78. Quoted in Anne Kornblut, "'Soul-searching' Inside the White House," *Washington Post*, November 14, 2010, A1.

79. Quoted ibid.

80. Alter, *The Promise*, 340-343; Wolffe, *Revival*, 225-226.

81. See the Heith chapter in this volume.

82. Sheryl Gay Stolberg, "Obama's Top Aide a Tough, Decisive Negotiator," *New York Times*, January 8, 2011, A1; and see also Eric Lipton, "In Daley, a Businessman's Voice in Oval Office," *New York Times*, January 7, 2011, A1.

83. Quoted in Karen DeYoung, "Despite Stature, Jones Was Awkward Fit," *Washington Post*, October 9, 2010.

84. Axelrod quoted in Peter Nicholas and Christi Parsons, "Rebuilding Staff, Obama Charts New Course," *Philadelphia Inquirer*, October 10, 2010, A4; Obama in Baker, "Education of a President," 87.

85. See, e.g., Eric Lichtblau and Robert Pear, "Rule Makers Emerge from the Shadows," *New York Times*, December 9, 2010, A28; Executive Order 13563, dated January 18, 2011.

More generally, see Andrew Rudalevige, "The President and Unilateral Powers: A Taxonomy," in Michael Nelson, ed., *The Presidency and the Political System*, 9th ed. (Washington, DC: CQ Press, 2009). Note that Obama made six recess appointments, including an ambassador to Syria and a deputy attorney general, on December 29, 2010.

86. Wolffe, *Revival*, 6.
87. Thomas Cronin, *The State of the Presidency* (Boston: Little, Brown, 1975), 138; and see Dickinson, *Bitter Harvest*.
88. Wolffe, *Revival*, 7; and see the extensive discussion of this point, including by former Clinton chief of staff John Podesta, in Luce, "Fearsome Foursome."
89. Quoted in Baker, "Education of a President," 86.
90. "President's Press Conference," Office of the White House Press Secretary, November 3, 2010.

CHAPTER 9

Doing Big Things: Obama and the 111th Congress

Barbara Sinclair

IN NOVEMBER 2008, Barack Obama was elected president, the first non-incumbent elected with a majority of the popular vote since 1988. He won by a substantial margin after a campaign promising big changes in policy and in how politics was practiced in Washington. Congressional Democrats won large majorities in both chambers.

These election results raised Obama's supporters' expectations to dizzying heights. Did Obama and the Democrats deliver legislatively? Why was it so hard? What was the public's verdict and how was it related to legislative performance?

The key determinants of a president's legislative success, I argue, are the context in which the president acts and the resources the president commands as a result of that context. This chapter begins with an examination of the political context; it then examines how Obama and congressional Democrats responded to the problems and opportunities the context presented. Finally, it considers the implications for the future of the electorate's verdict.[1]

The Contextual Determinants of Presidential–Congressional Relations

Understanding the relationship between a particular president and Congress and the policy outputs that ensue requires understanding how incentives and behavior are shaped by constitutional, institutional, and political context. Americans have come to expect the president to act as policy leader: to set the agenda and to engineer passage of legislation to deal with the country's major problems. The Constitution, however, establishes a relationship of mutual dependence between the president and Congress and, in terms of policymaking, puts the president in the weaker position.[2] The president is dependent on Congress not just for new programs but also for money to carry out already existing programs, for approval of top-level personnel to staff the administration, and for acquiescence in many of the decisions he makes that Congress, through legislation or less formal means, could hinder.

The Constitution and the undisciplined and decentralized party system that it fostered provide the president with no basis for commanding Congress, but they do give him leverage. By virtue of his veto power, his control of the executive branch, and his access to the media, the president can advance or hinder the goals of members of Congress. Given his dependence on Congress, his inability to command yet his potential capacity to influence, every president needs a strategy for dealing with Congress—a plan or approach for getting Congress to do what he wants and needs it to do in order to accomplish his goals.

A president's strategies vis-à-vis Congress are shaped and constrained by his legislative goals and by the resources he commands. The extent to which a president's policy preferences and those of a congressional majority coincide or conflict influences how a president sets out to get what he wants from Congress as well as his probability of success. So too do the resources the president commands for eliciting support beyond that based purely on policy agreement.

Even when US parties have been at their least cohesive, members of a party have tended to share policy preferences to some extent; consequently, when members of the president's party make up the congressional majority, they and the president will often agree on at least the general thrust of policy, providing a basis for presidential–congressional cooperation.[3] Further, the members of his party have an interest in the president's success that transcends any specific legislative battle. Because many such members believe a strong president will be able to help them attain various of their goals in the future, they may be willing to support him even when their policy preferences do not coincide with his. To the extent that presidential success in the legislative arena breeds a perception of strength that translates into future success, a member of the president's party may believe supporting the president today will pay off in terms of the passage of preferred legislation in the future. To the extent that presidential success has an electoral payoff—increasing the chances of holding the White House or increasing congressional representation—a fellow party member has an incentive to provide support for the president beyond that based purely on policy agreement.

Congressional leaders of the president's party are especially likely to see presidential success as in their best interest; they must concern themselves with the party's image and are likely to be judged by their success in enacting their leader's program.[4] Thus, when the president's party is in the majority, the very considerable institutional and procedural advantages of control of the chamber are usually available to the president.

Members of the other party, in contrast, are likely to see a strong successful president as a threat to their future goal advancement. They are less likely to share his policy preferences, so an increase in his legislative effectiveness may threaten their policy goals. Their electoral goals are diametrically opposed to his; the president wants his party to hold the White House and increase its congressional representation. To the extent that the president's legislative success advances his party's electoral success, contributing to that success is costly for members of the other party.

When the policy differences between the parties are not very great or the opposition party is ideologically diverse, the president may gain significant support from opposition party members solely on the basis of their agreement with his policy stances. However, for the president to elicit support from members of the opposition party beyond that based purely on policy agreement, such members must be persuaded that the costs of opposing the president are higher than the costs of supporting him. The most likely basis for that kind of persuasion is a possible threat to the member's chances of personal reelection. Circumstances that make that threat credible provide a president with significant resources for influencing Congress; their lack leaves a president with little leverage for persuading opposition party members to support him.

Under conditions of unified partisan control, cooperation is the dominant strategy for the president and the congressional majority. The president's success furthers the policy goals of members of his party directly (when they agree with him on the policy at issue) and indirectly (because they expect in the future to agree with him more frequently than they expect to disagree). Presidential success may indirectly further members' electoral goals by convincing the public that the party can govern effectively.

However, while the incentives to support the president are ordinarily considerable for members of his party, incentives to oppose him may also be present and may for some outweigh those dictating support. Neither of the major parties is monolithic; on any given issue, some members will disagree with the president. Policy priorities will certainly differ, and electoral priorities will differ as well. Members want to see their party do well in congressional and presidential elections, but their own reelection is their first priority. If the vote required to bring about the president's success would hurt a member's reelection chances, this direct cost may well outweigh the benefits to the member of presidential success. A member's best reelection strategy may dictate voting against a president of his own party on some major issues. The political context determines whether incentives to defect dominate and for how many members.

Consequently, although cooperation with and reliance on the members of his party is the best strategy for a president whose party controls Congress, the strategy does not assure success. In the American political system, numerical majorities in Congress do not automatically translate into policy majorities. Winning coalitions must be constructed. Depending on the issue, his party's cohesion, and the size of the partisan majorities, the president may need to reach across the aisle.

When one or both chambers of Congress are controlled by the opposition party, the president's strategic situation becomes even more complex, especially when the parties are ideologically polarized. Unless he has the resources to threaten the goals of a significant number of the members of the other party and thus induce them to support him, he will need to bargain and compromise with the opposition party. Yet doing so may alienate members of his own party.

The Political and Institutional Context at the Beginning of the Obama Presidency

Barack Obama won the presidency with 52.9 percent of the popular vote, carrying twenty-eight states. After a gain of thirty seats in the 2006 elections (and three subsequently in special elections), House Democrats added a net of twenty-one more in 2008, giving them a 257-to-178 margin in the 111th Congress. Senate Democrats picked up seven seats with one (Minnesota) undecided, for a majority of fifty-eight at the beginning of the Congress. Thus, the elections determined that the branches would be controlled by co-partisans and that the majorities in both chambers would be large by recent standards.

Further, congressional Democrats were ideologically homogeneous by American standards, certainly considerably more homogeneous than the Democratic congressional majorities that President Jimmy Carter or even President Bill Clinton faced. In the 110th Congress (2007–2008), the mean party unity score of House Democrats was 92 percent; that of Senate Democrats was 87 percent.[5] Only six House Democrats and four Senate Democrats had party unity scores below 80 percent.

Obama and congressional Democrats ran on quite similar issues, as one would expect when the political parties are relatively ideologically homogeneous. Thus they began with considerable agreement on a policy agenda. And the election results could be read as an endorsement of—if not a clear mandate for—that agenda. The economic crisis fueled a sense of urgency in the public and among policymakers alike, further focusing the attention of the new president and his congressional partisans on the same agenda.

The political context, then, encouraged cooperation between Obama and congressional Democrats. For the leaders of the 111th Congress the incentives to make passing Obama's agenda a central objective were especially great. Democrats had been in the minority in both chambers for most of the 1995–2006 period and, during that time, their policy preferences had been largely rebuffed; pent-up demand for policy change among Democrats was immense. As Speaker, Nancy Pelosi was a strongly policy-oriented leader whose basic goal was to pass major policy change.

When the Democrats did take back the majority in the 110th Congress (2007–2008), Pelosi and Senate Majority Leader Harry Reid often found their attempts to legislate frustrated by a president who profoundly disagreed with them and their membership on most major policy disputes. Now they had a president with whom they and their members mostly agreed.

Further, the public's high expectations and the dire economic situation made the likely cost of not delivering exceedingly high. Most of the senior Democratic leaders had served in Congress during the early Clinton presidency and were determined to avoid the mistakes they believed had led to the loss of the Democratic majorities in 1994.

Congressional leaders command organizational and institutional resources useful for putting together and holding together the support needed to pass legislation and thus assist the president in passing his—and his party's—agenda. In both chambers, party organization has become quite elaborate, consisting of a number of party committees and subordinate leadership positions; these provide assistance to the top leadership but also give other members an opportunity to participate in party efforts and thereby increase their stake in their success. Leadership staffs have grown significantly over the years and serve as the eyes and ears of—and sometimes negotiating surrogates for—the leaders.

The contemporary House majority party leadership, especially, commands formidable institutional resources. The increasing ideological homogeneity of the parties over the last several decades made possible the development of a stronger and more activist party leadership.[6] The majority party leadership oversees the referral of bills to committee, determines the floor schedule, and controls the drafting of special rules that govern how bills are considered on the floor. The leaders can bypass committees when they consider it necessary or orchestrate post-committee adjustments to legislation. They can work with (and, if necessary, lean on) committees to report out the party's program in an acceptable form and in a timely fashion; deploy the extensive whip system to rally the votes needed to pass the legislation; and bring the bills to the floor at the most favorable time and under floor procedures that give them the best possible chance for success. House floor decisions are made by simple majorities, and opportunities for minorities to delay, much less block, action are exceedingly limited. Thus a party leadership that commands a reliable majority can produce legislation.

Senate rules are a great deal more permissive than House rules and give individual members much greater prerogatives; a minority of forty-one or more can block passage if it uses its prerogative of extended debate. Because Senate rules do not require amendments to most bills to be germane, senators can force to the floor issues the majority leader might prefer to avoid. Consequently the Senate majority leader lacks many of the institutional tools the Speaker of the House possesses. Still, the majority leader does command the initiative in floor scheduling and is the elected leader of the majority party in the chamber.[7]

If the political context encouraged close cooperation between President Obama and congressional Democrats, did it provide any basis for cooperation between Obama and minority Republicans? Having promised to damp the bitter partisanship that voters at least claim to hate, Obama had some incentive to reach across the aisle. The ideological distance between the congressional parties on most major issues was, however, vast. The partisan polarization that developed in the 1980s and 1990s had resulted in a Republican congressional membership that was both more ideologically homogeneous and more conservative. Further, as the Republican party had shrunk as a consequence of the 2006 and 2008 elections, its center of gravity both coalesced and moved even further right. Republicans' and Democrats' beliefs of what constitutes good public policy were very far apart. The question, then, was whether with little policy agreement to provide a basis for the president to elicit support from members of the opposition party, such members might be persuaded that the costs of opposing the president were higher than the costs of supporting him. In essence, this would depend on how Republicans interpreted the message sent by the election and what they believed their choices would mean for their future electoral prospects.

Economic Crisis and Strategic Response

The Obama presidency began in the midst of the greatest economic crisis the United States has experienced since the Great Depression of the 1930s. Obama, congressional Democrats, and most economists agreed that a significant stimulus bill was essential. Passing such legislation would be the first big test for the new administration and its congressional allies. An examination of the effort reveals the president's and the major congressional actors' strategies that would characterize their interactions during the first Congress of the Obama presidency.[8]

Obama began working with Democratic congressional leaders on a stimulus package well before his inauguration. By mid-December 2008, Obama's transition team members and relevant Democratic congressional staffers were meeting almost daily. As would become a standard Obama strategy, he gave congressional Democrats great leeway, calculating that members who had a major role in shaping legislation would have a much greater stake in its enactment. He gave important jobs in the new administration to people with extensive congressional know-how and high respect on the Hill—as his chief of staff, Rahm Emanuel, a House member who had served as chair of both the Democratic Congressional Campaign Committee and the Democratic Caucus; Peter Orszag, director of the Congressional Budget Office, as head of the Office of Management and Budget;

Pete Rouse, a former chief of staff to Democratic Senate Leader Tom Daschle and then to Senator Obama himself, as a senior adviser; and, as his head of congressional liaison, Phil Schiliro, formerly chief of staff for senior House Democrat Henry Waxman, incoming chairman of the Energy and Commerce Committee.

Democratic congressional leaders and members were eager to work with and help their new president. To give President Obama popular legislation to sign soon after his swearing in, the House Democratic leadership engineered quick passage of the children's health insurance program (SCHIP) reauthorization and the Lilly Ledbetter Fair Pay Act, and the Senate followed—though a bit more slowly and with more difficulty.

Attempting to deliver on his promise of greater bipartisanship, Obama reached out to Republicans on the stimulus bill, sending high-ranking appointees to consult with them and visiting with both House and Senate Republicans himself on their own turf. Obama's initial proposal dedicated 40 percent of the stimulus package to tax cuts, in part to appeal to Republicans. Nevertheless, congressional Republicans demanded still more tax cuts and less spending. Conservatives in the media launched an all-out attack on the Democratic plan, arguing it was not a stimulus at all but just a lot of useless and expensive pork. When the House voted on the bill, not a single Republican supported it. The Republican whip system was aggressively employed to keep any Republican members from straying; even Joseph Cao, newly elected from a poor, majority-black district, was pressured into opposing the stimulus bill.[9]

Bipartisanship would be much harder to engender than Obama had hoped. Most House Republicans had little sympathy with Obama's approach on policy grounds. And further, despite Obama's high popularity, Republicans concluded that their electoral interests dictated all-out opposition. In a polarized environment, their activists demanded it. And Republicans believed that voters, already cynical about government, could be persuaded by the attacks on the bill that it represented venal politics as usual.

The stimulus bill passed the House by 244 to 188 with only eleven Democrats, mostly more conservative "Blue Dogs," voting against it. As would become a pattern, the House Democratic leadership adeptly used its institutional powers to ensure passage. The House committees marked up the stimulus bill during the first week of the Obama presidency and it passed in the second. The bill was considered under a rule that "self executed" (meaning no separate vote was necessary) an amendment making several last-minute changes to the bill; these post-committee adjustments included provisions striking family planning funds and money for reseeding the Mall. Democratic leaders had decided that these provisions, much derided by Republicans and the right-wing media, had become lightning rods that were not worth the pain they were causing their members.

Senate Leader Harry Reid would prove himself a steadfast and skillful ally to Obama as well, but the problems he faced in engineering passage were greater. With the Republican Senate leadership opposed to the bill, he would need a super-majority of sixty votes to break a filibuster. The previous Congress had set a record for minority-party obstructionism (70 percent of major bills encountered a filibuster-related problem); it now became clear that Republicans would continue along that path. In fact, with an opposition party president in the White House, they would feel even less constraint.

When Senate moderates Ben Nelson (D-NE) and Susan Collins (R-ME) began talks about possible revisions to the committee-reported bill, Reid, knowing he needed at least two Republican votes, encouraged their effort. Intense negotiations among these and a larger group of moderates and with Reid and White House officials finally yielded an agreement that could garner sixty votes. It cut the size of the stimulus, but the many Senate Democrats who supported a bigger package had no real choice but to go along.

After cloture was invoked on the compromise bill with the essential help of three Republicans—Susan Collins and Olympia Snowe, both of Maine, and Arlen Specter of Pennsylvania—and the bill passed the Senate, a compromise between the House and Senate bills was necessary. Although the Obama administration had left much of the detailed drafting to Congress, at this point the administration was deeply involved, with Chief of Staff Rahm Emanuel and OMB Director Peter Orszag acting as point men. Pelosi, too, was a key negotiator. And the Senate moderates had to be consulted and kept on board. When talks seemed to hit a wall over funding for school construction, the president phoned Pelosi and House Majority Whip Jim Clyburn to make sure that negotiations moved ahead.

The agreement reached called for a stimulus plan costing about $787 billion. The open conference committee meeting to approve the deal reached behind closed doors was tightly controlled by Democrats intent on holding together the package they had so painstakingly crafted; no amendments were allowed. As the leaders had promised, both chambers passed the conference report before the President's Day recess. Obama signed the bill on February 17, less than a month after his inauguration.

The strategies Obama pursued in the successful campaign to pass the stimulus bill would continue to characterize his relations with key congressional actors and his approach during other major legislative battles during the 111th Congress. He would work closely with the congressional Democratic leadership; he would reach out to Senate Republicans in an attempt to demonstrate a willingness to engage in bipartisan policymaking. He would not attempt to dictate the details of legislation to Congress. The Obama White House would work to help congressional Democrats to move legislation along, but so long as measures reflected Obama's policy views in general thrust, it would wait until the inter-chamber resolution process to play a major substantive role.

That the Senate would be the major obstacle to the enactment of the Democratic agenda was a lesson that clearly emerged from the stimulus battle. With its minority-empowering rules, it gave Republicans their greatest source of leverage in the national government. Although Republicans lost the legislative battle on the stimulus package when three of their members voted to cut off debate, the defectors had extracted significant policy concessions; more important, Republicans concluded that their vociferous opposition was the correct strategy electorally. Bolstered by the conservative media's assault on the bill, the strategy had begun to activate their demoralized base and to raise doubts about the Democrats' approach among the broader voting public.

The critical importance of controlling the terms of the debate illustrated by the stimulus battle was not lost on anyone. Despite commanding the bully pulpit, Obama, busy with establishing an administration and working on myriad pressing problems, saw his opponents seizing the initiative in defining the bill as simply wasteful pork. Urged on by the Democratic congressional leadership, Obama personally took over the job of selling the stimulus bill and did so aggressively and successfully, but some ground had been lost. When the economy did not immediately improve, Republicans built on the doubt they had sown to argue that the stimulus bill had been a costly failure.

Throughout the 111th Congress, Obama's use of the bully pulpit would be a point of friction between congressional Democrats and the White House. Congressional Democrats would regularly argue that Obama did not do enough to shape debate favorably. Some believed that he was too cautious about staking his prestige on such efforts and too concerned about wearing out his welcome with the public. The White House, on the other hand, was acutely aware that a president's ability to shape debate is, in fact, limited and that therefore a president has to be careful to pick his moments.[10]

Passage of the stimulus bill was an essential early victory and it did allow Obama and congressional Democrats to enact bits of their agenda—a program for the computerization of medical records, for example—and to bolster spending for some of their priorities that they believed had been neglected during the years of Republican government. Similarly the omnibus appropriations bill signed into law in March 2009 allowed Democrats to enact many of the domestic spending increases that had been blocked by veto threats from President George W. Bush in 2008. The Obama budget and the largely similar budget resolution passed by Congress also shifted resources toward Democratic priorities, especially toward education and scientific research. Still Obama and congressional Democrats knew that the 111th Congress and the early Obama presidency would not be judged legislatively successful unless they enacted significant health care reform.

Legislative Marathon: Passing Health Care

Obama, like all the other major Democratic presidential candidates, had strongly advocated health care reform throughout the lengthy presidential campaign. It figured prominently in the campaigns of many Democrats running for Congress and a great many incumbent Democrats had been working on the issue for years. But reforming the health care system presented an enormous challenge; the system is highly complex, so effective reform could not be simple—or simply explained. The economic stakes for major industries are huge and pressure from interest groups would be intense. The impacts of reform proposals were likely to vary by region, by urban versus rural, and by income, with the result that divergent interests and views within the Democratic congressional membership were inevitable.

Obama and the congressional leadership were determined to avoid the mistakes perceived as having sunk the Clinton effort to reform health care, and many of their strategic choices were shaped thereby. All of the major industry groups had fought the Clinton bill and that wall of opposition had killed the effort. Obama decided he would attempt to preempt the opposition by drawing the major interest groups into the process; getting and keeping those groups at the table and negotiating deals when possible was a major administration aim from the beginning.[11] Some of the agreements that the White House reached—notably with the pharmaceutical industry—caused problems with congressional Democrats. House Energy and Commerce chairman Henry Waxman believed the deal was too generous and required too little sacrifice from the drug companies, who would after all be gaining millions of new customers. The White House deal-making did, however, prevent monolithic opposition from industry groups; PhRMA, the drug companies' powerful trade association, became something of an ally in passing a bill.

Obama, unlike Clinton, would not send legislative language to Congress; side deals aside, he would set out general principles and let Congress fill in the details as he had on the stimulus bill. He would not draw lines in the sand that would make later compromise difficult.

Further, Obama and the Democratic congressional leadership agreed that the effort had to start quickly. The consensus was that Clinton had waited too long, thus running into election-year problems. Despite considerable advice (much but not all of it from conservatives) to postpone the heath care effort until the economy improved, Democrats began their push as quickly as they could.

Before the Tea Party: Drafting Legislation

To avoid the turf fights that had hindered the Clinton effort, Speaker Pelosi asked the chairmen of the three House committees with significant health case jurisdiction to negotiate a single bill that could then be introduced in all their committees. While the chairs worked, and continued until the bill was enacted almost a year later, Pelosi and her leadership team undertook an intensive campaign of consulting, educating, and negotiating with their members. Although the House Democratic majority was sizable (59%), the leadership knew that constructing a majority for such significant policy change would not be easy.

True, by historical standards the congressional Democratic party was ideologically homogeneous. But it was far from monolithic. The 111th House majority, in fact, included forty-nine members from districts that John McCain carried in the 2008 presidential election. These members tended to be moderates and most felt electorally vulnerable. The Blue Dogs, a grouping of moderate Democrats who could be expected to resist the more sweeping proposals, included a number of 2006 and 2008 freshmen. On the other end of the spectrum was a large group of liberal Democrats, many organized in the Progressive Caucus, who would have preferred a more radical approach than any that was on the table. At minimum, they wanted the bill to include a government health insurance program to compete with private insurance, which they believed essential to keep private insurance companies honest. Dubbed the "public option," it would soon become a center of controversy and, for many Democratic activists, its inclusion become the test of whether a bill represented true reform. Many other issues, based on policy preferences and on constituency interests, could be expected to arise as well.

The bill unveiled in mid-July, produced by the three chairs with some fine-tuning by the leadership, ran into trouble in the Energy and Commerce Committee. Enough Blue Dog Democrats on the committee opposed it as written to deny Committee Chairman Henry Waxman a majority to report the bill out. Their concerns included the form of the public option and what they believed were insufficient cost controls. In a pattern that would repeat itself throughout, the party leadership stepped in to craft a compromise and Obama helped out as well. Pelosi and Majority Leader Steny Hoyer held a series of meetings with all the groups that had concerns. Obama called Energy and Commerce Democrats to the White House for a meeting and a "verbal agreement" on the cost issue was reached. Finally on July 29, "after two weeks of very long and intense negotiations," as one Blue Dog said, a deal was reached.[12]

By late July all three House committees had reported health care reform legislation, as had the Senate Health, Education, Labor and Pensions (HELP) committee, one of the two Senate committees with jurisdiction. All the bills included a form of the public option, though the Commerce Committee's version had been weakened to appease the Blue Dogs. On none of these committees did even a single Republican vote for the bill.

Senate Finance chairman Max Baucus, however, was still trying to craft a bipartisan deal and had not yet begun his markup. Since early in the year, he had been negotiating with ranking member Charles Grassley; he later expanded the group, pulling in four other Finance members from both parties. One target date after another passed by and many Democrats began to voice their suspicion that Republicans had no intention of agreeing to a compromise and were just slowing the process down. Reid cajoled Baucus in private to move, and finally even pressured him in public, but then backed down. If Baucus could reach a bipartisan agreement it would make the task of passing the bill immeasurably easier; with the seating of Al Franken in mid-July (and the earlier switch of Arlen Specter from Republican to Democrat), Democrats had sixty members, but getting every one of them to vote for any bill would be a tall order. Further, Obama continued to send mixed signals. He had stated repeatedly that he wanted both chambers to pass a bill before the August recess; but he also signaled continued support for efforts to reach a bipartisan agreement.

On Thursday, July 30, Baucus announced that there would be no Finance markup before the August recess. Pressured by Reid and his Democratic colleagues who were growing increasingly frustrated, Baucus the next day set a deadline for reaching a bipartisan deal; on September 15 he would move forward with a markup whether or not such a deal had been achieved. The Senate delay led the House to put off a floor vote on a health care bill. Many moderate Democrats did not want to vote before they saw what the Senate Finance Committee produced; they wondered why they should take a tough vote on a liberal bill when the end result might be much less ambitious.

As many Democratic strategists had feared, the August recess proved to be a public relations debacle for Democrats. Since neither chamber had produced a unified bill, congressional Democrats lacked a proposal to defend and wild rumors about the reform gained currency. Opponents staged rowdy protests at some Democratic House members' town hall meetings and the media gave the most disruptive demonstrations enormous play. Republican leaders endorsed the protests and slammed the entire Democratic reform endeavor as an outrageously expensive big-government power grab. The Tea Party movement had become a force in national politics and especially in the politics of health care reform.[13]

Democrats had lost control of the debate and many began to blame Obama. By the time the recess ended, the media were declaring health care reform on life support, if not completely dead. The congressional Democratic leaders pressed Obama to respond more forcefully. During the summer of negotiations, Obama and his closest aides had repeatedly talked privately to various groups of members in an effort to keep the process moving forward; Obama himself had invited to the White House the Blue Dogs, the Baucus negotiating group of six Finance senators, together and individually, various other Republican senators, and, right before the recess, the entire Democratic Senate membership. At both the staff and the principal level, information sharing and discussion of strategy between the White House and leadership offices were continuous. Obama had also promoted health care reform publicly through statements and appearances. Yet the consensus was that he had failed to convey a "clear and coherent" message.

The Long Fall of 2009: Coalition Building and Floor Action

On September 9, Obama delivered a speech on health care to a joint session of Congress. His three goals, he emphasized, "were providing security and stability to individuals who already have coverage, extending coverage to those who don't, and slowing the growth of health spending."[14] The plan would cost $900 billion over ten years but, he promised, would be entirely paid for. The speech was well received by Democrats; the decline in public support for health reform stopped and Democratic members responded positively. "Everybody in the Caucus loved the speech," a moderate Democrat reported. "He made people feel a lot better."[15]

Once Finance reported a bill in mid-October, the next task was getting legislation ready for floor consideration. That required merging the multiple bills into a single bill in each chamber and, in the process, creating a bill that could pass that chamber. Here the party leaders would play the central role, but the White House would also be deeply involved behind the scenes.

The House party leadership had begun the process by the August recess, but the lack of a Senate Finance bill hampered the effort. The leaders knew they could expect no Republican votes at all so they could lose at most thirty-nine Democrats, which meant getting a considerable number of moderate to conservative Democrats on board. The core House negotiating group included the top party leaders and the three chairmen. But, as a Pelosi spokesman insisted, "Everyone is going to be in discussions on healthcare."[16]

A number of major disputes needed to be settled. Whether or not the bill would include a public option—and, if so, what its form would be—received the most media attention. Progressives, including Pelosi herself, strongly favored the so-called "robust" public option, a public insurance plan that would pay providers at the Medicare rate plus 5 percent. Many Blue Dogs preferred no public option at all; some were, however, willing to support the version contained in the Education and Commerce compromise; that called for a public insurance plan with rates negotiated by the secretary of Health and Human Services. The cost of the bill and how to pay for it were contentious issues. Blue Dogs worried about the total cost; junior Democrats from wealthier suburban districts opposed the Ways and Means bill's surtax on the wealthy to pay for a good part of the cost. When Obama in his September 7 speech called for a bill with a maximum cost of $900 billion dollars, the Democratic leaders knew they would have to reduce the price tag on their bill, but doing so created other problems, including ensuring that subsidies for the middle class remained high enough to make coverage affordable. Anti-abortion Democrats insisted on strong language to prohibit any federal funds from being used for elective abortions; pro-choice Democrats were outraged, claiming that this was an effort to make anti-abortion language more draconian than at present. In August, the Tea Party protesters and right-wing bloggers claimed that the Democrats' health care bill would provide benefits to illegal aliens; Republican Joe Wilson's infamous shout of "you lie" at Obama during his health care speech was in response to the president's assertion that this was not the case. Latino Democrats were concerned that, in attempting to assure that undocumented workers would not receive benefits, the bill would place onerous conditions on legal immigrants. Each of these controversies threatened, if not adeptly handled, to drain away crucial votes.

Based on many meetings, whip counts, and her own well-honed sense of where the vote stood, Pelosi made the final tough decisions. The votes for the robust public option were not attainable; the weaker form would go into the bill. Bart Stupak, a fervently anti-abortion Democrat, would be allowed to offer a stringent anti-abortion amendment on the floor; the US Conference of Catholic Bishops opposed the bill without the amendment and that would doom it. On both decisions, Pelosi came down against the position of her strongest supporters, the liberals, and against her own policy preferences. But as leader of her party in the House, she did what was necessary to pass a bill.

In the run-up to the floor vote, the top House leaders, the whip system, and the administration continued to focus on undecided members. One member reported that on the day before the scheduled vote alone he received calls from Obama, Pelosi, White House chief of staff Rahm Emanuel, Health and Human Services secretary Kathleen Sebelius, and Education secretary Arne Duncan.[17] Obama came to Capitol Hill on Saturday, November 7, to talk to the Democratic Caucus. He argued that this was a historic opportunity, perhaps the most important of their careers. He also warned them, a participant reported: "If you think the Republicans are not going to go after you if you vote no, think again."[18]

The bill passed the House on the evening of November 7. The vote was 220-215; thirty-nine Democrats voted against the bill; of those, thirty-one represented districts McCain had won in 2008. Twenty-four of fifty-three Blue Dogs voted against the bill.[19] One Republican, Joseph Cao, voted for the bill, but only after its passage was assured.

Pelosi and her leadership team had again shown themselves to be invaluable allies of the president. They had used their institutional powers to facilitate the bill's passage: their control over the floor schedule enabled them to bring the bill to the floor at the most favorable time; control of the Rules Committee allowed them to have the bill considered under a rule tailored to give the bill its best chance: the committee incorporated the various compromises reached into the bill without a separate vote; it allowed a vote on the Stupak amendment and on a Republican substitute but on no other amendments. Equally important, the leadership team employed its political savvy, its intimate knowledge of its membership and the House, and its prestige to engineer passage of a health care reform bill of major significance.

To the Senate

The task was even more difficult in the Senate. The two committee-reported bills were much further apart than the House bills had been, but more problematic still was the need to put together a bill that could command sixty votes. Finance had reported its bill with the support of only one committee Republican, Olympia Snowe, and she had made it clear her committee vote did not necessarily signal a positive floor vote. Further, many Democrats believed the Finance bill was significantly too conservative.

The core negotiating group in the Senate consisted of Reid, Baucus, Chris Dodd, representing the HELP committee, and, for the White House, Rahm Emanuel and Nancy-Ann DeParle, the president's top health care adviser. OMB Director Peter Orszag also sometimes participated. Reid kept the group small with the hope that would speed action. Nevertheless, the need for sixty votes required Reid to consult widely with his members. He, Baucus, and Dodd held daily meetings with various Democratic senators and occasionally with Olympia Snowe as well.[20]

With sixty votes needed to even bring a bill to the floor and with the likelihood of any Republican support increasingly remote, every Democrat had tremendous bargaining power. A small but crucial group of moderates including Joe Lieberman forced supporters to drop the public option; as the price of his vote, Lieberman also forced a compromise plan to allow people aged fifty-five through sixty-four to buy into Medicare that had been proposed as a partial substitute for the public option to be abandoned. To encourage Mary Landrieu to support the bill, Reid added a provision that would result in more Medicaid funds for still-struggling Louisiana. Ben Nelson negotiated several special deals for his state of Nebraska including one on Medicaid funding and then, at the penultimate moment, he insisted on stronger anti-abortion language.

With Vice President Joe Biden presiding, the Senate passed the health care bill in the early morning of Christmas Eve by a strict party-line vote of sixty to thirty-nine. The Senate had debated the bill for twenty-five days, without breaks for weekends since early December. It had taken thirty-eight roll call votes, some in the middle of the night, some at the crack of dawn. Democrats had had to win five cloture votes, the first just to bring the bill to the floor for consideration. Provisions that a large majority of the Democratic membership strongly supported had been dropped to get the requisite sixty votes. But the majority party had eked out a victory.

The White House was intimately involved in the process of putting together a bill that could garner sixty votes, both via deal-making and via persuasion. The White House sent Interior Secretary Ken Salazar, former Senate Majority Leader Tom Daschle, and Vice President Joe Biden, all former senators, to the Hill to help Reid work the bill. Rahm Emanuel conferred with Reid daily and Nancy DeParle essentially moved to Capitol Hill. Obama continued to meet with key senators individually and in groups. On December 7, at Reid's request, Obama went to Capitol Hill to give Democrats a "pep talk"; and on the 15th, Obama called all the Senate Democrats to the White House for a reprise. His message: we need to get this done; it is an opportunity to make historic progress and we cannot let it slip by.

Obama and the House and Senate Democratic leaders were convinced that Obama's presidency and the Democratic agenda—and likely also the Democratic congressional majorities—were at stake in the health care battle. In July 2009, GOP Senator Jim DeMint had said, "If we're able to stop Obama on this it will be his Waterloo. It will break him."[21] In this, if in nothing else, Democratic leaders agreed with the hyper-conservative DeMint. They believed their fates were closely intertwined with Obama's. They argued it vigorously and incessantly to their members, and persuaded most that failing once again on health care reform would have electoral consequences worse that any resulting from passing a less than universally popular bill.

The messy Senate passage—the result of having to amass a supermajority—took a toll on activists' and ordinary citizens' views of the bill. When the public option had to be dropped, many Democratic activists and liberal bloggers were outraged to the point of calling for killing the bill. Howard Dean proposed just that on television. The more politically savvy and many of those with the best grasp of the policy details responded that killing the bill would be folly, since even without those provisions, the bill represented a major step forward, and another chance was unlikely to come soon. Still, many liberal activists became less enthusiastic about the bill, while conservative activists' opposition remained fervent. Republicans and their media allies painted the deals Democrats had to make to get sixty votes as essentially bribes; the "Cornhusker Kickback," as the Nelson deal was named, was held up as an example of the worst of dirty politics. The public, always cynical about the political process and still suffering from the bad economy, largely bought the portrayal.

Still, significant reform had passed both chambers; the next step was working out the differences in the two bills and then passing the compromise in the House and the Senate. At this point the White House had always expected to be a key player. Obama himself presided over a series of marathon negotiating sessions at the White House during the second week of January.

After the Massachusetts Special Election:
Regrouping and Reconciliation

Most of the features of an agreement were in place when a special election outcome sent shock waves through Washington. On Tuesday January 19, 2010, Republican Scott Brown, running on an anti–health care reform and anti-Washington platform, won the Senate seat left vacant by Ted Kennedy's death in heavily Democratic Massachusetts. The loss deprived Democrats of their sixty-vote supermajority and came close to provoking panic among Democratic members in both chambers. Many commentators and Washington insiders declared health care dead.

Prodded by Pelosi, President Obama decided to double down on passing comprehensive health care reform: he had already bet his presidency on its success; pulling back might lessen the damage of a failure but not by much. In his State of the Union address on January 25, he called for passage, and on February 7, in a TV interview with Katie Couric right before the Super Bowl, he invited congressional Republicans to a health care summit. "I want to consult closely with our Republican colleagues," Obama said. "What I want to do is to ask them to put their ideas on the table. . . . I want . . . Republicans and Democrats to go through, systematically, all the best ideas that are out there and move it forward."[22] The summit would take place February 25, last half a day, and would be televised.

Congressional Democrats' responses ranged from head scratching (what does Obama think this is going to accomplish?) to dismissive (he's just stretching out a painful process with no hope of getting any GOP votes), but the invitation and the subsequent summit accomplished a number of useful things. It put a focus back on the substance of the issue, rather than on congressional maneuvering and dealmaking; it provided some breathing room for the congressional leaders to work with their members but also put pressure on members to come up with an agreement by the time of the summit; and it focused on the Republicans and their lack of health care solutions.

On February 23, in preparation for the summit, Obama released an eleven-page blueprint of what he wanted to see in a final health care bill. It made clear he continued to press for comprehensive reform, largely following the bills that had passed both chambers; it also provided guidance for resolving the remaining differences between the chambers and addressed some of the most serious House concerns with the Senate bill.[23] Republicans cried foul and again called for starting over. Democrats were encouraged by the administration's stronger public posture; and a pleased Pelosi asserted it would accelerate the process of reaching a final bill.

The summit, held at Blair House, lasted for seven hours. It was substantive, serious, and civil but, as expected, led to no breakthroughs. Republicans argued that Congress was incapable of making comprehensive policy effectively and that only small, incremental reforms should be attempted. Obama responded that, given the complexity of the health care system and the interdependence of its problems, only comprehensive change had a chance of working. Congressional Democrats responded favorably, bucked up by the strong case the president made.

The Republican victory in Massachusetts had complicated the procedural landscape. Democrats had lost their sixty-vote Senate margin and, without at least one Republican vote, an unlikely prospect, could not pass a compromise bill through any of the customary procedures. Pelosi had made it clear early on that one route suggested by a number of Senate Democrats and some White House aides was a nonstarter: the House would not simply pass the Senate bill; the votes were not there. Her members opposed the tax on "Cadillac plans"; they believed the subsidies for the middle class were too meager; and they would never vote for the various sweeteners that had become so unpopular. But a route already bruited about now increasingly looked like the only path: the House would pass the Senate bill, but also a bill with the compromises agreed to by the two chambers' negotiators; this latter bill would be a reconciliation bill and thus, under Senate rules, would be protected from a filibuster. Thus Reid would have to amass only fifty-one votes—not sixty.

Obama undertook to sell the health care bill to the public and to build support for the reconciliation path, which Republicans were arguing was underhanded and undemocratic. While Obama traveled around the country and met with many groups of Democrats at the White House, House and Senate Democratic leaders and senior White House staff including Chief of Staff Rahm Emanuel worked out the actual language of the reconciliation bill in a long series of meetings. The House leadership arranged another series of intensive staff briefings to make sure no members could claim not to know what was in the bill. Pelosi, Hoyer, and Clyburn talked to members individually, in small groups, and in the frequent Caucus meetings. They argued on substance and on politics, emphasizing that failing to pass health care would inflict "severe damage" on the Democratic party; they worked out individual, often constituency-related problems that certain members had with the legislation to the extent they could. They also coordinated their efforts with allied interest groups. Pelosi, for instance, in a meeting she called in early March, asked the leaders of national hospital associations for help. Hospitals are "influential employer[s] in most congressional districts, particularly in rural areas represented by many of the wavering House Democrats." According to a meeting participant, the Speaker said, "I don't have the votes. . . . I think we can get there, but I'm going to need help from any place I can get it."[24]

The White House political operation also went into high gear, gathering information and tracking member voting intentions, working with allied groups, getting influential constituents to lobby their members. Obama involved himself deeply in the effort and congressional Democrats who had criticized him for not committing completely gave him much credit for the eventual victory. "Taking it out into the country, the speeches, the rallies, taking on the insurance companies has been important," said Representative Raul Grijalva, co-chair of the Progressive Caucus.[25] The president spent many hours on the telephone and at face-to-face encounters at the White House attempting to persuade Democrats to vote for the bill; in the week before the House vote, he talked to sixty-four.[26]

On Saturday, March 20, with a vote scheduled for the next day, President Obama came to the Hill to speak to the Democratic Caucus. "Every once in a while a moment comes where you have a chance to vindicate all those best hopes that you had about yourself, about this country," he said. "This is one of those moments." The president declared: "We have been debating health care for decades. It has now been debated for a year. It is in your hands."[27]

Even as the countdown to the House vote progressed, the abortion issue continued to raise problems. The Stupak group considered the Senate language not strong enough even though it was the handiwork of staunchly anti-abortion senators, and Stupak threatened to bring down the bill if his stronger language was not somehow incorporated. But even if Senate liberals had been willing to accept the Stupak language, it could not be included in the reconciliation bill because only budget-related matters can go into such bills.[28] Obama broke the stalemate. On Sunday afternoon, the White House and the House leadership announced that, after the House passed health care reform, Obama would sign an executive order to make it clear that no federal funds would be used for abortions.[29] The executive order was to reaffirm the measure's "consistency with longstanding restrictions on the use of federal funds for abortion."[30]

With Stupak and most of the anti-abortion Democrats who had voted for the bill initially now on board, the House on Sunday evening passed the Senate bill on a vote of 219 to 212; thirty-four Democrats joined all the Republicans in opposition. Although a number of the marginal Democrats who supported the bill might have preferred to vote against it but still have it pass, voting against it and having it fail was unacceptable. The reconciliation bill passed a little later on an almost identical vote of 220 to 211.

On Tuesday morning, March 23, President Obama signed the Senate health care bill into law. The Senate then proceeded to consider the reconciliation bill. Republicans knew they could not stop the bill since only a simple majority was required, but they were determined to demonstrate their fervent opposition to their base. They stretched out the debate and offered a stream of amendments, many, Democrats charged, crassly political: an amendment by Tom Coburn, for instance, prohibited prescription coverage of erectile dysfunction drugs for child molesters and rapists. The bill finally passed on March 25 by a vote of 56 to 43. Fifty-six of the fifty-nine Democrats voted for the bill; no Republicans did.

On March 30, President Obama signed the bill into law, completing the enactment of the most far-reaching health care reform since the passage of Medicare in the 1960s. This was a huge policy victory for Obama and congressional Democrats but it was not without cost. The long and messy process had taken a toll on Obama's approval ratings as well as those of congressional Democrats—and on the public's view of the legislation itself.

Legislative Exhaustion and Reelection Dread

Congressional Democrats and the White House had been eager all year to move on to jobs legislation. The economy was improving slowly and, to many people, imperceptibly; jobs were the public's top concern and the public mood was sour. Obama's job approval numbers had declined and Congress's numbers were at a dismal low. Democrats' prospects in the 2010 midterm elections were looking dire. Their electoral fate was tied to the public's perceptions of the economy, they knew; yet Republican obstructionism in the Senate and, increasingly, dissension in their own ranks prevented bold action. Jobs bills passed by the House were stymied in the Senate; concern about deficits fostered in part by a vigorous GOP campaign then eroded Blue Dog support for jobs legislation in the House. By mid-June even an extension of unemployment insurance for the long-term unemployed was in legislative limbo.

Yet, at the same time, Obama and congressional Democrats racked up another major legislative accomplishment as financial regulatory reform legislation became law. The route to passage had been long and tortuous, especially in the Senate. However, as the bill took aim at Wall Street and the behavior that had led to the financial debacle, Senate Republican leaders were unable to block passage; a few moderate Republicans were unwilling to risk being seen as allies of Wall Street, now generally despised.

An extension of unemployment insurance did eventually pass later in the summer, as did a modest package of aid to the states for Medicaid and education. In September the Senate finally managed to invoke cloture on and pass a bill aiding small businesses that Obama had been advocating for months. Clearly, however, the period of big legislative achievements was over. The Senate was largely gridlocked; action on energy and climate change legislation, immigration reform, further ambitious jobs legislation, and even a broadly supported bill on food safety was stymied by the need to get sixty votes.

With the 2010 midterm elections looking more and more disastrous for their party, congressional Democrats increasingly questioned whether supporting their party's and their president's agenda would, in fact, help them at the polls. Obama and their leaders had been telling them since January 2009 that they and their president would sink or swim together; that, if the unified Democratic government did not deliver on its legislative promises, the result would be electoral defeat. Now, even though they had delivered on much of the agenda, it appeared they would sink anyway and perhaps because they had taken the tough votes. Democrats from marginal, more conservative districts and states were most worried and balked at voting for more spending—or on any measure that could be interpreted as raising taxes, even on the very well-to-do. Democrats across the ideological spectrum blamed the president for not doing a better job of selling their achievements, and House members complained that Obama concentrated his electoral help on senators and gave House members short shrift. House Democrats' unhappiness with Obama, however, paled in comparison with their anger at the Senate; progressives were furious that, in a Congress with such big Democratic majorities, many of their priorities had stopped short in the Senate. Moderates from red districts were equally upset that they had taken the tough votes on issues such as climate change only to see them, too, go nowhere in the Senate. And, of course, many of the moderates blamed their party leaders as well.

The poll numbers and pundits that predicted a big Republican win in November reinforced congressional Republicans' commitment to their strategy of all-out opposition. House Republicans could, by and large, only carp; but their Senate colleagues could bring the legislative process to a halt. "Sen. McConnell came to Sen. Reid several months ago and said, 'If you haven't noticed, it's over. You can stay as long as you want, but nothing's going to happen,'" Majority Whip Dick Durbin reported before the August recess.[31] And given Senate rules and forty-one members who saw major electoral benefits in blocking the majority from amassing achievements that might help them in the midterms, McConnell was, to a large extent, able to deliver gridlock.

The Verdict and Its Consequences

In the 2010 midterm elections, Democrats lost over sixty House seats and control of the chamber; they lost six Senate seats but maintained a majority, though one reduced to fifty-three. Obama and his party allies in Congress had promised to do big things and they did, yet the overall verdict of the voting public was resoundingly negative. Could Obama have prevented the electoral debacle and, if so, how?

Election interpreters, professional and amateur, have offered a variety of answers. Some contend that the legislative agenda was at fault; if Obama and congressional Democrats had concentrated on jobs and not on health care, the results would have been better. It is true that everything political scientists have learned about congressional elections confirms that if jobs legislation (or anything else) had lowered the unemployment rate from 9.5 percent to, say, 5 percent, Democrats would have fared much better at the ballot box. But it also indicates that jobs legislation that lacked such a dramatic impact would have made little difference. Senate rules and adamant Republican opposition made the prospect of a game-changing jobs bill unrealistic. Had Obama in early 2009 reneged on his promise to reform health care, the Tea Party phenomenon might have not have materialized, but the Democratic base and many congressional Democrats would have felt utterly betrayed. And the anger and anxiety that fueled the Tea Party phenomenon might well have focused on some other issue.

Perhaps it was process, not policy, that was at fault. If the process, especially but not only on health care, had been less messy, the public verdict would have been more favorable, some have argued. Specifically, Obama should not have "let" Congress draft the stimulus bill, the budget bills, and, of course, the health care bills. That argument is predicated on the counterfactual notion that a president has the power to dictate to Congress; a democratic legislative process does tend to be messy because legislators must be persuaded, not just told, what to do. To be sure, Obama and the congressional leaders might have done things to make the process look less messy; they might somehow have figured out a way to keep the health care fight from dragging on so long. But the changes and their effect would likely have been at the margins. And the evidence is overwhelming that a bipartisan process was never in the cards; the Republican leaderships in both chambers made their decision on strategy early: oppose, don't compromise.

The argument that the failure was one of PR, of framing and persuading the public, like the argument about process, holds a grain of truth: certainly Obama could have done a better job. But the political science literature indicates the impact would have been at the margins.[32] Presidential rhetoric cannot make the public feel good about their government and their leaders when the economy seems in a permanent slump and unemployment remains at 9.5 percent.

Elections have consequences, pundits like to say. What are the likely consequences of the 2010 midterms? Since the Republicans won by refusing to compromise, their incentives to change course would seem to be minimal. Their base—especially the Tea Party faction—is sure to be watching closely. Senate Minority Leader Mitch McConnell's repeated statement that his number-one priority was to defeat Obama in 2012 promises little softening in his approach. Even leaving aside electoral considerations, the very real and large differences between the parties in their notions of what is good public policy makes compromise on many major issues extremely painful at best.

The surprisingly productive lame-duck (postelection) session of the 111th Congress did raise hopes that the 112th might not be doomed to gridlock. The "New START" (Strategic Arms Reduction) treaty was ratified; the "don't ask, don't tell" policy of the military on homosexuals was repealed; and a deal on extending the Bush tax cuts and unemployment insurance was reached.

A galaxy of GOP foreign policy and defense superstars from past Republican administrations vocally supported the START treaty and yet Republican senators split 13 to 26 against. DADT repeal, which polls revealed to be broadly supported by the public, picked up eight GOP votes, but thirty-one voted against. The tax cut package, however, was negotiated between President Obama and Senate Minority Leader Mitch McConnell and was passed by bipartisan majorities in both chambers. Republicans got what they valued most—an extension of the Bush tax cuts for everyone, including the most affluent, and the estate tax set at a much lower rate than Democrats preferred. Obama got a continuation of the tax cuts for the middle class, an extension of unemployment insurance for thirteen months, and, instead of some tax reductions for the working poor that were expiring, a two-percentage-point cut for a year in employees' payroll taxes—all measures the administration considered crucial to keep the economic recovery on track. And both avoided the possibly devastating blame attendant on a big increase in most Americans' taxes come January. Liberal Democrats who objected to tax breaks for the affluent and very conservative Republicans who wanted the tax cuts made permanent disliked the package but were marginalized.

So is this a possible model for the 112th Congress? Might some significant bipartisan agreements addressing major problems—deficit reduction, entitlement reform, immigration—be reached?

What was done at the beginning of the 112th Congress as well as what did not get done in the lame duck suggest that is unlikely. House Republicans began the 112th by passing the "Repealing the Job-Killing Health Care Law" Act. Although Democratic control of the Senate means the repeal is unlikely to go further, Republicans have vowed to do everything in their power to block funding for implementing the Affordable Care Act. No room for compromise is evident. During the lame-duck session, Senate Republicans blocked legislation appropriating funds for the government through FY 2011; instead, a continuing resolution maintaining funding at current levels until March 2011 was enacted. Republicans did so because they had promised to cut hundreds of billions of dollars from the budget and intended to start delivering early in 2011. The necessity of raising the federal debt ceiling (to prevent the US government from defaulting on its debt) by late March confronts the new Republican House majority with a difficult vote but also provides them with a lever they hope to use to force Obama to accept deep spending cuts. To avoid alienating his own base, Obama needs to vigorously resist the House Republicans' most cherished initiatives. Democrats' control of the Senate serves as another barrier to the enactment of the GOP agenda, but with its smaller majority provides a weak basis for furthering a Democratic agenda.

Any hope of a productive 112th in which Obama and Congress work together to fashion broad-ranging bipartisan deals on domestic policy needs to identify areas where a compromise that furthers both parties' electoral and policy goals exists. In a period of such high partisan polarization that any significant ones do is questionable. Therefore, near gridlock is the most likely prognosis. What absolutely must get done will get done: Congress will fund essential services and programs, though there will be much controversy about what is essential. Congress will not allow the US government to default on its debts. But the 112th Congress will not "do big things," despite Obama's urgings in his 2011 State of the Union message.

In the longer term, the lessons politicians are likely to take from the elections are perhaps more important. With the GOP's "just say no" to compromise strategy having paid off so richly, emulation by future minority parties is likely. With Democrats' major legislative successes having certainly not paid off electorally, future majorities may well be leery of attacking big and complex problems with comprehensive, non-incremental legislation. For better or worse, then, Congress may not "do big things" again anytime soon.

Notes

1. In addition to the sources cited, this chapter is based on the author's interviews and conversations with members of Congress, staff, and informed observers, on congressional documents, and on newspaper reports.
2. Charles O. Jones, *The Presidency in a Separated System* (Washington, DC: Brookings Institution, 1994).
3. Jon Bond and Richard Fleisher, *The President in the Legislative Arena* (Chicago: University of Chicago Press, 1990).
4. Barbara Sinclair, *Majority Leadership in the U.S. House* (Baltimore: Johns Hopkins University Press, 1983), and *Legislators, Leaders, and Lawmaking* (Baltimore: Johns Hopkins University Press, 1995).
5. A member's party unity score is the percentage of times the member voted with his or her party colleagues on recorded votes on which a majority of Democrats voted against a majority of Republicans. Data are from *CQ Weekly* at cq.com, 2008, 3332-3342.
6. Sinclair, *Legislators, Leaders, and Lawmaking*; David Rohde, *Parties and Leaders in the Postreform House* (Chicago: University of Chicago Press, 1991). Barbara Sinclair, *Party Wars: Polarization and the Politics of the Policy Process* (Julian Rothbaum Lecture Series, University of Oklahoma Press, 2006).
7. Steven S. Smith, "Forces of Change in Senate Party Leadership and Organization" in *Congress Reconsidered*, ed. Lawrence C. Dodd and Bruce I. Oppenheimer, 5th ed. (Washington, DC: CQ Press, 1993), 259-290; Barbara Sinclair, "The New World of U.S. Senators," in *Congress Reconsidered*, 9th ed. (2009), 1-22.
8. See also the Weatherford chapter in this volume.
9. *The Hill*, December 13, 2009.
10. George C. Edwards III, *The Strategic President: Persuasion and Opportunity in Presidential Leadership* (Princeton, NJ: Princeton University Press, 2009).
11. See the Jacobs chapter in this volume.
12. *Politico*, July 29, 2009.
13. See the Jacobson chapter in this volume.

14. *Congressional Quarterly Weekly*, September 14, 2009.
15. Interview with author.
16. *Politico*, August 4, 2009.
17. *Washington Post*, November 7, 2009.
18. Quoted ibid.
19. *New York Times*, November 8, 2009.
20. *Roll Call*, October 22, 2009.
21. *Politico*, July 17, 2010.
22. *New York Times*, February 8, 2010.
23. *Washington Post*, February 27, 2010.
24. *Los Angeles Times*, March 8, 2010.
25. *New York Times*, March 20, 2010.
26. Ibid.
27. *New York Times*, March 21, 2010.
28. The Budget Act allows the yearly budget resolution to call for a reconciliation bill that cannot be filibustered in the Senate. The Senate's Byrd rule, however, limits what can be included in a reconciliation bill to budget-related matters. See Walter Oleszek, *Congressional Procedures and the Policy Process*, 7th ed. (Washington, DC: CQ Press, 2007), chap. 2.
29. *Roll Call*, March 21, 2010.
30. *New York Times*, March 21, 2010.
31. *Roll Call*, August 9, 2010.
32. Edwards, *Strategic President*.

CHAPTER 10

Obama and the Law: Judicial Restraint at the Crossroads

David A. Yalof

BARACK OBAMA'S FIRST OFFICIAL STATE of the Union address began like most previous ones: speaking before a joint session of Congress on January 27, 2010, the president reviewed his administration's accomplishments to date, then offered a list of proposals for the coming year, including renewed efforts at job creation, government spending freezes beginning in 2010, and continued efforts at passing comprehensive health care reform. Yet none of Obama's various agenda items captured nearly as much attention as when he chose to comment during the address on the Supreme Court's six-day-old ruling in *Citizens United v. Federal Election Commission*,[1] which held that corporate funding of independent political broadcasts in elections was protected by the First Amendment. Condemning the decision for reversing "a century of law" that would "open the floodgate for special interests," Obama took the unusual step of criticizing the court's decision in a venue where several of the justices were present—indeed, the chief justice and five of the eight associate justices were sitting less than twenty-five feet away from the president's rostrum. Certainly the court's more conservative members did not take their medicine without a fight. Justice Samuel Alito was caught on television cameras mouthing "that's not true" in response to the president's comments; as for Chief Justice John Roberts, he later told a crowd at the University of Alabama that the president's actions had been "troubling," helping turn the annual address into little more than a "pep rally" and raising the question of why the justices continue to attend this annual ritual at all.[2]

Obama's willingness to publicly scold the Roberts Court majority for revisiting long-standing precedents in campaign finance jurisprudence fits neatly into a broader story line pitting the young Democratic president against a conservative Republican chief justice with nothing less than the future constitutional landscape hanging in the balance. Though separated by six years in age (Obama was born in 1961; Roberts in 1955), both were magna cum laude graduates of Harvard Law School; both vaulted to the highest rung of their respective institutions of government after just a short apprenticeship below (Obama served as US Senator for four years; Roberts was a federal judge for two years). The mainstream media quickly gravitated to the story line of "Obama v. Roberts: The Struggle to Come," with Obama portrayed as battling Chief Justice Roberts and his allies' resort to "judicial activism" in support of conservative causes.[3] The emerging conflict seemed even more dramatic given their prior interactions, including Obama's vote against Roberts's confirmation as chief justice (one of just twenty-two Senators to do so), and their awkward exchange at Obama's January 2009 swearing-in as president, when both men botched their constitutionally prescribed lines.[4]

Such a story line would indeed be dramatic . . . if only it were true. Yet aside from the State-of-the-Union dramatics, Barack Obama's efforts to transform the constitutional landscape have actually paled in comparison to the efforts of many of his White House predecessors, including Franklin Delano Roosevelt, Richard Nixon, and Ronald Reagan. All three of those earlier chief executives utilized battles with the court as a fundamental tool in their respective administrations' arsenals for policy change. By contrast, Barack Obama has generally sidestepped the courts in his efforts to implement more sweeping policy reforms.

There are several possible explanations for the president's more cautious approach in this context. First, it may be a simple political calculation on his part: this president avoids the courts because he is not optimistic about his chances for victory in that venue. Early in his administration, the lower courts were rightly considered a conservative bastion, dominated by the appointees of conservative presidents who had held the White House for twenty of the previous twenty-eight years. As for the high court itself, the five-justice majority in *Citizens United* (Chief Justice Roberts and Justices Alito, Kennedy, Thomas, and Scalia) was the same conservative bloc that narrowly upheld the federal partial-birth abortion statute in *Gonzales v. Carhart*.[5] Those same five justices also voted to invalidate a race-conscious means of achieving educational diversity in *Parents Involved v. Seattle School District No. 1*.[6] Why would Obama look to such a conservative bench for redress?

Second, unlike Franklin Delano Roosevelt, who needed the court from the outset to rewrite constitutional law to protect his legislative initiatives, Obama benefits from favorable precedents dating back more than three-quarters of a century, which afford Congress considerable deference so long as legislation does not infringe on a clearly delineated constitutional right. Many of those precedents have taken firm hold within the American political system, and no longer require extensive litigation efforts in their defense.

A third explanation is perhaps the most likely: that Barack Obama's "skepticism about court-ordered change" may actually be driving him to look elsewhere as a matter of principle.[7] Principles of "judicial restraint" compel courts to defer to the policy decisions made by politically accountable government institutions. In the short term, where one stands on judicial restraint usually depends on what one stands to gain. Thus as a concept, judicial restraint is normally attractive to all those who agree with the decisions of the democratically elected legislatures and publicly accountable executives that are currently in power. During the 1920s and early 1930s, judicial restraint was the siren call of liberals frustrated with the court's willingness at that time to intervene against socially progressive legislation, including large chunks of the New Deal. Yet when the Warren Court revolution reached its peak in the 1960s, conservatives became the latest apostles of judicial restraint, celebrating the decisions made by state officials and state legislatures to limit defendants' rights and social privacy protections.

During the first part of the twenty-first century, politically active conservatives— most of whom affiliate with the Republican Party—have offered some notable contradictions in their approach to the question of judicial restraint. On one hand, most conservatives favor judicial restraint by federal courts as a general matter; Chief Justice Roberts himself has publicly extolled the virtues of "judicial minimalism," arguing succinctly that "if it is not necessary to decide more to dispose of a case, in my view it is not necessary to decide more."[8] Such minimalism amounts to a jurisprudence of deference, which "recognizes the limited role of the federal judiciary and makes a large space for democratic self-government."[9] And yet many of those same conservatives applaud the Roberts Court for its willingness to carve out exceptions in such areas as gun control, campaign finance regulation, and the use of eminent domain powers. They also hold out the hope of a judiciary willing to invalidate health care reforms when they come up for review. Of course, constituencies within the Democratic party assume contradictory positions on judicial restraint as well. Social liberals who celebrated judicial activism during the Warren Court era now hope the Roberts Court will exercise judicial restraint to leave those earlier precedents intact. Moderates within the party who tend to favor judicial restraint across the board should theoretically oppose judicial activism in support of same-sex marriage as yet another instance of the courts lurching ahead of the body politic as a whole; yet as a practical matter, many offer little or no opposition to such judicial forays.

As a candidate for president in 2008, then senator Barack Obama strongly opposed the war in Iraq; on other issues, however, he assumed the profile of a more moderate Democrat. He offered support for civil unions, but insisted that the issue of same-sex marriage be left to the discretion of state legislatures. Obama expressed support for the death penalty; he also declared his support for the USA Patriot Act and other aspects of anti-terrorism legislation, as modified by the Congress in 2006. None of those positions endeared him to the political left. Nevertheless, they did offer an early indication of the candidate's reluctance to invite judicial intervention in support of more liberal policies, or to seek solutions from courts more generally.

As president, Obama has not retreated from these campaign positions. His war on terrorism has been every bit as forceful as that of his predecessor, maintaining the Bush administration policy on holding certain prisoners indefinitely and without judicial recourse. The Obama administration has also invoked the so-called state secrets doctrine, whereby evidence may be classified and removed from litigation based solely on a government affidavit stating that court proceedings might disclose sensitive information which could "endanger national security." Amid the controversy surrounding Obama's highly public method of criticizing the Roberts Court, these critical realities are often forgotten.

Filling Two Supreme Court Vacancies In His First Two Years

Unlike most other events of major significance in American politics, Supreme Court vacancies tend to occur at unpredictable intervals. George W. Bush had to wait nearly five years for his first Supreme Court vacancy; Jimmy Carter never got the chance to name even one justice during his single term. By contrast, Presidents George H. W. Bush, Ronald Reagan, and Bill Clinton all appointed at least one justice before reaching the midpoint of their first terms. Barack Obama joins the latter list of more fortunate chief executives, having had the opportunity to fill a high court vacancy in each of his first two years as president.

David Souter and John Paul Stevens, the two justices who retired in 2009 and 2010 respectively, were both members of the moderate-to-liberal bloc on the high court. Both men expected Obama would replace them with similar-minded jurists, and the Democrats' strong hold on the Senate (at least fifty-eight caucusing members throughout the 111th Congress) afforded the president considerable leeway to make that happen. Senator Lindsey Graham (R-SC), explained that while he might disagree with the judicial philosophies of Obama's appointees, his votes would rest in part on the theory that Barack Obama won the White House and "elections matter." Yet because Obama replaced two relatively liberal Justices with their ideological equivalents, neither of his first two appointments afforded him the opportunity to transform the constitutional landscape to any significant degree.

The first vacancy of Obama's term occurred while the young president was still getting his feet wet. After privately notifying White House officials of his intention to retire in April of 2009, Justice David Souter made his intentions public in a formal letter to the president dated May 1, 2009. Barack Obama's role in the selection of Souter's successor differed from that of previous presidents. First, as a former constitutional law teacher, the president exhibited heightened interest in even the most archaic writings of potential high court candidates. Thus, unlike past chief executives who relied on aides to vet the candidates for their potential views,

Obama was in a position to make many of these judgments for himself. Second, as the first senator to be elected president in nearly four decades, Obama's views of the Senate's "advise and consent" functions were notably broad. Early in the selection process, the president called every member of the Senate Judiciary Committee (Republicans and Democrats) to solicit their suggestions for candidates. According to Senator Charles Grassley (R-IA), this was "the first time" he had "ever been called by a President on a Supreme Court nomination, be it a Republican or a Democrat."[10] With partisan wars over health care still looming in the future, Obama's first Supreme Court nomination marked an increasingly rare moment of cross-party consultation.

Long before Souter confirmed his plans to leave, White House counsel Gregory Craig was already preparing a short list of potential Supreme Court candidates.[11] Emphasizing demographic traits that had been underrepresented on the court to date, these early lists tended to emphasize female candidates in general, and Hispanic American candidates in particular. By the end of April, Craig's team had drafted sixty-page memoranda on several candidates, most of whom fell into one or both of those two critical demographic categories. Of those under consideration, Judge Sonia Sotomayor of the US Court of Appeals stood apart as the only candidate who managed to fulfill *both* demographic criteria. The short list of candidates also included two non-judges (Solicitor General Elena Kagan and Homeland Security secretary Janet Napolitano), as well as US Court of Appeals judge Diane Wood. Not since William Rehnquist's appointment in 1972 had a president successfully appointed a member of his current administration to the high court.[12]

Obama's determination to name a second female justice to the US Supreme Court was evident: All four candidates invited to the White House in May for interviews (Sotomayor, Wood, Kagan, and Napolitano) were women. The president's desire to appoint the first Latina in the court's history was also genuine, though not apolitical: Latino subgroups, among the fastest growing ethnic groups in the country, had favored Obama over John McCain by a 2-1 margin in the 2008 presidential election.[13] In key battleground states like Florida, where Latinos had historically supported Republican presidential candidates, Obama won by sizable margins. The chance to help secure that group in the Democratic column, while at the same time making history, proved irresistible to the new president. The only Latina on the final short list was Sotomayor; when her interview went well, she quickly moved to the head of this distinguished class.

If President Obama was concerned about confirmability, the choice of Sotomayor offered some reassurances. To members of the Senate committed to the need for judicial experience, Sotomayor offered nearly seventeen years of service on the federal bench. Among other Supreme Court nominees in the modern era, only Justice Alito (sixteen years) approached that length of service before arriving at the high court. During her five-year tenure as a prosecutor in New York City she was described as "fearless and effective," allaying fears that she might be too liberal on defendants' rights. Supporters of her nomination could also point to a level of bipartisan support in her past: a Republican president, George H. W. Bush, had been responsible for her first judicial appointment in 1992. Even sports fans had something to cheer about: in 1995 Federal District Judge Sotomayor had issued an injunction against Major League Baseball, effectively ending a seven-month-old baseball strike.

President Obama formally nominated Sotomayor to the US Supreme Court on May 26, 2010. Though her final confirmation was never in doubt, at least two controversial issues raised the prospect of more grueling confirmation hearings. First, critics pointed to a line from a 2001 speech, in which Sotomayor offered the hope that "a wise Latina woman with the richness of her experiences would more often than not reach a better conclusion than a white male who hasn't lived that life." At her hearings in July, the nominee termed the remark "a rhetorical flourish that fell flat" and stated that she did not believe any ethnic or gender group had an advantage in sound judgment. Though some Republican Senators feared her future rulings might reflect that initial sentiment, they were unable to generate much public furor for disqualifying her nomination on that ground alone. The other controversy arose over her dissenting vote in *Ricci v. Destefano*,[14] in which her appellate court upheld the claim by seventeen New Haven firefighters that they had been denied promotions because of their race. Sotomayor defended her vote as simply following applicable precedent. The Supreme Court had just a few weeks earlier affirmed the court of appeals' decision by a 5-4 vote; the fact that four Supreme Court Justices adopted the position in her dissent helped counter charges that her views on discrimination were too far outside the mainstream. On August 6, 2009, the Senate confirmed Sotomayor by a 68-31 vote.

On April 9, 2010, Justice John Paul Stevens announced his plans to retire from the court at the end of that court's term. The year 2010 proved different than 2009 in one important respect: with a second female justice now safely ensconced on the court, the White House was more open to male candidates than it had been a year earlier. Less than three weeks after Stevens's announcement, the *New York Times* reported that President Obama had interviewed two candidates for the vacancy: Judge Merrick Garland of the US Court of Appeals for the DC Circuit, and one new name, Judge Sidney Runyon Thomas of the US Court of Appeals for the Ninth Circuit in Montana.[15] A Stanford Law professor, Pamela Karlan, also drew White House attention despite the controversy inherent in appointing an openly gay candidate to the high court. Yet none of these names was able to displace two finalists from the previous year: Wood and Kagan. Both were reinterviewed for this second vacancy as well.

As media speculation focused heavily on Kagan during the first week of May, three aspects of her candidacy garnered the most attention: (1) the lack of any judicial experience in her background;[16] (2) a reputation for "accommodating and incorporating" conservative views as Harvard Law School dean; and (3) her open embrace of "broad wartime authorities" while testifying at her confirmation hearings for solicitor general in 2009. White House officials believed the first two objections could be overcome. As to the third, Kagan's faith in executive power had been cultivated in the late 1990s when she served as President Bill Clinton's associate White House counsel and deputy assistant to the president for domestic policy. In fact, far from its being a strike against her, President Obama was likely drawn to a candidate who might support his administration's broad authority to prosecute the war on terrorism.

President Obama formally introduced Kagan as his nominee on May 9, 2010. The only issue to cause so much as a stir at her confirmation hearings concerned her decision as Harvard Law School Dean in 2003 to enforce the school's policy of banning military recruiters from the Office of Career Services on the ground that its "don't ask, don't tell" policy discriminated against gays and lesbians. In response to tough questioning from Senate Republicans, Kagan testified that though she opposed the Pentagon's policy, the school was "never out of compliance" and that the military had alternative access to the law school. Kagan's responses satisfied few of her doubters, but that issue alone would not undermine her candidacy. The full Senate voted to confirm her nomination by a 63-37 vote on August 5, 2010.

Judged on the basis of two relatively easy confirmation battles, President Obama's selection of Supreme Court Justices Sonia Sotomayor and Elena Kagan rate as successful. In the case of Sotomayor, Obama made history by naming the first Latina justice, and helped to satisfy a key political constituency in the process. The administration also earned credit for breaking loose from criteria that had seemingly hamstrung recent presidents in the selection process: rather than simply making statements about the need for non-jurists to diversify the court, Obama interviewed several administration officials for the two vacancies, and he then named a non-jurist to the second vacancy that came available. Additionally, for the first time in history, a US president formally considered an openly gay candidate for a Supreme Court seat.

Yet in practical terms, President Obama did little to transform the Supreme Court along more liberal or progressive lines. In fact, the appointment of Kagan to replace Stevens may have actually moved the court to the right on some issues. This fact alone might frustrate Obama's more liberal constituencies unless they consider two key factors: (1) most presidents need at least two terms in office to create long-lasting change on the court; and (2) President Obama's own political philosophy tended to favor policymaking by democratically accountable branches rather than the judiciary. His choice of two less extreme Supreme Court nominees was not a bipartisan act on his part; rather, it was a manifestation of his own personal reluctance to fill the high court with judicial activists of any kind.

Successes and Frustrations in Lower Court Appointments

In the context of federal judicial selections as a whole, Supreme Court appointments consume a disproportionate amount of the public's attention, and in turn, the bulk of presidential resources as well. Lower court appointments, by contrast, tend to fly under the public's radar screen. Up through the 1980s, lower court appointments tended to proceed according to the unwritten custom of senatorial courtesy: the White House consults the senior US senator from the president's own political party before nominating any person to a federal vacancy within that Senator's state. So long as that tradition was followed, the president's lower court nominations rarely encountered legislative obstacles.

That norm of cooperation between the president and the Senate suffered its first real threat during the administration of Ronald Reagan, the first chief executive to recognize the true significance of the lower courts both as an influential policymaking entity and as a breeding ground for future Supreme Court justices. The following decade, Bill Clinton became the first chief executive to see his lower court nominations routinely locked up in committee based on ideological factors alone. Since then, the Senate minority has offered systematic resistance to the president's more extreme judicial nominees by exercising the filibuster on more than an occasional basis. The Senate did not outright reject these filibustered nominees; they simply remained in limbo, failing to receive an up-and-down vote from the Senate as a whole.

Given this transformation in lower court appointment politics over the past quarter century, it would be difficult to judge President Obama's selection process during his first two years in office against the performance of any presidents before 1988. Even by those earlier standards, however, the Obama administration's record of lower court appointments rates as a disappointment. During his first two years in office President Obama successfully appointed just sixty lower court judges (sixteen court of appeals judges and forty-four district court nominees). By comparison, during the first two years of his own presidency, George W. Bush secured the confirmation of one hundred lower court judges (seventeen court of appeals nominees and eighty-three district court nominees) from a Senate controlled mostly by the opposition.

Table 10.1 depicts changes in the relative success of presidents appointing lower court judges during their first two years in office.[17] President George H. W. Bush watched as 96 percent of the judges he appointed in 1989 and 1990 were confirmed by a Democratic Senate. President Clinton was similarly successful during his first two years in office: During the 103rd Congress of 1993–1994, Clinton successfully appointed 127 lower court judges out of 141 nominated for an overall 96 percent success rate. George W. Bush experienced a significant decline from these numbers, seeing just 85 percent of his district court nominees and a mere 72 percent of his lower court nominees overall confirmed during his first two years as president.

TABLE 10.1   Number of Nominees to US District and US Circuit Court Judgeships
during the First Congress of a Presidential Administration and Percentage
Confirmed, 1989–Present

Cong.	Years	President	District Court # nominees	District Court nominees confirmed		Circuit Court # nominees	Circuit Court nominees confirmed	
				No.	%		No.	%
101st	1989–90	Bush I	50	48	96%	23	22	96%
103rd	1993–94	Clinton	119	108	91%	22	19	86%
107th	2001–02	Bush II	98	83	85%	40	17	43%
111th	2009–10	Obama	65	44	68%	24	16	67%

Sources: Denis Steven Rutkus, "Judicial Nomination Statistics: U.S. District and Circuit Courts, 1977–2003," CRS Report for Congress; website of the US Senate Committee on the Judiciary (http://judiciary.senate.gov/nominations/111thCongress.cfm), last accessed April 28, 2011.

Even by these declining standards, Obama's judicial confirmation before a Senate in which the Democrats throughout held at least fifty-eight seats is hard to fathom: Obama secured confirmation for barely two-thirds of his lower court nominees.

The Obama administration's early failure to appoint more lower court judges was a product of several factors. First, the successful appointment of a Supreme Court justice in each of President Obama's first two years in office undoubtedly exhausted considerable resources that the White House and the Senate Judiciary Committee might otherwise have directed toward the lower court approval process. Presidents Nixon and Clinton faced the similar challenge of balancing the need to fill multiple Supreme Court vacancies early in their respective first terms with the need to fill many open seats elsewhere in the judiciary; neither of those two chief executives had an especially easy time finding Supreme Court justices who fit the bill. In Obama's case, his Supreme Court selection process offered mostly smooth sailing, while his lower court nominations may have suffered from neglect.

Second, while the filibuster has always been a potent tool for the Senate minority, its use skyrocketed in frequency during the first two years of the Obama administration. In absolute terms, the Democratic Senate rejected few judicial nominees outright. In fact, the Senate returned just five judicial nominees to the president during his first eighteen months as president. Rather, the 111th Congress broke the record for the number of filibusters in a session, passing one hundred cloture votes during its first eleven months. As Senator Sheldon Whitehouse (D-RI) remarked, "Not even in the bitter sentiments preceding the Civil War, was such a thing ever seen in this body."[18] As a consequence, the fifty-nine-seat Democratic majority often was as helpless in practical terms as a forty-nine-seat minority. Further, once a filibuster ends, Senate rules require an additional thirty hours of debate for each nominee, adding yet another obstacle to the speedy confirmation of judicial nominees.

Yet perhaps the most significant factor of all in this judicial appointment atrophy was foot-dragging by the White House itself. In naming lower court judges, President George W. Bush was quick out of the box, announcing eleven nominees by May of his first year in office. President Obama, by contrast, submitted nominees at a far slower pace, failing to nominate his eleventh judge until November 2009. Moreover, President Obama waited over eighteen months to nominate someone to one of the two highly prized vacancies on the prestigious US Court of Appeals for the DC Circuit. Why would a president so keenly interested in constitutional law move so slowly to staff a judiciary that might well transform the constitutional landscape for decades to come? The president's decision to tackle nearly all aspects of his administration's legislative agenda at the outset may have discouraged White House aides from leaning too heavily on the Senate majority leader and his allies to move large numbers of judicial appointments through the Senate machinery at the same time. An official with the Center for American Progress, a liberal think tank friendly to the Obama administration, speculated as follows:

> If Majority Leader Harry Reid were to cancel all recesses on August 1, 2010 and then require the Senate to work 24 hours a day, seven days a week, doing nothing but considering judicial nominees, the last nominee would not be confirmed until well into autumn—and that's assuming that the Senate passed no bills, confirmed no other nominees, and took up no other matters for this entire period.[19]

Of course the Senate *was* still wrestling with other items during the summer and fall of 2010, including more than 250 unconfirmed executive branch nominees. President Obama's foot-dragging on lower court nominees may just have been the price his administration had to pay to avoid a fatal logjam in the Senate and to keep all his legislative initiatives on track.

Despite President Obama's slow approach to judicial appointments, his administration still made significant inroads in transforming the judiciary as a whole. Federal judges with lifetime appointments are independent actors. Yet in resolving a wide range of legal issues, judges must exercise considerable discretion. Not surprisingly, judges appointed by Democratic presidents tend to exercise that discretion more in line with Democratic party preferences, while the appointees of Republican presidents tend to exercise their discretion in line with Republican preferences. By this measure, circuit courts have been especially susceptible to the new president's influence. In January of 2009 the US Court of Appeals for the Fourth Circuit based in Richmond (traditionally dominated by Republican appointees) had five vacancies on its fifteen-member court. By the end of the 111th Congress, President Obama had successfully appointed four judges to that Court, giving the Democrats a 9-5 advantage among its membership with another Obama appointee expected to arrive at some point before the end of 2012. The Second Circuit based in New York City also garnered considerable White House attention: Obama successfully appointed three judges to that thirteen-member court during the 111th Congress, giving the Democrats a 6-5 edge in membership. (Two more vacancies remained for Obama to fill during the 112th Congress.) President Obama also flipped the Third Circuit in favor of the Democrats, and the First Circuit is likely to follow during the remainder of his first term. President Obama has brought greater diversity to the lower courts as well: nearly half of his nominees have been women, more than a quarter have been African Americans, and 10 percent have been Asian Americans.[20]

Still, critics of the administration remain unimpressed. Even presidents who were apathetic about the federal judiciary made their imprint by filling many of the vacancies placed in front of them. Has President Obama sacrificed important opportunities by failing to make judicial appointments a greater priority in his administration? Ilya Shapiro of the libertarian Cato Institute captured the frustration of many Obama supporters:

> It's been surprising because he's a constitutional lawyer, he knows how courts work, how important they are . . . it seemed like an easy bone to throw to his base to make a mark, a lasting mark.[21]

Historically, it has normally taken two full terms to create a lasting legacy on the judiciary. As two-term presidents, Ronald Reagan and Bill Clinton appointed 375 and 372 judges, respectively. Those are the two highest lower court appointment totals ever recorded. More recently, George W. Bush appointed 322 lower court judges during his eight years as president. By contrast, George H. W. Bush appointed just 190 lower court judges during his single four-year term. Even those who fear that the Obama administration's slow pace might hamper liberal goals know that his successful reelection in 2012 will do more for their cause than all other factors combined. That holds true even if Obama chooses judges who favor staying out of matters of public policy, deferring to legislatures and electorally accountable officials instead.

Prosecuting Wars on More than One Front: President Obama Goes to Court

Though President Obama's first two years in office offer little evidence of a determination to use the courts for larger ends, the Obama Justice Department has routinely utilized the courts to fulfill its traditional function as the nation's chief law enforcement agency. For example, questions surrounding the decision to prosecute terrorists in civil courts or to mount a legal challenge against Arizona's immigration policy ultimately fall to Attorney General Eric Holder, who in turn answers to the president. Certainly Attorney General Holder is no stranger to public conflict, having survived a grueling Senate confirmation process in January of 2009, which focused on his controversial recommendation that President Clinton pardon financier Marc Rich in 2001. Still, there was no preparation for the heat that would come his way over his handling of these and other litigation decisions during the first two years of the Obama administration.

Guantanamo Detainees, Military Tribunals, and Civil Trials

With regard to the war on terrorism, the Obama administration was forced to resolve a fundamental question once the president's hand-picked officials assumed the reins of the Justice Department: Should the newly staffed department reverse course from the previous administration in its approach to the legal treatment of unlawful detainees? Under the leadership of Attorneys General John Ashcroft and Alberto Gonzales, Department of Justice lawyers had pursued several avenues in the war on terrorism: (1) they routinely suspended constitutional rights for detainees classified as "unlawful combatants"; (2) they expanded the policy of "extraordinary rendition," whereby CIA agents transfer select terrorism suspects to third-party states such as Egypt and Jordan for further interrogation; (3) they defended, through internal memoranda and in the court of public opinion, the legal right to torture detainees (in part by careful redefinition of "torture"); and (4) they steadfastly maintained the executive branch's power to hold trials of select detainees in military commissions rather than in civil courts.

Holder's Justice Department declared at the outset that the Bush administration's broad treatment of unlawful combatants and its policy of rendition would remain intact. While the administration tried (and ultimately failed) to close the Guantanamo Bay Military base in Cuba, it never sought to upend the general rules governing detention or the transfer of detainees there and elsewhere. Both Holder and Solicitor General Elena Kagan testified at their respective confirmation hearings that those who support Al Qaeda should be subject to so-called "battlefield law," under which they could be detained indefinitely without a trial, whether or not they are captured in an actual physical battle zone.[22] To that end, Holder's Justice Department argued successfully in the US Court of Appeals for the DC Circuit that the high court's decision in *Boumediene v. Bush* (2008)[23] applied only to the rights of habeas corpus, and that no additional rights extended to detainees therefrom.[24]

Meanwhile, a shift in direction from one administration to another was obvious on other fronts. Fulfilling a campaign promise that the administration would not "compromise its ideals" to fight terrorism, on January 22, 2009, President Barack Obama signed an executive order which expressly banned the use of torture by the US government in interrogations, bringing executive branch policy in line with section 1003 of the Detainee Treatment Act of 2005.[25] The Obama administration also repudiated the so-called torture memos from 2002, in which Justice Department officials had advised the CIA and the Defense Department that torture might be legally permissible under an expansive interpretation of presidential authority. Though some critics contend that the CIA's continued use of "extraordinary rendition" has the effect of transferring the use of torture overseas, administration officials counter that prior to all transfers, they have sought assurances from foreign officials that such detainees would not be mistreated in any way.

The debate over the use of military commissions to try unlawful combatants detained at Guantanamo Bay and elsewhere presents a more muddled picture. On October 28, 2009, Obama signed into law the National Defense Authorization Act for Fiscal Year 2010.[26] The new law retained the basic structure of the then-existing military commissions: a military judge continues to preside and decide issues of law, while a panel of five to twelve US armed forces members effectively determines the guilt or innocence of individuals on trial. The 2009 law did, however, introduce some modest changes to the earlier rules: (1) statements obtained through torture would thereafter be inadmissible; (2) defendants now received the right to attend their own trial, confront their accusers, and call witnesses; and (3) military prosecutors would thereafter be forced to disclose exculpatory or other helpful evidence. In addition, the convicted can appeal to the US Court of Military Commission Review, and ultimately to the US Supreme Court.

Still, a central question remains about these tribunals: When and under what conditions would the Obama Administration resort to them, if at all? According to data collected by New York University's Center on Law and Security, in the eight years following 9/11 the criminal courts convicted approximately 150 suspects on terrorism charges; during this same time period, the federal government successfully prosecuted just three detainees (all apprehended abroad) in military commissions located at Guantanamo Bay.[27] Moreover, at the time of this writing the military commissions had not yet tried a murder case of any kind.

Attorney General Eric Holder's first two years in office were often occupied with questions of how and where to try such detainees. The triggering event in the controversy that ensued was the Justice Department's decision on November 13, 2009, to transfer the case of five detainees including Khalid Sheikh Mohammed (alleged to have been a principal architect of the 9/11 attacks) to the US District Court in Manhattan for trial. Politicians including Senator Dianne Feinstein (D-CA), Senator Joseph Lieberman (I-CT), and New York City Mayor Michael Bloomberg all expressed opposition to holding the latest "trial of the century" in downtown Manhattan, complaining that it was either too dangerous, too expensive, or both. The fear of an undeserved acquittal had no basis at that point in time. For example, civil courts had successfully convicted such high-profile terrorists as John Walker Lindh, said to be a member of the so-called American Taliban, who was captured as an enemy combatant in Afghanistan. (Lindh is currently serving a twenty-year sentence.)

The case of Ahmed Khalfan Ghailani, wanted for his participation in the 1998 US embassy bombings, fueled passions on both sides of this debate. Ghailani was tried in the US District Court in Manhattan in 2009. Critics of the decision to try him in civilian court soon complained that the judge disallowed a key witness in the case and severely constrained prosecutorial attempts to introduce what he saw as tainted evidence. The jury eventually acquitted Ghailani on 284 of the 285 counts brought against him, including all murder counts. Still, the administration's defenders were quick to note that Ghailani was nonetheless sentenced to life without parole on the basis of that sole remaining count in January of 2011.

The administration clarified its position on the use of military commissions in an executive order issued on March 7, 2011. President Obama—now resigned to the reality that the Guantanamo Bay facility would continue to hold detainees for the immediate future—declared that military commission trials would resume once again at the controversial facility in Cuba. The order offered some protections for detainees, including a periodic review process for those who could not be tried or released because they represent a "continued threat to national security." Detainees tried under a newly reformed military commission process would also be able to retain a voluntary lawyer or hire private counsel.[28]

Though former vice president Dick Cheney has complained publicly that Holder was giving "aid and comfort to the enemy," the weight of evidence points to more continuity than change from one administration to another. If so, that is once again reflective of the more moderate views of the commander-in-chief himself.

National Security, Confidentiality, and the "State Secrets Doctrine"

As commander-in-chief of the US armed forces and head of the US government's foreign relations establishment, the president has benefited from some form of executive privilege to guard "state secrets" since the beginning of the republic. When former vice president Aaron Burr was tried for treason in 1807, President Thomas Jefferson refused to divulge a potentially exculpatory letter from a US general to himself on the ground that it contained state secrets. The US Supreme Court formally recognized the doctrine in 1953, when it held that only the government can claim or waive the state secrets privilege, and that it is "not to be lightly invoked."[29] After the September 11th attacks, the George W. Bush administration relied repeatedly on the doctrine to dismiss entire court cases, including those brought by former detainees who claimed they were abused while in US or foreign custody.

Although the Obama administration has acknowledged that the state secrets doctrine can be abused, it too has relied on it in numerous instances on the ground that certain evidence should not be made public if it endangers national security.[30] In one high-profile case, administration officials invoked the privilege in response to a lawsuit filed by the American Civil Liberties Union (ACLU) on behalf of Anwar al-Awlaki, a US-born cleric who resides in Yemen and was implicated in numerous terrorist attacks. The Obama administration has also used the doctrine to dismiss lawsuits contending that the US government illegally kidnapped a German national, engaged in unlawful rendition, and engaged in unlawful surveillance. In defense of this position, one Justice Department spokesman offered that "it strains credulity to argue that our laws require the government to disclose to an active, operational terrorist any information about how, when and where we fight terrorism."

Unlike his predecessor, President Obama was forced to defend the state secrets doctrine before the US Supreme Court as well. At the time of this writing, the high court was actively considering claims by aerospace companies Boeing Co. and General Dynamics Corp. that the federal government's refusal to provide essential information about stealth technology—a critical element in a twenty-year-old contract dispute against the Department of Defense—violated the companies' legal rights. Of course the implications of their claims go well beyond that particular case: The Obama administration's willingness to invoke the doctrine so often has done more than simply disappoint its more libertarian constituencies; it has left the administration at the mercy of the Supreme Court to accept its more expansive view of the executive privilege doctrine.

A Shift in Policy on Civil Rights and Immigration

Of the major divisions within the Department of Justice, none has undergone as significant a shift in culture and personnel during recent years as the half-century-old Civil Rights Division. An audit of the division covering the years 2001 through 2006 revealed a significant drop in the enforcement of several major antidiscrimination and voting rights laws during that period. In particular, lawsuits brought by the division to enforce laws prohibiting race or sex discrimination in employment fell from about eleven per year under President Clinton to about six per year under President Bush during his first six years in office.[31] The study also discovered a sharp decline in enforcement of a section of the Voting Rights Act that prohibits electoral rules with discriminatory effects, down from more than four cases a year under Clinton to fewer than two cases a year under Bush. Justice Department lawyers were already disillusioned by the embarrassing discovery that so many US attorneys were illegally fired for partisan reasons after the 2004 election. For many holdouts, the last straw, however, was the revelation that political appointees sought to hire conservatives and block liberals for career positions in direct violation of civil service laws.[32] The agency reported losing 236 of 350 civil rights lawyers between 2003 and 2007.

Congress increased the Civil Rights Division's budget by $22 million (up 18 percent) in 2010, the largest such increase in the division's history. Department officials promised to use the increase to bring over a hundred new people (including fifty additional lawyers) to the understaffed office.[33] The administration's first Civil Rights Division chief, Thomas E. Perez, publicly committed his agency to restoring the frayed relationship between career staff and the political leadership. Yet while a renewed foundation of staff and resources offered an important first step in reviving a flagging division within a demoralized department, would the Obama administration simply return the division to the status quo that prevailed at the end of the Clinton administration, or would it go further?

Some changes occurred immediately. Within just six months of Obama's taking office, the Civil Rights Division filed ten "friend of the court" briefs in private discrimination-related lawsuits; meanwhile, the acting division chief sent a memorandum to every federal agency urging more aggressive enforcement of regulations that forbid recipients of taxpayer money from policies that have a disparate racial impact. It also eliminated rules that previously restricted front-line career lawyers from making recommendations on whether to approve proposed changes to election laws.[34] In other areas, however, changes in civil rights enforcement practices proved slow-going thanks to the staff turnover of a few years earlier: Many of the replacement lawyers hired by the Bush administration after the exodus now enjoy the protection of civil service laws, and thus cannot be fired simply because they possess weak credentials. That is why even Attorney General Eric Holder admits that the various efforts to improve the division may offer more of a "restoration" than any kind of real change.[35]

Still, a handful of lawsuits can shape the image of a president and his administration. Among their successes, Perez's civil rights division has obtained the largest ever settlement of rental discrimination claims under the Fair Housing Act from a group of landlords in Los Angeles ($2.7 million).[36] In pressing certain civil rights claims, Justice Department officials may also be eyeing the looming battle over the constitutionality of comprehensive health care. Though that issue is not directly related to civil rights initiatives, the administration must assiduously maintain the current constitutional rules that afford Congress considerable deference in regulating the economy and securing the nation's borders if it hopes to prevail in federalism battles that will emerge later.

The administration's fears for the future at least partly explain its willingness to lead the charge against Arizona's controversial new immigration law in court.

Passed in April 2010, the state law (known in Arizona circles as SB 1070) makes it a misdemeanor for any alien to be in Arizona without carrying certain required documents, and it gives the police broad power to detain anyone suspected of being in the country illegally. It also cracks down on those sheltering, hiring, and transporting illegal aliens.[37] Though Obama has often objected to the law publicly, the decision to intervene did not come easily: White House officials in early 2010 debated whether it made sense to thrust the administration into a fierce national debate over immigration policies with midterm elections just around the corner. Yet President Obama ultimately decided in favor of intervention. Accordingly, the Justice Department filed its own lawsuit against the state of Arizona on July 6, 2010, seeking a court order declaring the measure invalid on the ground that power to implement immigration regulations is "exclusively vested in the federal government."[38] The administration's efforts were initially successful: on July 28, 2010, a district court judge blocked several provisions of the law, including the controversial requirement that police check the immigration status of those they stop for suspicious activity or arrest. The US Court of Appeals, in April 2011, upheld this injunction, setting the stage for a potential battle in the Supreme Court.

The Arizona immigration law provides a case study in why President Obama dreads taking political issues to court. Since its passage, the Arizona law has tarnished America's image in Latin America.[39] While the lawsuit might help repair America's relationship with Mexico, it opens the administration up to complaints that it has been trumping states' rights. Of course the federal government has brought similar lawsuits alleging discrimination against state governments in the past. Most notably, it took several states to court in the late 1950s and 1960s when they refused to segregate their public schools in line with the Supreme Court's landmark decisions.

Looming large on this horizon is the legal battle over congressional health care reforms passed in 2010. In fact, fears of current lawsuits challenging health care reform may have played a role in the administration's legal strategy over immigration: stated simply, Obama's administration could not stand by and countenance incursions into federal power by state authorities. On December 13, 2010, US District Judge Henry Hudson of Virginia ruled that Congress exceeded its constitutional authority by requiring Americans to start buying health insurance in 2014 or risk paying a substantial fine.[40] In the months following Hudson's ruling, at least one other federal judge (in Florida) deemed the bill unconstitutional, while three others upheld the constitutionality of the landmark legislation. Even as a reluctant litigant, President Obama cannot just appeal the occasional unfavorable ruling; he must counter challenges to federal authority wherever they crop up, lest he risk seeing his administration's signature legislative accomplishment slowly undermined.

Obama versus the Courts: The Battle That Wasn't

As a United States Senator, Barack Obama did not simply oppose President George W. Bush's two Supreme Court nominees. In the case of Samuel Alito's nomination in early 2006, Obama went a step further, joining a broader Democratic effort headed by Senators Edward Kennedy (D-MA) and John Kerry (D-MA) to filibuster Alito's nomination and deny him an up-and-down vote on the merits. This effort gathered just twenty-five signatures (sixteen short of the forty-one necessary to survive cloture), and Alito was ultimately confirmed by a 58-42 vote. Based on that episode alone, one might assume Obama to be a classic legal progressive, determined to remake the constitutional landscape along the more liberal lines favored by Chief Justice Earl Warren and Justices William Brennan and Thurgood Marshall, among others. Chief Justice Roberts and Judge Alito represent the opposite approach to the law, and Obama's opposition to their candidacies fits that assessment to a 'T.'

Yet just a few months later Obama was already backtracking from his position on those nominations. In his 2006 book, *The Audacity of Hope*, then senator Obama wrote of the mixed feelings he expressed at the time over his role in the confirmation process:

> I had a conversation with a friend in which I admitted concern with some of the strategies we were using to discredit and block nominees. . . . I wondered if, in our reliance on the courts to vindicate not only our rights but also our values, progressives had lost too much faith in democracy. . . . Our system of self-governance is an intricate affair; it is through that system, and by respecting that system, that we give shape to our values and shared commitment.[41]

Even then, Senator Obama believed that "elections meant something."[42] It was a sentiment that translated to Obama the national candidate, and more recently to Obama the chief executive. Democratically elected officials, and not courts, are the driving influences in Barack Obama's policymaking vision. In that sense his views align closely with those of Franklin Delano Roosevelt, who believed in a liberal government unhampered by an activist judiciary. Obama was just a toddler when the Warren Court was at its peak; he was barely fourteen years old when the US Supreme Court ended Richard Nixon's stalling tactics in *United States v. Nixon*.[43] If the Democratic party of the 1960s and 1970s learned to lean on the courts as a means of short-circuiting excesses by government, President Obama represents a new generation of Democratic party thinking about the more limited role of courts in general, and of the Supreme Court in particular.

The forty-fourth president's reluctance to resort to the judiciary to help create sweeping policy change leaves his critics from the left frustrated with what they perceive as undue moderation—or even worse, capitulation. His first two Supreme Court justices came accompanied with olive branches to the right: Sonia Sotomayor cut her teeth as a hard-core prosecutor in New York, and thus was less likely to become a blanket vote for defendants' rights; Elena Kagan sported a reputation for accepting broad executive authority, much to the delight of many conservatives, and perhaps to the satisfaction of President Obama himself. Both were confirmed easily, with moderate Republicans joining the entire Democratic caucus to put to rest any notion of a Republican filibuster. As for lower court appointments, White House foot-dragging and the failure to more promptly forward names to a supportive, Democrat-controlled Senate offer a clear indication that the administration's priorities lie elsewhere. President Obama's Justice Department has been anything but aggressive in support of liberal principles. It has waged the war on terrorism on terms that are remarkably similar to those of Bush's Justice Department. Civil rights enforcement has increased somewhat compared to the previous eight years, but it hardly signifies a heroic new approach. Finally, Department of Justice lawsuits filed to enjoin Arizona's immigration law are as much about creating precedents for future battles (over health care, for example) where the Court's position on federalism may prove vital to defending Obama's own legislative initiatives from constitutional attack.

For a former constitutional law teacher, Barack Obama has exhibited remarkable reluctance to take steps that might forcefully shift the constitutional landscape. This may have ironic consequences as Obama's legislative majorities diminish in the 112th Congress and perhaps beyond. If *Citizens United* is not an aberration, and the high court continues its activism in a politically and economically conservative direction, his reluctance to directly engage the judiciary may prove more costly to Obama than any other of the administration's early missteps.

Notes

1. 558 U.S. 50 (2010).
2. "Roberts Questions SOTU Attendance," *Politico*, March 9, 2010 (http://www.politico .com/politico44/perm/0310/very_troubling_f90ec36f-c19d-4360-81c8-f72bdd227b3a .html), last accessed on April 28, 2011.
3. See, e.g., Peter Baker, "Obama v. Roberts: The Struggle to Come," *New York Times*, April 16, 2010; Jeffrey Toobin, "Activism v. Restraint," *New Yorker*, May 24, 2010, 19-20.
4. At the inauguration Chief Justice Roberts incorrectly asked President-Elect Obama to repeat, "that I will execute the office of President *to* the United States . . . *faithfully*"; Once Obama reached the word "execute," he paused. Roberts then tried to correct his mistake by reciting "faithfully the Office of President of the United States." Obama

then repeated Roberts's initial, mistaken, prompt, with the word "faithfully" inserted after the "United States" instead of after the word "execute." Although many constitutional experts argued that the oath was not technically a precondition for the exercise of presidential power, Chief Justice Roberts administered the oath the next day at the White House out of what White House aides called "an abundance of caution."

5. 550 U.S. 124 (2007).

6. 551 U.S. 701 (2007).

7. See Jeffrey Toobin, "Bench Press: Are Obama's Judges Really Liberal?," *New Yorker*, September 21, 2009, 47.

8. Chief Justice John Roberts, delivering the commencement address at Georgetown University Law Center, May 21, 2006. Webcast of address can be found at http://www .law.georgetown.edu/webcast/eventDetail.cfm?eventID=144 (last accessed on April 28, 2011).

9. Cass Sunstein, *Radicals in Robes* (New York: Basic Books, 2005), xv.

10. Peter Baker and Adam Nagourney, "Tight Lid Defined Process in Selecting a New Justice: Using Past Battles to Avert Pitfalls," *New York Times*, May 28, 2009, 1.

11. Peter Baker and Adam Nagourney, "Sotomayor Pick a Product of Lessons from Past Battles," *New York Times,* May 27, 2009, A1.

12. President George W. Bush nominated White House Counsel Harriet Miers to the US Supreme Court on October 3, 2005, but Miers withdrew her nomination less than a month later.

13. Mark Hugo Lopez, "How Hispanics Voted in the 2008 Election," *Pew Research Center Publications*, November 5, 2008 (No. 1024).

14. 530 F.3d 87 (2d Cir. 2008)

15. Sheryl Gay Stolberg, "Obama Interviews Potential Supreme Court Nominees," *New York Times*, April 30, 2010.

16. Though Bill Clinton had nominated her to the US Court of Appeals for the DC Circuit in 1999, her nomination never received a hearing in the then Republican majority Senate.

17. This data is drawn from Denis Steven Rutkus, "Judicial Nomination Statistics: U.S. District and Circuit Courts, 1977–2003," CRS Report for Congress, updated August 28, 2003 (accessed at http://www.policyarchive.org/handle/10207/bitstreams/1549 .pdf).

18. Carl Hulse and David Herszenhorn, "Senate Debates on Health Care Exacerbates Partisanship," *New York Times*, December 20, 2009.

19. Ian Millhiser, "Judicial Confirmation Rates Have Nosedived in the Obama Presidency," Memo for the Center for American Progress, July 30, 2010, http://www.american progress.org/issues/2010/07/judicial_confirmations.html, last accessed on October 1, 2010.

20. Russell Wheeler, "Judicial Nominations and Confirmations in the 111th Senate and What to Look for in the 112th," *Governance Studies at Brookings*, January 4, 2011, accessed at http://www.brookings.edu/~/media/Files/rc/papers/2011/0104_judicial_ nominations_wheeler/0104_judicial_nominations_wheeler.pdf (last accessed on April 28, 2011).

21. Mark Sherman, "Obama Getting Fewer Judges Confirmed than Nixon," *Associated Press*, September 7, 2010.

22. Charlie Savage, "Obama's War on Terror May Resemble Bush's in Some Areas," *New York Times*, February 18, 2009, p. A20.

23. 553 U.S. 723 (2008).

24. See *Maqaleh, et al., v. Gates* (D.C. Cir. No. 09-5265), decided May 21, 2010.

25. 42 U.S.C. 2000dd. Obama's executive order effectively revoked President George W. Bush's order of July 20, 2007.

26. Pub. L. 111-84 (2009).

27. Center for Law and Security, *Terrorist Trial Report Card: September 11, 2001–September 11, 2009* (NYU School of Law, 2010); Jane Mayer, "The Trial: Eric Holder and the Battle over Khalid Sheikh Mohammed," *New Yorker,* February 15, 2010.

28. Executive Order 13567. For a sense of the extensive complications involved in assessing the status of detainees, see Charlie Savage, William Glaberson, and Andrew W. Lehren, "Classified Files Offer New Insights into Detainees," *New York Times*, April 24, 2011.

29. See *U.S. v. Reynolds*, 345 U.S. 1 (1953).

30. Jess Bravin, "High Court to Consider State Secrets Doctrine," *Wall Street Journal*, January 18, 2011.

31. Charlie Savage, "Report Examines Civil Rights during the Bush Years," *New York Times*, December 3, 2009, A26.

32. An inspector general's investigation into the matter was released to the public on January 13, 2009. See US Department of Justice, Office of the Solicitor General, *An Investigation of Allegations of Politicized Hiring and Other Improper Personnel Actions in the Civil Rights Division* (July 2, 2008).

33. Jerry Markon, "Justice Department Steps Up Civil Rights Enforcement; Division Reshapes Itself after Employee Exodus during Bush Era," *The Washington Post*, June 4, 2010, p. A16.

34. Charlie Savage, "Justice Department to Recharge Civil Rights Enforcement," *New York Times*, September 1, 2009, A1.

35. Ibid.

36. Jerry Markon, "Justice Department Steps Up Civil Rights Enforcement," *Washington Post*, June 4, 2010, A16.

37. Randal C. Archibold, "Arizona Enacts Stringent Law on Immigration," *New York Times*, April 24, 2010, A1.

38. Complaint of the US Government, *United States of America v. The State of Arizona*, Case No. 2:10-cv-01413-NVW, U.S. Dist. Ct. Dist. Arizona (Filed July 6, 2010).

39. A Pew Research Center poll found that the percentage of Mexicans who viewed the United States favorably dipped from 62 percent before the law to 44 percent immediately afterwards.

40. *Commonwealth of Virginia v. Sebelius* (Civil Action No. 3:10CV188-HEH) E.D. Va., December 13, 2010.

41. Barack Obama, *The Audacity of Hope* (New York: Crown Publishers, 2006), 83-84.

42. Ibid., 83.

43. 418 U.S. 683 (1974).

CHAPTER 11

Ambition, Necessity, and Polarization in the Obama Domestic Agenda

Christopher H. Foreman, Jr.

COMPLEX FORCES SHAPE EACH PRESIDENCY and the most important of them lie beyond the president's control. The system is famously separated.[1] In the best of times Congress can be cajoled but never commanded. Nomination may (and once did), but today regularly does not, lead to prompt Senate confirmation. The Office of Management and Budget (OMB) may assiduously scrub and fine-tune a departmental or program budget with the result merely an opening bid, rarely matching a final outcome.

Beyond such permanent systemic challenges lie specific legacies bequeathed by a president's predecessors. Barack Obama might be thought to have drawn from history's deck a very bad hand indeed: two questionably executed wars; a catastrophic financial meltdown that yielded the bailed-out banks, sluggish credit markets, stubbornly high unemployment, and anemic growth widely labeled the Great Recession; a Middle East threatening to evolve into a nuclear tinderbox; and challenges on immigration and climate change that would resist policy consensus even in a world devoid of Democrats.

On the other hand, as Franklin Roosevelt, Ronald Reagan, and George W. Bush exemplify, crisis can empower a presidency, creating energizing focus and political space for policy innovations otherwise unlikely, even unimaginable. Could Obama tame the cascade of economic woes that had boosted his election prospects and enact some version of his campaign agenda? Doing so would certainly position him among the most consequential of presidents. Or would the effort devour his presidency, perhaps after a single embattled term? As the 2010 midterm elections approached Obama had certainly achieved some substantial (and hard-won) legislative victories. Yet largely because the more electorally energizing prize of a strong economy proved elusive, with unemployment hovering just under 10 percent,

Obama watched the loss of the Democratic majority in the House of Representatives and saw six precious Senate seats fall to the Republicans.[2] And Republicans viewed that as only a beginning. In late October Senate minority leader Mitch McConnell (R-KY) had made the party's central political objective abundantly clear: "The single most important thing we want to achieve is for President Obama to be a one-term president."[3]

Whether McConnell would get his wish was of course then unknowable. To be sure, a successful path around the multiple challenges facing Obama's domestic presidency was hard to judge as well. More certain when he took office were three fundamental parameters of the political problems facing him.

Policy Ambition

The ambitious agenda on which Obama had run, and the Democratic Party's pent-up policy appetites, posed one facet of the problem set. At the time of his victory, Democrats had been out of the White House for eight years and had not controlled both ends of Pennsylvania Avenue since 1994. Moreover, even the brief period of all-Democratic national governance that prevailed in 1993–94 had been an enormous disappointment to many partisans, as key elements of the Clinton domestic agenda had foundered. To be sure, Clinton had won two terms, survived impeachment, and overseen both a prospering economy and the end of crippling budget deficits, but his mixed record (including a bout of decidedly unhelpful personal behavior) offered a weaker-than-expected launching pad for his putative successor. George W. Bush, after prevailing over Al Gore despite losing the popular vote, then stunned and frustrated Democrats by assuming a commanding first-term position, aided by disciplined congressional majorities and the political tailwind of a war on terror. Deficits returned as a "compassionate conservatism" mutated into a "big-government conservatism" focused on cutting taxes but unwilling to trim spending in equal measure. Meanwhile, climate-change legislation and immigration reform stalled and bipartisan education reform (the No Child Left Behind legislation) yielded a profusion of implementation problems. Change-hungry Democrats rode a wave election that took back the Congress in 2006, somewhat reviving the moribund practice of administrative oversight and enacting a 2007 energy bill that both raised automotive fuel economy standards and targeted the incandescent light bulb for extinction.[4] All of this, combined with Bush's plummeting popularity, whetted Democrats' appetite for an even broader resurgence that came in 2008.

Over two consecutive election cycles (2006–2008) Democrats picked up a total of fifty-two House and fourteen Senate seats and won back the presidency with a small but decisive 53 percent popular vote margin, magnified into a 365-vote Electoral College victory. Combine this with Obama's formidable personal skills and organizational assets and it was no wonder that by Election Day and shortly thereafter many Democrats, especially the young, were hugely expectant, even euphoric. Legislation to address climate change (and the nation's widely bemoaned dependence on fossil fuels) now seemed within reach, as did a new regime for immigration, a matter of top concern to the Democrats' pivotal Latino constituency. In short, there was, for Democrats, policy aplenty to pursue. That the ambitious agenda would demand the setting of priorities, that Democrats might not easily coalesce around the detailed legislation to pursue them, that the very problems boosting Obama's candidacy might soon impair his presidency—these hurdles were quickly apparent to the incoming administration but understandably lost, for a time, on many supporters.

Legacy Crises

The second key feature defining the political landscape as Obama came to power was the Great Recession, a development covered in greater detail in Stephen Weatherford's chapter in this volume. The economic meltdown had begun with the bursting of a huge "bubble" in housing prices in 2006–2007. It continued into the election year with a startling series of events: the unraveling and liquidation of one major investment firm (Bear Stearns), the government takeover of mortgage lenders Fannie Mae and Freddie Mac, the termination of another major investment bank (Lehman Brothers), and the seizing-up of credit markets that precipitated a Republican treasury secretary's unprecedented proposal for a $700 billion bailout of major banks' "toxic" investments, the Troubled Assets Relief Program (TARP). As matters came to a head in September 2008, candidate Obama had managed to appear far steadier than his opponent McCain, who surprised virtually everyone by proposing to suspend his campaign and postpone planned presidential debates.[5]

The economic downturn that helped seal McCain's fate would vastly complicate Obama's governance problem. It necessarily diverted time and political capital from the aforementioned agenda, requiring that Obama expend that capital very early—indeed, he would tie himself to the Bush administration's bank bailout effort even before being inaugurated—on stimulus and economic recovery. The crisis would justify major government action, but the total domestic agenda thus created, including both recovery measures and the long-term investments and reforms Obama contemplated, would make for a very full plate of policy for voters to swallow and would produce inevitable charges of overreaching, even arrogance. Big strategic choices were unavoidable. Should Obama postpone or scale back his plans for health care reform or climate-change policy to concentrate on recovery? And how should the administration calibrate and sell a message that incorporated doing some very big things temporarily (for banks and the auto industry) while also pursuing other permanent shifts in the way major sectors of the economy (health and energy) functioned?

Party Polarization

Navigating this difficult path, Obama would find few Republican allies. The deep partisan divide was the third element profoundly shaping the new president's domestic policy world.

Candidate Obama had launched his campaign on two key premises, one solid but the other flawed. In announcing his candidacy in February 2007, Obama had understood the strong hunger in the electorate for "change" and cast himself successfully as its agent and embodiment. But the faulty premise lay in his promise to transcend the partisan divide. He spoke then, and throughout the campaign, of a politics "that's divided us for too long" and of "the smallness of our politics—the ease with which we're distracted by the petty and the trivial . . . [and] our preference for scoring cheap political points instead of rolling up our sleeves."[6] This was music to the ears of many, especially independent voters and youthful idealists. But in his book reviewing Obama's first year, the journalist Jonathan Alter would astutely observe that "from the start [he] was boxed in not only by the mess that Bush left him but by the contradictions at the center of his appeal. He had promised something that he couldn't deliver—a capital culture where Democrats and Republicans worked together."[7]

By the time the 2008 presidential campaign got underway the gulf between the political parties, and especially among the professionals and activists constituting partisan elite cadres, had solidified into common knowledge among social scientists, journalists, pundits, and the public.[8] Even though some analysts disputed the extent to which polarization extended to the electorate as a whole—most voters remained near the moderate center in expressed preferences—nearly all agreed that a decided "sorting" of voters had occurred.[9] As William Galston and Pietro Nivola express it: "Fewer self-identified Democrats or liberals vote for Republicans than they did in the 1970s, fewer Republicans or conservatives vote for Democratic candidates, and rank-and-file partisans are more divided in their political attitudes and policy preferences."[10] Indeed, Obama's election and subsequent policy reach would trigger an intensified and rhetorically aggressive grassroots opposition consisting mostly of likely Republican voters and styling itself as the Tea Party movement. Understandably (if temporarily) alienated from the Republican party label, Tea Party activists opposed the bank rescue efforts of both Bush and Obama as well as the latter's initiatives on economic stimulus and health care. Tea Party activists believed government was too large, too wasteful, too deficit-ridden, and too tax-hungry. Like many grassroots movements, some members proved partial to extreme beliefs and rhetoric (e.g., that Obama was a "socialist" or even not a "natural-born" citizen and thus not legitimately president). This was public opinion polarization at its starkest.

In addition, Obama would contend with congressional Republicans who were all too aware of their previous path to power in 1994: confrontation with Democrats.

A failed Democratic health care proposal had helped leverage a Republican congressional majority once and some doubtless hoped that it would do so again. In any case it appeared unlikely, as the November 2008 election drew closer, that Obama would lose or that his winning would have a more than momentary effect in taming Republican opposition. Supplementing the challenge of contrasting partisan ideologies would be strong and continuing incentives for what political scientists call "strategic disagreement," the well-documented inclination of politicians, as John B. Gilmour describes it, to deliberately "avoid reaching an agreement when compromise might alienate supporters, damage their prospects in an upcoming election, or preclude getting a better deal in the future."[11]

Easy Targets:
Executive Orders, Wage Discrimination, and Children's Health

Notwithstanding the structural and political challenges facing the new administration, on a few fronts at least, Obama could quickly prevail. Such matters inhabited two categories: (1) administrative actions (such as new or revised executive orders) not requiring congressional assent, and (2) legislative initiatives for which congressional Democrats could quickly muster majorities for a supportive president.

Just as Clinton had, with relative ease, altered the White House regulatory review process he inherited from his Republican predecessors, so Obama could, with the stroke of a pen, perform the same feat—albeit moving the ball in the opposite direction. Thus did a perennial Republican focus on "regulatory relief" give way to Democratic "regulatory effectiveness," a scant ten days after Obama's inauguration.[12]

Barely a week later came another executive order recasting one of Bush's signature initiatives, the Office of Faith-Based and Community Initiatives, as pursuing instead "neighborhood partnerships" with an emphasis on the preservation of "our fundamental constitutional commitments guaranteeing the equal protection of the laws," the free exercise of religion, and "rigorous evaluation" of performance.[13] The Bush executive order curtailing federal support for embryonic stem-cell research was likewise revoked the following month (although a pre-existing appropriations rider, the Dickey-Wicker Amendment, would create grounds for challenging the Obama order in federal court).[14]

Nine days after the inauguration Obama enjoyed an easy legislative victory in the Lilly Ledbetter Fair Pay Act, his first bill signing. Reacting to a 2007 Supreme Court decision holding that Ms. Ledbetter, who had worked at an Alabama tire factory, had been too late in pressing her claim of unequal compensation, Congress extended the period within which such lawsuits could be filed.[15] Bush had opposed the bill, as had many congressional Republicans, believing it encouraged unnecessary litigation and excessive judgments. With Obama at the helm, a bipartisan coalition for the bill quickly prevailed.[16]

Reauthorization of the Children's Health Insurance Program (CHIP, formerly known as S-CHIP) presented a somewhat similar political situation. A Democratic congressional majority was primed to deliver. Originally enacted in 1997 S-CHIP had been created with significant bipartisan support; the Senate's famous "odd couple" of Edward M. Kennedy (D-MA) and Orrin Hatch (R-UT) had been key promoters.[17] A state-run, federally supervised program intended to cover uninsured children in families with incomes that, while modest, remained too high to qualify for Medicaid, S-CHIP had, a decade after enactment, some 6.6 million enrollees.[18] The purpose and targeting of the program made it popular, but Bush had twice vetoed S-CHIP expansions intended to cover up to ten million children.[19] Bush objected to the very features that helped give the proposals traction in Congress: they aimed beyond the poor, embracing middle-class families, and would expand (with financing via cigarette taxes) the federal role in health care.

Enter Barack Obama, happy to sign what Bush had vetoed—and assisted by combative chief of staff Rahm Emmanuel anxious to put "points on the board" as a kind of down payment toward (and, perhaps, temporary substitute for) broader health care reform.[20] The administration had been internally divided on this, with some advisers hoping to use the children's program to politically sweeten broader legislation. In the end, Obama saw the virtue of a quick victory and made the S-CHIP renewal his second bill signing. But he made plain that S-CHIP was only a beginning, "only a first step," as Obama reminded his audience at the ceremony. "The way I see it, providing coverage to 11 million children through CHIP is a down payment on my commitment to cover every single American."[21]

Stimulating the Economy and Opposition: The American Recovery and Reinvestment Act

Fulfilling that commitment would have to wait, however, because recession and unemployment approaching 10 percent quickly became the lens through which pundits and public alike began to rate (and berate) Obama's performance. Whatever else he might wish to pursue, or perceive as important in the long term, Obama like all presidents would be hostage to current economic conditions and expectations, rational and otherwise.

Conditions were so severe, and expectations so high, that Obama did not wait for Bush's formal January exit to begin exerting himself. In a brief period of informal "transition presidency" Obama wielded unprecedented informal power. As Jonathan Alter recounts: "Never before in American history did a president-elect make so many presidential-level decisions before being sworn in. Obama signed off on the largest public investment since World War II and lobbied a huge bank rescue bill through Congress while he was still technically a private citizen."[22]

The stimulus (formally the American Reinvestment and Recovery Act or ARRA, Public Law 111-5) was omnibus legislation on a vast scale. Even Democrats would think it a "monster," and Republicans, a monstrosity. As with health care reform later, Obama would endorse a broad vision, encouraging congressional Democrats to fill in the details. Democrats saw the bill as a vehicle not only for Keynesian economic stimulus but also (and perhaps more significantly) for the redress of a wide array of previously under-funded Democratic priorities. At its signing reporters could tally more than a hundred categories of assistance totaling $787 billion. House Appropriations Committee chairman David Obey (D-WI) worked full-bore for weeks on the package, which emerged to a polarized reception: every House Republican voted no.[24]

The very wide-ranging nature of the stimulus legislation may also have had the ironic political effect of understating Obama's achievements early in the new administration. A more drawn-out FDR-style "Hundred Days" of separate bill-signings might have helped to convince the public that Obama was getting more done. Rolling so many priorities up into one bill made for an irresistible juggernaut on the Hill but reduced the number of photo-ops. Michael Waldman, Bill Clinton's former speechwriter, saw the bill as multiple pieces of landmark legislation for which Obama would strain to claim credit. As Alter recites:

> If the bill had been split into the biggest tax cuts for the middle class since Reagan, the biggest infrastructure bill since the Interstate Highway Act in the 1950s, the biggest education bill since Lyndon Johnson's first federal aid to education, the biggest scientific and medical research investment in forty years, and the biggest clean energy bill ever, then Obama would have looked like Superman, or at least more like FDR.[25]

Though harboring a germ of truth, that statement is likely overwrought. More likely the fundamental influence of widely shared economic misery would have overwhelmed any series of headline-grabbing legislative wins. In any case, as Weatherford suggests later in this volume, the stimulus would turn out to be a significant (if under-powered) success economically even as it failed in broad political terms to recast the public's fundamental perception of government performance.

Education

The education component, however, allowed Obama and his secretary of education Arne Duncan the resources for significant policy innovation. Quietly eschewing the "No Child Left Behind" rubric that had dominated education policy discourse in the Bush era, the Obama administration took a different tack. The stimulus legislation made available $4.35 billion for a new initiative, announced in July 2009, trumpeted as "Race to the Top" under which states could compete for funding. "To win the race," announced Duncan, "states have to have standards and tests that prepare students to succeed in college and careers . . . recruit and reward excellent teachers and principals . . . have data systems to track students' progress and to identify effective teachers . . . [and] identify their lowest-performing schools and take dramatic action to turn them around."[26] More importantly from the standpoint of state governments in extreme fiscal distress, the stimulus also allowed the Obama administration to claim credit, by fall 2009, for saving "at least 250,000 education jobs across the country."[27] By March 2010, Obama had sent to Congress a proposed revision of the existing NCLB framework to emphasize student outcomes over time (as opposed to the "adequate yearly progress" formulation, widely reviled as excessively rigid because it penalized arguably successful schools) and dispensing with the previous demand that all students be proficient in reading and math by 2014.[28] The administration's new goal would be to ensure that all students graduate from high school prepared for college or a career by 2020.

Not surprisingly political resistance arose, not all of it from conservatives. Teacher unions still felt they were being scapegoated for larger societal failings. Tennessee and Delaware made out well in the first round of Race to the Top awards, but some states were unable to coalesce their education establishments around a proposal and others simply scored too poorly (in the 500-point multi-criteria rating system) to be competitive. Texas resisted even trying, with Republican Governor Rick Perry asserting that "we would be foolish and irresponsible to place our children's future in the hands of unelected bureaucrats and special interest groups thousands of miles away in Washington, virtually eliminating parents' participation in their children's education."[29] Education historian and school-reform apostate Diane Ravitch saw Race to the Top, like NCLB, as another initiative grounded in faulty assumptions. "Today there is empirical evidence," she wrote, "and it shows clearly that choice, competition and accountability as education reform levers are not working. But with confidence bordering on recklessness, the Obama administration is plunging ahead."[30] Other reform advocates had more positive reviews, though, and the administration remained committed to its education course even after the 2010 midterm elections. As of the 112th Congress the ultimate fate of NCLB reauthorization remained to be determined; complicating matters, the end of the stimulus funds combined with state fiscal constraints put education budgets nationally under great pressure.

A Giant Gamble

ARRA, along with the banking and auto industry bailouts, amounted to a colossal bet on bigger government—mere "big government" would endure in any case—and one that any Democratic president, working with a Democratic congressional majority, almost certainly would have had to take given the circumstances. The blend of political and policy rationales would necessarily exert an enormous force on Democrats. The Federal Reserve's tools of first resort for interest-rate cuts were unavailable; rates were already about as low as they could go. To enact their long-run priorities, Democrats would have to spend (or "invest") big and hope that doing so would help create jobs, restore confidence, and thus capture some political and economic breathing space for additional measures down the road. And if big enough, ARRA itself would offer a substantial down payment on the very priorities that a bolstered economy would make sustainable farther into the future. Nineteen ARRA expenditure categories (including tax credits, biomedical research, electricity grid and transportation modernization, Medicaid help for states, unemployment assistance, and much else) would *each* receive $10 billion or more.

Meanwhile, congressional Republicans could afford to stand aside and reap a rich harvest if things did not go well. Indeed, prompt and dramatic improvement appeared unlikely. Supporting Obama to any appreciable degree would gain Republicans little collectively and could cost them, as individuals, very dearly back home: campaign money would dry up; primary challengers would materialize; angry messages would pour into the offices; and town meetings would morph into public torture. Fifty days into his term, Obama already had "the most polarized early job approval ratings of any president in the past four decades" with a 61-point partisan gap in job performance approval.[31] And as the electoral clock ticked toward an ever-more-likely November 2010 comeback election, the smart Republican move seemed simple enough: hang tough or get hanged by the Tea Party.

Near-Death Politics: Winning on Health Care Reform

Whether Obama serves one term or two, his most durable domestic policy legacy is probably already apparent: the Patient Protection and Affordable Care Act (Public Law 111-148) signed on March 23, 2010. Hostile Republicans (not one of whom voted for it) would likely either subside or fail in their initial promise to overturn it, if only because overriding a sure Obama veto would prove impossible, leaving court challenges by Republican state attorneys general as the immediate point of active resistance.[32] In winning broad reform conferring insurance coverage on more than thirty million additional recipients, Obama overcame not only unified Republican opposition but also a constant threat of Democratic defections. From before the inauguration until early 2009 some Democrats (and Obama's own chief of staff) had strongly inclined toward a modest bill as necessary given the public rancor and the sheer complexity of health care. Yet others positioned farther to the left deemed the Senate bill ultimately enacted (in contrast with the more expansive

House product) too compromised by corporate influence. Obama and House Speaker Nancy Pelosi (D-CA) had to work hard for every vote.

A comprehensive health care overhaul had escaped all prior Democratic presidents, most recently Bill Clinton, and came very close to eluding Obama as well. Definitive accounts of health care reform's genesis, evolution, and larger meaning will come later. For present purposes it will suffice to indicate briefly (here, and in more detail in the chapter by Barbara Sinclair) what the administration won and how, why it almost lost, and why the battle for a genuinely transformed health care regime has only begun.

Three primary concerns have anchored the health care policy discourse in recent decades: coverage, cost, and quality. Throughout the 1990s and beyond, one could reliably hear a single claim recited again and again: the United States lagged behind other advanced industrial nations with some forty-five million persons lacking health insurance.[33] In the postwar era, while Britain was embracing (and later struggling with) its National Health Service, and Canada was committed to a "single-payer" system (with health care as a closely managed right), the United States had stayed, largely, with a private insurance-supported fee-for-service model. A familiar triad of special programs for the elderly and the poor (Medicare and Medicaid, both launched in 1965) and for veterans constituted significant exceptions.

This regime proved durable largely because it offered at least tolerable (and often more than tolerable) results for the elderly, the poor, veterans, and the working middle class. If one had a minor or readily treatable health condition, or needed routine preventive care, and could pay for that (or, crucially, have a third party pay) there seemed little reason for complaint. Public hospitals, community health centers, and emergency rooms supplemented the fee-for-service apparatus as what came to be called the health care "safety net." Ideally, uninsured persons (especially young adults, part-time workers, unauthorized residents including many Hispanic adults, the unemployed, and workers whose employers did not offer health insurance) were caught by the net. A crucially important feature of health care politics is that this heterogeneous and ever-shifting category of persons was unorganized and had little collective influence in the policy process. There existed nothing resembling a "National Organization of the Uninsured," though a diverse network of committed advocates kept the cause alive. Meanwhile, most people (including certainly an overwhelming majority of Republican voters) were reasonably content with the health care they had: they might want more if they could get it (or at least hold what they had), but were hardly interested in radical system change even if that might permit extending insurance coverage to the millions without it. Ironically, Medicare, understandably seen as a progressive victory over organized medicine at its enactment, would later siphon away the political energy that millions of sympathy-inducing and politically active senior-citizen beneficiaries might later have delivered for broader reform.[34]

By 1993, with public confidence in government well below what had prevailed when Medicare had passed, the Clinton administration offered what Democrats imagined to be a politically shrewd bargain. There would be no dreaded Canadian-style single-payer; private insurance would be preserved, but with consumers empowered to shop around. But, in Jonathan Cohn's summary of the fate of the Health Security Act, "Under Clinton's plan, most working-age people had to dump existing insurance to buy one of the new regulated private plans. Yes, Americans craved security—they wanted to know coverage would be there if they lost a job and provided for them if they got sick. But, by and large, they didn't want government forcing them to change their coverage, even if it was change for the better."[35] Staunch opposition from the insurance lobby, which took to the airwaves with a now-famous series of doubt-raising "Harry and Louise" ads, also helped kill the measure. And while prominent congressional Democrats most associated with the cause of expanded health care access tended to back reform, Congress as a whole was unmoved, as was the influential Senate Finance Committee chairman Daniel P. Moynihan (D-NY). In the aftermath of reform's defeat the Republicans gained control of Congress (and leadership of the House for the first time in forty years).

At the start of his presidential campaign, health care had not been a defining issue for Obama. But by his election he was both knowledgeable and committed to acting, doubtless influenced by his campaign rivals and perhaps, too, by Senate colleague Edward Kennedy (D-MA), a pivotal early endorser. The key strategic question, however, was how to avoid the fate of previous efforts: how, as Cohn put it, "to get the policy and the politics right next time."[36]

One clear departure from the Clinton approach lay in inducing Congress, early on, to take ownership of the issue. After the Clinton effort, in which the First Lady had overseen a relatively closed deliberative process that yielded an ultimately unpalatable proposal, Obama took the opposite tack, letting Congress drive the detailed legislative drafting, with the White House weighing in on broad direction. Another difference from 1993–94 lay in the early cultivation of sufficient industry support to head off the sort of well-funded media campaign that had helped doom the Clinton plan. This time America's Health Insurance Plans and PhRMA, the Pharmaceutical Research and Manufacturers of America (led, respectively, by the formidable Karen Ignani and former Louisiana Republican congressman Billy Tauzin, renowned for his deal-making savvy) cooperated, more or less, with the White House. Not surprisingly, however, their acquiescence came at a price. Ignani's group, though rhetorically roughed up by Obama at various points, clearly saw the advantage of a reform that would generate millions of new customers; it firmly opposed any competition from a government alternative or "public option" passionately pursued by liberals. Coverage would be compulsory (to prevent the financial "death spiral" that plans could face if healthier citizens could opt out of insurance altogether, taking their premium payments with them) but government would subsidize coverage for those who could otherwise not afford it. PhRMA, on the other hand, wound up cutting a more explicit deal, agreeing to offer up $80 billion in cost savings over a decade.[37] If the Obama administration saw agreeing to such terms as pragmatic necessity, the bargains would strike many political progressives as odious.

Unlike the Baucus bill, the House legislation included, as Jacob Hacker recounts, "a public plan modeled after Medicare . . . a national exchange in which the public plan would be offered alongside regulated private plans . . . and a tough requirement for employers that ensured that all but the smallest . . . either had to provide coverage or pay to cover their workers through the exchange."[38] But in the weeks leading up to the Senate vote erstwhile Democratic Senator Joe Lieberman (I-CT) had made clear his unwillingness to support any version that included such a government-sponsored insurance plan, and his vote (like that of every other Senate supporter) was critical.

After Democrats lost Ted Kennedy's old Senate seat to Republican upstart Scott Brown, suddenly the sole plausible path to enactment lay in House Democrats agreeing to pass a Senate bill about which many had deep misgivings, especially regarding the lack of a public insurance option meant to exert competitive pressure on private insurers.[39] The House and Senate could then amend the legislation through a budget reconciliation procedure automatically immune to the filibuster. A simple Senate majority would suffice.

Obama prevailed in the end for several reasons. First, he remained steadfast, unwilling to lower his sights even when knowledgeably (indeed plausibly) counseled to do so, deploying his formidable public presentation skills (augmented by old-fashioned Oval Office arm-twisting) at various points sufficiently to come back from the brink of disaster. Obama also had formidable help, none more crucial than Pelosi, who at first proclaimed the Senate bill a "nonstarter" in the House but who ultimately weighed in to count and corral votes with, by all accounts, a zealous efficiency. Rank-and-file House Democrats rationally relented. There was only one way forward: with a bill many disliked but that offered the promise of correction and enhancement. Even if, for supporters of abortion rights, that meant accepting restrictive legislative language (and a negotiated presidential executive order) that pro-life Democrats insisted on to win their support. Perhaps the most persuasive argument was simply that the bill constituted a major improvement over the status quo that voters would ultimately see benefits from—the sooner the better!—and demonstrated that Democrats could "get things done," even if that meant settling for a program of state-based exchanges instead of a unified national one, a tough requirement for individuals to have private-insurance coverage, no "public option," and only the barest architecture for the future promotion of either quality enhancement or cost control. In the end a combination of institutional rules, partisan incentives, and interest-group milieu allowed, to be sure, a non-incremental national policy breakthrough on a matter of basic provision for millions of Americans. Yet key fears, stakes, and veto positions imposed real constraints.

Bank Shot: Winning on Financial Reform

Proceeding at the same time as health care legislation, albeit with notably less grass-roots and partisan rancor, major financial regulatory reform moved toward final passage. Obama and the Democrats scored a major success with the Dodd-Frank Wall Street Reform and Consumer Protection Act (Public Law 111-203) signed on July 21, 2010, thirteen months after Obama formally called on Congress to remake a disastrously failed regulatory system. The new regime, he claimed, would be more stringent in policing the complex financial instruments that had proved disastrous, more comprehensively and proactively "systemic" in regulatory outlook, and more consumer-friendly (an orientation to be institutionalized in a new consumer financial protection agency).[40] The final legislation, although overwhelmingly a Democratic enterprise, reflected months of serious inter-party bargaining, with Republicans toward the end "focusing their objections on specific tenets of the legislation rather than on its overall thrust, allowing for more compromise [than was possible on health care]."[41] South Dakota Senator John Thune (R) observed that "a lot of Republicans want to be for this. . . . We realize that, in the end, something is going to pass."[42] In contrast to health care reform, Republicans had much less opportunity to leverage grassroots rage against Democrats. Indeed, it was Republicans who risked being publicly portrayed by Democrats as patsies of the same Wall Street wizards who had engineered financial calamity and outrageously undeserved bonus payments. Moreover, Senate Banking Committee chairman Christopher Dodd (D-CT) was determined not to become a Baucus-like hostage to a vain search for strategically disagreeing Republicans.[43] After a three-day filibuster in late April 2010 (one that Democrats likely would have relished to see continue a while longer, as it actually helped sell the Democratic message), Senate Republicans reversed course and agreed to let the legislation reach the floor for debate.[44]

While Obama could also use the bully pulpit to chime in with supportive rhetoric casting himself and his party as standing up for the middle class, he was not necessarily destined to prevail. Unless congressional leaders took extreme care in counting votes, the ship might well have run aground. As with health care, one or two pivotal senators might object strongly enough to some particular item in the mammoth bill (or to something its drafters had omitted) to set the stage for either a successful filibuster or defeat on the floor, notwithstanding the weeks of painstaking negotiation and legislative craftsmanship. For example, enhanced oversight of, and transparency within, the derivatives market might conceivably impair not only

Wall Street's speculative "casino" (widely blamed for having helped precipitate and deepen the economic crisis) but also Main Street's access to financing. Certainly Senate Banking Committee ranking minority member Richard Shelby (R-AL) thought so.[45] And the Senate's most conservative Democrat, Ben Nelson of Nebraska, had similar concerns, apparently stemming from the interests of Berkshire Hathaway, the Omaha-based company run by billionaire Warren Buffett, a major Nelson donor.[46] Such forces, along with the sheer scale of the undertaking, and the bicameral compromises necessary to achieve passage, might have been enough to stall matters indefinitely. The Senate bill, for example, included tougher rules on derivatives trading and the so-called Volcker Rule, intended to inhibit banks from much proprietary trading and investing in hedge funds and private equity. The House version envisioned a more potent consumer regulator than the Senate.[47]

Prospects for passage brightened noticeably with two developments.[48] One was the April 16 announcement that the Securities and Exchange Commission (SEC) was charging Wall Street's spectacularly profitable investment house Goldman Sachs and one of its vice presidents with "defrauding investors by misstating and omitting key facts about a financial product tied to subprime mortgages as the U.S. housing market was beginning to falter."[49] The barrage of negative commentary was predictably immediate and neatly played into the Democratic narrative of the need to rein in such behavior. A related development was simply framing the legislation as "Wall Street reform" which much more readily evoked a useful villain than the "financial regulatory" labeling. In the end, Maine's two Republicans joined Senator Brown of Massachusetts in voting for the bill, enough cross-aisle support to ensure passage.

The Dodd-Frank legislation also marked a second prominent legislative victory for consumer advocates during Obama's first two years. In May 2009, Obama had signed the Credit Card Accountability, Responsibility, and Disclosure (CARD) Act (Public Law 111-24) restricting card issuers' options in charging interest and fees and mandating greater clarity and disclosure for the benefit of customers. The companies had long engaged in practices widely perceived as deceptive and even predatory.[50] So widespread and long-standing were the complaints that many Republicans were inclined to back the legislation and, with strong Democratic majorities in each house of Congress, the likely outcome was in little doubt. One of the Dodd-Frank bill's most prominent features, hotly debated throughout its congressional consideration, was the Bureau of Consumer Financial Protection (an idea promoted by Harvard Law School professor Elizabeth Warren) established independently within the Federal Reserve. Obama's September 2010 appointment of Warren as a dual-hatted assistant to the president and special adviser to treasury secretary Timothy Geithner, with responsibility for setting up the bureau, triggered a severely mixed response. Everyone understood that Obama had wanted her for bureau director but that opposition stoked by the financial industry might have made the required Senate confirmation impossible. Yet in elevating someone other than Warren to the new position Obama risked offending his liberal base only weeks before the midterm elections. By making Warren interim director in all but name, Obama attempted to have it both ways even as some commentators deemed the politically creative move an abuse of the appointment process.[51]

Out of Gas: Energy and Environment

On energy and the environment Obama and the Democrats encountered a mostly frustrating search for a dramatic path forward. The 2009 stimulus provided some creative long-range nods in the direction of green energy. Meanwhile, the Environmental Protection Agency, recently unshackled by the Supreme Court in a 2007 decision, appeared poised to intervene administratively against greenhouse emissions. But as the fall 2010 elections loomed, legislative success had proved elusive. By privileging health care reform, Obama unavoidably demoted climate change as a priority.[52] But forces beyond Obama's control contributed mightily as well.

Simple bad luck intervened. Every president must face unpredictable "in-box crises" (e.g., a terrorist attack, a seized vessel or hostage, an exploding spacecraft, a destructive storm). Resulting expectations regularly exceed a president's authority or influence. This time it was the April 20, 2010, explosion aboard the Deepwater Horizon oil rig in the Gulf of Mexico, which precipitated a major environmental and commercial disaster usually known as the BP oil spill. Besides deploying the relevant federal assets, Obama could do little other than rhetorically reflect and magnify the public demand for an expeditious plugging of a catastrophic leak that eroded lives and livelihoods by the day.

The incident was especially ill-timed for Obama as it came shortly after his call for new ocean exploration.[53] The crisis was clearly not Obama's fault, and the administration responded with breakup of the Minerals Management Service, an agency intensely criticized for a pervasive coziness with industry. However, given the administration's subsequent call for a six-month drilling moratorium, intensely conflicting environmental and commercial perspectives were amplified in a context bound to yield pointed displeasure with Obama's leadership, especially in a region of the country where he was already politically weak. The hole was plugged, eventually, but only after placing the president on the defensive much of the summer and prompting his first national address from the Oval Office. Even this did little to plug another leak, that of the president's approval ratings on the issue.

The BP imbroglio contributed to a vastly more significant policy development with the simultaneous collapse of climate change legislation.[54] In June 2009 the House of Representatives passed, by a vote of 219-211, the proposed American Clean Energy Security Act (aka the Waxman-Markey "cap-and trade" bill) with forty-four Democrats opposing and only eight Republicans in support. Among other ambitious provisions, the bill contemplated a cap-and-trade regime for reducing greenhouse gas emissions among covered sources, by 2050, to 83 percent below 2005 levels. Moreover energy productivity would, by 2012, increase at least 2.5 percent per year through 2030. Retail electricity suppliers would have to ramp up both their efficiency and reliance on renewable energy sources.[55]

The path of corresponding Senate legislation, however, was predictably more tortuous. Senator Barbara Boxer (D-CA) steered an arguably tougher climate change bill, co-sponsored with John Kerry (D-MA), through the Environment and Public Works Committee without Republican votes. Kerry had pointedly jettisoned the increasingly politically toxic "cap-and trade" terminology, branding the measure instead a "pollution reduction" bill.[56] It was, nevertheless, ultimately abandoned, and a so-called "tripartisan" group consisting of Kerry, Lieberman, and Lindsey Graham (R-SC) attempted to formulate an alternative. But Graham soon announced his withdrawal, peeved at what he deemed a "cynical, political" effort by majority leader Reid to advance immigration reform before climate legislation.[57]

Kerry and Lieberman continued on, but their labor yielded little. In mid-June, as the oil still hemorrhaged in the Gulf, Obama devoted his first Oval Office address to calling for an end to the country's "addiction to fossil fuels," a clear attempt both to get ahead of the continuing crisis and to use it to leverage public opinion toward his long-term energy goals.[58] But reaction was notably tepid with many commentators critical at the absence of specifics in the speech. A few weeks later the push for climate change legislation was officially shelved by Democratic leaders, a casualty of Republican and industry opposition, the sheer scope of the overall legislative agenda, a weak economy, and the lack of time remaining before the fall elections. More modest legislation proposed by Jeff Bingaman (D-NM), chair of the Energy and Natural Resources Committee, to accelerate use of renewable energy sources in electric power generation, enjoyed a decidedly more bipartisan Senate reception. But many environmentalists dismissed it as a climate change response and other analysts believed that the collapse of cap-and-trade, ironically, undermined the states' incentive to embrace the Bingaman proposal.[59]

A Lame Duck Flies But Hard Arguments Remain

The predictable second-guessing and speculation started well before the Republican wave hit. Had health care taken too long? Should Obama have pushed harder, or sooner, on health care or climate change? Should he have been tougher on Wall Street? Should he have vetoed some "pork-ulus"? Why couldn't he connect better with white working-class voters? Would Nancy Pelosi's continuation as leader of the House Democrats pose a net liability? What areas of common ground might Obama forge with Speaker John Boehner?

These questions would come to the fore during the 112th Congress. For present purposes it is important mainly to understand how we got to the point of posing them.

The short answer is that President Obama had choices both before and after the 2010 elections but he also faced massive constraints. The three-legged stool of policy ambition, legacy crises, and party polarization constituted an inherently unstable platform for his domestic presidency, notwithstanding Obama's formidable skills and durable personal popularity. The political context was simply very challenging for the White House, which had to set priorities, hold together a restive coalition, and navigate between the Scylla of unified opposition and the Charybdis of the Senate's peculiar characteristics.

Ironically, in the weeks after massively losing the House in the November "shellacking" of 2010, Democrats would rebound to rack up significant legislative victories. To the chagrin of liberals, Obama cut a December deal with Republicans on the soon-to-expire Bush tax cuts, an agreement that left intact rate reductions for high-income earners. Yet the administration could boast that the agreement had also won "an employee-side payroll tax cut for over 155 million workers" worth $112 billion in 2011, various other tax benefits assisting middle-income families, and a thirteen-month extension of unemployment benefits.[60] December also brought a long-overdue upgrade of the Food and Drug Administration's authority to safeguard the food supply, new legislation policing child nutrition in schools (a cause dear to the First Lady), and a measure offering a long-delayed $4.3 billion to defray health care expenses for rescue workers and others exposed to the toxic stew unleashed by the September 11, 2001, terror attacks.[61]

Perhaps most striking was the enactment of legislation initiating the reversal of the long-contentious "Don't Ask, Don't Tell" (DADT) policy inhibiting the ability of gays and lesbians to serve in the military while openly acknowledging their sexual orientations. In that instance the Obama administration benefited critically from seventeen years of frustrating experience with a policy forced on the previous Democratic president, lengthy bureaucratic preparation, and strong public assurances by both the chairman of the Joint Chiefs of Staff and a holdover Republican secretary of defense that the new policy could be successfully implemented.[62]

Some of this progress rested on potentially wobbly foundations. Congressional conservatives might starve the FDA of sufficient funds to function effectively; child eating habits (like much of public health generally) offers a target for which available policy tools are weak at best; and some rank-and-file resistance to openly gay service members is all but certain to outlive DADT.

Obama had by the end of 2010 been placed in the unenviable position of having to make a series of inherently difficult arguments to voters. The combination of spending both to realize policy ambitions (i.e., health care, the stimulus) and to boost the economy (i.e., the stimulus, plus the bank and auto industry rescues) in a larger context of massive budget deficits (reaching $1.4 trillion in fiscal 2010) was easy for Republicans to present, cumulatively, as profligate and misguided, especially when near-term employment and growth remained anemic. Prominent economists might opine that the stimulus, however massive, was actually too small (and perhaps not carefully enough designed) but, as often happens, voter intuition ran in a different direction from expert opinion.

In the case of health care, the stimulus, the industry rescues, and unemployment, Obama was regularly in the difficult position of posing very challenging arguments to voters. On the stimulus, he wanted them to perceive a counterfactual, that any pain families felt would have been worse (as economic analysts regularly opined) without the government's intervention. Similarly, in the case of looming health insurance premium increases he would have to get voters to perceive transition pains as inevitable, not a consequence of his reform effort. In the former case Obama would have to get voters to forge a connection that did not come naturally. In the latter he would have to sever a connection (*post hoc ergo propter hoc*) that voters could embrace all too easily, especially with aggressive Republican prompting.

For health care as a broad political project, Obama and reform supporters had the task of explaining (mostly to the already insured) that present circumstances, however imperfect, would worsen considerably absent reform.[63] Obama also had to argue, again counterintuitively, that covering more people could save money in the long run and not degrade service quality. Many voters found that an impossible stretch, or at best a risk not worth taking.

Obama plumped for immigration reform in his 2011 State of the Union address, but a similar challenge may bedevil him there, if a reform bill moves: he may be placed in the position of suggesting, for example, that in some respects easing up on border control may improve matters (i.e., by allowing unauthorized residents to exit more easily after entering).[64] Likewise on energy: ramping up fossil fuel production and keeping gasoline prices low are the easy and popular answers that only worsen an existing problem over the long term. (In April 2008 candidate Obama had stood apart from opponents Hillary Clinton and John McCain when both called for a "gas tax holiday" in response to spiking pump prices.) But as gas prices shot upwards in spring 2011, partly in response to Middle East turmoil, they took a toll on Obama's approval ratings. Being repeatedly on the wrong side of voter perception and intuition is bound to take a toll on a presidency.

Notwithstanding the remarkable legislative record on domestic policy during his first two years, Obama's future appeared uncertain as the new House Republican majority arrived in January 2011 to claim its berth in the cabin of power. As both Jimmy Carter and George H. W. Bush can attest, severe economic woes pose terrible electoral consequences for any president running for reelection. A rising economy, combined with a more favorable 2012 electorate, may lift Obama to a second term. A sputtering economy would likely sink him, notwithstanding his landmark victory on health care and even if Republicans continue in their tacit abandonment of the attack that had once looked most likely—that an Obama presidency poses a security risk, that he can't be trusted to keep the country safe. Such is the power of economic pain in politics.

Obama and congressional Republicans could almost certainly find areas of cooperation; trade, infrastructure, energy, and education were all regularly mentioned immediately after the midterm debacle. Even here, plans to act administratively against climate change via Environmental Protection Agency rule-making were all but certain to provoke a Republican counterattack via the appropriations and oversight processes. And so the key question was not whether deals were possible but whether each side had sufficient incentive to pursue them in good faith, overcoming or at least muting the inclination to strategic disagreement. Given Senator McConnell's declared intention to drive Obama from office and the hostility to the president among resurgent House Republicans, the way forward was uncertain although tax reform looked promising to some astute observers.[65]

Divisions between and within the national political parties also render any substantial attack on the deficit an especially treacherous exercise. Among congressional Democrats, Blue Dog "deficit hawks" remain vastly outnumbered by colleagues who see all the good that spending can do, an imbalance only enhanced by the 2010 midterm elections. Republicans, especially when out of power, more easily coagulate around a rhetoric that highlights the perils of spending but cannot bear to sacrifice tax cuts or security-related appropriations as part of any plan to trim it. Neither party relishes attacking entitlement spending except in the always-receding future. In all these respects, politicians reflect a mass public harboring little taste for sacrifice and no perception of the deficit as a near-term pocketbook issue (unlike taxation, inflation, and unemployment). The Congressional Budget Office estimated that the fiscal 2011 deficit would again exceed $1.4 trillion.[66] Neither the postelection agreement to continue the Bush tax cuts nor the dismissive reaction greeting the aggressive plan drafted by the bipartisan National Commission on Fiscal Responsibility and Reform appointed by Obama indicated much progress. The plan won the backing of only eleven of eighteen commission members, too few to propel it as the centerpiece of a broader congressional debate, though potentially providing useful future political cover.[67] Some steps, at least, toward utilizing that cover came in the spring of 2011, both in the Republican plan to cut discretionary spending, fundamentally change the nature of Medicare and Medicaid, and rule out tax increases, and in Obama's subsequent speech rejecting much of that approach while putting on the table long-term defense cuts, broad tax restructuring, and higher tax rates on those earning over $250,000 per year.[68]

Ongoing partisan rancor and public misgivings notwithstanding, health care reform appears likely to last (albeit amended) as Obama's signature domestic achievement. Even if the Obama presidency were to fall to Republican assault in 2012, a complete repeal of the Patient Protection and Affordable Care Act would be exceedingly tough to engineer, not least because of insurance company opposition. For the present, Obama's veto and continued (though narrow) Democratic control of the Senate would impede any such effort. The Senate filibuster would, on this one matter at least, powerfully assist the president. And the longer the law remained on the books the less likely a wholesale rollback would become. Unless Obama's Republican successor (if there is one) could muster sufficient strength and motivation to attack the law in his (or her) first year in office, the long-term durability of at least a revised reform law would seem assured. And with that, Obama's domestic legacy may itself have important durability.

Notes

1. Charles O. Jones, *The Presidency in a Separated System* (Washington, DC: Brookings Institution, 1994).
2. http://www.npr.org/templates/story/story.php?storyId=131093849.
3. Major Garrett, "After the Wave," *National Journal*, October 23, 2010.
4. On the characteristics of the Republican Congress and the changes wrought by the 2006 election, see Barbara Sinclair, "Spoiling the Sausages? How a Polarized Congress Deliberates and Legislates," in Pietro S. Nivola and David W. Brady, eds., *Red and Blue Nation? Consequences and Correction of America's Polarized Politics* (Stanford, CA, and Washington, DC: Hoover Institution and Brookings Institution, 2008), 55-87. On Public Law 110-140, the Energy Independence and Security Act of 2007, see John M. Broder, "House, 314-100, Passes Broad Energy Bill; Bush Plans to Sign It," *New York Times*, December 19, 2007.
5. Elisabeth Bumiller and Michael Cooper, "Obama Rebuffs McCain on Debate Delay," *New York Times*, September 25, 2008; and see the Campbell chapter in this volume.
6. "Illinois Sen. Barack Obama's Announcement Speech (As Prepared for Delivery)" *Washington Post*, February 10, 2007.
7. Jonathan Alter, The Promise: President Obama, Year One (New York: Simon & Schuster, 2010), xv.
8. See the Jacobson chapter in this volume.
9. Morris P. Fiorina with Samuel J. Abrams and Jeremy C. Pope, *Culture War? The Myth of a Polarized America* (New York: Longman, 2004).
10. William A. Galston and Pietro S. Nivola, "Delineating the Problem," in Nivola and David W. Brady, eds., *Red and Blue Nation? vol. 1, Characteristics and Causes of America's Polarized Politics* (Palo Alto, CA, and Washington, DC, Brookings 2006), 1-2.
11. John B. Gilmour, *Strategic Disagreement: Stalemate in American Politics* (Pittsburgh and London: University of Pittsburgh Press, 1995), 4.

12. Executive Order 13497. Note that in January 2011 Obama issued a subsequent executive order (EO 13563) "improving regulation and regulatory review" by seeking to weed out "burdensome" rules.
13. Executive Order 13498.
14. Executive Order 13505. See Gardiner Harris, "U.S. Judge Rules against Obama's Stem Cell Policy," *New York Times*, August 23, 2010.
15. Public Law 111-2 stipulates in the preamble the intent "to clarify that a discriminatory compensation decision or other practice that is unlawful under [the relevant civil rights statutes] occurs each time compensation is paid pursuant to the discriminatory compensation decision."
16. Sheryl Gay Stolberg, "Obama Signs Equal-Pay Legislation," *New York Times*, January 30, 2009.
17. Shailagh Murray and Jonathan Weisman, "Both Obama and Clinton Embellish Their Roles," *Washington Post*, March 24, 2008.
18. David Stout, "Bush Vetoes Children's Health Bill," *New York Times*, October 3, 2007.
19. See Stout, ibid., and Christopher Lee, "President Again Vetoes Children's Insurance Bill," *Washington Post,* December 13, 2007.
20. Alter, *Promise,* 244-245.
21. The White House, Office of the Press Secretary, "Remarks by President Barack Obama on Children's Health Insurance Program Bill Signing," dated February 4, 2009, accessed at http://www.whitehouse.gov/the_press_office/RemarksbyPresidentBarack ObamaOnChildrensHealthInsuranceProgramBillSigning/.
22. Alter, *Promise,* 77. Obama had resigned from the Senate shortly after the election and so held no office in the weeks leading up to his inauguration.
23. http://projects.nytimes.com/44th_president/stimulus.
24. Carl Hulse, "Defense and No Apologies from Author of Fiscal Bill," *New York Times,* January 27, 2009.
25. Alter, *Promise,* 131.
26. The White House Blog, "Race to the Top," posted by Secretary Arne Duncan on July 24, 2009. Accessed at http://www.whitehouse.gov/blog/2009/07/24/race-top-0.
27. The White House, Office of the Press Secretary, "State Governments Expected to Credit Recovery Act with Creating, Saving at Least 250,000 Education Jobs Nationwide," dated October 19, 2009, accessed at http://www.whitehouse.gov/the-press-office/state-governments-expected-credit-recovery-act-with-creating-saving-least-250000-ed.
28. Gail Russel Chaddock, "Obama's No Child Left Behind Revise: A Little More Flexibility," Christian Science Monitor, March 15, 2010, at http://www.csmonitor.com/USA/Politics/2010/0315/Obama-s-No-Child-Left-Behind-revise-a-little-more-flexibility.
29. http://governor.state.tx.us/news/press-release/14146/.
30. Diane Ravitch, "The Big Idea—It's Bad Education Policy," *Los Angeles Times*, March 14, 2010. See also Ravitch, *The Death and Life of the Great American School System: How Testing and Choice Are Undermining Education* (New York: Basic Books, 2010).
31. Pew Research Center, "Partisan Gap in Obama Job Approval Widest in Modern Era" (April 2, 2009) available at http://pewresearch.org/pubs/1178/polarized-partisan-gap-in-obama-approval-historic; and see the Jacobson chapter in this volume.

32. Peter Slevin and Rosalind S. Helderman, "GOP State Leaders Say They'll Fight Health-Care Legislation," *Washington Post,* March 23, 2010. As of April 2011, three federal district courts had decided in favor of the law's constitutionality, and two others against it; that same month the Supreme Court rejected a request by Virginia's attorney general to expedite its own consideration of the law.

33. A 2003 Congressional Budget Office study reported that while "it is frequently stated that about 40 million Americans lack health insurance," that number "overstates the number of people who are uninsured all year." CBO estimated that between twenty-one million and thirty-one million people were uninsured throughout 1998. See CBO, "How Many People Lack Health Insurance and for How Long?" (May 2003), accessed at http://www.cbo.gov/ftpdocs/42xx/doc4210/05-12-Uninsured.pdf.

34. Jacob S. Hacker, "The Road to Somewhere: Why Health Reform Happened, Or Why Political Scientists Who Write about Public Policy Shouldn't Assume They Know How to Shape It," *Perspectives on Politics* 8(3) (September 2010): 867.

35. Jonathan Cohn, "How They Did It: The Inside Account of Health Care Reform's Triumph," *New Republic,* June 10, 2010, 16.

36. Ibid.

37. David D. Kirkpatrick, "White House Affirms Deal on Drug Cost," *New York Times,* August 6, 2009.

38. Hacker, "Road to Somewhere," 868.

39. Again, see Sinclair's chapter in this volume for additional detail.

40. The White House, Office of the Press Secretary, "Remarks by the President on 21st Century Financial Regulatory Reform," dated June 17, 2009, accessed at http://www.whitehouse.gov/the_press_office/Remarks-of-the-President-on-Regulatory-Reform/.

41. Brady Dennis and Paul Kane, "Senators near Deal on Financial Overhaul," *Washington Post*, April 22, 2010.

42. Ibid.

43. David Rogers, "Senate Insider Seeks to Retire as a Reformer," *Politico,* April 19, 2010, 12.

44. Shailagh Murray and Brady Dennis, "GOP Halts Financial Overhaul Filibuster," *Washington Post,* April 29, 2010.

45. Ibid.

46. Brady Dennis and Lori Montgomery, "Suspicion Greets Democrat's Opposition to Bill," *Washington Post,* April 29, 2010.

47. David Cho, "6 Questions on the Financial Regulatory Overhaul," *Washington Post,* April 25, 2010.

48. Dana Milbank, "Washington Sketch: The Wall Street Gunslingers Shoot Themselves in the Foot," *Washington Post,* April 29, 2010.

49. Securities and Exchange Commission, "SEC Charges Goldman Sachs with Fraud in Structuring and Marketing of CDO Tied to Subprime Mortgages" (press release 2010-59 dated April 16, 2010). Available at http://www.sec.gov/news/press/2010/2010-59.htm. Goldman would, three months later, agree to pay $550 million to settle the suit.

50. "A Gift to Credit Card Companies" (editorial), *New York Times,* November 19, 2009.

51. "Elizabeth Warren: President Obama Gets His Choice . . . By Thumbing His Nose at the Senate" (editorial), *Washington Post*, September 19, 2010.

52. Stephen Stromberg, "How Washington Failed on Climate Change," *Washington Post*, July 29, 2010.

53. The White House, Office of the Press Secretary, "Obama Administration Announced Comprehensive Strategy for Energy Secuity," dated March 31, 2010, accessed at http://www.whitehouse.gov/the-press-office/obama-administration-announces-comprehensive-strategy-energy-security.

54. John M. Broder, "Oil Rig Blast Complicates Push for Energy and Climate Bill," *New York Times*, April 27, 2010.

55. See http://www.govtrack.us/congress/bill.xpd?bill=h111-2454&tab=summary.

56. Alexis Simendinger, "Gang of Three," *National Journal*, April 17, 2010. On Kerry's rejection of "cap-and-trade" labeling see John M. Broder, "'Cap and Trade' Loses Its Standing as Energy Policy of Choice," *New York Times*, March 25, 2010.

57. Juliet Eilperin, "Climate Legislation Suffers Setback," Washington Post, April 25, 2010.

58. Scott Wilson and Anne E. Kornblut, "Obama Presses for Action on Energy Bill," *Washington Post,* June 16, 2010.

59. Timothy Gardner, "US Renewable Energy Bill Faces Battle in 2010," Reuters online at http://www.reuters.com/article/idUSN2115966820100921?loomia_ow=t0:s0:a49:g43:r1:c0.142857:b37504052:z0.

60. See http://www.whitehouse.gov/taxcut.

61. On the FDA Modernization Act see http://www.govtrack.us/congress/bill.xpd?bill=s111-510&tab=summary. On the Healthy, Hunger-Free Kids Act see http://www.whitehouse.gov/blog/2010/12/13/president-first-lady-child-nutrition-bill-basic-nutrition-they-need-learn-and-grow-a and on the health benefits for 9/11 responders see Sheryl Gay Stolberg, "Obama Signs Bill to Help 9/11 Workers," *New York Times,* January 2, 2011.

62. On the breakthrough on gays in the military see http://www.whitehouse.gov/blog/2010/12/22/president-signs-repeal-dont-ask-dont-tell-out-many-we-are-one.

63. Jonathan Rauch, "The Health Care Bill Is Worth Saving," *National Journal,* January 23, 2010.

64. See testimony by Douglas S. Massey at Senate Committee on the Judiciary hearing on May 20, 2009. Available at http://judiciary.senate.gov/hearings/testimony.cfm?id=3859&wit_id=7939.

65. Jackie Calmes, "Obama Weighs a Broad Tax Overhaul," *New York Times*, December 9, 2010, accessed at http://www.nytimes.com/2010/12/10/us/politics/10tax.html?_r=2&scp=19&sq=deficit%20panel&st=cse. See also William A. Galston, "The Only Way President Obama Can Win in 2012," *New Republic*, December 8, 2010, accessed at http://www.brookings.edu/opinions/2010/1208_obama_galston.aspx.

66. Jay Heflin, "CBO Deficit Projection Lower But Still Gloomy," *The Hill*, August 19, 2010, accessed at http://thehill.com/blogs/on-the-money/budget/114977-cbo-deficit-projection-lower-but-still-gloomy.

67. Brady Dennis and Lori Montgomery, "Deficit Plan Wins 11 of 18 Votes; More Than Expected But Not Enough to Force Action," *Washington Post,* December 3, 2010. See http://www.washingtonpost.com/wp-dyn/content/article/2010/12/02/AR2010 120205913.html.

68. See, e.g., The White House, Office of the Press Secretary, "Remarks by the President on Fiscal Policy," dated April 13, 2011, accessed at http://www.whitehouse.gov/the-press-office/2011/04/13/remarks-president-fiscal-policy.

CHAPTER 12

Continuity and Change
in Obama's Foreign Policy

Robert S. Singh

BARACK OBAMA'S victory in the 2008 presidential election was greeted at least as enthusiastically outside as within the United States. After one of the most controversial and divisive periods in the history of American foreign policy under President George W. Bush, the Obama administration was expected to make decisive changes for the better in the style, substance, and results of US relations with the wider world. Not only had America confronted its painful racial past in electing an African American president, but it thereby embraced new international leadership by a progressive who grew up in Hawaii and Indonesia, a self-proclaimed "citizen of the world"[1] mindful of how non-Americans often resent what he called "our tireless promotion of American-style capitalism and multinational corporations" and "tolerance and occasional encouragement of tyranny, corruption and environmental degradation when it serves our interests."[2] As Obama predicted to his wife in his White House campaign's earliest moments, "The day I take the oath of office, the world will look at us differently,"[3] a claim confirmed by opinion surveys during his first two years as president and by the award of the 2009 Nobel Peace Prize.[4] Rarely has a change of administration generated such broad excitement or high expectations.

Still, as the Obama administration progressed, those expectations were substantially—perhaps permanently—tempered. The international problems confronting the president appear more intractable than malleable, especially with the US stretched economically and militarily: gains in Afghanistan remain "fragile and reversible," as a late 2010 policy review concluded; Israeli–Palestinian negotiations remain fraught with difficulties; Iran steadfastly rejects compromise on its nuclear ambitions; popular uprisings across the Arab world threaten to derail long-standing American allies; Russian–US relations remain uneven; China and India have been minimally supportive of US priorities, especially on climate change; trade liberalization has stalled; Iraq's democracy remains fragile; the prison at Guantanamo Bay remains open; and despite the audacious killing of Osama bin Laden by U.S. Navy SEALS in his Abbottabad compound on May 2, 2011, al Qaeda remains active, from Pakistan to Yemen.

The president rapidly achieved one key objective: reestablishing much of the international confidence in US leadership that was badly eroded during the Bush presidency. And the administration's approach was widely—though not universally—welcomed as a return to the multilateral, consultative, and pragmatically realist tradition that Bush was perceived to have abandoned. But the pronounced distance from the euphoria of November 2008 flows from the fact that signature elements of Obama's foreign policy reflected continuity with George W. Bush's, rather than fundamental change: more a recalibration than a repudiation. Though the emollient tone and powerful symbolism of the new administration's diplomacy confirmed Obama's election campaign promise of "hope," questions of policy substance and results were more mixed. Indeed, by the summer of 2010 some respected US foreign policy observers were cautioning that Obama had "yet to bank a significant foreign policy success."[5] Former national security advisor Brent Scowcroft, while crediting Obama as an extraordinary communicator successfully changing international attitudes toward America, cautioned, "I'm still not sure, however, that he's the kind of chief executive that can take ideas, turn them into programs and initiatives, and then successfully execute and sell them."[6]

No definitive judgment can be delivered on a foreign policy in a volume devoted to first appraisals. Volatile elements in the international system can prompt unexpected events, policy reversals, and innovations that reshape evaluations overnight. Moreover, the hyper-partisan and sharply polarized nature of contemporary US politics both erodes the notion that "politics stops at the water's edge" and impedes dispassionate assessments of presidential leadership.

Nonetheless, it is important to attempt a balanced appraisal of Obama's strategic choices and achievements. In this chapter, Obama's foreign policy is assessed in four stages. The Obama inheritance and its prospects for foreign policy change are appraised, followed by the administration's strategic approach and the personnel chosen to carry it out. Third, the administration's progress in addressing key foreign policy challenges is evaluated. The concluding section asks how, and how far, Obama's foreign policy has departed from his predecessor's—and assesses its future prospects.

Change We Can Believe In, Part I: Foreign Policy Principles

Obama's election promised major changes in foreign policy and a new era in America's international relations, calibrated to the arrival of what Fareed Zakaria termed a "post-American world."[7] The president's public statements and speeches, from his book *The Audacity of Hope* through the 2008 election campaign, had emphasized several distinct but interrelated themes that implied a decisive break with the Bush years. He stressed America's interdependence with the world; the persistence and centrality—for good and ill—of globalization; the need to strengthen alliances and international institutions to tackle shared global challenges, from terrorism to climate change, nuclear proliferation to pandemics; the desirability of engaging US adversaries; and the restoration of the link between America's internal values and external policies. "We reject as false," Obama said in his inaugural address, "the choice between our safety and our ideals." Such commitments both repudiated his predecessor and signaled a willingness to adapt to the emergence of a more multi-polar and interconnected world.

Simultaneously, though, Obama seemed to reaffirm a traditional presidential commitment to preserving US primacy. Although recognizing a "changed world" in his inaugural address, Obama stated explicitly that "we are ready to lead once more."[8] In her Senate confirmation hearings as secretary of state one week earlier, Hillary Clinton had stressed "we must strengthen America's position of global leadership" to ensure America remains "a positive force in the world."[9] The administration took office conscious the world had changed, yet committed to renewing US leadership in ways that, directly and indirectly, implied it had not. This inherent tension, and the accompanying adjustment to an era of limits on US leadership, influence, and global reach, emerged as constant features of the administration's first two years.

From the outset, Obama's foreign policy inheritance was at least as problematic as his domestic "in-box." US forces were deployed in two major interventions of uncertain course and Obama was the first president since Richard Nixon to assume office with a shooting war in progress. After eight years of an aggressive "war on terror" the threat of mass fatality attacks from al Qaeda, its affiliates, and Western "homegrown" Islamist terrorists remained serious. Rising autocratic powers and petrodollar states from Latin America to Central Asia were increasingly assertive. Iran's and North Korea's ambitions for nuclear weapons threatened regional desta-bilization in the Middle East and East Asia. The festering Israel–Palestine conflict fueled Muslim extremism and threatened further wars. Failed, failing, and weak states continued to export lethal violence. International cooperation to advance free trade, combat climate change, and prevent pandemics had hardly advanced.

The international challenges facing Obama were therefore multiple, grave, and urgent—but after the Bush era, Washington's leverage in the international order appeared diminished. American power was widely resented and US judgment questioned. The financial crisis and recession compounded the spiraling budget deficits from 2001 to 2009, raising serious questions regarding the economic foun-dations of US power. Attempts at increased burden-sharing with NATO and other allies were only fitfully successful.

Moreover, the American public was disinclined to back major foreign commitments. A 2009 Pew Research Center/Council on Foreign Relations poll found 49 percent of Americans believed the United States should "mind its own business internationally"—the largest-ever plurality Pew had recorded in favor of an isolationist stance. Forty-four percent of Americans also inclined toward unilateralism, agreeing "we should go our own way in international matters, not worrying about whether other countries agree with us or not," the highest proportion since Gallup first asked the question in 1964.[10]

Politically, Obama therefore faced three contextual dilemmas. One was that, as David Sanger noted:

> The world he is inheriting from Bush will constrain his choices more than he has acknowledged, and certainly more than the throngs of supporters believed as they waved their signs proclaiming CHANGE. His biggest risk is that he will take the anti-Bush turn too far—that his cool, analytic approach will be seen, in times of crisis, as a lack of resolve; that his control and calmness might be viewed, over time, as a mask for an absence of conviction.[11]

That related to the second: the febrile pressures of Beltway life. Could Obama "change the nation before the nation's capital changed him"[12] and, by extension, exert a serious influence on the "arc of history" in the wider world, despite domestic priorities and the sharply polarized politics on Capitol Hill?

The third was that the urgency of the geopolitical problems confronting Washington sat uneasily with the need for sufficient patience to bring about concerted international action to resolve them. Precisely because US hard and soft power resources were strained, the instruments by which the administration could effect unilateral, decisive, and rapid global change were relatively weak.

The cumulative result meant that renewing US leadership in an increasingly multi-polar—perhaps even "non-polar"[13]—world required an imaginative approach. Obama's response was to emphasize a pragmatic but ambitious strategy that attended to a new era of limits. The term most commonly invoked during 2009–10 to define Obama's foreign policy was "engagement." The National Security Strategy (NSS) document of May 2010 defined this loosely as "the active participation of the United States in relationships beyond our borders."[14] A more exact definition might include employing positive and negative inducements to convince or cajole others that changing their behavior is their most rewarding or least harmful course of action. (Although a "pure" policy of engagement would abandon negative inducements or threats altogether,[15] I will use "engagement" to cover both variants.)

Engagement's underlying logic post-Bush was clear. First, organizing US foreign policy around threats such as al Qaeda and "rogue states" marginalized globalization as the primary driving force in twenty-first-century geopolitics. This was especially true since, second, a "global war on terror" elevated terrorism to an unwarranted preeminence among multiple foreign policy challenges while alienating the world's 1.5 billion Muslims. Third, in an international environment of rising powers and transnational challenges, an overemphasis on American exceptionalism weakened Washington's capacity to persuade other states to adequately share the burden of policing the international order. As Secretary Clinton declared on the NSS's publication:

> We are looking to turn a multi-polar world into a multi-partner world. I know there is a critique among some that somehow talking this way undercuts American strength, power, leadership. I could not disagree more. I think that we are seeking to gain partners in pursuing American interests. We happen to think a lot of those interests coincide with universal interests.[16]

By emphasizing shared interests that required every stakeholder in the international order to exercise rights and responsibilities, engagement sought to give others incentives to take a greater role in establishing and enforcing norms of international conduct. This would send clear signals to those—terrorist networks, failed states, outlaw regimes, and others—who refused to follow the order's rules, and ease the path to their effective isolation by the broader international community. As the NSS stated, "Rules of the road must be followed, and there must be consequences for those nations that break the rules—whether they are non-proliferation obligations, trade agreements, or human rights commitments."[17]

Engagement embraced the international order's shifting tectonics. By "resetting" relations with other powers, abandoning the war on terror's militaristic frame, pledging the United States to adhere to common norms and shared conventions, and addressing not only allies but adversaries—and, further, appealing to individuals and civil societies as well as governments—the administration sought to convey a powerful symbolic and substantive contrast to its ill-loved predecessor. Democracy promotion and the Bush "freedom agenda" were now secondary. Force took a back seat to vigorous diplomacy. Open markets required global coordination and enhanced regulation. Sovereignty needed to incorporate shared responsibilities.[18] Seeking greater balance and reciprocity in his foreign policy, Obama repeatedly stressed its essence as forging new global relationships "on the basis of mutual interests and mutual respect."[19] To translate these theoretical underpinnings into a coherent "Obama Doctrine" depended, of course, on their effective practice and concrete results.

Change We Can Believe In, Part II:
Foreign Policy Principals and Practice

The success of US foreign policy depends critically on presidential attention; the principal officials appointed by the president; his management of their inevitable tensions, conflicts, and rivalries; and the effective execution of the policy decisions reached. Obama's avowed intention during his transition was to ensure that his foreign policy principals operated as a "team of rivals"[20] rather than rival teams, as had too often characterized prior administrations (Democratic and Republican). If an implicit model existed, it was that of George H. W. Bush, whose foreign policy team from 1989–93 was experienced, cooperative, and generally effective, as well as unashamedly pragmatic rather than doctrinaire in its approach.

Obama's selections were widely approved within the Beltway, representing a blend of experience and freshness, policy expertise and political *nous*. The appointments drew on experts from the academy and think tanks such as the Brookings Institution and the Center for American Progress, with an eye toward bridging the distinct realist and liberal internationalist foreign policy strands within the Democratic Party's coalition.[21] With a strong Democratic Party majority in the Senate, few encountered confirmation problems. Clinton's selection as secretary of state was bold, imaginative, and unifying. Retaining Robert Gates as secretary of defense made both political and policy sense, as a bipartisan pick who ensured continuity of control in the Pentagon during wartime. The choice of retired Marine General James Jones, a former adviser to John McCain, as assistant to the president for national security, consolidated the centrist cast of the team. Vice President Joseph Biden, a former chair of the Senate Foreign Relations Committee with extensive experience and contacts, promised to play an important role as well. With White House chief of staff Rahm Emanuel and adviser David Axelrod contributing the more overtly political calculations, Obama's original selections suggested a chief executive comfortable with a broad array of views and advice, albeit from a relatively narrow, centrist (and non-business) spectrum of opinion.

From the outset, these principals engaged in one of the most concerted efforts at strategic engagement and renewed diplomacy seen by a new administration. Clinton's first overseas visit was to China and Southeast Asia, while specially appointed envoys such as George Mitchell and Richard Holbrooke made several missions to their respective regions of Israel and "Af-Pak" (Afghanistan and Pakistan). In only his first year, Obama announced his intention to have the United States close the Guantanamo Bay detention facility, end torture, rejoin the UN Human Rights Council, and catch up on its UN dues. The president initiated a major push on nuclear nonproliferation that resulted in his chairing a UN Security Council session in September (the first time a US president had done so) and convening thirty-eight heads of government in a DC security summit in

April 2010. He traveled to Ankara and Cairo to open a new dialogue with the Muslim world, to Accra to reach out to Africa, and to Prague and Oslo to advance the cause of a non-nuclear world and accept the Nobel Peace Prize, respectively. He opened a bilateral diplomatic initiative to Tehran and spoke directly to the Iranian people. He announced a firm date of August 2010 for the withdrawal of all US combat forces from Iraq, while approving a new "surge" (and timeline for withdrawal) as part of a comprehensive revised strategy for Afghanistan. He pledged to "reset" relations with Russia and advance strategic arms reductions. In terms of global perceptions, the effort to establish a new beginning could hardly have been clearer.

To this end, too, Obama visited more countries in his first year of office than any other president, making ten trips to twenty-one nations; his closest competitor was George H. W. Bush, who visited fourteen countries in 1989. The speeches the president made were crucial in transforming the tone of US foreign policy, especially those in Prague, Cairo, and Oslo. The Nobel Prize, while admittedly premature (and politically problematic at home), testified to the positive attitudes outside America toward Obama.

As Table 12.1 shows, Obama's restoration of US favorability ratings was not universal. Obama's immense popularity in western Europe and Africa was somewhat lower in central and eastern Europe, India, and Israel. But the most conspicuous and consequential exceptions were those where he made the greatest effort to project an empathetic image, namely, the Muslim world. From his inaugural declaration that America was not at war with Islam, through the decision to give his first television interview to Arab language channel *Al Arabiya*, to his offer of an "outstretched hand" to Iran and speeches emphasizing America's eagerness for relationships based on mutual interest and respect, Obama prioritized changing Muslim attitudes toward the United States. But his success was slight. While polls documented a higher level of approval than had obtained under Bush, this increase occurred from a very low base and still registered strong animus in many Muslim states, not least those formally classified as US "allies," such as Egypt, Turkey, Jordan, and Pakistan. A serious and long-standing tension between American interests and values in the Middle East could not be talked away, as Obama's cautious response to the popular protests in Tunisia, Egypt, Yemen, Bahrain, and Syria in the spring of 2011 appeared to confirm. The reluctant decision to accede to US participation in another military intervention in the region, against a Muslim regime in Libya, also highlighted the difficulty in balancing ideals, alliances, and interests.

The president rarely spoke to domestic audiences about international affairs.[22] But his travels earned him trenchant criticism at home. Obama, his critics charged, was conducting an "apology tour." Worse, they argued, the president was weak yet

TABLE 12.1 US Favorability Rating 2010 (percentage of respondents expressing "very favorable" and "somewhat favorable" attitudes)

	1999/2000	2002	2003	2005	2006	2007	2008	2009	2010
US	–	–	–	83	76	80	84	88	85
Britain	83	75	70	55	56	51	53	69	65
France	62	62	42	43	39	39	42	75	73
Germany	78	60	45	42	37	30	31	64	63
Spain	50	–	38	41	23	34	33	58	61
Poland	86	79	–	62	–	61	68	67	74
Russia	37	61	37	52	43	41	46	44	57
Turkey	52	30	15	23	12	9	12	14	17
Egypt	–	–	–	–	30	21	22	27	17
Jordan	–	25	1	21	15	20	19	25	21
Lebanon	–	36	27	42	–	47	51	55	52
China	–	–	–	42	47	34	41	47	58
India	–	66	–	71	56	59	66	76	66
Indonesia	75	61	15	38	30	29	37	63	59
Japan	77	72	–	–	63	61	50	59	66
Pakistan	23	10	13	23	27	15	19	16	17
South Korea	58	52	46	–	–	58	70	78	79
Argentina	50	34	–	–	–	16	22	38	42
Brazil	–	–	–	–	–	–	–	–	62
Mexico	68	64	–	–	–	56	47	69	56
Kenya	94	80	–	–	–	87	–	90	94
Nigeria	46	76	61	–	62	70	64	79	81

Source: Pew Research Center, Pew Global Attitudes Survey of Twenty-Two Nations, Q7a, 92-95: "Please tell me if you have a very favorable, somewhat favorable, somewhat unfavorable or very unfavorable opinion of: The United States"; 1999/2000 survey trends provided by the Office of Research, US Department of State.

arrogant—since to believe his mere appearance and oratory could alter the deep-seated attitudes of tens of millions of people was narcissistic but also naive about the way the world works. Even if Obama "still retains an aura of charisma abroad," James Ceaser complained, "to date it has yet to bring any of the benefits that were promised." Ceaser continued:

> This kind of soft-power realism hardly bespeaks a foreign policy conducted on the basis of "a decent respect to the opinions of mankind," where principles are set down as markers designed to help open eyes to the rights of man. It represents instead a foreign policy based on promoting an indecent pandering to an evanescent infatuation with a single personality.[23]

It was unsurprising that a sharp conservative critique should rapidly emerge of Obama's foreign policies, which effectively amounted to calibrated strategic retrenchment: minimizing unilateralism, encouraging multilateralism, and espousing less rather than more assertiveness abroad. Its central charge was that efforts to gracefully manage an inevitable decrease in US power were misguided since, as Charles Krauthammer put it, "Nothing is inevitable. . . . For America today, decline is not a condition. Decline is a choice."[24]

Attacks on this purported choice rested on three claims. First, it was foolish to "normalize" America in the community of nations, because America was not "normal." As Bush administration official John Bolton argued,

> Central to [Obama's] worldview is rejecting American exceptionalism and the consequences that flow therefrom. Since an overwhelming majority of the world's population would welcome the demise of American exceptionalism, they are delighted with Obama. One student interviewed after an Obama town hall meeting during his first presidential trip to Europe said ecstatically, "He sounds like a European." Indeed he does.[25]

Second, backtracking from the aggressively militaristic approach of the Bush administration was ill-conceived and counterproductive, damaging allies' confidence in US commitments while unduly weakening key elements of homeland security.

Third, Obama's instrumental view of alliances—stressing their relevance to current US strategic challenges rather than to historical bonds of common experiences or shared values—neglected crucial relationships and allowed traditional ties to fray.[26]

As Mitt Romney—former Massachusetts governor, and past and future Republican presidential aspirant, summarized it,

> [Obama] envisions America as a nation whose purpose is to arbitrate disputes rather than to advocate ideals, a country consciously seeking equidistance between allies and adversaries. We have never seen anything quite like it, really. And in positioning the United States in the way he has, President Obama has positioned himself as a figure transcending America instead of defending America.[27]

Many of these critiques fell flat. After all, Obama was never so naive as to believe that speeches alone could secure substantive policy changes. His conviction was instead that by demonstrating outreach, humility, and appreciation of other cultures and peoples the necessary, and possibly sufficient, geopolitical space could be established to restore US standing and credibility. As Walter Russell Mead argued, Obama's tightrope walk required him to judge carefully how to blend his Jeffersonian instincts—to limit commitments abroad, strengthen the US economy, and renew the example of American democracy at home—with his Wilsonian idealism in support of universal values of human rights, the rule of law, and constitutional liberal democracy.[28]

Key Challenges

Even if elements of conservative criticism were excessive, Obama's policy results were decidedly mixed. It is to those results we now turn. In a variety of regions, Obama's incremental achievements confirmed the limits on Washington's influence in an era of exacting geopolitical and economic constraints.

Pakistan, Afghanistan, and the War on Terror

The most immediate foreign policy challenge was South Asia. In June 2010, almost nine years after its launch, Afghanistan succeeded Vietnam as the longest war in American history.[29] Candidate Obama had labeled the Afghan war a necessary and just one, unlike the "war of choice" on Iraq. As commander-in-chief, the task of winning—and/or ending—the war fell to him. But despite two surges in US troops, two changes of military leadership in theater, and a shift from a counterterrorism to a hybrid counterinsurgency approach, the war remained unresolved. Moreover, coalition casualties increased significantly during 2009–10, fighting became more intense, and the Taliban became increasingly confident of prevailing. Obama confronted the dilemma of waging a difficult, increasingly unpopular military campaign that—especially after December 2009—he now owned in full.

Anticipating that Afghanistan would shortly become "Obama's war," the president approved the deployment of 21,000 additional US troops in March 2009, the largest increase since the war began in 2001. In May, Secretary of Defense Gates sacked General David McKiernan, the top US and NATO commander in Afghanistan, after less than a year in post. McKiernan's replacement was General Stanley McChrystal, who had conducted counterinsurgency operations in Iraq. The same month, Obama hosted a trilateral meeting with Presidents Asif Ali Zardari of Pakistan and Hamid Karzai of Afghanistan where they agreed on a common objective: to disrupt, dismantle, and defeat al Qaeda. After a new strategy review from McChrystal—deliberately leaked to the media to pressure the White House—asked for some 40,000 additional troops, in August 2009 Obama launched an immensely detailed personal review of the situation.

The protracted deliberations over the course of three months reflected the acute difficulties posed by the war and profound divisions within Obama's foreign policy team. The more hawkish principals supporting a broad counterinsurgency strategy (especially Clinton, Gates, and Admiral Mike Mullen, chair of the Joint Chiefs of Staff) were opposed by several officials favoring a narrower and more limited counterterrorism approach (most notably, Biden, Jones, Emanuel, Holbrooke, and the US ambassador to Afghanistan, Karl Eikenberry). Proponents of counterinsurgency, aimed at protecting and winning over the Afghan population, cited the success of General David Petraeus's "surge" in Iraq from 2007 to 2009. Building a credible government in Kabul was necessary, if not in itself sufficient, to prevent al Qaeda's return and the restoration of a Taliban Afghanistan as a terrorist training haven. Advocates of a more limited strategy they called "Counter terrorism Plus" focused instead on targeting al Qaeda operatives via Unmanned Aerial Vehicles (UAVs or, more commonly, "drones") and special forces units. They stressed the problems surrounding counterinsurgency: the limited reach and rampant corruption of the Kabul government; Karzai's rigged reelection in August 2009; and the presence of insufficient Afghan army and police forces to keep order in a notoriously ungovernable nation. Since it was estimated that only some 400 Al Qaeda *jihadists* remained in Afghanistan, a counterterrorism strategy could facilitate the exit of most US forces within a short time frame.

Obama's political pressures and the major divisions among administration principals ultimately resulted in a compromise, announced at West Point in December 2009. The additional increase of 30,000 troops was—in a rare outbreak of bipartisanship—strongly endorsed by congressional Republicans, for whom "victory" in Afghanistan remained a strategic necessity. But many Democrats were unconvinced. By offering a review after one year to determine the strategy's efficacy, and promising the beginning of a troop drawdown from July 2011, Obama sought to reassure his supporters and set a favorable political framework for his 2012 reelection campaign. McChrystal had been granted more troops, but Obama and Biden had narrowed the mission from "defeating" al Qaeda to "denying" al Qaeda a safe haven, effectively mandating both a rapid escalation and prompt withdrawal.

The compromise was, at once, both eminently rational and not quite coherent. The West Point address was distinctly low-key—explicit on the financial as well as human costs entailed, echoing not Churchillian vigor but Dwight Eisenhower's calls for budgetary prudence and balance, and directly contesting parallels with Vietnam—and it made one deliberate omission: "any definition of victory."[30]

As one Obama adviser explained, "Our Afghan policy was focused as much as anything on domestic politics. He would not risk losing the moderate to centrist Democrats in the middle of health care reform and he viewed that legislation as the make-or-break legislation for his administration."[31] But the geopolitical price of preserving political capital for domestic ends was substantial and potentially dangerous, in signaling to key regional players (the Taliban, al Qaeda, the Afghan government, Pakistan, and Iran) that a US exit was on the horizon. As one US Marine recalled, the most popular saying among Afghan tribesmen was "The Americans have the watches, but we have the time."[32] In effect, the new strategy echoed Nixon's "Vietnamization" approach from 1969–74: "Afghanizing" the conflict to draw down US forces and, ultimately, exit completely. But, while pointedly abandoning the language of a global war on terror, Obama proved no more able than his predecessor at squaring a problematic circle: al Qaeda was no longer a major force in Afghanistan but was increasingly active in Pakistan, Yemen, and Somalia. As Gideon Rachman put it, "The west is fighting a war on terrorism in Afghanistan. But the terrorists are somewhere else. Meanwhile, our ability to combat threats around the world is sapped by the huge drain on resources caused by the Afghan war."[33] Spending hundreds of billions of dollars on the fifth-poorest nation on earth had not won over civilian hearts and minds. Afghan attitudes to US forces ranged from wary to hostile, while al Qaeda's prize target—nuclear-armed Pakistan—remained anything but a stable and reliable US ally. Nor were American hearts and minds convinced, with 57 percent disapproving of Obama's handling of Afghanistan by August 2010.[34]

The Obama administration rightly refocused US strategy to embrace Pakistan as the key to stabilizing Afghanistan ("I think Afghanistan and Pakistan are the same problem," the president told an interviewer in late 2010).[35] The Enhanced Partnership with Pakistan Act of 2009 provided $7.5 billion in aid over five years, tripling economic aid and rebalancing military and civil society contributions. Frustratingly, this increased priority did little to extend US leverage or accelerate a definitive and lasting resolution. Islamabad resented being lumped together with Afghanistan as "Af-Pak." The internal pressures that the US military campaign fueled caused consternation within Pakistani society and the military. When asked in a July 2009 *Al Jazeera*-Gallup poll, "Some people believe that the Pakistan Taliban are the greatest threat to the country, some believe India is the greatest threat, whereas some believe the U.S. is the greatest threat. Who do you think is the greatest threat for Pakistan?," only 11 percent cited the Pakistan Taliban. Eighteen percent suggested India—and 59 percent identified the United States.[36]

US drone strikes on border areas, incursions within Pakistani sovereign territory, and the relocation of al Qaeda leaders to Pakistani cities and towns abetted the rise of a radicalized Pakistani Taliban. While some elements of the state, especially within the military and the ISI intelligence service, were willing (under heavy US pressure) to deal coercively with the Pakistani Taliban and al Qaeda forces targeting the Pakistani government in some border provinces, they were much less interested in the Afghan Taliban. With the conflict with its existential enemy, India, still Islamabad's top priority, and the perceived need to maintain "strategic depth" in Afghanistan as and when the United States withdrew (to prevent either chaos or enhanced Indian influence), Pakistan continued to play a decades-long double game.[37] Lacking incentives to induce Pakistan's compliance, and unwilling to use sanctions that might conceivably force cooperation, Washington remained effectively in a state of limbo. That the U.S. operation to kill Osama bin Laden had to be undertaken without notifying Pakistan in advance illustrated the glaring lack of trust between Washington and Islamabad.

By midterm, Obama's evolving South Asia strategy was therefore mired in a double irony. First, Obama's engagement strategy was premised on the notion that terrorism was merely one of many dilemmas, yet (as journalist Jonathan Alter noted) he "was acutely conscious that protecting the country was his first responsibility, and he devoted more time to confronting al Qaeda and other terrorist groups than to any other challenge of his presidency."[38] But Obama was also unwilling to be defined as a war president, given that he saw real needs at home; global conflicts were less existential than "problems that need managing," unfortunate distractions from his domestic "nation-building" priorities.[39]

Second, the success of the strategy relied on the same individual to whom Bush had previously turned to salvage Iraq. In July 2010, *Rolling Stone* magazine ran a long story on "The Runaway General," exposing the contempt of General McChrystal and his team for the administration's leadership. The revelations posed a crucial test for civil–military relations.[40] With no real choice—and already resentful of what he saw as the military leadership's efforts to limit his policymaking options—Obama exercised the most direct assertion of presidential authority over the military since Truman had sacked General MacArthur in 1951. He fired McChrystal, replacing him with the only credible alternative, General David Petraeus, architect of the surge strategy in Iraq that Obama had opposed as a US Senator.

The president thereby effectively tied his most pressing security concern to the assessments of Petraeus. Obama appeared at West Point to promise an early end to the war but, given subsequent qualifications about "conditions on the ground" and the acute problems in building Afghan forces, some knowledgeable observers estimated that at least 50,000 troops would still be in Afghanistan through 2012.[41] Indeed, the December 2010 policy review made 2014 a more likely date. As Major General Bill Mayville, McChrystal's chief of operations, conceded, the eventual outcome might more likely resemble Vietnam than Desert Storm: "It's not going to look like a win, smell like a win or taste like a win. . . . This is going to end in an argument."[42]

Iran

Obama became the latest in a succession of presidents since 1979 to be confronted by the dilemma of relations with the Islamic Republic of Iran. Iran was "Exhibit A" as a test case for the administration's engagement approach, which saw several public and private overtures to the Iranian leadership and people during 2009. The opaque features of Tehran's governing regime make it difficult to assess how far internal deliberations seriously entertained any "grand bargain" with Washington.

What is clear is that the outcome of such discussions was a decisive rejection of Obama's outstretched hand.

Iran's domestic political crisis complicated the outreach effort, notably with the popular demonstrations that erupted after the June 2009 presidential election was widely seen as having been stolen by President Mahmoud Ahmadinejad. The violently repressive reaction to the protests reflected longer-term trends in which the theocratic regime was increasingly morphing into a security state or quasi-military dictatorship, with the Iranian Revolutionary Guards Corps (IRGC) assuming ever greater influence in economic policy, politics, and foreign policy-making.[43] Obama's open-hand policy in some ways assisted the protests, since the regime could not credibly blame a United States transparently seeking *rapprochement* with Tehran of malign intent or pursuing regime change. Indeed, many Iranian protestors were disappointed with Obama's initially muted response. Many reform-minded Iranians and American proponents of regime change favored a greater emphasis on enriching human rights than on opposing uranium enrichment, arguing for ceasing engagement to deepen the legitimacy crisis and hoping that a successful Green Movement would at least prove more willing to negotiate on the nuclear issue.

The increasingly repressive regime response caused a steady shift in the administration's approach by early 2010, with a renewed emphasis on economic sanctions and diplomatic attempts to increase Iran's isolation. The UN Security Council resolution adopted in June 2010 (over the objections of erstwhile US allies Turkey and Brazil) imposed new targeted sanctions on Iran, albeit not the "crippling" sanctions sought by the United States, UK, and France. Obama also signed legislation that summer imposing new sanctions on foreign entities involved in refined petroleum sales doing business with key Iranian banks or the IRGC.

As in the Clinton administration, the well-intentioned efforts to engage Iran were ultimately unproductive, a case of "giving futility its chance." The administration did entertain from the outset the prospect of Tehran refusing to soften its hard-line approach. The additional sanctions, the decision to exclude Iran from the US policy not to employ nuclear weapons against states that were not nuclear-armed,[44] and the subsequent revival of speculation about possible military action—whether genuine or a tactical bluff—therefore occurred after a number of transparent tests of Iran's leadership had failed. By September 2010, the abandonment of engagement in favor of promoting regime change was complete, with Clinton calling for "some effort inside Iran, by responsible civil and religious leaders, to take hold of the apparatus of the state."[45] Meanwhile Arab alarm at Iran's growing power escalated[46]—as did the Iranian nuclear program and a reassertion of Iranian influence across its region. The secret diplomatic cables published by WikiLeaks in November 2010 confirmed that states such as Saudi Arabia had privately urged the United States, under both Bush and Obama, to take military action against Iran.[47] Iran's approach to Iraq and Afghanistan, especially, amounted to systematically promoting "managed chaos": assisting indigenous insurgents to cause sufficient problems for US and allied forces to hasten their withdrawal without bringing about a state collapse that could threaten Iranian interests.

The fundamental dilemma for US policymakers was therefore no closer to resolution at midterm than at the outset of the Obama administration. If an Iranian nuclear capacity, or actual weapon(s), represented a strategic "red-line" for Washington, what coercive measures would the White House contemplate to prevent it, given the inevitable Iranian military response across the region to American or Israeli strikes, the effect such strikes would have on Iranian domestic opinion (still relatively pro-Western), and the limited international support for another US use of force against a Muslim state? Increasingly, administration signals suggested a resigned acceptance of a nuclear-capable Iran and a nascent shift to a Cold War–style strategy of containment and deterrence. But, facing what Tel Aviv perceived as the genuine threat of another *Shoah*, how long Israeli tolerance of Iran's efforts would last remained to be seen. The worst case was laid out by Dana Allin and Steve Simon in their book-length review of the increasingly parlous predicament: "The compressed coil of disaster linking Iran, Israel and the United States is not the only problem facing the Obama administration, and it may not even be its worst problem. But Iran's defiance and Israel's panic are the fuses for a war that could destroy all of Obama's other ambitions."[48]

Israel–Palestine

This issue was hard to separate from broader American policy vis-à-vis Israel and the Arab world. Obama had pledged to focus from day one on advancing a lasting settlement of the Israel–Palestine conflict, both for its intrinsic importance and because he viewed rapid progress as essential for US national interests. But few issues proved as stubbornly intractable. Obama himself considered the conflict the one area of foreign policy "failure" in 2009, conceding that his administration had "overestimated our ability to persuade" the two parties to take steps to advance the peace process "when their [domestic] politics ran contrary to that."[49]

American diplomacy here was especially ineffectual. The focal point for Obama's effort was Jewish settlements, a potentially shrewd choice to exert leverage on Tel Aviv (since most Israelis are not strongly supportive of further expansion, especially in the West Bank). But the diplomatic execution was poor, with an inexperienced White House staff overestimating presidential influence while misjudging the dynamics of Israeli coalition politics. Obama's capacity for persuasion was undercut by popular Israeli distrust and declining confidence in the two-state solution and land-for-peace formula. Obama's Cairo speech exacerbated this, since it was not accompanied by a visit to Israel—an apparent indication of indifference to Israeli interests—and his demand for a settlement freeze was not echoed by calls on Arab states to take commensurate risks for peace. The president's courageous attempt to confront Arab and Muslim Holocaust denial also fell short, since his grounding of support for Israel in the World War II genocide rather than wider biblical and historical claims to Palestine (and any implicit comparison of Palestinian suffering to the *Shoah*) struck Israelis as insulting. Since political pressure on Binyamin Netanyahu's coalition came from the right, the issue also allowed the prime minister to stand firm on settlements.

An eventual compromise, reached in November 2009, for a ten-month freeze excluding Jerusalem generated a new crisis when Clinton declared it "unprecedented" and a demonstration of Israeli "restraint," which most Arabs found farcical. The Obama administration was then incensed when Vice President Biden was humiliated on a visit to Jerusalem in March 2010 during which the Israeli housing minister declared the construction of 1600 new units in East Jerusalem. The rebuke was returned when Obama abruptly left Netanyahu alone in the Oval Office on a subsequent meeting in Washington. The resumption of direct peace talks in Washington on September 2, 2010, with regular fortnightly efforts scheduled thereafter, did offer tentative hopes of progress, subject to a formidable array of obstacles on the Israeli (extremist religious and right-wing parties in the coalition), Palestinian (the division between Fatah and Hamas), and American (competing congressional, AIPAC, J Street, and other lobbies) sides.

But the prospects for conflict resolution remain weak, not least since the gulf in US–Israeli relations that developed over 2009–2010, while not unprecedented, was deep and alarming for supporters of close bilateral ties. While American warmth toward Israel remains steadfast, fewer than half of Americans support defending Israel against an attack by its neighbors,[50] and an increasing partisan polarization has arisen, with Republicans far closer to near unconditional support than an increasingly skeptical cohort of Democrats.[51] For all of Obama's attempts at outreach to Muslims, the chaotic efforts to pressure Tel Aviv—along with the continued US military presence and activity in Muslim lands—substantially undercut symbolic signs of reconciliation with and renewed respect for Islam. Those outreach efforts, absent comparable concern for Israeli sentiments, in turn compounded the acute mistrust in Israel.

Resolving this basic tension in Obama's approach constitutes a necessary if insufficient condition of regional progress, but it is a tension deeply resistant to resolution. A growing American debate as to whether Israel is more a liability than an asset to national security is increasingly echoed in Israel. Most clearly, if—despite Obama's repeated assertions that a nuclear-armed Iran is "unacceptable"—Israel's closest ally is not going to disarm its one existential threat, the broader relationship faces serious challenges with profound regional implications. This was only emphasized as the "Arab spring" of 2011 threatened to replace authoritarian but "friendly" regimes in Egypt, Tunisia, Yemen, and elsewhere with less reflexively pro-American, and more strongly anti-Israeli, governments that reflected the hostile sentiments of the "Arab street." Obama's response, from initially being wary of the uprisings to eventually expressing selective support for democratic transitions and even intervening militarily (if multilaterally, after securing a United Nations Security Council Resolution and Arab League support) in Libya[52]—ostensibly to protect civilians against the Gadaffi regime but with an unsubtle eye to regime change—instilled little confidence in Israel of a coherent strategic vision from Washington.

Iraq

Obama's opposition to the Iraq war helped to secure his victory over Hillary Clinton, an early supporter of the war, in the 2008 Democratic primaries and caucuses. But the success of the "surge" strategy under Petraeus had also defused the issue for the general election, with Obama and McCain occupying broadly similar positions on Iraq's future. The Bush administration negotiated the Status of Forces Agreement and the Strategic Framework Agreement at the end of 2008. The latter accord provided parameters for US–Iraqi partnership in education, trade, diplomacy, culture, and science and technology. The former provided for the full withdrawal of US forces by December 31, 2011. Obama increased the exit's momentum by committing to withdraw all combat troops by August 2010, leaving some 50,000 for training purposes and selective combat operations with Iraqi forces. Although six months after the March 7, 2010, parliamentary elections a new government had yet to be agreed on and the incidence of violence began again to increase, the withdrawal of US combat troops proceeded apace. Troop levels dipped to 47,000 by March 2011, and Obama remained committed to a total withdrawal by the end of that year. But the post-election stalemate and the uncertain transition to Iraqi-provided security meant that while the broad parameters of the post-invasion political settlement were clear, the notion that all US forces would be home by 2012 remained in question.

China

China, America's most important bilateral relationship, remains one of Washington's most testy and fragile. Where the Bush administration had aspired to China becoming a "responsible stakeholder" in the international order, Obama's initially behaved as if that had already transpired. While avoiding the terminology, its approach to Beijing implicitly suggested that a de facto G-2 was emerging, with China being actively encouraged to assume a greater leadership role and responsibilities. Washington initially sought to deepen cooperation in 2009 on multiple fronts: multilaterally through the G-20, and bilaterally through a revamped annual Strategic and Economic Dialogue; via a presidential visit in November 2009 (making Obama the first US president to visit China during his first year of office); by deferring the traditional meeting between the US president and Tibet's Dalai Lama in the fall of that year; and by examining revisions of US relations with India to accommodate Chinese concerns.

But this policy effectively collapsed by early 2010. China was perceived to bluntly resist pressure to cease manipulating its currency, one cause of financial imbalances with the US. Obama's visit was more tightly controlled than prior presidential ones, with few tangible accomplishments. China's hard line at the Copenhagen climate change summit in December 2009 snubbed Obama while leaving Washington with the blame for the negotiations' failure. In January 2010 Google declared its intention to withdraw from China amid allegations of cyber attacks from Chinese nationals. By early 2010 the administration had concluded that the financial crisis had convinced Beijing of America's accelerating decline and the cost-free option of greater assertiveness. The administration thus shifted tack, effectively abandoning the premise of strategic engagement: that China shared the same interest in addressing challenges to the global order as America. In January 2010 Clinton made a major speech defending Internet freedom. In February, Obama met the Dalai Lama. The United States also agreed to punitive tariffs on all Chinese car and light truck tire imports and to sell defensive weapons to Taiwan. Ironically, these less emollient approaches induced some shift in Beijing, with President Hu Jintao attending the Washington nuclear security summit in April 2010 and the Chinese agreeing to the new round of UN sanctions on Iran in June.

US–China relations continued a pattern set since at least 1989. While Washington and Beijing may "objectively" share interests, neither party shares the other's priorities or values. Selective cooperation is possible where some convergence can be created, but increased cooperation in some areas coexists with a basic competitive dynamic and instances of increased competition in others. Most obviously, China's failure to exert pressure on North Korea to return to the six-party talks reflects its concern about state collapse, a secondary issue for Washington to North Korea's nuclear arsenal. Obama's policy toward Asia-Pacific has been "fundamentally similar" to Bush's in that it is intended to consolidate US strategic primacy in Asia, maintain a presence to hedge Chinese military power, and reassure Japan, South Korea, and India while seeking greater cooperation on global concerns.[53] Increasing mutual dependence coexisting with serious ideological differences mandates increased emphasis on the relationship as well as a continued policy of "modified hedging." This aims to encourage China to be a strategic partner and develop a shared strategy to that end, but also to respond judiciously to an increasingly proactive China that challenges US influence in key parts of the world.

Russia

Perhaps more than in most bilateral relations, Obama's policy to "reset" relations with Russia enjoyed substantial success, facilitated by a Moscow that—owing to the impact of a severe recession in 2009 and the partial eclipse of Vladimir Putin by the more pragmatic Dmitry Medvedev as president—was less activist, assertive, and obstructive during 2009–2010.

Russia nonetheless remained a difficult and frequently reluctant partner. As with China, Russian interests are multiple and only selectively overlapping with Washington's. Moscow's attitude to Tehran is a clear example. While the prospect of Iranian nuclear capacity to its south is not welcome, neither is it of the importance that it is to America. Moreover, improved Iranian relations with the United States and EU would not serve Russian energy interests if it undercut Russia's near monopoly supply of natural gas to several EU states. As such, partial isolation but limited rather than comprehensive sanctions represented a reasonable outcome for Moscow: while Russia voted with the United States for new sanctions on June 9, 2010, its price was to substantially narrow their scope and impact.

Nonetheless, relations between Obama and Medvedev were good and Obama's visit to Moscow in July 2009 assisted a warmer bilateral atmosphere. Washington also removed two serious irritants in the relationship by reconfiguring prior commitments to install a missile defense shield in Poland and the Czech Republic and generally downgrading its engagement in post-Soviet nations. Washington and Moscow cooperated effectively in encouraging the normalization of Turkish–Armenian relations in 2009 and managing the Kyrgyztan crisis of spring 2010. Most notably, although they missed the December 5, 2009, deadline for replacing the START I (Strategic Arms Reduction) treaty, and while ambiguities and tensions remained over the status of missile defense, Obama and Medvedev signed a "New START" agreement on April 8, 2010. Although ratification by the US Senate was not achieved until late December 2010, the progress was notable for the presidents' personal involvement, the agreement's rapid completion (in forty-five weeks, compared to the nine years of START I), and its bipartisan bolstering of Obama's broader nonproliferation efforts.

Europe

Transatlantic relations suffered substantially during the Bush years. On the surface, Obama restored much of the pre-Bush status quo, as reflected in his high approval ratings, the enthusiasm of most European leaders to bask in his reflected glow, and a high level of common purpose on nonproliferation, counterterrorism, climate change, Iran, Iraq, and Afghanistan. Beneath the surface, though, important differences of interest, policy, and values remained unaltered. The global economic crisis drew contrasting approaches as to the merits of stimulating growth (the Obama preference) versus prioritizing fiscal sustainability in the context of mounting sovereign debt (the European course). But broader differences remained that reflected deeper divisions. While Washington was increasingly keen on crafting a "global NATO," for instance, most European member states preferred a more Euro centric focus. As the European contribution to the Afghanistan mission—already more symbolic of transatlantic comity than the outcome of a genuine sense of shared threat—became even more limited in the face of the US troop surge and the operation's increasing unpopularity, Secretary Gates lamented Europe's "demilitarization" as "an impediment to achieving real security and lasting peace" in a February 2010 speech.[54] Although it was the UK and France, rather than the United States, that were most vocal for military intervention to prevent Gadaffi's repression of the Libyan uprising in the spring of 2011, the United States remained central to the military operations. Divergent threat perceptions, and contrasting approaches to policy challenges, remained intact. Moreover, a widespread perception gained ground that US priorities downgraded Europe while upgrading Asia, fears compounded by Obama's not attending the US–EU summit in Madrid in May 2010.

Conclusion: Continuity We Can Believe In?

Abroad as well as at home, Obama employed his extraordinary gifts as a friend rather than enemy of the English language to present himself as the "un-Bush": self-consciously cerebral, cool, and cosmopolitan. His conservative critics endorsed this, though angrily. Mitt Romney claimed that the result was "much more than a departure from his predecessor, George W. Bush; it is a rupture with some of the key assumptions that have undergirded more than six decades of American foreign policy."[55]

But in fact, in many ways, what Obama offered as president was less a wholesale rejection of the Bush Doctrine than a promise of its more competent execution. As Stanley Renshon argues, the pervasive national security tension in the Obama administration is between Obama's instinctive liberal internationalism and his reluctant embrace of some of Bush's security policies.[56] Especially where vital national interests are at stake, change has been limited and sometimes cosmetic: former US ambassador to Iraq, Ryan Crocker, observed of America that "patience is not our strong suit" but commended, in relation to Afghanistan and Iraq, the "welcome and extremely important" continuity in policy from Bush to Obama.[57] While in his inaugural address Obama boldly rejected as false "the choice between our safety and our ideals,"[58] as president he made precisely those necessary and inevitable trade-offs; and although the administration abandoned the assertive language of the war on terror as counterproductive, its reversal of supposedly constitutionally suspect policies was only partial.[59]

Ironically, while Dick Cheney and many conservatives castigated the president's alleged "softness" on national security, many on the left instead condemned Obama's "neo-imperialist presidency"[60] for continuing Bush policies and, in the ACLU's words, "establishing a new normal": escalating the Afghan war; vastly expanding the use of Predator and Reaper UAV drones there—and also in Pakistan, Yemen, Somalia and Libya; continuing indefinite detention and the use of military commissions; citing "state secrets" privileges to block judicial review of counterterrorism policies; continuing intrusive domestic surveillance programs; and authorizing the CIA and US military to execute extra judicial targeted assassinations.[61] Former Bush administration official Jack Goldsmith dismissed the "Cheney fallacy" that Obama had reversed Bush precedents:

> The truth is closer to the opposite: The new administration has copied most of the Bush program, has expanded some of it, and has narrowed only a bit. Almost all of the Obama changes have been at the level of packaging, argumentation, symbol, and rhetoric. . . . The main difference between the Obama and Bush administrations concerns not the substance of terrorism policy, but rather its packaging.[62]

To be clear, this is not the whole story. The changes that Obama initiated in foreign policy were consequential. In tone, emphasis, and symbolism, the re-embrace of multilateralism, diplomacy, and engagement, and the de-emphasis of confrontation, unilateral actions, and preventive war were appropriate for a new era of constrained internationalism.

The return of a restrained pragmatic realism in place of a militarized Wilsonian idealism was unsurprising. Indeed, arguably it actually began in 2005, with the result that Obama's foreign policy resembled more that of Bush's second term than the Bush second term had resembled its first. As one authoritative account argued, for example, "Both the Pentagon's Quadrennial Defense review (released in February 2010) and the White House's National Security Strategy (released in May 2010) were evolutionary rather than revolutionary."[63] Even Obama's much-lauded Nobel Peace Prize speech, "which among other things underlined the sober necessity of war, sounded in some ways not unlike the philosophy of George W. Bush."[64]

The legacy of the deep recession that followed the 2008 financial crisis compounded the longer-term geopolitics that rendered cash-strapped America a "frugal superpower."[65] As such, Obama was left with incremental means to pursue transformational ends, a predicament that rather suited his pragmatic blend of Jeffersonian realism and Wilsonian idealism. Obama's engagement strategy therefore has had much to commend it. Global Obamamania has receded but the prestige of the US "brand" is now substantially restored and the toxicity of the Bush era mitigated. Engagement's key weaknesses, however, are threefold.

First is the erroneous assumption that shared interests represent not only necessary but also, given appropriate diplomacy and incentives, sufficient conditions of alignment and cooperation on key global problems and threats. However skilled, diplomats cannot convince other governments of the merits of policies or actions that the latter do not regard as necessary, desirable, or feasible. Sovereign, as well as shared, interests matter; while not all foreign relations are zero-sum games, some are (and most are relative sum games). The notion that a new great power consortium could be corralled proved mistaken and neglectful of the key role that values and regime type play in constructions of the national interest and threat perceptions, from Israel through Turkey to China. Moreover, if politics in Washington is a "two-level game," so it is in the capitals of America's allies.[66] A greater appreciation of the domestic constraints facing US allies, especially, appeared to have emerged by the latter part of 2010. But the administration's de-emphasis of established allies in favor of "partners" compounded the disaffection in several traditional client states while gaining little buy-in from less familiar interlocutors. While the United States under Obama has a retinue of partners that would make Charlie Sheen envious, the quality of the relationships remains markedly varied.

Second, "soft power" has profound limits. Obama's approach has at times drifted away from the incentives and sanctions framework most commonly evoked by the notion of "engagement" and ignored the role of negative inducements. As a result, the perception that the president, and by extension his nation, were "weak" gained increased credence in a number of capitals. While the United States was regarded favorably, presidents rarely have the persuasive powers commonly attributed them in relation to US public opinion.[67] In terms of international relations, the utility of the "bully pulpit" is even less pronounced. Not only, for example, did the lack of suasion in regard to Iran, North Korea, Myanmar, and Pakistan undercut the broader nuclear nonproliferation effort but, as the Graham-Talent Commission on the Prevention of Weapons of Mass Destruction Proliferation and Terrorism noted, the administration displayed "no equal sense of urgency" regarding the most probable source of WMD attack: biological weapons.[68]

Third, as suggested above, engagement cannot be fully effective without attending to foreign policy's domestic foundations. The need to articulate a compelling vision for America's world role is integral to sustaining public support for internationalism. To the extent that Obama's "Cosmopolitan-in-Chief" role championed a contrite admission of historical errors, and a hedged view of American exceptionalism, more Americans might have accepted the bargain had they seen a clearer return on the investment.[69] But the substantive results have been modest. As even Zbigniew Brzezinski, a campaign adviser, conceded of Obama's foreign policy, "So far, it has generated more expectations than strategic breakthroughs."[70] Foreign policy did not cause the heavy Democratic losses in the 2010 midterms. Nor need Republican gains preclude further bipartisan progress on international affairs, especially on security matters and trade. But the election results did raise serious obstacles to Senate ratification of the Comprehensive Test Ban Treaty and renewed legislative efforts on climate change, immigration reform, and energy independence, among many others.

For every president, translating a strategic vision into operational reality is a difficult work in constant progress. Obama's statecraft is subtle, serious, and ambitious in scope but, at least thus far, with the notable exception of Osama bin Laden's elimination, modest in accomplishments. It may yet be the case that Guantanamo is closed, Afghanistan and Pakistan stabilized, Iran persuaded to abandon its military nuclear ambitions, corrupt autocracies across the Arab world replaced by pro-American liberal democracies, and Israelis and Palestinians coaxed and cajoled into a permanent peace. But so far, Obama's diplomatic outreach, downsizing of militarism, and demotion of democracy promotion have yielded mostly tentative and faltering steps toward long-term objectives. Of course, as John F. Kennedy cautioned in his 1961 inaugural address, "All this will not be finished in the first one hundred days. Nor will it be finished in the first one thousand days."[71] By its nature, a policy of engagement requires time to bear fruit. Where this does not occur, the diplomatic and political contexts for future policy corrections can still be altered, to permit revisions to more coercive or confrontational approaches.

Like presidents before him, Obama may find that foreign policy assumes a more prominent and problematic place in coming years—on the one hand, as congressional opposition to his domestic agenda proves difficult to overcome; and on the other, as gathering storms in Afghanistan, Pakistan, Iran, Israel, and various Arab states loom increasingly large. The worry also remains that "Obama's wars" may yet eclipse or unhinge his domestic priorities, as Vietnam did to Lyndon Johnson's. As one view from abroad put it, "In the war on terror, as in much else, this president's pragmatic search for the middle way is in danger of satisfying nobody. It is turning into the recurring pattern, and may become the ultimate tragedy, of his presidency."[72]

Notes

1. Barack Obama, "A World That Stands as One," Berlin, Germany, July 24, 2008, available at http://hotlineoncall.nationaljournal.com/archives/2008/07/a_world_that_st.php.
2. Barack Obama, *The Audacity of Hope* (New York: Crown, 2006), 279.
3. Richard Wolffe, *Renegade: The Making of Barack Obama* (New York: Crown, 2009), 20.
4. In the middle of 2009 Obama's popularity in ten nations was higher than in the United States: Kenya, 94 percent; Germany, 93 percent; France, 91 percent; Canada, 88 percent; Nigeria, 88 percent; Britain, 86 percent; Japan, 85 percent; South Korea, 81 percent;

India, 77 percent; Brazil, 76 percent; United States, 74 percent. See Jonathan Alter, *The Promise* (London: Simon & Schuster, 2010), 224.

5. James Traub, "The Two Obamas," at http://www.foreignpolicy.com/articles/2010/08/06/the_two_obamas?page=0,0; see also Stephen Walt, "Obama Is Zero for Four and Republicans Are Sitting Pretty," at http://walt.foreignpolicy.com/posts/2010/07/30/obama_is_zero_for_four_and_republicans_are_sitting_pretty%20.

6. Quoted in James Kitfield, "The Thirteenth Crisis," *National Journal*, August 7, 2010.

7. Fareed Zakaria, *The Post-American World* (London: Allen Lane, 2008).

8. Barack Obama, Inaugural Address, January 20, 2009, at http://whitehouse.gov/blog/inaugural-address/.

9. Statement of Senator Hillary Rodham Clinton, Nominee for Secretary of State, Senate Foreign Relations Committee, January 13, 2009, at http://foreign.senate.gov/testimony/2009/ClintonTestimony090113a.pdf.

10. *America's Place in the World 2009*, Pew Research Center/Council on Foreign Relations (December 2009), 3-4.

11. David E. Sanger, *The Inheritance: The World Obama Confronts and the Challenges to American Power* (London: Bantam, 2009), 448.

12. Wolffe, *Renegade*, 328.

13. The most prominent case for non-polarity is Richard Haass, "The Age of Non-Polarity," *Foreign Affairs* 87, 3 (2008): 18-43.

14. *National Security Strategy May 2010* (cited henceforth as NSS 2010), 11.

15. For a fuller discussion of the distinction, see Kenneth M. Pollack, Daniel L. Byman, Martin Indyk, Suzanne Maloney, Michael E. O'Hanlon, and Bruce Riedel, *Which Path to Persia? Options for a New American Strategy toward Iran* (Washington, DC: Brookings Institution, 2009).

16. Hillary Clinton, "Remarks on the Obama Administration's National Security Strategy," Brookings Institution, Washington, DC, May 27, 2010, at http://www.state.gov/secretary/rm/2010/oS/142313.htm.

17. NSS 2010, 3.

18. Henry R. Nau, "Obama's Foreign Policy—The Swing Away from Bush: How Far to Go?," *Policy Review*, 160 (April/May 2010) at http://www.hoover.org/publications/policy-review/article/5287.

19. NSS 2010, 11.

20. The reference was to Doris Kearns Goodwin, *Team of Rivals: The Political Genius of Abraham Lincoln* (New York: Simon & Schuster, 2005). See the Rudalevige chapter in this volume.

21. Excepting "global rejectionists," Obama's team included all of the tendencies identified by Kurt Campbell and Michael O'Hanlon within the Democratic foreign policy coalition: "hard power advocates," "globalists," and "modest-power Democrats." See Campbell and O'Hanlon, *Hard Power: The New Politics of National Security* (New York: Basic Books, 2006), 241-245.

22. Even his speech at West Point regarding Afghanistan policy quickly pivoted to domestic policy. Obama did not address international affairs in a televised Oval Office broadcast until August 31, 2010, when he announced the end of combat operations in Iraq.

23. James W. Ceaser, "The Unpresidential President," *Weekly Standard*, August 2, 2010, at http://www.weeklystandard.com/articles/unpresidential-president?page=4.

24. Charles Krauthammer, "Decline Is a Choice: The New Liberalism and the End of American Ascendancy," *Weekly Standard*, October 19, 2009, at http://www.weeklystandard.com/Content/Public/Articles/000/000/017/056lfnpr.asp.

25. John Bolton, "The Post-American Presidency," *Standpoint*, July/August 2009, 42-45.

26. See, for example, Charles Krauthammer, "Obama's Policy of Slapping Allies," *Washington Post*, April 2, 2010, at www.washingtonpost.com/wp-dyn/content/article/2010/04/01/AR2010040102805.html; and Robert Kagan, "Obama's Year One, Contra," *World Affairs Journal* (January/February 2010), at http://www.worldaffairsjournal.org/articles/2010-JanFeb/full-Kagan-JF-2010.html.

27. Mitt Romney, *No Apology: The Case for American Greatness* (New York: St. Martin's, 2010), 25.

28. Walter Russell Mead, "The Carter Syndrome," *Foreign Policy*, Jan./Feb. 2010, 58-64.

29. This dates the Vietnam war from the introduction of US combat troops in 1965, though some argue that war began much earlier.

30. Alter, *The Promise*, 391.

31. Quoted in Peter Baker, "For Obama, Steep Learning Curve as Chief in War," *New York Times,* August 28, 2010.

32. Cited in Paul Kennedy, "A Time to Appease," *National Interest* 108 (July/August 2010): 7-17.

33. Gideon Rachman, "Somali Lessons for Afghanistan," *Financial Times*, 27 July 2010, 11.

34. According to a Gallup poll, at http://www.gallup.com/poll/141836/Issues-Obama-Finds-Majority-Approval-Elusive.aspx. Later data: http://www.gallup.com/poll/144944/americans-less-pessimistic-progress-afghanistan.aspx.

35. See the transcript of his interview with the *National Journal*, October 24, 2010, at http://nationaljournal.com/whitehouse/complete-transcript-of-obama-interview-20101024.

36. http://english.aljazeera.net/focus/2009/08/2009888238994769.html.

37. For an authoritative account of this in relation to Pakistan's nuclear weapons program, see Adrian Levy and Catherine Scott-Clark, *Deception: Pakistan, the United States and the Global Nuclear Weapons Conspiracy* (London: Atlantic Books, 2007).

38. Alter, *The Promise*, 347.

39. See: Peter Baker, "For Obama, Steep Learning Curve as Chief in War," *New York Times,* August 28, 2010; and Bob Woodward, *Obama's Wars* (New York: Simon & Schuster, 2010).

40. In the article, Obama had been described as "uncomfortable and intimidated" in an initial Pentagon meeting with senior military officials; Vice President Biden was derided; Jim Jones was referred to as a "clown" who was "stuck in 1985"; and Richard Holbrooke was described as a "wounded animal." See Michael Hastings, "The Runaway General," *Rolling Stone*, July 8–22, 2010, 90-97, 120-21.

41. See Michael O'Hanlon, "Staying Power: The US Mission in Afghanistan beyond 2011," *Foreign Affairs* 89, 5 (2010): 63-79.

42. Quoted in Hastings, "The Runaway General," 93.

43. Ali Ansari, "The Revolution Will Be Mercantilized," *National Interest* 105 (Jan./Feb. 2010): 50-60.

44. States in violation of their Non-Proliferation Treaty obligations, such as Iran, were excluded from the assurance of no US nuclear strikes in the new Nuclear Posture Review of 2010.

45. Quoted in Giles Whittell and Alexandra Frean, "Ahmadinejad Goes on the Offensive at UN as Clinton Calls for Regime Change," *The Times*, September 20, 2010, 29.

46. Arab states in the Gulf embarked on a $123 billion purchase of US arms to increase their deterrent capacity against Iran in 2010–2011. See Roula Khalaf and James Drummond, "Gulf in $123bn US Arms Spree," *Financial Times*, September 21, 2010, 1.

47. Tom Coghlan, "Arabs Urged US to Bomb Iran," *The Times*, November 29, 2010, 1.

48. Dana H. Allin and Steve Simon, *The Sixth Crisis: Iran, Israel, America, and Rumors of War* (New York: Oxford University Press, 2010), 165.

49. Joe Klein, "Q and A: Obama on His First Year in Office," *Time*, January 21, 2010, at http://www.time.com/time/politics/article/0,8599,1955072-6,00.html.

50. *Constrained Internationalism: Adapting to New Realities* (Chicago: Chicago Council on Global Affairs), 72.

51. Paul Starobin, "The Israel Divide," *National Journal*, January 16, 2010.

52. Obama also approved CIA covert actions inside Libya.

53. Mayang A. Rahawestri, "Obama's Foreign Policy in Asia: More Continuity Than Change," *Security Challenges* 6, 1 (2010): 109-120, at 110.

54. "Gates Speech on the NATO Strategic Concept," February 23, 2010, at the National Defense University; available at http://www.cfr.org/publication/21518/gates_speech_ on_the_nato_strategic_concept_february_2010.html.

55. Romney, *No Apology*, 22.

56. Stanley A. Renshon, *National Security in the Obama Administration: Reassessing the Bush Doctrine* (New York: Routledge, 2010).

57. Ryan Crocker, "Dreams of Babylon," *National Interest* 108 (July/August 2010): 18-23, at 22-23.

58. Barack Obama, Inaugural Address, January 20, 2009, at http://whitehouse.gov/blog/ inaugural-address/.

59. See the Yalof chapter in this volume.

60. Stephen Chan, *The End of Certainty: Towards a New Internationalism* (London: Zed Books, 2010), 316.

61. ACLU, "Establishing a New Normal: National Security, Civil Liberties, and Human Rights under the Obama Administration: An Eighteen-Month Review" (ACLU, July 2010). See also Paul Street, *The Empire's New Clothes: Barack Obama in the Real World of Power* (London: Paradigm, 2010).

62. Jack Goldsmith, "The Cheney Fallacy: Why Barack Obama Is Waging a More Effective War on Terror Than George W. Bush," *The New Republic*, May 18, 2009, at www .tnr.com/story_print.html?id=1e733cac-c273-48e5-9140-80443ed1f5e2.

63. "The United States: Obama's New Balance," *Strategic Survey 2010: The Annual Review of World Affairs* (London: International Institute for Strategic Studies), 83-100, at 85.

64. Ibid., 99.

65. Michael Mandelbaum, *The Frugal Superpower: America's Global Leadership in Cash-Strapped Era* (New York: Public Affairs, 2010).

66. Robert D. Putnam, "Diplomacy and Domestic Politics: The Logic of Two-Level Games," *International Organization* 42 (Summer 1988), 427-460.

67. George C. Edwards, *The Strategic President: Persuasion and Opportunity in Presidential Leadership* (Princeton, NJ: Princeton University Press, 2009); and see the Edwards chapter in this volume.

68. Bob Graham and Jim Talent, *Prevention of WMD Proliferation and Terrorism Report Card* (January 2010), 2.

69. While Obama has at times downplayed America's unique qualities, at others he has championed them, not least in using his own election as proof of the special place of the United States. Interestingly, the 2011 State of the Union address strongly emphasized American exceptionalism.

70. Zbigniew Brzezinski, "From Hope to Audacity: Appraising Obama's Foreign Policy," *Foreign Affairs* 89, 1 (2010): 16-30, at 28.

71. John F. Kennedy, Inaugural Address, January 20, 1961, at http://www.jfklibrary.org/Research/Ready-Reference/JFK-Miscellaneous-Information/Inaugural-Address.aspx.

72. "Lexington: 9/11 plus Nine," *Economist*, September 11, 2010, 48.

CHAPTER 13

Economic Crisis and Political Change: A New New Deal?

M. Stephen Weatherford

A DECISIVE ELECTION, bringing a major partisan shift in government, inevitably gives rise to debate about the historical significance of the change. Needless to say, this debate as applied to the 2008 presidential contest has centered on the economy and economic policy—this was the most salient campaign issue, and the Great Recession and the continuing impacts of the financial crisis crowded most other issues off the agenda during President Obama's first two years. The resemblance of economic conditions to the 1930s is unmistakable; it is little wonder that the debate has pivoted around whether Obama's economic program will measure up to Roosevelt's New Deal. But could it? Or will the economic emergency inevitably consume the administration's energies in ad hoc reactions to events, or will a recalcitrant Senate and a skittish public reduce innovative plans to incremental adjustments, rather than lasting change? This chapter seeks to take the measure of the opportunity history has given the president, and of the president's skill at shaping a coherent set of economic policy accomplishments.

The Warrant for Change: A Mandate Election, or Only an Unpopular Incumbent?

Two polar positions bound the various readings of the historical moment. One side holds that the message of the election amounted to little more than the rejection of an unpopular incumbent, whose policy failures temporarily tarred his co-partisans but did not alter the underlying landscape of beliefs and affiliations that favored conservative identifiers.[1] GOP campaign strategists were guided by this reading of the political alignment, as McCain and Palin distanced themselves from President Bush while claiming to be the true representatives of the Reagan legacy.

On the other side are those who hold that the election endowed President Obama with a mandate for change. Nearly every new president claims a mandate, and it is appropriate to greet the claim skeptically. A mandate election starts with the rejection of the previous incumbent, but it also carries an identifiable statement of where the government's policy failures have stimulated opposition and what expectations will center the public's judgment of the new administration.

The retrospective message of the 2008 election was resounding.[2] And the prospective message was equally clear: over the year preceding the election, public concern came to focus almost exclusively on the economy.[3] The Obama campaign, moreover, portrayed the election as a turning point, taking aim at the Reagan legacy of conservative individualism and invoking transformative presidents' responses to similar crises in the past. Obama traced the roots of his economic program from Theodore Roosevelt's attack on Gilded Age grandees to Franklin Roosevelt's leadership in crafting "a new social compact," broadly inclusive and committed to limiting economic inequalities—"a bargain between government, business, and workers that resulted in widespread prosperity and economic security for more than fifty years." Writing more than two years before his presidential campaign, Obama gave Reagan credit for advancing a well-timed corrective to an overambitious federal government. But conservatives' continued fealty to an old orthodoxy had yielded a legacy that left most Americans worse off:

> Without any clear governing philosophy, the Bush administration and its congressional allies have responded by pushing the conservative revolution to its logical conclusion—even lower taxes, even fewer regulations, and an even smaller safety net. But in taking this approach, Republicans are fighting the last war, the war they waged and won in the eighties, while Democrats are forced to fight a rearguard action, defending the New Deal programs of the thirties.[4]

The Bush economic program had worsened income inequality, and his tax cuts had deprived the government of the resources to advance widely shared public goals such as affordable health care. Just as Reagan's emphasis on individualism created the impetus of ideas and beliefs for a post–New Deal conception of government and the economy, so Obama framed his campaign around a "new economic consensus" intended to shift the balance toward the societal or communitarian side of the equation.[5]

The evidence is strong that the message of the election went beyond disapproval of the incumbent to a resounding call for changing the economic policy course. Surveys of voters' issue concerns and their images of the candidates' positions on economic issues; the unprecedented level of grassroots involvement in the campaign; the spike in voter turnout; and the Democrats' enlarged majorities in

Congress all give evidence that Obama's campaign connected with the electorate in a way that went beyond simply rejecting the incumbent government.[6]

If Obama's campaign responded to the electorate's call for a new approach to pressing problems, to what extent was he able to channel earlier transformative presidents, from Lincoln and Roosevelt to Reagan, to look beyond transient opinion? Was he able to discern—and shape—the public's understanding of the electoral mandate, by laying out an interpretation of the state of the nation and a vision of how his program will enhance the long-run public interest?[7]

A Plan for Change: Obama's Economic Agenda

Three economic issues defined the agenda of problems facing the president. Two were unambiguous emergencies: the recession and its impacts on jobs and businesses, and the financial crisis of 2007–2008 and its imperative to repair the credit system and avoid a similar calamity in the future. The third constituted a different type of economic challenge, a slowly developing but historically transformative problem of the sort that popular governments are notoriously hesitant to acknowledge and address: the growing inequality of income and wealth. The White House was sensitive to the fact that a changeable public opinion plus a polarized opposition gave them only a brief window for significant policy change, and they rejected the idea of putting off big initiatives until the immediate problems were laid to rest.[8]

Each problem has its own characteristic trajectory, and addressing them would require calling on different constellations of policy ideas and instruments. In the campaign, both Obama and McCain spoke frequently about the recession and the financial crisis. But Obama alone framed an interpretation of the problem of rising economic inequality that pointed toward an ambitious, multidimensional agenda of economic innovations. In this section, I briefly review these three economic challenges, then describe the way the new president shaped his agenda to address them.

A Faltering Economy

For most Americans, the new century had marked a slow decline in their economic fortunes. Although overall GDP growth was positive during the Bush years, at an annual average of 0.3 percent it was the lowest of any postwar president, enough to absorb only 14 percent of the yearly growth in new workers. The stock market declined by an average of 5.6 percent annually. The economy tipped into recession in 2007, more than a year before the election, but the downturn was much worsened by the financial collapse. In the year following October 2007, the stock market lost a third of its value; homebuilding and exports fell by more than 20 percent;

the GDP declined by 6.2 percent in the final quarter of 2008. When President Obama entered office, the economy was losing jobs at the rate of 750,000 a month, and Americans' economic expectations had fallen to levels not seen since the oil embargo of the 1970s.[9]

The difference between the two candidates' policy proposals was stark. McCain placed the blame for the recession on government spending, asserted that the Bush tax cuts had made the country more prosperous than it was in 2000, and proposed to repeat a round of tax cuts like President Bush had enacted in his first year. Obama responded by claiming that Bush had "squandered the surplus" left by Clinton, and he called for "bottom-up economics instead of trickle-down economics."[10] But as president he sought to craft a stimulus bill that Republicans could support, allotting a substantial portion to tax cuts and reaching out personally to GOP legislators. In the end, with the Republican leadership pressing its partisans for unified opposition and the economy continuing to decline, Obama struck bargains with just enough GOP Senators to pass the economic stimulus bill as his first major legislative initiative.

The Financial Crisis

When the market for sub prime mortgages collapsed in the summer of 2007, many banks were left holding assets that could not be sold at any price. The most precarious institutions were those that had speculated aggressively in the mortgage market, and when the investment bank Lehman Brothers failed in September 2008, the financial markets froze up. With no trustworthy mechanism for valuing assets, banks refused to advance loans not only to other financial institutions but even for traditional commercial purposes. Bush treasury secretary Henry Paulson quickly put together a plan to bail out the financial sector, finally gaining the reluctant approval of Congress to spend up to $700 billion in taxpayers' money on the strength of his promise that buying distressed mortgage securities from the banks would help ordinary Americans by stabilizing the housing market. When the financial panic continued to worsen, Paulson changed course: rather than bail out mortgage-holders, he opted to invest $250 billion directly in bank equity in order to keep financial institutions afloat. Although this had some calming effect on the markets, it perplexed the public and set in motion a spiral of incredulity and populist anger: "The Bush administration, after eight years of preaching the virtues of free markets, tax cuts, and small government, had turned the U.S. Treasury into part owner and the effective guarantor of every big bank in the country. . . . It had stumbled into the most sweeping extension of state intervention in the economy since the 1930s."[11]

Both candidates denounced Wall Street greed, and McCain even suspended his campaign and urged President Bush to convene a summit of leaders from both parties. But beyond the similarity of their concern, the two candidates gave very different impressions of their mastery of the problem. President Bush, whose massive bank bailout was stalled in Congress, did bring the candidates and the congressional leadership together with his economic team at the White House on September 25, 2008. While McCain had initiated the meeting, he appeared baffled by the complexity of the issues and the ideological implications of Bush's newfound drive to backstop the banks. Obama, on the other hand, proved to be more engaged and knowledgeable than Bush or McCain, and more comfortable in a politicized context than Paulson. He pressed the legislative leaders toward mutual concessions that would permit bipartisan support of the administration's proposal. At the end of the day, Paulson and most of the other political and economic notables in the room concluded that Obama was the clearly preferred candidate for pulling the economy out of the financial crisis.[12] As president, Obama introduced his financial reform plan in mid-2009; it was passed by Congress in August 2010.

Economic Inequality

Unlike the Great Recession and the Wall Street meltdown, inequality has grown slowly and does not have the feel of a crisis. Yet the rising concentration of income going to the most affluent has not only widened the gap between the rich and the rest, it has made it increasingly hard for middle-class families to afford the material standard of living their parents' generation achieved. Still, there is little agreement on its political significance, and Obama's drive to integrate it into his policy program undoubtedly posed the greatest challenge for the new administration. The raw material for framing an agenda includes changes both in the economy and in the views of the public.

Whether one looks at income, wealth, or the prospects for economic mobility, the distribution of the rewards from work has become much more concentrated and economic opportunity much more limited over the last three decades. From the 1930s through the 1970s, the richest 10 percent of the population received just over 30 percent of the nation's total income. A long period of stability ended in the 1980s, and by the end of the century, the richest 10 percent received some 44 percent of total income. The bulk of this increasing concentration is accounted for by disproportionate gains at the very top: the share of national income going to the most affluent 1 percent rose from less than 8 percent in the 1970s to over 23 percent in 2007.[13] Inequality has increased even more in the distribution of wealth. Of the total gain in wealth accrued in the US economy from 1980 to 2004, 89 percent went to the richest fifth of the population, and only 1.9 percent to the middle fifth; the wealth of the bottom two-fifths actually shrank by 0.7 percent. The share of the nation's total net worth owned by the richest 1 percent now exceeds the combined wealth of the bottom 90 percent of the population.[14] At the same time opportunity for upward mobility has seemingly diminished. As recently as the 1970s, some 23 percent of men whose fathers were in the bottom quarter of the

FIGURE 13.1   Real Family Income Growth by Quintile, 1947–2004

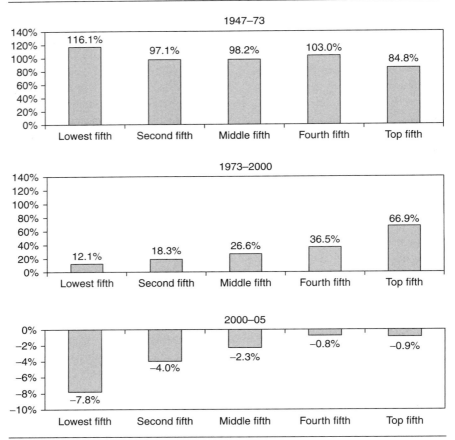

Source: Authors' analysis of U.S. Census Bureau data. Figure 11 from: Mishel, Lawrence, Jared Bernstein, and Sylvia Allegretto, *The State of Working America 2006/2007.* An Economic Policy Institute Book. Ithaca, NY: ILR Press, an imprint of Cornell University Press, 2007.

income distribution had risen to the top quarter; by the 2000s, that figure had fallen below 10 percent. "The U.S. economy," worried the conservative journal *Business Week* in 2003, "is slowly stratifying along class lines."[15] Figure 13.1 summarizes these trends, showing the growth of family income (corrected for inflation) over key segments of the period.[16]

By the end of the Bush years, increasing inequality was no longer a concern limited to left-wing sociologists and editorial writers, nor voiced only by envious have-nots or liberal politicians. Drawing on new research plus historical data spanning several decades, Benjamin Page and Lawrence Jacobs show that: (a) Americans are aware of exceptionally high and growing inequality; (b) large majorities (from two-thirds to nearly 90 percent) are in favor of concrete programs to strengthen economic opportunity and security; and (c) a majority are willing to pay taxes to support targeted programs.[17] Moreover, there is surprisingly little variation in these beliefs across political party or social class—majorities of Democrats and Republicans, rich and poor, agree on the salience of today's exceptional inequality and the need for government to address it. These findings do not contradict Americans' long-standing individualism and skepticism about government: the consensual support is for programs that expand economic opportunity rather than directly redistribute income. "[Americans] want opportunities for economic success and want individuals to take care of themselves when possible. But they also want *genuine opportunity* for themselves and others, and a measure of *economic security* to pursue opportunity and to insure themselves and their neighbors against disasters beyond their control."[18]

The new president could call on a more or less familiar script in responding to the recession, but acting to reverse the growth of inequality would require using the tools of the rhetorical presidency to frame a political issue out of an inchoate problem. Obama's first move was to subtly reshape the Democratic Party's traditional attack on inequality.

Defining the Mandate: Obama Frames His Agenda

Departing from the New Deal appeal on the basis of class competition, President Obama couched the problem of inequality in terms that emphasize pragmatism rather than ideology—a "new economic consensus . . . guided by what works"— and society-wide gains rather than redistribution. Speaking on tax policy during the campaign, Obama singled out the Bush administration's priorities, rejected the "class war" trope as a laughable defense of privilege, and recalled the American dream of unitary, cooperative interdependence:

> At a time when income inequality is growing sharper, the Bush tax cuts gave the wealthiest one percent of Americans a tax cut that was twice as large as the middle class. At a time when Americans are working harder than ever, we are taxing income from work at nearly twice the levels that we're taxing gains for investors. If you talk about this in polite society, sooner or later you'll get accused of waging class warfare, and it's distasteful to point out that some CEOs made more in 10 minutes than a worker makes in 10 months. Or, as my friend Warren Buffett put it to me, "If there's class warfare going on in America, then my class is winning."

Now, what Warren Buffett knows is what all Americans have to remember: to get through these uncertain times, we have to recognize that we all have a stake in one another's success. . . . We've gone too far from being a country where we're all in this together to a country where everyone is on their own.[19]

Rejecting the narrow individualism of Bush's "ownership society," Obama centered his economic program around themes that conservatives have long assumed they owned: growth, not redistribution, is the goal; and responsibility, rather than empathy, is its normative rationale. Obama's pre-presidential writings and even the Inaugural Address noted the contribution of faster growth to raising living standards, moving toward a more equal division of economic gains, and paying off the deficit without having to raise taxes. But the bubble economy of Wall Street speculation and rising consumer debt yielded only the illusion of growth, while sustained prosperity entails change "from an era of borrow and spend to one where we save and invest, where we consume less at home and send more exports abroad."[20] Reversing the "investment deficit," Obama proposed, starts with building human capital. Investments in education and research have a special place in Obama's agenda, because they strengthen both markets and equality—building workers' skills fosters greater productivity and competitiveness at the same time that it equips workers with enhanced bargaining leverage to even out the distribution of gains from growth.[21]

President Obama framed the case for his economic agenda in a major address at Georgetown University in April 2009, stepping back from day-to-day politics to place his program—and specifically the financial crisis—in the context of ideas and values.[22] The frame is unabashedly normative, and the theme is the traditionally conservative idea of *responsibility*. He begins by describing America's economic culture as it once was: ordinary people saved and lived in the same house most of their lives; banks lent on the basis of solid information about the borrower's reputation and promise; insurance companies used traditional standards and shunned speculation. These norms collapsed over recent years, succumbing to irresponsibility as "short-term profits" and "reckless speculation" displaced investment, financial manipulation triumphed over making and selling useful goods, consumption replaced saving. Calling to mind a story from the Sermon on the Mount, Obama argues that it is past time to build the American economy on rock rather than sand. By purposely situating his economic program as a quest to defend middle-class morality and strengthen treasured small-town values such as personal responsibility and mutual obligation, Obama intended to cast the appeal to cultural conservatives.[23]

In the short term, at least, that audience was (to borrow another biblical metaphor) stony ground. We cannot know whether the administration will produce a sea change in American politics. But the economic crisis when Obama took office prompted a widespread call for change: the economy had underperformed for nearly a decade; the financial crisis dragged the nation deeper into recession at the same time that it revealed significant weaknesses in the government's capacity to restrain socially harmful speculation by banks and other financial firms; and the growing concentration of income and wealth undermined the prosperity and optimism of America's middle class. Obama consciously framed the problems and shaped his policy agenda so as to expand the political coalition in support of progressive initiatives. But political change is never easy, and several barriers stood (and stand) in the way of altering the status quo.

Opportunity and Agenda versus Structure and Interests

The historical image of critical junctures calls up heroic presidents—Jackson, Lincoln, FDR, Reagan—with the implication that success requires a leader of rare political skill and character, who can marshal or manipulate the government toward accomplishment. This vantage neglects the structural factors—organized interests, taken-for-granted ideas, and institutions—that provide the more solid and systematic account of the difficulty of converting the potential for change into the real thing.[24]

Organized Interests

Economist Mancur Olson's theory of *The Rise and Decline of Nations* gives an account of how the forces blocking significant policy innovation can defeat even popularly elected leaders. He argues that, over time, stable, affluent countries give rise to a policymaking process increasingly dominated by interest groups, who obtain favorable laws and lax regulations. These arrangements benefit narrow interests at the expense of everyone else: subsidies and tax exemptions allow politically powerful industries to capture a larger share of the pie; and by discouraging competition they keep the pie from growing. Over time, an encrusted system of interest groups stifles the vigor of an open economy and weakens the nation's ability to compete. But because the benefits are narrowly concentrated and the costs widely dispersed, and because the slow glide toward inefficiency and inequality is not readily perceptible, it is difficult to mobilize the constituency for change. Only a crisis—war, economic depression, financial collapse—will disrupt vested interests sufficiently to open the possibility of significant reform.[25] The oft-quoted remark of Rahm Emanuel, Obama's chief of staff, captures this political truth: "You never want a serious crisis to go to waste. What I mean by that is that it's an opportunity to do things you could not do before."

The analogy between Olson's theory and contemporary American politics is hardly perfect, but it should compel a closer look at both economic conditions and the configuration of interests. Compared to the 1929 crash and its aftermath, recent economic conditions differ in two politically salient ways. First, attribution of blame for the crisis and its consequences enabled Roosevelt but constrained Obama. Roosevelt entered the presidency well after the crisis began, and after Hoover's attempts at amelioration had failed. In the eyes of the public and most of the mass media, it was Hoover's Depression. Obama came to power just as the impacts of the financial meltdown were spreading to the wider economy: although the public perceived that the crisis had begun under Bush, it quickly became Obama's to fix.

Second, unlike the Depression, which was deep and broad and persisted for years, the effect of the financial crisis, although sharper and deeper than the 1929 Crash, was countered by aggressive monetary and fiscal policy, and converted into something like a conventional but severe recession.[26] Although the White House had played the key role in reversing the downturn, Obama received little political credit; media commentators and the public quickly picked up on Republican allegations that the president was to blame for the slow pace of recovery.

Third, while the New Deal reforms surely faced interest group opposition, the density and influence of the contemporary interest group system is qualitatively greater: many more interests are organized; they can mobilize a larger quantity and wider range of resources; and their formal and informal connections to the administrative and regulatory process are pervasive.[27] In each of the policy areas the White House has targeted for reform, well-heeled and well-connected interests have grown up over the years: organized teachers, oil companies and coal producers, insurance and pharmaceutical manufacturers, and—perhaps most daunting of all—Wall Street bankers. Historically, the financial sector is by far the largest source of campaign contributions to federal candidates and parties, and also leads all other sectors in spending on lobbying. The bulk of the sector's contributions (around two-thirds) go to Republicans, although the Democratic Party and national Democratic candidates also depend on the financial sector for a substantial share of their campaign funds. Without attempting to decide the question of whether that dependency directly limits the ability and desire to aggressively regulate business, observers agree that it assures business and finance a privileged hearing in the economic policymaking process.[28]

The Dominant Ideas

Although Barack Obama handily won the candidate contest in 2008, the dominant ideas about the role of government in the economy were largely unchanged: they owe less to Obama's progressive sentiments than to Ronald Reagan's campaign against taxes and big government. The 1980 election did not initiate the tax revolt, but Reagan sharpened the anti-tax message, raised it to the national level, and expanded it into a broad-gauge anti-government platform that united the various strands of the Republican coalition. Since then, the conservative movement has developed a coherent ideological alternative and successfully recruited and installed sympathetic legislators and judges at virtually every level of the system. The simple mantra to cut taxes anchored the Republican Party's image as the better manager of the economy, and as a campaign plank it posed irresolvable difficulties for Democrats seeking to address societal needs. The step from anti-tax to anti-government rhetoric was a small but significant one that has fostered not only an unprecedentedly disciplined Republican opposition but also a populist movement historically unusual in that the opposition to government is not twinned with similar opposition to concentrated economic power.[29] In this context of ideas, Obama's presidency is an opposition interregnum, not the overthrow of the dominant conservative ideology. The president cannot, in short, count on deep or persistent support for an agenda of significant change, or indeed for initiatives that deviate much from the tone of his Republican predecessors.

Institutional Curbs on Innovation

Although powerful status quo interests were disrupted by the financial crisis and the electoral defeat of the incumbent Republicans, opponents of change can draw strength from standing institutional rules, as well as—ironically—Obama's own initiatives to increase the transparency of the government's budget. Arguably the most intractable barrier is the US Senate, where the filibuster and other rules empower a minority to block legislation that is clearly favored by the majority.[30] The requirement of a supermajority has only recently become a regular element of party competition, occasioned not simply by party polarization but in recent years by the intensity of the Republican opposition to Democratic initiatives.[31] The intensity differential is important because both carrying out and stopping a filibuster entail substantial time and energy. For Democrats the opportunity costs of matching the Republicans' commitment are high: given their ambitious agenda, it often makes sense to drop an intensely opposed bill in order to move on to another salient initiative.[32] The status of economic policy as the defining cleavage between the parties, along with the fact that political economic initiatives are central to Obama's agenda, fuels competitive intensity and heightens the incentive to use the Senate's supermajority rules to their obstructive utmost.

Additionally, President Obama gave a crucial hostage to the opposition in moving to ban four accounting gimmicks that President Bush had used to make deficit projections look smaller. Obama's first budget explicitly included spending on the wars in Iraq and Afghanistan, Medicare reimbursements to physicians, and the cost of disaster responses, as well as (in the largest adjustment) omitting phantom revenues from the alternative minimum tax (AMT).[33] Enacted in 1969 to prevent the wealthy from using tax shelters to avoid paying any income tax, the AMT was never indexed for inflation and now affects millions of middle-class taxpayers. If the government levied the tax, it would bring in additional revenue—and past budgets have projected this. But it would fuel a tax revolt, and to forestall that, recent presidents and Congresses have added a one-year "patch," adjusting the AMT for inflation and wiping out the budgeted extra revenue. The White House assumed this would continue, to the tune of omitting $1.2 trillion in revenue over ten years, plus an additional $218 billion to reflect the interest on the resulting additional debt over the next decade. At a time when the rising deficit gives opponents of Obama's policy initiatives their most broadly attractive argument, the price of more honest bookkeeping is a budget that is $2.7 trillion deeper in the red over the next decade than if the administration had continued the Bush administration's approach to accounting.[34]

The Change Agenda:
An Innovative Stimulus and Cautious Banking Reform

Every president has felt that having to attend to the immediate emergency of recession or inflation sapped his ability to put a stronger stamp on economic policy, but no postwar president has entered office facing an economic crisis as wrenching as the one Obama faced in January 2009. The admonition not to let a crisis go to waste made good sense in the abstract, but advancing the president's long-term goals could hardly take precedence when economic activity was already dropping steeply. There was little alternative but to put his administration's efforts into enacting an anti-recession package that would halt the slide and restore growth.

Thus the economic stimulus was the first order of business, and in that legislation Obama sought to combine aggressive anti-recession actions with significant long-run initiatives that amounted to a "down payment" on his substantive policy agenda. Banking reform, on the other hand, could be delayed. Although keenly aware that the opposition of financial interests to his banking reforms would only grow stronger as the postelection honeymoon faded into the past, Obama set aside financial regulation to focus on health care reform as the great initiative of his first year. When he unveiled his proposal for banking regulation, it faced the opposition of a financial sector that—aided by the government bailout—had returned to profitability much faster than the economy as a whole and was prepared to mount a well-coordinated lobbying blitz. The processes through which the White House formulated its two major economic policies, and then worked to build legislative coalitions to enact them, offer a window on the way the president's agenda of change played out against unfavorable economic trends, interest group opposition, and partisan obstruction.

The Economic Stimulus

By November 2008, the worsening economic crisis had galvanized the public's concern, and the Democratic sweep underlined the imperative to enact an anti-recession program big enough to meet the worst economic downturn since the Great Depression. But the new president faced a dilemma. His campaign had outlined a wide-ranging agenda that included proposals to address health care, climate change, education, financial regulation, and immigration; and the Democrats' decisive electoral victory afforded the opportunity of an open policy window. However, that window could not accommodate a large agenda, and the prospects for moving innovative legislation would decline steeply with the passage of time. The president-elect and his team recognized that the need for a stimulus package and his desire to make health care his top priority in the first year meant that other initiatives could not be advanced during the same period.[35] President Obama resolved the dilemma with an assertive but risky strategy for a carefully crafted bill—the American Recovery and Reinvestment Act (ARRA)—that addressed three quite different goals: short-term stimulus; tax cuts given to congressional Republicans in an effort to shape a bipartisan coalition; and Democratic commitments, both to his own "change agenda" and to targeted economic relief for individuals.

Obama met with congressional leaders before the inauguration, and all agreed that stimulating recovery was the top priority and that it would be possible to enact a bill before President's Day on February 13. But jockeying for partisan advantage began almost immediately, with Republican leaders warning that the stimulus could be as high as $1.8 trillion. Obama, acknowledging the importance of minimizing additions to the deficit, announced that he was appointing Nancy Killefer as the administration's "Chief Performance Officer" with instructions to "scour the budget, line by line," and promised to bring his stimulus in at "the low end of economists' range."[36] Meeting with his economic team daily, the president compiled a list of "preferences but not a detailed plan" to send to Congress, and then met with Democratic and Republican leaders at the White House. The administration's proposal included funding for hard-hit state governments, and provisions to shore up the safety net, for instance by expanding unemployment compensation and extending Medicaid and health insurance eligibility to unemployed workers.[37] The bill immediately faced complaints from liberals—who objected that the $775 billion the White House estimated for the stimulus was much too small to cover a drop in the GDP of some $2 trillion—and conservatives, who wanted a much smaller bill centered on permanent tax cuts.

The president used his first speech since the election to emphasize his commitment to take the lead toward a bipartisan bill. Obama's outreach started with his commitment that some $300 billion (40 percent of the total) would be allotted to tax cuts, which would be drafted in consultation with the Republican leadership.

He then went to Capitol Hill to meet with the Republican caucus, declaring that he had "no stake in pride of ownership" but was open to compromise; and he invited GOP leaders to the White House for a Super Bowl party. Republican leaders seemed taken aback by the administration's push for collaboration, and found it difficult to move out of campaign mode. When Speaker Nancy Pelosi thanked Republicans for proposing a job-creating tax credit, Minority Leader John Boehner denied paternity, and Boehner's second in command, Eric Cantor, accused the president of repackaging old liberal-spending plans by extending the tax credit to families and individuals who pay Social Security and Medicare taxes but who don't make enough to pay income taxes. Although Boehner gave Obama "high marks for outreach," he adamantly urged all his party colleagues to vote against the bill.[38] As the bill moved toward a vote, Obama continued to float ideas intended to defuse Republican opposition, but he vowed not to compromise on essential priorities including safety net funding and directing the bulk of the tax cuts to middle- and lower-income families.[39]

Although the White House stressed the immediate importance of the bill's stimulus measures, the package also included provisions intended to strengthen the national economy over the long run. President Obama gave pride of place to these components, noting, "This is not just a short-term program to boost employment. It's one that will invest in our most important priorities like energy and education, health care and a new infrastructure that are necessary to keep us strong and competitive in the 21st century." They included funding for research and development in green energy, extending broadband to underserved areas, improving medical records, shifting the tax burden back toward the affluent, along with school construction and an increased commitment to education reform.[40] House Republicans were adamant in opposing the administration, and Boehner railed against the bill in his response to Obama's weekly address. But Senate Republican leader Mitch McConnell warned against blanket rejection of compromise, worrying that this would result in "a state of permanent legislative gridlock. And that is simply no longer acceptable to the American people."[41]

The debate over the stimulus, as with most such legislation over the last fifty years, focused on its size and whether it would impact the economy quickly enough to keep unemployment from worsening. When January's statistics on macroeconomic activity showed continuing decline, this news, coming at a crucial point in the legislative debate, refocused attention on the need for prompt action and propelled the bill toward passage by a comfortable margin in the House.[42]

The bill bogged down in the Senate, where Democrats lacked the sixty votes needed to end a filibuster. Although commentators had suggested that the Republican Party's weak electoral showing would make the leadership more amenable to cooperating with the new president, particularly on an emergency measure, by the first week of February it was clear that Obama's outreach toward the opposition was producing little easing of partisan tensions. Senate Democrats announced that they were open to amendments on Republican issues, and Republican governors joined their Democratic counterparts in lobbying for the administration's bill, but congressional Republicans rebuffed offers for compromise and Minority Leader Mitch McConnell marshaled fierce pressure on GOP senators to deny the president a victory.[43] The administration strategy focused on conservative Democrat Ben Nelson (D-NE), Maine's two moderate Republican senators, Susan Collins and Olympia Snowe, and Pennsylvania Republican Arlen Specter, who sought to pare down the bill's size. President Obama personally joined the negotiations to cut some $110 billion from the Senate version. The stimulus cleared the Republican filibuster on February 10 and gained Senate passage the next day.[44]

Even after the Senate passed the bill, the White House faced difficult negotiations: not only did the Senate and House bills differ, but the GOP continued to harp on items it considered "pork" while conservative "Blue Dog" Democrats insisted on further cuts to the overall size of the package. At a news conference on February 10, Obama emphasized the economic importance of passing the stimulus, and he again dispatched Rahm Emanuel and Office of Management and Budget head Peter Orszag to the Capitol, where they negotiated well past midnight, finally cementing a coalition for a stimulus totaling $787 billion ($501b in spending; $286b in tax cuts). The bill was passed by both houses on February 13, 2009, less than a month after its introduction. The end product was nearly the same size as the president's proposal and included initiatives in education, energy and the environment, science, safety net enhancements, health, taxes, and infrastructure.[45]

Assessing the stimulus: economic success and political nullity. As President Obama's first significant economic initiative, the stimulus carries important information about the White House policy process, the president's political strategy in negotiating with Congress in an era of extreme polarization, and how the public learns about and responds to policy change. If passing the stimulus in the face of concerted opposition was an achievement worth remarking, even more surprising is the evidence that it succeeded economically but utterly failed to generate any political reward for the president and his allies in Congress.

Judging from the experience of other presidents, the need to devote his administration's first significant legislation to an anti-recession stimulus seemed to sound the death knell for Obama's ambitious program of long-term economic change. But the stimulus bill played effectively both with and against the conventional pattern of narrowly circumscribed legislation. The administration's draft bill conformed to the norm in its emphasis on "shovel-ready projects;" in directing spending toward hard-hit social groups, such as the unemployed and working poor, sure to put the benefit back into economic circulation quickly; and in allotting more than a third of the stimulus to tax cuts in a good faith gesture to the Republican opposition. But it pushed the envelope of convention by leavening the short-term stimulus with initiatives designed to set in motion projects—standard-setting and reform in K–12 education, clean-energy, broadband access, medical comparative effectiveness research—that would speed up the pace of change and build momentum for public goods that the private market cannot supply. Betting on the magnitude of the crisis, the electoral popularity of his change agenda, and the fact that the Republicans were still regrouping after their losses, President Obama succeeded in pushing through a program that met the recession with a strong dose of proven counter-cyclical medicine, but that also laid down the first markers of a potentially transformative disruption of the economic policy status quo.[46]

The bill nearly failed in the Senate, and although Obama's political strategy of flexing on details while sticking firmly to his core goals (for instance, regarding the distribution of spending and tax rebates across income classes) kept the broad outline intact, the eventual legislation was smaller and its allocation more conventional than the administration had planned. Votes were won by extending district benefits that undercut the wider message of change; the cuts that won the votes to defeat the Republican filibuster came largely from the investments in the bill—for instance, funds to help local school districts renovate deteriorating school buildings—and from inter-governmental transfers intended to shore up state and local budgets. Arguably more important in shaping the public's perception of the stimulus was the messy, contentious fight, as the slow cumulation of arcane bargains only served to fulfill the popular stereotype of Washington politics mired in narrow partisanship. Even before it was implemented, the American Recovery and Reinvestment Act's exceptional combination of short-run palliatives with substantive initiatives had been simplified to the stylized narrative of ideological competition between the parties.

A year and a half later the evidence is strong that the economic impact of the stimulus was a clear success. Judged not against the easy but empty impatience of a partisanized demand to "fix it now," but rather against an econometric analysis that takes into account the depth of the recession and the turnaround capacity of the private economy, the record is good. The Congressional Budget Office (CBO) estimates that it raised the real (inflation-adjusted) GDP by between 1.7 and 4.5 percent since mid-2009, reduced unemployment by more than a full percent, and increased the number of full-time jobs by between 2 and 4.8 million. The more econometrically demanding study by Alan Blinder of Princeton and Mark Zandi of Moody's Analytics distinguishes the effect of monetary/financial market policies from the president's fiscal program: it shows that ARRA, along with several smaller stimulus measures enacted in late 2009 and early 2010,[47] raised real GDP by about 3.4 percent and lowered the unemployment rate by at least 1.5 percent.[48] Comparing the Obama stimulus to similar measures by other presidents, and taking into account the historic magnitude of the Great Recession, the administration's recovery program merits substantial praise.

Politically, however, the policies made no difference to the public's perception of government's performance.[49] A majority of voters believe the stimulus was ineffective or worse, and while Republicans still rate more poorly than Democrats as managers of the economy, the hostility to additional stimulus is palpable. Two quite different streams account for the gap between economic effectiveness and political blame. One is the campaign by Republicans, which associated the stimulus with the federal deficit and with the widely unpopular bank and auto bailouts.[50] The other has to do with the design of the policy: for many of the key components, the administration opted to implement the stimulus with policy instruments that maximized economic effectiveness but hampered political visibility—and hence befogged the credit that usually accrues to the party orchestrating a successful recovery. This included allocating the tax cuts over several paychecks (rather than as a lump sum, which past research shows that recipients hoard instead of spending); directing money to state governments (where it saved jobs, but did not create them); extending benefits to unemployed workers (out of sight for most of the employed); spreading expenditures into 2010 (making for a smaller impact in 2009 but lessening the risk of a double-dip recession); and allocating a portion to R&D investments (which are likely to have a transformative impact on education and industries such as clean energy and broadband, but are much less visible than, say, the public works projects of the New Deal). In the face of an opposition strategy directed toward painting the solution as the problem, the fact that the Obama administration has taken ownership of the recession by acting to combat it—but has neither produced an immediate recovery nor created a record of visible changes in the lives of most voters—appears to show that in today's polarized political environment, no good deed goes unpunished.

Financial Regulation

Financial reform was crucial in mobilizing the Democrats' electoral victory in 2008. Once in office, President Obama and his advisers, knowing that enacting stronger regulations would bring the administration into direct conflict with the country's richest and most powerful interests, delayed their efforts until the stimulus had been approved and health care reform was well on the way. The material resources of the banking sector are magnified by the status of finance in the iconography of national prosperity and international competitiveness—an immensely powerful but impenetrably complex set of forces only partly amenable to the control of governments. This configuration of strengths insulates the financial sector against government regulation in normal times. The financial crisis and the Great Recession impacted not only investors but also ordinary Americans, eliminating jobs and health insurance, homes and equity, for millions of the working poor and middle class; it aroused the public and embarrassed the economists and business commentators who had assumed that market forces would ensure continued prosperity.[51]

Thus there were two centers of political energy: the financial community, the ultimate "inside player," rich in resources and channels for influencing policy; and an energized populist outrage—powerful but clumsy, angry but incoherent and ripe for leadership. Together they constituted the field on which financial reform would be fought out. Unlike health care reform, where the Obama administration invited Congress to take the lead in drafting proposals, the executive branch worked out the details of the financial reform proposal and shaped the agenda of issues in the debate. Drafted by the Treasury Department and released in June 2009,[52] the White House document was well-attuned to the complex regulatory issues and the traditional line-up of interests that would have to be taken into account in the congressional process. But the administration was strangely insensitive to the possibility that in this political fight the public could be less an audience and more a participant.

Financial reform involves two sorts of issues that animate different patterns of politics: those centering on risk to the banking system versus those that have to do with consumers' transactions. Systemic activities are the bank-to-bank relationships that define the difference between Wall Street and the world of local banks and credit unions, and that, via products such as collateralized debt obligations, hedge funds, derivatives, and securitized assets and mortgages, leveraged interdependent borrowing relationships into the huge and unstable debt structure that finally collapsed in mid-2007. Consumer-to-bank relationships involve home mortgages, pensions, consumer and auto loans.

The administration's reform bill addressed systemic risk with new regulations on capital requirements and derivatives. The proposals provoked intense lobbying by banks, large insurance companies, and mortgage lenders, but for the most part the issues were too complex and arcane to generate much public involvement.[53] This was not the case with issues that directly implicated consumers' future welfare, including the bank bailout, which encapsulated populist anger at bankers who had profited when risky lending paid off but were bailed out by taxpayers when their bets fell through; the Consumer Financial Protection Agency; and the proposal to separate ordinary commercial transactions (backed by the government's guarantee to depositors) from speculative activities such as foreign exchange trading or hedge fund management.[54]

Setting capital requirements was the primary instrument for regulating the amount of risk banks would be allowed to take on. In the run-up to the collapse, it was not uncommon for banks to have outstanding loans thirty times their capital, a leverage ratio that left firms like Lehman Brothers no alternative to dissolution once a few large counter-parties defaulted. The Treasury document called for stronger "prudential standards" in general and for more stringent capital requirements for "large, interconnected firms," and it proposed that these requirements be set by a new interagency body, the Financial Services Oversight Council. Congressman Barney Frank (D-MA), chair of the House Financial Services Committee, was uncomfortable with delegating authority over this key regulation, and the House approved his specification of a 15-to-1 ratio, with less leverage allowed for the most problematic firms. In the Senate, Finance Committee chair Christopher Dodd was more sympathetic to the Treasury's position and launched an effort to remove the Frank provision, but when Maine's Senator Susan Collins proposed an even stronger capital requirement, the White House and the Treasury relented in order to avoid alienating Collins, whose vote was crucial to defeating the promised Republican filibuster.[55]

Derivatives include some of the most complex and profitable of Wall Street's recently invented financial products. A derivative is simply a contract whose value is linked to the future price of some underlying asset. Derivatives were initially used to hedge against fluctuations in the prices of agricultural commodities, and it was speculation in agricultural markets that led to establishing the Commodity Futures Trading Commission (CFTC) as the regulator of these contracts. With the expansion of the range of assets to which derivatives are linked, the opportunities for risky speculation—against stocks, currencies, and even bundles of mortgages—multiplied. When CFTC chair Brooksley Born sought to regulate financial derivatives in the 1990s, she met fervent opposition from bankers, the chair of the Federal Reserve Alan Greenspan, and officials in the Clinton Treasury.[56] The 2009 Treasury proposal contained no clear authority for regulating derivatives, and the House, after rejecting moves to require trading on a federally regulated exchange and to expand the authority of the CFTC or SEC, adopted a relatively weak requirement that most derivatives be traded on a private exchange.

Once again, the action of a single senator upset the calculations of industry lobbyists, committee leaders, and the White House. Blanche Lincoln (D-AR), facing a primary challenger who framed the regulation of derivatives as a fight between the people and the banks, proposed to require that banks holding guaranteed deposits "spin off" their derivatives trading operations. With public anger at the banking industry on the rise, her amendment passed the Senate and survived the conference committee; it was included in the final bill in only slightly weakened form. In the case of both capital requirements and derivatives, the final legislation was tougher than the administration's bill.[57]

Proposals to restrict proprietary trading and to establish a consumer agency were more visible to the public and generated more aggressive opposition from the industry. Proprietary trading, exercised by setting up a hedge fund or private equity fund within the bank, had become the most profitable line of business for large banks, in part because traders regularly took highly leveraged risks, confident that the government would back them up if they lost the bet. The Treasury proposal included no significant limitation on such activities, and the House bill carried this stance forward. Although several well-known policy-oriented economists had advocated restoring a separation of banks' commercial and speculative activities,[58] it was widely believed that such a proposal could not survive the opposition of banking interest groups and might spell the death of the full bill. Former Federal Reserve chair Paul Volcker, renowned for his stolid stand against inflation during the Carter and Reagan years and now a leading public intellectual in international finance circles, had persistently advocated separating the two functions. In spite of opposition from Timothy Geithner and other Treasury officials, President Obama was persuaded and announced his support for including the "Volcker Rule" in the bill, and it quickly picked up the backing of five former Treasury secretaries. The rule was watered down in a bargain for the vote of Senator Scott Brown (R-MA); the "three-percent Volcker rule" allows large financial firms some leeway, but the constraint on proprietary trading is substantially restrictive.[59]

The idea of a "Financial Product Safety Commission" owes its wide dissemination to Harvard law professor Elizabeth Warren, whose 2007 article on the topic had brought her to the attention of then senator Obama. Appointed by the president to head the oversight panel for the Troubled Asset Relief Program (TARP) bailout, Warren came to symbolize the liberal populist alternative to the Republicans' Tea Party mobilization. Obama made the consumer agency the centerpiece of his financial reform proposal, and it attracted the most intense opposition from banking interests and the GOP.[60] Financial interests have argued that the agency's regulations would restrain competition and discourage the development of new financial products, and Republicans in Congress have portrayed it as a government takeover of a key economic sector. The agency was nearly lost to a pitched battle among "status quo regulators," including the FDIC, FTC, and the Fed. In the end, the Fed's yearlong campaign to capture the agency paid off when Chairman Dodd announced the support of both his Senate colleagues and Elizabeth Warren for placing the consumer agency in the Federal Reserve.[61] Formally, the agency claims considerable autonomy within the Fed, but almost alone among regulatory agencies its proposed rules can be reviewed by a board representing other financial regulators.

Assessing financial reform.   Although it is too early to gauge its full impact—the new law remained a target for the House Republican majority well into the 112th Congress—the Dodd-Frank Act, which combines significant changes in the law with a substantial amount of delegated discretion over rule-making and enforcement, has already stimulated activity within the executive branch and the financial sector. Some of the new regulatory authority is assigned to new agencies, and they will be competing with established bodies which are well staffed, have regularized channels for communicating with major financial firms and organizations, and participated actively in seeking to shape the form and scope of delegation written into the bill. There is no question that the Obama administration's financial reforms have disrupted standing arrangements: some of the country's largest banks have begun to bring their balance sheets into line with new capital requirements and spin off their proprietary trading and derivatives operations. Banks and organizations representing financial firms, meanwhile, have moved from lobbying Congress to lobbying the bureaucracy over the rule-making process and appointments to key positions in new agencies. The most prominent battle has focused on the president's selection of a head for the new consumer protection bureau, with liberals and progressive organizations advocating the appointment of Elizabeth Warren, and conservatives and Republican leaders vowing to oppose her (in the short term, Warren was moved to a White House position overseeing the bureau's implementation); but the Treasury's barely supportive stance toward the Volcker rule promises an equally important, if much less visible, fight over the regulation of proprietary trading.[62]

Although the immediate attention will rightly focus on political and bureaucratic competition over draft regulations, appointments, and the vigor of early enforcement actions, the stakes—and the criteria for success—hinge on larger changes. Over the last several decades, politicians and administrators set aside laws and relaxed oversight of trading and lending, allowing banks to grow larger, less transparent, and much more profitable. But the crisis showed that banks had used their market power and informational advantages to manipulate transactions, and this revelation has knocked the wind out of investors' confidence that financial markets could be trusted to produce fair results.[63] Three years after the beginning of the financial meltdown, bank profits have resumed their previous level but the flow of credit to businesses and homeowners is still slowed by the lack of confidence between lenders and borrowers. Inasmuch as the goal of Obama's financial reforms is to repair the structure of transparency and prudential limits that markets need to function effectively, its success will be signaled by the actions of businesses, home buyers, investors, and banks.[64]

After the Midterm Elections: Changing Direction

After the midterm elections, a new issue loomed: if legislation was not passed to renew them, the Bush tax cuts of 2001 would expire on December 31, 2010, raising taxes across the board and undercutting the recovery. Moreover, the election results made it clear that the public was dissatisfied with the trajectory of job creation, and Obama emphatically set strengthening the pace of recovery as his top priority.

GOP opposition, however, had stymied a succession of White House fiscal initiatives during 2010, whether directed at jobs, aid to the states, or even aid for small business, and now Obama found the way blocked once more by an election-emboldened Republican minority determined to force him to endorse their version of the tax bill.

The gulf over the Bush tax cuts was deep but not wide: both parties agreed that the lower rates should be extended for middle- and working-class taxpayers, but they differed bitterly over whether rates should be allowed to expire for the most affluent. Obama had campaigned for raising the top-bracket rate (on incomes over $250,000) and Democratic liberals, arguing that the wealthy were not paying their fair share, saw it as essential to the party's mission. As the salience of the federal deficit grew during 2010, the president also emphasized that restoring Clinton-era rates on that top bracket would yield $700 billion in deficit-reducing savings over the next decade.

Republicans were just as committed to extending the lower rates for all income groups, and they had an unmistakable strategic advantage. They read the election results as signaling the popularity of obstructing the president's program, and Mitch McConnell vowed that no legislation would pass the Senate until the Republican position on taxes was enacted. The Republican minority was quite happy to watch the rising pressure on Obama as the economy's slow recovery soured public opinion and the backlog of stalled legislation provoked increasingly outspoken criticism from the Democratic caucus.[65]

Two Democratic senators gamely offered compromises. Charles Schumer of New York proposed extending the Bush tax cuts for incomes up to $1 million, and Mark Warner of Virginia wanted to keep the $250,000 cutoff but designate the annual savings as a new tax cut for small business. The Republican leadership confidently rebuffed every such proposal. And while liberal commentators continued to demand that the president "get tough" and let all the Bush tax cuts expire, it was likely that—with a Democrat in the White House—Obama's party would bear most of the blame when taxes went up. The president, it seemed, was holding a visibly weak hand, and some conservatives predicted that the Bush tax cuts could be extended without offering the Democrats any quid pro quo.

Surveying the strategic prospects, Obama embarked on a campaign focused on job creation, moving away from his earlier insistence on restoring the upper-bracket tax rates and framing a potential bargain that would agree to temporarily extend all the tax cuts, in exchange for a package of other stimulus measures that he felt would have a quicker and more direct effect on economic activity. As with his attempt to win Republican votes for the stimulus, Obama went against the consensus among expert economists, who advised that spending programs would have the greater immediate impact, to propose a set of initiatives weighted toward the GOP preference for tax cuts. With liberal Democrats threatening to vote against the president, and Senate Republicans resolute in their determination to block action on any legislation, White House negotiators minimized the party's retreat on the tax issue and, noting that unemployment now stood at 9.8 percent, centered their strategy on strengthening stimulus measures and gaining more aid for the jobless. In the end, the Republicans pushed a hard bargain, requiring that any increase in unemployment aid be offset by spending cuts, a move that nearly drove a wedge between the president and congressional Democrats.[66] But the package, finalized in talks between Vice President Joe Biden and McConnell, fulfilled the president's hope for a second stimulus bill even as it severely disappointed his partisans in Congress.[67]

As 2011 began, the economy's halting progress dictated that President Obama turn from policy reformer to economic manager, and the Republican gains in Congress transformed his status from the leader of a legislative majority to a separation-of-powers president constrained by divided government. Obama took advantage of the usual midterm staff turnover to rebuild his economic team, shifting the focus from innovation and reform to pragmatism and political adjustment. Drawing on notable alumni of the Clinton administration, Obama tapped Gene Sperling to direct the National Economic Council and Jacob Lew as Budget Director. With Christina Romer's return to academe, Obama promoted Council of Economic Advisers member and former campaign adviser Austan Goolsbee to head the Council, and tapped Katharine G. Abraham, who had served as Commissioner of Labor Statistics, to fill the vacant seat.[68] And, in perhaps the most significant signal of a pro-business turn in his orientation toward economic policy, Obama named the chairman of General Electric, Jeffrey Immelt—who has been an influential advocate for strengthening American manufacturing and exports—to head the panel of outside advisers previously chaired by Paul Volcker.

But in a late 2010 press conference after the lame-duck session, Obama continued to stress the problems of income inequality and the threat it posed to a "thriving, booming middle class." He subsequently spent most of his 2011 State of the Union address focused on economic recovery, touting deficit reduction even as he held firm to enhanced "investments" in education, R&D, and clean energy. In response, top Republicans suggested that "investment is the Latin for more Washington spending" and pledged to make battles over spending levels and the national debt the key issue leading into 2012.[69] Those competing priorities would soon spill over into intensive arguments over the long-delayed fiscal 2011, and pending fiscal 2012, budgets and the vote to increase the United States' debt limit.

Conclusion

The signature economic initiatives of President Obama's first two years, the anti-recession stimulus and the financial reform, drew on his core economic beliefs and goals and form part of a coherent program intended to change the trajectory of the American political economy. But they also differ in ways that illuminate the strengths and weaknesses of Obama's leadership style in guiding a proposed project of governance centered on change toward an economy in which prosperity is more equally shared.

Obama aspired to shift from a course that elevates individual preferences to one that foregrounds equalizing opportunity and building social capital. Although the conservative regime never did succeed in shrinking the size of government, the Reagan and Bush administrations dramatically altered its fiscal profile. By reducing taxes on the affluent, relaxing regulations on business and finance, and cutting social programs, their policies enlarged income inequality; the change President Obama envisions aims to move not forward into uncharted territory but back, to restore the configuration of economic rewards that typified the thirty years beginning with Eisenhower's presidency.

The stimulus addressed inequality both in its short-run anti-recession provisions and in its "down payments" on productivity-building investments. As a counter-cyclical measure, the stimulus drew on standard policy instruments, such as temporary tax cuts, public infrastructure projects, and extended unemployment insurance. But it also included less conventional steps specifically intended to strengthen the safety net and lessen the recession's impact on workers and their families—including health insurance for the unemployed, a further extension and expansion of unemployment insurance in light of the exceptional depth of the recession, and fiscal assistance for state governments intended to minimize cuts in education, income assistance, and Medicaid. Obama's purpose in combining the stimulus with long-run growth-oriented initiatives was to begin to build a foundation for future growth that would be more solidly grounded and produce more widely shared benefits than the "bubble economy" of recent years. The education program is the most visible of these,[70] but increased funding for research, green energy, and broadband all act on the long-standing consensus of economists that education and technology are the main drivers of economic growth. By broadening and upgrading the educational opportunities of workers, and jump-starting industries outside of Wall Street, the program is intended to reverse the pattern in which the bulk of the gains went to the financial sector. The financial reform law reshapes the regulatory environment toward the same goals, increasing the transparency of exchanges and setting limits on the opportunities for financial firms to profit by taking risks at taxpayers' expense.

President Obama's economic project is also distinguished from his conservative predecessors' by its focus on public goods, collective benefits that cannot be supplied by markets. Investments in public education and basic research are classic examples, but so are public infrastructure and subsidies for start-up industries where high initial costs and delayed payoff deter private investors.

The administration's banking reform bill takes a similar tack: strong financial regulation, although it constrains individual firms' opportunity to profit from their informational advantage over consumers and investors,[71] benefits both borrowers and lenders in the long run. By correcting informational asymmetries and limiting the concentration of market power, it enhances the efficient use of capital and strengthens investor confidence—but all this can be accomplished only if government steps in to constrain market competition.

If the programmatic narrative of the Obama economic agenda provides a common thread linking the stimulus and financial regulation, the similarity also extends to the political process by which they were enacted. Both were blocked by Republican opposition in the Senate, and, in order to gain the two or three votes needed to move past the filibuster, they were modified in ways that weakened their potency at achieving the administration's core goals. The cuts from the stimulus, for instance, fell most heavily on Obama's proposed investments in education and human capital; opposition to the financial reform bill led to situating in the Federal Reserve what had been intended as an independent consumer agency, and to diluting the Volcker rule's initially unambiguous separation of commercial and speculative activity.

But the differences between the politics of the stimulus and financial reform are also worth noting, for they reflect both White House legislative leadership and the configuration of opposing interests. With the stimulus, Obama achieved more than most observers would have thought possible—a substantial anti-recession effort, plus down payments on public goods that never could have been enacted in separate legislation. The stimulus was historically ambitious, and more than a few thought the president had overreached and would be defeated. But the process, including bargaining with the legislature and reaching out for public support, was orchestrated with a deft sense of how much the economic crisis would permit the White House to squeeze substantive accomplishment out of an inhospitable political environment.

The president's financial reform proposal, by contrast, asked for less than was needed, and got more than it requested—not because the White House was directing the process, but because other actors had a better sense of the potential for leveraging a populist appeal into more robust reform. Each of the key moves toward strengthening the legislation—by Frank and Collins on capital requirements, Lincoln on derivatives, Volcker on proprietary trading, and Warren and her supporters on consumer protection—was an initiative crafted to respond to the popular wish to rein in the banks. Whether the White House underestimated the potential of a populist frame, or rejected it as blatant and inappropriate, or whether Obama and his key advisers—notably Treasury secretary Geithner and NEC chair Lawrence Summers—were simply more respectful of Wall Street's sensibilities than the legislators, the executive branch was typically playing catch-up, where it had been in command of the stimulus process.

If President Obama's economic agenda has mapped out a coherent, program-matic rebuttal to the Reagan legacy, how should its significance be judged?[72] First, it is important to note that the administration's policies have accepted some of the most salient features of Reagan's program. The centrality of market-based themes to Obama's health care reforms, his education initiatives, and his posture toward the financial sector could not be more different from the tone of policies under Roosevelt, Johnson, or even Nixon. On the other hand, the stimulus, and especially its long-term investments in research and education, along with the financial reform, set in motion new incentives and government–market relations that will continue to resonate into the future. Moreover, given the difficulty of enacting any major legislation in the gridlock of American national politics, the president and his advisers deserve credit for prevailing over structural odds arguably more daunt-ing than any modern administration has faced.

Taken all together, President Obama's legislative accomplishments during his first two years do not come up to the broad and fundamental change enacted dur-ing the New Deal. And that they garnered for the administration little in the way of political benefit is undoubtedly frustrating for the White House. But they do rank with three exceptionally productive historical moments that transformed sig-nificant portions of the political economy—the immediate postwar years, when the GI Bill vastly broadened the opportunities for upward mobility and the inter-state highway system transformed the efficiency of the economy's transportation network; the 1960s, when civil rights laws, Medicare, and Medicaid reduced vast inequalities of political rights and economic risk; and the Reagan years, when tax cuts and deregulation swept away decades of incremental but bipartisan moves to limit inequality, and set in motion the historic shift toward America's current place as the most economically unequal of developed democracies. Thus Obama's first years can rightly claim to be a period of great accomplishment—political entrepre-neurs pushed politicians and the public to acknowledge problems; coalitions were constructed around solutions; and laws were enacted and funded to accomplish visible changes in the lives of ordinary people.

Notes

1. See the Edwards and Campbell chapters in this volume. The Republicans' ideological advantage—around 38 percent of the electorate identify as very or somewhat conser-vative, while about 21 percent identify as very or somewhat liberal—has remained stable since the 1990s. The shift in party identification has been more ambiguous: from 2004 to 2008, the proportion claiming a Republican party identification declined from 33 percent to 27 percent, while the Democratic proportion rose from 35 percent to 36 percent. See Juliana Horowitz, "Winds of Political Change Haven't

Shifted Public's Ideology Balance," http://pewresearch.org/pubs/1042/winds-of-change-haven't-shifted-publics-idology-balance (November 5, 2008); Kate Kenski, Bruce W. Hardy, and Kathleen Hall Jamieson, *The Obama Victory: How Media, Money, and Message Shaped the 2008 Election* (Oxford: Oxford University Press, 2010), figure 1.4, 20.

2. The referendum on the incumbent was clear: only 11 percent believed that Bush would be remembered as "an outstanding or above-average president," and his 25 percent final approval rating was compared with Nixon's 24 percent on the eve of his resignation and Truman's low of 22 percent. Lydia Saad, "Democratic Party Winning on Issues," Gallup Poll, http://www.gallup.com/poll/103102/democratic-party-winning-issues .aspx (December 7, 2007); Pew Research Center for the People and the Press, "Bush and Public Opinion: Reviewing the Bush Years and the Public's Final Verdict," http://people-press.org/report/478/bush-legacy-public-opinion (December 18, 2008); John Maggs, "Despite Crisis, Bush's Legacy Isn't Written Yet: The Financial Meltdown Has Sent Bush's Approval Ratings near Truman's Record Low," *National Journal Magazine*, October 18, 2008.

3. Voters' policy focus evolved and clarified through the course of the campaign: early in 2008, the economy displaced the Iraq War and terrorism as the most important problem, and from January to October the plurality naming the economy as the most important problem grew from just over 30 percent to almost 70 percent (Kenski, Hardy, and Hall, *Obama Victory*, fig. 1.2, p. 18). Not only was the economy the most salient issue, voters' evaluation of the government's economic policy was equally unambiguous, as approval of the president's handling of the economy fell to a historic low on the eve of the election (http://www.sca.isr.umich.edu/documents.php?c=ty).

4. Barack Obama, *The Audacity of Hope* (New York: Crown, 2006), 158.

5. Obama's "history" speeches include June 22, 2007, "Taking Our Government Back"; July 18, 2007, "Changing the Odds for Urban America"; and September 17, 2007, "Our Common Stake in America's Prosperity." The tax program is typically twinned with his plans for human capital investment; for instance, June 15, 2007, "Strengthening Families in a New Economy"; September 18, 2007, "Tax Fairness for the Middle Class"; and May 3, 2008, "A Plan to Fight for Working Families and Take on Special Interests in Washington." As the economy deteriorated and the financial crisis worsened, his criticisms of Bush's policies and McCain's promises became sharper: see January 22, 2008, "Economic Speech"; May 16, 2008, "Confronting an Economic Crisis"; and October 13, 2008, "A Rescue Plan for the Middle Class." See http://origin.barackobama.com/speeches/.

6. Obama's victory over John McCain, in a contest with an exceptionally high voter turnout, made for a clear contrast with recent close elections. Obama received 53 percent of the popular vote and 365 electoral votes, to McCain's 46 percent and 173 electoral votes; turnout exceeded that of every federal election back to the 1960s. Among the flurry of media commentary, Jonathan Woon presented a sophisticated political science analysis of the probability of policy change in "Change We Can Believe In? Using Political Science to Predict Policy Change in the Obama Presidency," *PS* 42 (2009): 329-444.

7. Patricial Heidotting Conley, *Presidential Mandates: How Elections Shape the National Agenda* (Chicago: University of Chicago Press, 2001); Robert Dahl, "The Myth of the Presidential Mandate," *Political Science Quarterly* 105 (1990): 355-372. On the president's role in interpreting the "sense of the people" and giving voice to the considered interests of the public, see Hamilton in *Federalist 71* and Madison in *Federalist 63*, and Jeffrey K. Tulis, *The Rhetorical Presidency* (Princeton, NJ: Princeton University Press, 1987). See the Edwards chapter in this volume for a different view.

8. Mark Halperin, *Game Change* (New York: Harper, 2010).

9. For business cycle dates, see http://www.nber.org/cycles.html; GDP: http://www.bea .gov/national/nipaweb/; personal financial condition and consumer sentiment: http:// www.sca.isr.umich.edu/main.php.

10. Key moments include the Republican debate at Reagan Library (January 30, 2008) and the second Presidential Debate (October 7, 2008), accessed at http://www.ontheissues .org/default.htm.

11. John Cassidy, *How Markets Fail: The Logic of Economic Calamities* (New York: Farrar, Straus and Giroux, 2009), 4.

12. On the basis of interviews with several participants, Alter describes Obama as giving a "lengthy and well-informed overview," specifying Democratic concessions in the interest of moving the plan toward speedy implementation, while McCain, after initially deferring the opportunity to speak, "was reduced to a series of platitudes about how . . . everyone needed to 'work together' and 'move forward'. . . . When he was asked explicitly what he thought of Paulson's [three page-long] plan, he said he hadn't read it." Jonathan Alter, *The Promise: President Obama, Year One* (NY: Simon & Schuster, 2010), 9-12.

13. Thomas Piketty and Emmanuel Saez, "Income Inequality in the United States," *Quarterly Journal of Economics* 118 (2003): 1-39 (updated through 2008 at http:www.elsa .berkeley.edu/~saez); Lane Kenworthy, *Jobs with Equality* (Oxford: Oxford University Press, 2008).

14. Edward N. Wolff, *Poverty and Income Distribution*, 2nd ed. (Malden, MA: Wiley-Blackwell, 2009). Wealth includes ownership of housing, businesses, savings and checking accounts, stocks and other financial assets.

15. Aaron Bernstein, "Waking Up from the American Dream," *Business Week*, December 1, 2003, 54-58; Daniel Aaronson and Bhashkar Mazumder, "Intergenerational Economic Mobility in the U.S., 1940 to 2000," Federal Reserve Bank of Chicago, Working Paper 2005-12; Piketty and Saez, "Income Inequality"; Lane Kenworthy, "The High-Employment Route to Low Inequality," *Challenge* 54 (2009): 77-99; Lawrence R. Jacobs and Theda Skocpol, *Inequality and American Democracy* (New York: Russell Sage Foundation, 2005).

16. Lawrence Mishel, Jared Bernstein, and Sylvia Allegretto, *The State of Working America, 2006/2007* (Ithaca, NY: Cornell University Press, 2007 [updated to 2010 at http://www .epi.org/]); William G. Gale et al., "Distributional Effects of the 2001 and 2003 Tax Cuts: How Do Financing and Behavioral Responses Matter?", Brookings Institution, paper prepared for the National Tax Association's Spring Symposium (June 2008), available at http://www.brookings.edu/~/media/Files/...taxcuts.../06_taxcuts_gale .pdf. Benjamin I. Page and Lawrence R. Jacobs in *Class War? What Americans Really*

Think about Economic Inequality (Chicago: University of Chicago Press, 2009) find a similar pattern in recent national surveys showing an increasing proportion of the public denying that "the distribution of money and wealth in this country is fair" and supporting "a more even distribution of money and wealth."

17. Such programs include raising the minimum wage and expanding job training programs, improving public schools and access to college, and strengthening the quality and coverage of health care and retirement pensions. Page and Jacobs, *Class War?*

18. Page and Jacobs, *Class War?*, 99; cf. Kenworthy, *Jobs with Equality*; Nolan McCarty, Keith T. Poole, and Howard Rosenthal, *Polarized America: The Dance of Ideology and Unequal Riches* (Cambridge, MA: MIT Press, 2006); Larry Bartels, *Unequal Democracy: The Political Economy of the New Gilded Age* (Princeton, NJ: Princeton University Press, 2008).

19. Barack Obama, "Speech on the Economy, Opportunity, and Tax Policy" (Washington, DC: Urban Institute—Brookings Institution Tax Policy Center, September 18, 2007); cf. Barack Obama, *The Audacity of Hope* (New York: Three Rivers Press, 2006), 159; 177-186.

20. Obama, *Audacity of Hope*, chap. 5; http://www.whitehouse.gov/video/President-Barack-Obamas-Inaugural-Address-January-20-2009.

21. Classic expositions of the rationale for government investment in education and research as public goods include Robert Solow, "Technical Change and the Aggregate Production Function," *Review of Economics and Statistics* 39 (1957): 312-320; Robert Solow, "The Last Fifty Years in Growth Theory and the Next Ten," *Oxford Review of Economic Policy* 23 (2007): 3-14; and Paul M. Romer, "Economic Growth," in *The Concise Encyclopedia of Economics*, ed. David R. Henderson (New York: Liberty Fund, 2007). The contemporary argument has been invigorated by Claudia Goldin and Lawrence Katz in *The Race between Education and Technology* (New York: Cambridge University Press, 2008), whose research shows that slower economic growth over the last thirty years is in part due to the decline in investment in education and the corresponding decline in Americans' gains in educational attainment. Nathan Kelly, *The Politics of Income Inequality in the United States* (New York: Cambridge University Press, 2009), and Bartels, *Unequal Democracy*, trace the historical pattern of party differences.

22. Barack Obama, "Address on the Economy" (April 14, 2009), http://www.whitehouse.gov/the_press_office/Remarks-by-the-President-on-the-Economy-at-Georgetown-University/. David Leonhardt's interview ("Time to Steer 'Forceful Course' for Stimulus Bill," *New York Times*, February 4, 2009) two weeks later is invaluable in fleshing out the president's thinking.

23. Obama frequently hearkens back to FDR's use of the metaphor of the social compact, and draws on recent research on the relationship between inequality and social fragmentation: "The welfare state [along with charitable giving, and support for progressive taxation] rests on enlightened self-interest in which people can look at beneficiaries and reasonably say, 'There but for the grace of God . . .' As income differences widen, this statement rings less true." Frank Levy, *The New Dollars and Dreams: American Incomes and Economic Change* (New York: Russell Sage Foundation, 1998), 155; cf. Frank Levy and Richard Murnane, *The New Division of Labor* (Princeton, NJ: Princeton University Press, 2004).

24. Several decades of research have cumulated strong evidence that structural variables provide a more valid account of presidential success than personal characteristics, and this section focuses on three key structural constraints. For thoughtful discussions of the structure/agency distinction, see Stephen Skowronek, *The Politics Presidents Make* (Cambridge, MA: Belknap Press, 1993); Jon R. Bond and Richard Fleisher, *The President in the Legislative Arena* (Chicago: University of Chicago Press, 1990); William G. Howell, *Power without Persuasion* (Princeton, NJ: Princeton University Press, 2003); M. Stephen Weatherford, "Comparing Presidents' Economic Policy Leadership," *Perspectives on Politics* 7 (2009); and Lawrence R. Jacobs, "Democracy and Capitalism: Structure, Agency, and Organized Combat," *Politics and Society* 38 (2010): 243-254. On path dependency and critical junctures, see Jacob S. Hacker, *The Divided Welfare State* (New York: Cambridge University Press, 2002), 59; Paul Pierson, *Politics in Time: History, Institutions, and Social Analysis* (Princeton, NJ: Princeton University Press, 2004); and John Kingdon, *Agendas, Alternatives, and Public Policies* (Boston: Little, Brown, 1984).

25. Mancur Olson, *The Rise and Decline of Nations* (New Haven, CT: Yale University Press, 1982). Olson's history compares three nations in the decades after World War II: Britain, economically dominant for a century or more and with an entrenched system of organized interests; and Germany and Japan, where defeat in war destroyed the established system of political economic influence and necessitated rebuilding without the pressure of vested interests. The great paradox of Olson's argument is that the defeated countries grew faster not in spite of the crisis of wartime destruction but because of it.

26. Barry Eichengreen, "Macroeconomic and Financial Policies before and after the Crisis," prepared for the East-West Center/KDL Conference on the Global Economic Crisis, August 19-20, 2010.

27. Allan J. Cigler and Burdett Loomis, eds., *Interest Group Politics*, 7th ed. (Washington, DC: CQ Press, 2007), chap. 1. Skowronek, *Politics Presidents Make*, argues that the density of organized interests' connections to national policymaking have qualitatively diminished the possibilities for presidents to advance a "reconstructive" agenda.

28. For data on lobbying and campaign expenditures by different economic sectors, see Center for Responsive Politics (http://www.opensecrets.org/influence/index.php). Simon Johnson and James Kwak in *Thirteen Bankers: The Wall Street Takeover and the Next Financial Meltdown* (New York: Pantheon Books, 2010), and Jacob S. Hacker and Paul Pierson in "Winner-Take-All Politics: Public Policy, Political Organization, and the Precipitous Rise of Top Incomes in the United States," *Politics and Society* 38 (2010): 152-204, chronicle the political rise of the financial sector beginning in 1970s. Some commentators have suggested that business may be employing another, more insidious, mode to pressure the government. By August 2010, the economy's five hundred largest corporations had accumulated a historically high level of cash on their balance sheets—"By any calculation (for example, as a percentage of assets), this is higher than it has been in almost half a century": Fareed Zakaria, "Obama's CEO Problem," *Newsweek,* July 6, 2010, http://www.newsweek.com/2010/07/06/obama-s-ceo-problem .html. This has prompted the suggestion that businesses may be hoarding cash that

could be spent on new plants, equipment, or hiring additional workers. By hampering the recovery, such a move would weaken popular support for a government whose policies they oppose. Others reject the implication of a political motivation, emphasizing market uncertainty (James Surowiecki, "The Financial Page: The Blame Game," *New Yorker*, August 2, 2010).

29. Isaac William Martin, *The Permanent Tax Revolt: How the Property Tax Transformed American Politics* (Stanford, CA: Stanford University Press, 2008); Kimberly J. Morgan, "Constricting the Welfare State: Tax Policy and the Political Movement against Government," in *Remaking America: Democracy and Public Policy in an Age of Inequality*, ed. Joe Soss, Jacob S. Hacker, and Suzanne Mettler (New York: Russell Sage, 2007); Fred Block, "Read Their Lips: Taxation and the Right-wing Agenda," in *The New Fiscal Sociology: Taxation and Comparative and Historical Perspective*, ed. Isaac William Martin, Arjay Mehrortra, and Monica Prasad (New York: Cambridge University Press, 2009); Steven Teles, *The Rise of the Conservative Legal Movement: The Battle for Control of the Law* (Princeton, NJ: Princeton University Press, 2008); Jill Lepore, *The Whites of Their Eyes: The Tea Party's Revolution and the Battle over American History* (Princeton, NJ: Princeton University Press, 2010).

30. Bringing floor debate to an end requires sixty votes to invoke "cloture"; other dilatory possibilities are "holds," in which as few as one senator can (anonymously) block measures from coming to the floor; or objection by one or more senators to the unanimous consent needed to hold committee hearings while the Senate is in session. See also the Sinclair chapter in this volume.

31. Until the 1970s, there were fewer than one cloture vote per year. When the annual average rose to about a dozen, the Senate in 1975 changed the threshold from two-thirds to sixty votes. The average increased to about 25 per year until 2007, when the Republicans, in the minority after the 2006 election, adopted the practice of filibustering (or threatening to filibuster) virtually every bill of substance. In the 110th Congress (2007–2008), there were 112 cloture votes, and in the 111th (2009–2010) there were 136, a new record. Even the threat of a filibuster frequently keeps a bill from reaching the floor or a particularly ambitious provision from being included in the final legislative vehicle. See http://www.senate.gov/pagelayout/reference/cloture_motions/111/shtml; Francis E. Lee, "Senate Deliberation and the Future of Congressional Power," *PS* 43, 2 (April 2009): 227-229; Barbara Sinclair, *Unorthodox Lawmaking: New Legislative Processes in the U.S. Congress*, 3rd ed. (Washington, DC: CQ Press, 2007); Gregory J. Wawro and Eric Schickler, *Filibuster: Obstruction and Law making in the U.S. Senate* (Princeton, NJ: Princeton University Press, 2009); George Packer, "The Empty Chamber: Just How Broken Is the Senate?," *New Yorker*, August 9, 2010, 38-51.

32. David Mayhew, "Supermajority Rule in the U.S. Senate," *PS* 36 (2003): 31-36, emphasizes the importance of the intensity differential (which traditionally separated only the legislative politics of civil rights from the norm), and Packer ("Empty Chamber," 48) invokes the same reasoning to account for the success of Minority Leader Mitch McConnell in keeping moderate Republicans voting with their more extreme co-partisans.

33. James J. Calmes, "For Obama, Rare Chance for Bold Start on Big Task," *New York Times*, January 19, 2009.

34. President Obama intended that his frank approach to the deficit would bring Republicans into a constructive conversation over the shape of economic policy once growth was restored. The president established the National Commission on Fiscal Responsibility and Reform in February 2010. It issued its final report, "The Moment of Truth," on December 1, 2010 (http://www.fiscalcommission.gov/sites/fiscalcommission.gov/files/documents/TheMomentofTruth12_1_2010.pdf). Although the report of the deficit commission underlines the importance of more transparent accounting, to date Obama's hope has elicited little engagement from the GOP.

35. With too many proposals on the agenda at the same time, members of Congress, the media, and the public would become distracted and attention would be diverted from the president's priorities; several proposals would have to pass through the same committees (e.g., health care and education fall within the jurisdiction of the same House and Senate committees); and the Republican leadership's promised opposition would slow the legislative process.

36. Edmund L. Andrews, "A Crisis Trumps Constraint," *New York Times*, January 8, 2009.

37. D. E. Sanger, "Spending More Than $800 Billion Is the Easy Part," *New York Times*, February 9, 2009; J. Calmes and C. Hulse, "Obama, Visiting G.O.P. Lawmakers, Is Open to Some Compromise on Stimulus," *New York Times*, January 28, 2009; J. Calmes and D. M. Herszenhorn, "Obama Pressing for a Quick Jolt to the Economy," *New York Times*, January 24, 2009; David Leonhardt, "Time to Steer 'Forceful Course' For Stimulus Bill," *New York Times*, February 4, 2009.

38. E. L. Andrews and D. M. Herszenhorn, "Plan to Jump-Start Economy with No Instruction Manual," *New York Times*, January 10, 2009; J. Calmes and C. Hulse, "Obama Considers Major Expansion in Aid to Jobless," *New York Times*, January 4, 2009; S. Otterman, "Republicans Are Resistant to Obama's Stimulus Plan," *New York Times*, January 26, 2009; J. Zeleny, "Obama Woos G.O.P. with Attention, and Cookies," *New York Times*, February 5, 2009; J. Zeleny and D. M. Herszenhorn, "Obama Seeks Wide Support in Congress for Stimulus," *New York Times*, January 6, 2009.

39. Calmes and Hulse, "Obama Considers."

40. Calmes, "For Obama"; P. Baker, "Sternly Taking On His Critics, Obama Puts Aside Talk of Unity," *New York Times*, February 10, 2009; Obama, weekly radio address, January 24 and 31, 2009 (http://www.whitehouse.gov/video/YWA012409).

41. Calmes and Herszenhorn, "Obama Pressing."

42. The House approved the bill, now totaling $819b, on January 29. No Republicans voted for and eleven Democrats voted against the bill.

43. John Harwood, "Plotting Path in Congress for Economic Plan," *New York Times*, January 26, 2009; Otterman, "Republicans"; Jennifer Steinhauer, "As Aid Vote Nears, Cash-Pressed Governors Are Dialing for Dollars," *New York Times*, February 10, 2009.

44. D. M. Herszenhorn, "Party Lines Barely Shift as Package Is Approved," *New York Times*, February 14, 2009.

45. Jane Gravelle, Thomas L. Hungerford, and Marc Labonte, *Economic Stimulus: Issues and Priorities*, Report R40104 (Washington, DC: Congressional Research Service, November 9, 2009); D. M. Herszenhorn, "Bipartisan Push to Reduce Costs of Stimulus Plan," *New York Times*, February 6, 2009; D. M. Herszenhorn, "Senate Clears Path

for Vote on the $838 Billion Stimulus," *New York Times*, February 10, 2009; D. M. Herszenhorn, "By Narrow Margin, Economic Measure Clears Senate Hurdle," *New York Times*, February 10, 2009; D. M. Herszenhorn, "A Smaller, Faster Stimulus Plan, But Still with a Lot of Money," *New York Times*, February 14, 2009; D. M. Herszenhorn, "Party Lines Barely Shift as Package Is Approved," *New York Times*, February 14, 2009; J. Zeleny and D. M. Herszenhorn, "Obama Seeks Wide Support in Congress for Stimulus," *New York Times*, January 6, 2009; D. M. Herszenhorn and C. Hulse, "House and Senate in Deal for $789 Billion Stimulus," *New York Times*, February 12, 2009. The vote in the House was 246 to 183 (all Republicans and seven Democrats voted against); the Senate vote was 60 to 38 (three Republicans, two Independents, and all Democrats voted in favor).

46. The two components of ARRA—expenditures and tax cuts directed toward short-run relief of individuals and state governments, versus public investment—trace different time paths, with the short-run stimulus starting immediately on enactment and then tailing off by mid-2010 while investment ramps up more slowly but sustains the recovery longer (Council of Economic Advisers, "The Economic Impact of the American Recovery and Reinvestment Act of 2009, Fifth Quarterly Report," November 18, 2010).

47. These include the cash-for-clunkers tax incentive (fall 2009), the extension and expansion of the housing tax credit (through summer 2010), the job-creation tax credit for small business (through 2010), and several extensions of emergency unemployment insurance benefits.

48. The CBO report is available at http://cboblog.cbo.gov/?p=1326; Alan S. Blinder and Mark Zandi, *How the Great Recession Was Brought to an End* (Princeton/*Moody's Analytics*, July 27, 2010), at http://www.economy.com/mark-zandi-documents/End-of-Great-Recession.pdf.

49. The Campbell chapter in this volume shows relevant survey data.

50. Mike Pence (R-IN), chair of the House Republican Conference, fostered this misconception by coining the quotable "bailout stimulus" to refer to a public policy that never existed (http://mikepence.house.gov/index.php?option=com_content&view=section &id=1&Itemid=55). The GOP also made effective use of talk radio and conservative media outlets, as exaggerated claims were voiced first by commentators in partisan but more marginal media outlets and then picked up by mainstream media whose coverage of the allegation typically got more media play than the evaluation of its accuracy (W. Lance Bennett et al., *When the Press Fails,* Chicago: University of Chicago Press, 2007).

51. Alan Greenspan's mea culpa came to symbolize the excessive faith in financial markets. Responding to the question of Henry Waxman, the Chair of the House Oversight Committee, "My question for you is simple. Were you wrong?", Greenspan said: "Partially . . . I made a mistake in presuming that the self-interests of organizations, specifically banks and others, were such that they were best capable of protecting their own shareholders and their equity in the firms. . . . Something which looked to be a very solid edifice, and indeed a critical pillar to market competition and free markets, did break down. And . . . that shocked me. I still do not fully understand why it happened and, obviously, to the extent that I figure out what happened and why, I will

change my views" (US Congress, House Committee on Oversight and Government Reform, Hearings "The Financial Crisis and the Role of Federal Regulators," Washington, DC, October 23, 2008). Greenspan's testimony: http://oversight.house .gov/images/stories/documents/20081023100438.pdf. The exchange with Waxman: http://wn.com/Waxman_to_Greenspan_Were_You_Wrong.

52. US Treasury, "Financial Regulatory Reform: A New Foundation," June 21, 2009. (http://www.financialstability.gov/docs/regs/FinalReport_web.pdf). The Treasury website also includes an extensive collection of analyses of the proposal from the financial press. Sewell Chan, "After Health Care Win, Democrats Put Financial Overhaul at Top of Agenda," *New York Times*, March 25, 2010; Joe Nocera, "A Financial Overhaul Plan, But Only a Hint of Roosevelt," *New York Times*, September 26, 2009.

53. Other provisions, such as the regulation of credit rating agencies, also addressed systemic risk. They are omitted simply for reasons of space.

54. In the academic and business press, these issues were gathered under the "moral hazard" label (referring to the situation in which the gains from some transaction accrue to the actor, but the losses are indemnified by a backer who is not a party to the risky decision), and in the distinction between commercial banking and "proprietary trading" (the more risky and speculative activities associated with investment banks). The Glass-Steagall Act of 1933 had separated commercial banking from proprietary trading and, until its successive weakening and then repeal in 1999 (via the Gramm-Leach-Bliley Act), is usually credited with preserving the conditions for the historically unprecedented seventy-year period without a major financial crisis. Cassidy, *How Markets Fail*; Carmen M. Reinhart and Kenneth Rogoff, *This Time Is Different: Eight Centuries of Financial Panics* (Princeton, NJ: Princeton University Press, 2009).

55. Kim Dixon and Rachelle Younglai, "U.S. House Panel Seeks to Weaken Bank Capital Rules," Reuters (June 17, 2010), http://www.reuters.com/article/idUSN1727326320 100617; Damian Paletta, "Financial Overhaul Likely to Be More Restrictive on Banks' Capital Requirements," *Real Time Economics* (June 17, 2010), http://politifi.com/news/ Financial-Overhaul-Likely-to-Be-More-Restrictive-on-Banks-Capital-Requirements-1039667.html; Joe Nocera, "From Obama, G-20's Mission, As Tim Sees It," *New York Times*, September 26, 2009.

56. Derivatives trading is dominated by half a dozen very large banks, and their success at defeating the CFTC attempt at regulation led to increased growth in the size and riskiness of this component of their business. Brooksley Born, "Regulatory Responses to Risks in the OTC Derivatives Market," Remarks to the Committee on Federal Regulation of Securities, ABA Section of Business Law, Washington, DC, November 13, 1998, available at http://www.nuuzer.com/forum/index.php?action=printpage;to pic=227.0; Bloomberg.com, "Brooksley Born 'Vindicated' as Swap Rules Take Shape" (November 13, 2008), http://www.bloomberg.com/apps/news?pid=newsarchive&sid=aXcq .r6xLf4g.

57. Edward Wyatt, "Veto Threat Raised over Derivatives," *New York Times*, April 17, 2010; D. M. Herszenhorn, "Senate Liberals Move to Toughen Bill Regulating Wall Street," *New York Times*, May 22, 2010; Sewell Chan, "Finding the Way to the Final Bill," *New York Times*, June 11, 2010.

58. As required by the Glass-Steagall Act passed during the Great Depression, but revoked in the late 1990s.

59. W. Michael Blumenthal et al., "Congress Should Implement the Volcker Rule for Banks," *Wall Street Journal*, February 22, 2010; Simon Johnson, "The Treasury Position on the Volcker Rule," *Baseline Scenario*, August 5, 2010, http://baselinescenario .com/2010/08/05/the-treasury-position-on-the-volcker-rule/; Louis Uchitelle, "Volcker's Voice, Often Heeded, Fails to Sell a Bank Strategy," *New York Times*, October 21, 2009; John Cassidy, "The Volcker Rule," *New Yorker*, July 26, 2010, 25-30; Paul Volcker, "The Time We Have Is Growing short," *New York Review of Books*, June 24, 2010, 12-14.

60. Elizabeth Warren, "Unsafe at Any Rate," *Democracy* 5 (2007), http://www.democracy journal.org/5/6528.php; Huffington Post, "Goldman Sachs—SEC Settlement," July 15, 2009 (http://www.huffingtonpost.com/2010/07/15/goldman-sachs-sec-settlem_n_ 648045.html).

61. Daniel Carpenter, "Institutional Strangulation: Bureaucratic Politics and Financial Reform in the Obama Administration," *Perspectives on Politics* 8 (2010): 825-846.

62. Jia LynnYang, "Banks Gird for Financial Overhaul's Ban on Speculating with Their Own Money," *Washington Post*, August 14, 2010; Helene Cooper, "Obama Signs a Contentious Overhaul of the U.S. Financial System," *New York Times*, July 22, 2010; Johnson, "Treasury Position."

63. Olson's model of entrenched interests captures the extent to which the financial sector's campaign contributions and lobbying, along with long-standing ties to regulatory agencies and congressional committees, had over the preceding three decades led to the relaxation or removal of one after another of the regulatory strictures put in place in the wake of the 1929 crash. See Cassidy, *How Markets Fail*; Justin Fox, *The Myth of the Rational Market* (New York: Harper Collins, 2009); Reinhart and Rogoff, *This Time Is Different*; Simon Johnson and James Kwak, *Thirteen Bankers: The Wall Street Takeover and the Next Financial Meltdown* (New York: Vintage, 2010).

64. Again, with Republicans taking over the House, financial reform has come under close scrutiny in the 112th Congress. The new chair of the Financial Services Committee, Spencer Bachus of Alabama, admonished that "Washington and the regulators are there to serve the banks"; the majority whip, Kevin McCarthy of California, and Frank Lucas whose Agriculture Committee will have jurisdiction over derivatives, have pressed regulators to avoid "overly prescriptive" interpretations of rules on derivatives speculation or the Volcker rule.

65. In addition to the tax bill and a spending measure needed to keep the federal government running, the president had high hopes that the lame-duck session could pass several stalled initiatives. He successfully sought Senate ratification of the New START nuclear arms treaty with Russia, and Senate approval of House-passed bills to update the nation's food safety system, and to repeal the military's "don't ask, don't tell" policy. House Democrats also intended to pass and send to the Senate a bill protecting workers from sexual discrimination, and an immigration bill setting out a citizenship path for undocumented residents brought to the US when they were children; these did not become law. C. Hulse and J. Steinhauer, "Looking to Next Year, Republicans Stymie Democrats' Efforts on Top Measures," *New York Times*, November 20, 2010.

66. House Speaker Nancy Pelosi described as "grossly unfair" the Republicans' insistence on finding spending cuts to offset unemployment benefits while being willing to add the $700 billion cost of extending tax cuts on the highest incomes for the next decade. D. M. Herszenhorn and J. Calmes, "Obama Seeking Aid for Jobless in Any Tax Deal," *New York Times*, December 3, 2010.

67. The $858 billion tax plan passed the Senate on December 15 by a vote of 81 to 19, the House the next day by 277 to 148. For the Republicans, along with extending the Bush tax cuts across the board, it set new, more generous, estate tax parameters. The White House gained a thirteen-month extension of benefits for the long-term unemployed, a one-year cut in the Social Security payroll tax, continuation of the college tuition tax credit initiated in the 2009 stimulus, expansions of the child tax credit and the earned income tax credit, a two-year adjustment to prevent the Alternative Minimum Tax from impacting middle-class families, and expanded allowances for business hiring and equipment purchases.

68. Obama's decision to replace Rahm Emanuel as chief of staff with Bill Daley, whose background in investment banking is twinned with a history of strategically sophisticated management of various centrist Democratic initiatives, is emblematic of this shift in orientation.

69. Press Conference of the President, Office of the White House Press Secretary, December 22, 2010. The Republican quoted is Senator Mitch McConnell; see Michael D. Shear, "Obama Subtly Adopts the Language of Business," *New York Times*, January 25, 2011, available at http://thecaucus.blogs.nytimes.com/2011/01/25/obama-adopts-language-of-business/.

70. McDonnell and Weatherford 2010. The health care reform, the largest expansion of the safety net in forty years, continues the theme. The health care bill also included a provision that ended subsidies to banks for making student loans, and redirected the funds toward increased college financial aid.

71. The most notable example is Goldman Sachs's creation of investment vehicles that packaged subprime mortgages for sale to investors, when the firm believed the vehicles would not pay off and was in fact taking speculative positions that bet against their clients. The details of this case came to light with the SEC's civil lawsuit against Goldman Sachs and Goldman's eventual settlement with the payment of $550m. in fines and the promise to reform its business practices. Louise Story and Gretchen Morgenson, "S.E.C. Accuses Goldman of Fraud in Housing Deal," *New York Times*, April 16, 2010; Huffington Post, "Goldman Sachs."

72. Cf. David Leonhardt, "After the Great Recession," *New York Times Magazine*, May 3, 2009; and "A Progressive Agenda to Remake Washington," *New York Times*, May 21, 2010, for thoughtful discussions of this question.

CHAPTER 14

Presidential Style
and the Obama Presidency

Bert A. Rockman, Eric N. Waltenburg, and Colin Campbell

THE INDIVIDUAL WHO COMES TO THE OVAL OFFICE in the White House typically draws extraordinary attention and commentary in the popular media. The cult of the leader looms large in how we assess presidencies. Biographies of presidents, as well, point to how their particular subject handled difficult events and, often, how prior experiences shaped the handling of those events.

On the whole, political scientists are fairly skeptical about the impact of personal characteristics on the success or failure of presidencies.[1] They tend to see larger and more powerful forces at work: those influencing the economy, the ability to generate political coalitions in an institutional system designed to deter ambition, the short attention spans of mass publics, and the political and environmental forces and path dependencies that constrain movement off of existing policy equilibria. The preceding chapters in this book more frequently than not suggest a skeptical perspective about the impact of individual presidents in the absence of massive systemic political change.

In addition, political scientists are often perplexed by the analytic softness of gauging how individuals differ and what difference individual variability might make. On the whole, political scientists are driven to understand powerful rather than marginal forces at work in policy outcomes, in presidential achievement or the lack thereof, and in the political viability or its absence among various presidencies. Individual variability in the presidential office—the so-called style of leadership— is usually regarded as one of those marginal forces. Moreover, it is often regarded as squishy, soft, and unable to provide a generalizable theory about what difference variation in style makes for effective leadership. The mass market equivalent might be the "leadership books" that one finds in airport bookshops suggesting ways that are often contradictory as to how to be an effective leader. A leading behavioral scientist and Nobel Prize winner, Herbert Simon, once referred in a different context to these sorts of scientifically unfounded and sometimes contradictory observations as "proverbs."[2]

What, in other words, can we make of someone's leadership style? What can we observe? How can we connect what we observe to the way in which a president's administration conducts its affairs, influences outcomes, and assesses conditions? What are the conditions and contexts in which presidential leadership styles may make a decisive difference? Despite the attention we give to these personal driven factors, they may be only a modest part of the story of an administration's fate. Strategic political considerations are likely to be a lot more relevant. For example, was the crucial part of Lincoln's commitment to preserve the union—and later to end slavery—the consequence of his being a Republican, a party that then owed no political fealty to the South?

A president's style might, as a candidate, electrify crowds or put them to sleep (in which case the candidate may be less likely to make it to the White House), it might appeal to concord and collaboration and compromise or it might appeal to the passions of its supporters. In reality, a lot of both goes on in many cases. A president in office might be a delegator or a hands-on, detail-oriented manager of process. A president may set aside the briefing books if one has powerful preconceptions and if facts get in the way of those preconceptions—or if one simply gets bored by the seemingly inexhaustible supply of details. Another kind of president might well devour the briefing books but fail to define clearly goals or a vision. One kind of president might well make decisions from the heart or the gut or fail to ask challenging questions of his advisers. Holding to a course may be viewed as the essence of leadership. After all, if you do not believe in where you are heading or are hesitant in holding to a direction, it may make others hesitant to follow you. Such a view was espoused by President George W. Bush but also, at least indirectly, by two other modern predecessors, Ronald Reagan and Harry Truman. Another style of leadership, however, might emphasize careful vetting, adaptation, interdependence, and analytic acuity. Carried to an extreme, the one style emphasizes action and assertion whereas the other emphasizes caution, prudence, and complexity. The first one tends to fit the intuitive definition of leadership whereas the second suggests the sort of person one would want hanging around the leader as a trusted adviser whose qualms should be occasionally overcome.

The reality is that styles can vary quite a bit. Presidents over time get a better bead on which advisers they can trust more and which less. Decisions in an administration are a compound of inputs, sometimes hardly engaging the president at all—though that too is, in part, a function of how presidents go about their business, see the stakes of choices, and are willing or not to put their fortunes in the hands of others.

The way in which presidents conduct themselves in the presidency is sometimes attributed to deep-seated personality characteristics formed by their temperaments or by profound personal experiences in their individual development. Those connections are probably better left to speculation, biography, or to developmental psychologists. Our focus is on patterns, especially those that characterize the presidential style of Barack Obama. Any effort, of course, to understand the patterns of Obama's leadership at this point is inevitably a first take on a history that will unveil a deeper record. By definition, therefore, it is a first word, not a last word.

Are Leadership Styles Random or Systematic?

Although each individual president has some unique qualities, modern presidencies going back at least to the presidency of Franklin D. Roosevelt (1933–45) seem to reflect some systematic characteristics among occupants of the office. First, there seems to be some product differentiation among successive presidencies. Presidents who tend to delegate and be hands off, who emphasize the orderly management of processes through a top-down hierarchical system, are frequently succeeded by presidents who are much more absorbed in detail, involved directly in the way choices are managed, and who want those choices to flow directly to them. The reverse is equally true. One might surmise that criticisms of any given president for being too (or too little) immersed in detail produces an opposite effect in the successor. So, Dwight Eisenhower (1953–61), who liked orderly processes and meetings with his entire cabinet, was succeeded by John F. Kennedy (1961–63), who thought too much order cut off the circulation of ideas and frank talk. Jimmy Carter (1977–81), who was involved in managing even the tennis court schedule at the White House, was succeeded by Ronald Reagan (1981–89), who had the big picture colored in black and white but little grasp of, or curiosity for, detail. Bill Clinton (1993–2001) had a restless and inquisitive mind and liked the give and take that came from detailed policy discussions, but often seemed paralyzed in making decisions. No such affliction befell George W. Bush (2001–09). Bush liked meetings that started on time and the appearance of orderliness, but it is unclear that he used these meetings to challenge assumptions or engage varied perspectives or even gain operational closure on a plan of action. Bush seemed to emphasize his instincts more than analytics. But his instincts often led him onto unsustainable courses and a lack of clarity as to what followed. Bush's father's emphasis on prudence (George H. W. Bush, 1989–93) was in some ways replaced by the son's impetuousness. Bush the younger's style, in turn, was succeeded by the detached and more cerebral pattern that significantly characterizes Barack Obama.

While presidential temperaments and leadership styles seem to come in starkly contrasted pairs, it may be that these sequential differences are mostly attributable to differences in the presidents' parties. In recent history, Republican presidents have been more interested in extracting government from policy than in activating it. In contrast, Democratic presidents are interested in problem solving (or problem creating, depending on one's perspective) that utilizes governmental tools as part of the solution. This difference by no means completely explains differences in leadership style or presidential temperament but it does help explain some differences. If Republicans want to disengage (Nixon having been an especially notable exception), they are more likely to focus on international affairs, on budgetary controls, and to have a top-down management style. They may be less prone, on the whole, to thinking through policy implications in detail, especially if it means more regulation or more expenditure. Democrats, on the other hand, may be more likely to think through the details and implications of policy initiatives, because that is what their party's policy agenda leads them to do. They also may organize their White House operations to lead more to the flow of ideas than to controlling those inclined to stray. Again, major exceptions appear. Harry Truman reputedly asserted that he was hoping to find a one-armed economist who wouldn't qualify advice with "on the one hand and on the other hand" complexities. Lyndon Johnson, before the era of hyper-analysis in Washington, also saw his opportunities to create the "Great Society" legislation, and he took them. While there were policy advocates for his programs and analysis of the problems the programs were designed to address, there was not a heavy emphasis on addressing trade-offs between costs and benefits. As a legislative strategist, Johnson was into cajoling others, finding the openings, and ramming through what the opportunities presented. He was into reading people and opportunities, not analytics. For better or for worse, however, at least from Jimmy Carter onward, Democratic presidents have tended to be policy wonks, not to mention the party's losing candidates such as Michael Dukakis, Al Gore, and John Kerry.

Complexity, however, is difficult to explain, whereas straightforward if simple messages are easier to express. From that standpoint, Republican presidents may have an advantage in the messaging wars. But from the perspective of accounting for leadership style, the larger point is that the fashion in which leadership is exercised may well be a function of the distinctive agendas of the political parties, the individuals they attract to lead their forces into political battle, and the alternative visions they have for defining achievement. The enemy of a purist vision is the devil that resides in the details.

Obama's Leadership Characteristics

There are several limitations evident in studying President Obama as a leader. One that we earlier noted is the incompleteness of the record—a matter that may or may not contradict the current record of evidence. Second, a good bit of what we have to work with comes from sources that appear to be relatively sympathetic to this particular president or who have spoken mainly to people who populate the Obama administration. In other words, there is a potential bias. Much of this bias, if such there be, is apt to be the byproduct of journalists' general sympathies toward Democratic presidents and general antipathies toward Republican ones. The journalists try mightily to be objective and professional, but their own values and who they speak to lead them to be, say, more sympathetic to a Barack Obama than to his predecessor, George W. Bush. Of course, the different levels of sympathy and antipathy may also reflect an underlying reality. It is not always easy to tell them apart or even to pull them apart. Third, it is impossible to get inside someone else's head even when one has already written about it as Obama has in the autobiography of his personal development.[3] So, we have to look at observables and see what patterns emerge. To be sure, however, two people of differing or even similar persuasions can see different things. In the case of President Eisenhower, for instance, the notable presidential scholar, Richard Neustadt, saw a political naïf who was readily manipulated by others. Some years later, however, another notable presidential scholar, Fred Greenstein, saw in Eisenhower a nuanced set of political skills seemingly concealed by a style of indirection. Unless one is dealing with an utterly noncontroversial (and therefore uninteresting) figure, it is likely that there will continue to be differences of perspective about the subject's personal characteristics and style of leadership.

It is certainly the case that Barack Obama is a controversial political figure. This could be for many reasons, most of all perhaps that he is president in politically tempestuous times in which there seems little room for compromise or bargaining. Political postures are hardened across party lines and political leaders are often demonized by their opposition. Strident differences in policy position—or often posture—rarely make for dispassionate assessments of leaders. To some of his more strident opponents, Obama is a radical socialist who is bent on redistributing the benefits of the social order while busily using government to bankrupt the economy and control private transactions. Who he is as a person may mean a great deal less than what he does or proposes to do as a politician. In the rogue's gallery of the political right, Obama may even be a lesser villain than Nancy Pelosi, the current Democratic minority leader in the House of Representatives and former Speaker of the House who was used as the Republican poster child for Democratic "sins" during the 2010 midterm elections. In that regard, to the right, Obama may be to Pelosi what, to the left, Bush was to Vice President Dick Cheney.

To his own partisans, however, Obama is an entirely different character. Some people—excited by his oratorical flourishes, by his novelty, by the aspirations reflected in his being the first member of a racial minority to become president, by his relative youth, and by his cool demeanor—saw in him something inspiring and hopeful. These hopes and aspirations were likely to be dashed by the toxic political climate that transpired and by the inevitable compromising and wheeling and deal-ing that looked a lot like the "old politics," but which is typically the way things get accomplished in the ordinary course of American politics. Especially after the mid-term elections, Obama had to reposition himself, following in the footsteps of Bill Clinton, as a budget-cutting and tax-cut compromising moderate. Inevitably, this repositioning, however tactical, would create discontent among Obama's left-lean-ing supporters.

Putting aside the substance of Obama's positions, however, and the tactical adjustments that changes in political circumstances bring, is there a set of charac-teristics that can be said to define Obama's temperament and style of leadership? Is there, in other words, an essential Obama? The answer to that is yes, there is. Here, we identify some of the core aspects of Obama's leadership style. Then, we turn to how some of these are exemplified in aspects of his presidency.

Political Style: The Inspirational Obama

Obama's long campaign for the presidency mobilized groups that are ordinarily not highly mobilized. He did especially well with people of color, the young, and the well educated. Part of this is attributable to his own ethnic identification, his rela-tive youth, his freshness on the political scene, and the new style of organization his campaign brought to bear on the ground and through digital media. Obama, like any successful politician, could weave a story and deliver it in a way that made many people think a better day was coming. Obama did not speak in the cadences of a Martin Luther King nor did he speak in the vernacular of other great African American orators. His style was more reminiscent of John F. Kennedy. He found the right notes of challenge and triumph suggesting that if we all put our shoulders to the wheel we could find our common aspirations. His hope and change message also had the good fortune to be articulated just as anxiety over an economic collapse was soaring. A speech is ordinarily just a speech putting someone else's words into one's own mouth and quickly forgotten. And fiery speeches are often dismissed as excessively partisan and combative. There is no doubt that Obama was partisan, but his message was about facing the future together at a time when the future didn't look so good and about the challenges to come.

Finding our commonality as Americans was a theme that launched his politi-cal career in his keynote speech at the 2004 Democratic National Convention. It was also a reflection of his personal journey, which helped make it feel genuine. Ironically, Obama's stress on communitarian values was an old conservative mes-sage in a new wrapping. Social solidarity is an underlying theme for communal cohesion. Obama took that forward in an American context teeming with different identities by trying to build a new narrative of diverse backstories in search of a common vision, the theme of his 2004 speech. In an environment of seemingly endless partisan bickering and political polarization, the message seemed hopeful, as though Obama could be a breakthrough political figure turning political swords into the proverbial ploughshares.

No doubt this was a pipe dream, as previous chapters, in various ways, have noted. The parties are too far apart and the blocking opposition too cohesive. Those were the conditions of Obama's first two years when the Democrats controlled both chambers of Congress. This meant that Obama, for almost all of those two years, had to work within his own party to achieve his goals. He did, however, get some Republican support in the lame-duck session of the 111th Congress after the 2010 elections for the updated START treaty with Russia, the compromise tax-stimulus package, and the repeal of "don't ask, don't tell." But notably, the Democrats still had the House majority and a larger Senate majority in those waning days of their grip on legislative power. Some additional compromises, most notably the agreement on the budget averting a government shut-down in early April of 2011, have been reached in the partially divided government that exists after the 2010 election. It is likely, however, that unless Obama were to travel much further to the Republicans' side, the structural divides between the political forces and the opportunism that motivates them are too great for further and more transformative compromises. Jimmy Carter, Bill Clinton, Richard Nixon, and, to some extent, both Bush presidencies tried to meet in the middle or more from time to time—several of them in less heated political environments—but mostly to little avail. If you travel too far, you lose your base. If you travel insufficiently far, you lose pivotal centrist voters and typically fail to gain sufficient legislative support. But the base plays a critical role, because that is where challenges may arise, where financial support is rooted, and where enthusiasm lies.

The paradox of Obama is that he is *goal-oriented* as a politician but also *consensus-oriented* and *pragmatic* in his political style. There is, as a consequence, a continuing tension once past the first immediate phase of his presidency between achieving his policy ends and sustaining his political viability. All presidents experience this tension to varying degrees. It is an inevitable part of politics in a system where elections are rarely conclusive even, as in 2008, when they seem to be. American political institutions proliferate veto points and the arcane rules of the Senate can be used to regularly stall or kill legislation preferred by a substantial majority. In some ways, divided government legitimizes compromise and makes it easier for each party to claim that its hands were tied. This is not an inevitable outcome, however, and gridlock may be even more likely to result, as well as intense incrimination. Clinton seemed relatively comfortable in adjusting to having Republican Congresses—at least until the Republican House sent up articles of impeachment in 1998. However, Clinton campaigned as a third-way politician and while he achieved considerable political success, it was largely at the cost of his party's policy ambitions. How this all plays out with Obama remains to be seen but, as we note below, his commitment to policy goals seems to be an intrinsic part of his presidential style.

Decisional Style: The No-Drama Obama

In political speeches to his followers, Obama had a tag line, "Are you fired up and ready to go?" That was Obama at his most dramatic, Obama as the so-called rock star. As a decision maker, however, Obama seems to be anything but dramatic. A number of accounts, without notable dissent, have portrayed him as calm, even-tempered, focused, prepared, deliberative, analytical, and intelligent. As we noted, it is possible, if not necessarily plausible, that the early accounts reflect journalists in the thrall of Obama-mania or that they have spoken to the same sources, many of whom have a vested interest in portraying their principal in a way that reflects well. It is also the case that journalists are typically well-informed people who prize the "uncommon touch" of intellect, preparation, focus, and analysis. It is certainly possible that these factors have influenced the accounts of Obama's decisional style but it is unlikely that such influences have portrayed an Obama significantly at odds with the underlying reality. There seems to be no serious dispute that Obama's style is characterized by careful preparation and focus, by moving meetings to an outcome that produces operational choices, and by an emphasis on scouring alternative options. Despite these seeming intellectual assets, Obama left several friendly critics wondering if his intellectualism was devoid of an underlying moral project[5] or whether he was unable to connect the politics of campaigning to the politics of governing.[6] One other critic wondered if, in Obama's effort to bring all the big stakeholders to the table on his health care initiative and work out incentives for each of them to provide political cover for his plan, he overlooked significant cost savings that could be had by no longer protecting the domestic market of the pharmaceuticals—a choice unlikely to sit well with the big pharmaceutical manufacturers.[7]

No president, whatever his style, is immune from criticism. Presidents who ponder alternatives carefully may be subject to indecisiveness. Presidents who make decisions forthrightly may be subject to doing so without due consideration of adverse consequences. But Obama has been on top of the facts, if not always the narrative, and has typically faced down his critics in direct confrontation. His journey to the Republican House Conference retreat in Baltimore in January of 2010 parrying questions from his Republican opponents was a showcase for Obama's skills, his preparation, his understanding of the arguments, and his ability to articulate them. But in the end, this counted for naught as Obama's approval declined, distrust of incumbents spiraled, and the high unemployment rate remained stagnant. As with most other politicians, presidents are more captive of events than free agents. They may have skill sets and leadership styles that promote healthy debate and lead to fact-based (or best-estimate-based) choices, but typically only a small set of the cognoscenti are watching, and about half of them are trying to bring the incumbent down. So, virtue—if that is what it is—must be its own reward. Luck, at least as frequently as not, determines one's political fate, but how leaders decide often determines our own. Democracy, sad to say, does not necessarily guarantee that virtuous leaders be rewarded or that indolent or incompetent ones be sanctioned. Scoundrels usually do get shown the door ultimately but not always expeditiously. Those who take political risks for longer-term objectives may well fall through the trap door.

The nature of presidents' preferred policies, of course, also has a lot to do with how they are perceived publicly. But mass publics rarely understand the details of those policies, nor what policies are attributable to whom. More than we would like to think, how good or effective a politician is at governing or thinking about the future may have little to do with his or her political success. Even presidents' much ballyhooed personalities may have little to do with their success or lack thereof. No one could disagree that Ronald Reagan was an amiable fellow, but amiable or not, Reagan's approval ratings were sinking as fast as the economy was falling until the economy bounced back in 1983.

So far, we have talked about leadership styles, the difficulties in reliably inferring them, the ones that seem to characterize Barack Obama, and the limitations of leadership and personal qualities in determining the political success or failure of presidents or politicians, in general, and of Obama in particular. Now we try to place Obama's characteristics in the context of his political circumstances from the campaign through the first half of his term in office.

Obama: The Person and the System

In the 2008 presidential election contest, Barack Obama exploded on the national political scene as the "candidate of hope." He sent chills up the legs of at least one seasoned, if partisan, political journalist[8] and connected with millions of voters on an emotional, even personal level. Yet, Obama, so capable of inspiring intense passions among his electoral supporters, has evinced a style of presidential leadership that is at least several degrees separated from passion. Obama's approach to the presidency is best characterized as cool, cerebral, and resolute. He is highly organized and far more often than not in command of the facts that are relevant to the policy question at hand. Consequently, he is able to engage in and guide the discussion so that conclusions most proximate to his preferences are reached. As David Brooks, a moderately conservative columnist for the *New York Times,* put it after observing Obama's daylong summit on health care reform, "The man really knows how to lead a discussion. He stuck to specifics and tried to rein in people who were flying off into generalities. He picked out the core point in any comment. He tried to keep things going in a coherent direction."[9] Obama's decisions are deliberate and marked by careful and sober consideration of their logic and consequences, but a conclusion nonetheless is reached. To put it concretely, Obama is decisive. In this sense he is quite different from his immediate Democratic predecessor, Bill Clinton. Clinton also examined all the angles and consequences of a policy, but often left decisions dangling.

Not surprisingly, Obama's presidential style seems wholly consistent with his temperament. Maureen Dowd, the *New York Times* columnist, has occasionally referred to Obama as "Mr. Spock," and several political cartoonists have caricatured him as the starship *Enterprise's* first officer, pointy ears and all. Like Mr. Spock, Obama appears to be analytical and detached. He is neither fiery nor given to public displays of anger. He does not wear his passions on his sleeve. None of this is to say that Obama is without passion. Quite the opposite, his positions and actions as president reflect a strong commitment to his party's orthodoxy toward a more activist role for the government on matters of business regulation, social welfare, and protection of the environment. While he is pragmatic and somewhat flexible in the methods he employs to achieve his goals, he has laid down markers he intends to meet. Thus, he has not used Clinton's language of centrism, and so far he has not found it necessary (or perhaps even possible, given his dedication to Democratic orthodoxy) to pursue a Clintonian strategy of "triangulation." To the degree he has been willing to compromise with his political opponents, he has done so only so long as they move more toward his position than he to theirs in the ensuing give and take.[10]

The Past as Predictor:
The Campaigns for Nomination and Election

It is a worn-out psychological saying that the best predictor of future behavior is past behavior. Now, one reason sayings become threadbare is that there tends to be a large element of truth behind them, and this is certainly the case for the predictive qualities of Obama's performance as a candidate with respect to his style as president. The outlines of the most notable attributes of his presidential style—highly knowledgeable of both the situation and process, analytical, calm, deliberative, and cautious—are evident in his behavior during the Democratic primary and general election contests.

Races for the presidency are more akin to marathons than to dashes. They place a premium on a candidate's strategic capacity, resources, and discipline. And on all three counts, Obama scored well. As a candidate for his party's nomination, Obama demonstrated an intimate knowledge of the intricate and arcane rules structuring the Democrats' nomination process. He understood the byzantine allocation of delegates to candidates through both primary elections and party caucuses. With this understanding, he was able to pursue a strategy that was predicated on exhausting his opponents' (chiefly Hillary Rodham Clinton's) financial resources. Early on, Clinton was the expected Democratic nominee, and her financial support was drawn from traditional Democratic sources, a relatively small number of very wealthy donors. Their support for Clinton's nomination, however, could be ephemeral. The money would continue to flow so long as she appeared to be the odds-on favorite. Her strategy, therefore, was to score an early knockout. By contrast, Obama drew his financial support from a very large base of intense, passionate contributors. Their support was not tactical; it was the product of loyalty and commitment. They would be there for the long haul, and as Obama accumulated and then maintained a slim delegate lead, their support only grew. This was not the case for Clinton. With each delegate Obama gained, her support become more fragile. Finally, as the nomination season drew to a close, Obama was the clear front-runner, in both the number of pledged delegates and the stability of financial supporters. At this point the party's "super delegates"—office holders whose inclusion in the process is intended to promote the nomination chances of the most electable candidate—moved inexorably toward Obama as well. With their votes in hand, Obama was lifted to the Democratic party's nomination in Denver.[11]

Along with an intimate understanding of the process, Obama's candidacy for the nomination is notable for its organization and discipline. Throughout the grueling process, Obama's drive toward the nomination moved with a precision rarely matched in modern campaign politics. Ill-timed gaffes, self-inflicted or otherwise, are not unusual in presidential elections, and some have become the stuff of electoral legend—Jimmy Carter beating back a "killer rabbit" while fishing; Michael Dukakis, helmet and all, photographed riding in a tank; Gary Hart caught with attractive consort Donna Rice aboard, of all things, the pleasure craft *Monkey Business* (after issuing a challenge to the media to catch him in just such an act). Often there are rumors of unrest and dissent within a candidate's campaign staff. Arguments occur over the political message, or campaign strategy, or over who gets access to the candidate, that bubble into media reports. Key campaign aides leave or are fired. These incidents are generally framed as evidence of a campaign ship in heavy seas and taking on water. By contrast, Obama had smooth sailing for the most part. His team worked well together. By spring of 2008 the media had noticed the almost preternatural calm and order that suffused the Obama candidacy and began referring to him as "no drama Obama."

This is not to say that the primary and general election contests were without incident for Obama. At about the same time some media voices began using the "no drama" sobriquet, the Obama campaign faced its first serious threat of being torpedoed. In March 2008 excerpts of sermons made by Obama's long time pastor, Jeremiah Wright, appeared in the media. In these sermons, Wright made racially inflammatory statements about the United States, among other things effectively blaming America for the 9/11 attacks, calling on God to damn the nation, and referring to America as the "US of KKK-A." The danger for Obama was that he would be linked to Rev. Wright's "angry Black" rhetoric, certainly a fatal connection for a minority candidate who up to that point was amassing large swaths of support from the majority white electorate.

Obama's response to the Jeremiah Wright controversy is illustrative of his style and personal demeanor. On March 18, five days after the Wright story first gained national attention, Obama eloquently delivered a thoughtfully crafted speech in which he calmly and analytically brought into context Wright's incendiary remarks.[12] Early in the speech, Obama disavowed Wright's comments, identifying them as a "profoundly distorted view of this country,"[13] but he did not disown Wright.[14] Instead, Obama explained that Rev. Wright and his expressions were the products of a different time in American history, a time marked by black humiliation, fear, anger, and bitterness. With rhetorical skill, he walked his listeners through the nation's historical racial divide. He described the emotional energy that flowed from the Sunday sermons in Wright's church. And he pointed out that, as a nation, America continues to move toward a more perfect union.

The take away points here lie in the nature of Obama's reaction to the hazard Rev. Wright suddenly presented to his candidacy. First, Obama did not immediately comment on the Wright controversy. Instead, he remained calm and worked to produce a speech that would contextualize Wright's statements, explaining them while simultaneously distinguishing Wright from himself. Second, along with its soaring rhetoric, Obama's speech contained a strong dose of logic. According to Obama, Wright's incendiary comments are best understood almost in terms of cultural relativism. They are the residue of a different political time, a different political culture. Obama would not and could not accept them, but logically, he could comprehend their origin, in the same way that he could comprehend his white grandmother's occasional confession of fear of black men passing her on the street.

At times, Obama's calm, analytical demeanor and tendency to ascend to (descend to?) a law professor's style of ratiocination could get him in trouble, as when he attempted to explicate his difficulty in attracting white, working-class support among midwestern small-town voters.[15] More often than not, however, these qualities served him well during the campaign. This certainly seems to be the case when comparing his response to the global economic meltdown near the end of September 2008 to that of Republican presidential nominee, John McCain.

The outlines of the financial crisis the world experienced in the waning months of 2008 are fairly well established.[16] An economic downturn that had begun in late 2007 became a full-scale financial implosion with the bankruptcy filing of Lehman Brothers on September 15, 2008. Lehman's filing, the largest in US history, exposed banks worldwide to massive losses. To protect their liquidity, the banks abruptly stopped lending to each other, effectively freezing the credit markets and making business all but impossible to conduct. The US Federal Reserve and central banks in Europe and Asia attempted to restore interbank lending by pumping nearly $200 billion into world money markets, but to little or no avail. On September 19, US Treasury Secretary Henry Paulson announced the outlines of the so-called Troubled Assets Relief Program (dubbed TARP), a financial rescue package totaling $700 billion intended to stabilize the nation's financial system. The sheer cost of Paulson's plan was daunting, and despite the severity of the crisis, there was no guarantee Congress would approve it. Moreover, even the approval of TARP (or some version of it) did not guarantee that the downward spiral of the financial system would be arrested.

With the global economy on the brink of depression, McCain inserted himself and presidential politics into the mix. McCain suddenly and impetuously announced that he was suspending his campaign and returning to Washington to work on the financial rescue package. He also called on Obama to delay their scheduled debate until Congress passed legislation addressing the mounting crisis. Obama responded in typical Obama fashion. He demurred with respect to a delay of the debate and coolly pointed out that presidents must be able to deal with more than one thing at a time. Obama also consulted with Bush administration officials on the proposed financial package and communicated his priorities on the legislation to congressional Democrats. To many, the episode made McCain appear erratic and unprepared, while Obama came across as calm and analytical, ready to be president.

Following this episode, President Bush called a meeting at the White House for September 25 with both presidential contenders, the congressional leadership and relevant congressional players, and Secretary Paulson among the principals. According to one vivid account of this meeting, McCain said little, exposing his lack of knowledge; President Bush was unacquainted with details and appeared detached from decisions his own administration would have to make. Obama wound up taking over the meeting asking detailed questions. The appearance of Obama's readiness to be president was reinforced by his command of knowledge and emphasis on getting answers that neither the incumbent president nor Obama's opponent in the election seemed capable of.[17]

Style as President

Legislatively, two issues dominated the first fourteen months of the Obama administration—enactment of an economic stimulus package in response to the deep recession gripping the nation and health care reform.[18] The stimulus passed the legislative gauntlet with relative speed. Less than one month transpired between Obama's inauguration and his signing of the American Recovery and Reinvestment Act of 2009 into law. Health care legislation, however, followed a much more daunting and tortuous path. Assumed dead at various points, the Patient Protection and Affordable Care Act was introduced in September 2009 after a lot of molding across four different committees involving both the House and the Senate. It finally was signed into law six months later. The stories associated with each piece of legislation illustrate some of the basic elements of Obama's presidential style—pragmatic and flexible in method yet resolute, willing to reach out to political opposition, and deferential to Congress. They also reveal the systemic dysfunction of the present legislative and political process in which presidents must toil.

The severity of the economic crisis made enactment of a stimulus package the most immediate concern on Obama's legislative agenda. Even before taking the oath of office, Obama moved to set the legislative foundations for a stimulus plan. In November, shortly after his election, he began discussions with congressional leaders over the basic elements of a plan, and in January he met with Speaker Pelosi to lay out the package's broad outlines. Once the new Congress came into session, however, Obama largely deferred to his party's congressional leadership on the legislation. His White House did not draft the legislation nor did he attempt to guide the stimulus bill through Congress. Obama's initial interaction with Congress, and then his subsequent deference to it, is consistent with the way the system is supposed to operate. That is, the president establishes the broad parameters of a policy and then leaves it to Congress to act. Moreover, deference to Congress was probably the wisest strategy. Since enactment of a stimulus bill was perceived as essential and urgent, Obama needed the input of key congressional committee leaders to tell him what the bill required to gain sufficient votes for a rapid passage.[19] Reliance on the Democratic leadership did move the bill quickly, but it also guaranteed the bill would be replete with Democratic legislative priorities. Given the Democrats' large majorities in the House and Senate, there was no need to attract Republican votes, and congressional Democrats made no real effort to do so. Consequently, despite Obama's efforts to enlist Republican support, not a single Republican House member voted for the bill, and only three Republican senators, one soon to become a Democrat (Arlen Specter, PA), were willing to do so.

Still, it was not clear that congressional Republicans would have supported the bill even had Obama taken ownership of it and sculpted it more in tune with Republican tastes for tax cuts. In reality, about one-third of the stimulus package consisted of tax cuts reflecting Obama's effort to at least make a first move toward the Republicans or, more likely, to outmaneuver them rhetorically. As matters turned out, however, the Republican strategy seemed to be to position itself implacably in opposition to Obama's initiatives whatever they were.[20] As a result, the stimulus and the bail outs, which were mostly initiated during the Bush administration, became part of a Republican mantra that Obama was madly spending money and moving the government toward bankruptcy. Despite the Democrats' massive losses during the 2010 midterms, they still fared better than the Republicans on most issues. However, public opinion data indicate that among the few issues in which Republicans did better than Democrats was the belief that they would be more likely to reduce the budget deficit. Further, a plurality of the public also thought that President Obama had expanded the role of government too much.[21] Whatever the merits of the case, the Republicans clearly were successful at getting out the message they wanted to.

Although a sense of impending economic disaster moved the stimulus bill to the front of Obama's legislative queue, the complex health care reform act was the signature piece of legislation during the first two years of the Obama Presidency.[22] Something approaching universal health care has been a goal largely of the American left since at least the 1940s. Expansion of health care coverage did periodically occur. The elderly gained coverage through Medicare in 1965, and the poor were covered through Medicaid that same year. Health care coverage was extended to the children of lower-income families through CHIP during the Clinton administration and expanded, however reluctantly, during the George W. Bush administration. Universal coverage, however, was yet to be achieved despite the efforts of a string of presidents.

Aside from the moral imperative of providing for the poor and sick, the motivation for near universal coverage is a fiscal one. The United States, far and away, has the most expensive health care system in the western industrialized world.[23] The most obvious way to reduce or at least control health care costs is a single-payer system, in which costs and expenditures are strictly set and defined. However, that would have to be done upfront, and the experience with Health Maintenance Organizations (HMOs) in the 1990s indicated that the American public would resist this and hold its perpetrators politically accountable. In addition, and perhaps even more important, the entrenched system of private, for-profit health care special interests and pressure groups (insurance companies, doctors, hospitals, pharmaceutical companies) in the United States makes the nation's political process especially resistant to a single-payer formula. The Obama administration quickly recognized this and moved to strike bargains with the various interests in order to gain their support. Insurance companies, for example, were convinced that the increased costs they would incur by providing coverage to at-risk populations would be more than offset by the surge of new customers that the legislation's compulsory insurance requirement would create, customers who were disproportionately young and healthy.[24]

For Obama, convincing elements of the health care complex to accept his plan was one thing; convincing congressional Republicans to do so was quite another. Certainly since the New Deal, the Republican party has been opposed to the expansion of entitlement programs, and to Republicans, universal health care was the mother of all entitlements. Consequently, they put up a furious wall of resistance. In the House, where majorities rule, Republicans could do little to stop the legislation. Democrats held a seventy-seven-seat advantage, and on November 7, 2009, the House passed the bill with only one Republican vote, a vote that eventually disappeared during the Senate reconciliation process. In the Senate, Republicans could exert greater influence. The Upper Chamber's rules, procedures, and norms make it more likely that the minority party can maintain some voice. Specifically, the filibuster (unlimited debate) enables a determined minority to block majority action by preventing a vote on a piece of legislation. A Senate rule, however, permits a supermajority to overcome the minority's dilatory actions. Rule 22 (cloture) calls for debate to be ended with the vote of sixty senators. In 2009 Democrats did hold sixty seats, making their majority filibuster-proof. It was a razor-thin margin, however. Republicans could be ignored only if every Democratic senator supported the legislation. Obama and the Senate leadership recognized this and tried to attract some Republican support on their health care bill. This resulted in several months' delay in bringing the legislation to the Senate floor as the chair of the Senate Finance Committee entered into extended negotiations with three GOP senators, negotiations that came a cropper. Ultimately, the Senate passed its version of a health care bill on December 24, 2009, without a single Republican vote. Before it could be presented to the president, however, the bill had to pass in identical form in both chambers. At this point, the delay that the futile negotiations in the Senate caused almost proved to be the legislation's undoing.

On January 19, 2010, Massachusetts held a special election to fill the late Ted Kennedy's Senate seat.[25] Scott Brown, a Republican, won, ending the Democrats' filibuster-proof majority. Moreover, Brown explicitly campaigned as *the* Republican vote in the Senate that would halt Obama's health care legislation. Political observers all but declared the reform effort dead, and there seemed to be meager political payoff in pushing it along. One interpretation of the Massachusetts election was that Brown's victory was a product of deep public animus toward the proposed health care reform, and national soundings on public opinion seemed to give this interpretation credence. Between the end of December 2009 and the beginning of March 2010, national public opinion was consistently opposed to the legislation.[26] Some of Obama's closest advisers as well as some members of the Democratic congressional leadership reacted to Brown's election by urging the adoption of a scaled-down bill, one that might collect some GOP votes. Obama himself initially signaled a willingness to move toward a compromise on the legislation. In a television interview the day after the Massachusetts election, he stated, "I would advise that we try to move quickly to coalesce around those elements of the package that people agree on."[27] Republicans, however, indicated no willingness to compromise on the versions of the bill that had passed the House and Senate. Even after Obama held a televised summit in February to draw attention to the many points of agreement between the parties and to the fact that his bill contained many Republican suggestions, the Republicans remained obdurate.

Ultimately, Obama was too committed to the passage of a far-reaching health care measure like the bills that had passed both the House and Senate and were awaiting conference, for him to give up. In the face of united and unyielding Republican opposition, Obama and Speaker Pelosi convinced a majority of Democrats in the House to accept the Senate bill so that Reconciliation, a special Senate procedure designed for budget bills and requiring only a simple majority, could be used.[28] In other words, Reconciliation effectively would render the outcome of the Massachusetts special election irrelevant to the enactment of health care reform. On March 23, 2010, Obama signed the bill into law. While it was not entirely the law that Obama and many on the Democratic left had wanted (for example, it did not contain a "public option" provision), the health care reform act did mark the most expansive piece of social legislation enacted in the United States in over four decades.

A characteristic trait of Obama's presidential style is pragmatism and flexibility of method. And this was certainly on display in the health care reform effort. It was Obama's recognition and willingness to strike bargains with the various interests in the health care system that created the possibility of simultaneously expanding access and portability while containing costs (although this latter result's actually occurring is open to substantial debate). To put it concretely, Obama was willing to make deals where deals could be made. As a pragmatic politician, results motivated Obama rather than rigid commitment to a specific approach.[29] At the same time, Obama was steadfast in his campaign for this major legislative accomplishment. Despite the utter absence of bipartisan support, a significant electoral loss, suggestions to pare down the effort, and mounting public opinion opposed to the legislation, Obama never gave up. He recognized that both his own political capital and his party's numerical strength in Congress had discrete shelf lives. If health care reform of the type he envisioned was to be enacted, it had to be enacted in this Congress.

The passage of both health care and economic stimulus also reveals important features of the toxic partisanship crippling the legislative process. Traditional differences between the parties have deepened over the course of the last several decades, and the nation has entered a period of hyper-partisanship where the parties have become polarized blocs, and essential voting coalitions cutting across those blocs are nearly impossible to cobble together.[30] In part, this is a consequence of electoral accountability, as both parties, but especially the Republicans, have become more homogeneous internally, and their partisans will not brook compromise. It is also a consequence of legislative leaders recognizing that their party's position on the president's legislative agenda has electoral consequences. Legislators of the president's party have an electoral stake in seeing the president's agenda items enacted. This demonstrates to their constituents their unity and legislative skill. Legislators from the opposition party, on the other hand, want to see the president's agenda defeated. This displays their own vitality as a party and the incompetence of their counterparts.[31] Given this environment, it is not especially surprising that despite repeated overtures, Obama and Democratic congressional leaders were almost never able to enlist Republican support. Republican leaders recognized that their journey back into the majority would not be along the path of Democratic legislative success.

Finally, both legislative efforts illustrate the outsized and increasingly anti-democratic role of the Senate. The longer terms of individual senators and the fact that only one-third of them face reelection at any one time were designed to insulate the Upper Chamber from democratic passions. As a result, the Senate would act as a "cooling saucer" of legislation, ensuring that only well reasoned and broadly popular bills would become the law of the land. Today, however, the Senate has moved beyond a cooling saucer to a deep freezer. Supermajorities now are routinely required to enact legislation. Consequently, a very small number of senators effectively can determine the fate of any given piece of legislation. Indeed, the seating of one senator (Scott Brown's special election victory in Massachusetts) compelled Obama and Democratic congressional leaders to resort to an extraordinary legislative tactic, despite holding a seventy-seven-seat advantage in the House and a nine-seat advantage in the Senate. The rules and normative structure operating in the US Senate have cheapened legislative majorities and the elections that produce them.

What Difference Do Presidents Make?

The classic question of leadership is what difference does a leader make stripped of all the situational, systemic, and party-based forces against which he or she must push? The answer is not clearly known because it always has to be in comparison with a hypothetical other. In the popular eye, leaders are omnipotent if also incompetent and corrupt. They are supposed to exercise magical powers to move the economy and create general happiness among the population. No one in a constitutional political order exercises any such authority or would be so flawlessly prescient that they could push all the right buttons. Most often leaders struggle against resisting forces. In the US political system, our presidents seek to sustain their agendas and their political fortunes under conditions that typically make it difficult for them to achieve their goals.

And yet, despite the stark partisan controversies that Obama encountered and the difficult economic circumstances that defined his first two years in office, his record has been one marked by remarkable legislative achievement in the face of a highly cohesive opposition. In part, this is testimony to the political circumstance of Obama's party nominally controlling majorities in both chambers during the first two years. But it also is testimony to Obama's persistence, focus, and goal orientation.

Presidents' leadership styles are most in evidence and apt to have powerful impact when the degrees of presidential discretion are greatest. Mostly, this has to do with process. Does a president have knowledge or know how to attain it? Can a president ask the right questions and be his or her own best skeptic? Can a president be, as George H. W. Bush liked to say, "prudent" but willing to take calculated risks? Obama may have lacked traditional experience, but whether one agrees or disagrees with his policy agenda he has demonstrated a capacity for clear thinking, for focusing sharply on the issues involved, and for leaving few stones unturned. At the same time, he has been criticized for losing his narrative and for having too much faith that he could successfully appeal to bipartisanship. When Lyndon Johnson expanded health insurance coverage to the senior citizen population, he mainly had to be concerned about coverage expansion rather than coverage *and* cost containment wrapped up in the same piece of legislation. Obama had to create a package based on interdependencies, because that was the only way the political system could bring together and cut a deal with powerful interests already vested in the health care system. Obama is not one to tilt at windmills.

Obama has been president during trying times. He inherited two wars, a very deep recession with stubbornly high rates of unemployment, and a toxic political atmosphere. In large part, he came to office as the beneficiary of these misfortunes. Ultimately, he will be judged by how rapidly and effectively he is able to extricate the country from its economic problems and its military entanglements. The reality is that there are no buttons to press to create jobs, especially well-paying ones. If there were, they already would have been pressed. Obama has managed largely to move US forces out of Iraq, but Afghanistan may get more complicated since the Obama administration itself largely built up the US military presence there. It is notable, of course, that the lengthy process by which Obama made the decision to surge troops into Afghanistan was typical of the focus, consideration of alternatives, and deliberativeness that he brings to the decision-making process. In the end, however, the process focused on the exit strategy rather than a clear definition of what would constitute a winning strategy.[32]

The take away, therefore, is this. Presidents' leadership styles are a function of their temperaments and their intellects. Curiosity, skepticism, focus, and bringing issues to a head with a strategic plan and contingency plans make for careful decision-making processes that reduce, but do not guarantee the elimination of, the prospect of error. Image management is also helpful but not ultimately central. People did not trust Clinton so much as a person, but they thought he was competent as a president. That, however, mainly had to do with the prosperity of the country. In the end, presidents get judged by their circumstances, over which they may not necessarily have much control. We assess presidents by the condition of the country. But that is probably the wrong metric. The proper one would be what they can control—that is, how they manage the processes of decision-making and balance the ingredients of governance and politics in those processes. This is a less grand benchmark but a more appropriate one, and by this standard Obama has brought to the presidency a leadership style that concentrates the mind, brings evidence and analysis to bear, and leads to operational, if imperfect, outcomes. That could be about as good as it gets.

An Epilogue

The successful assassination of the al Qaeda leader, Osama bin Laden, in early May of 2011 reflects both the organic continuity of government and also the essential role of a leader in focusing effort and bringing that effort to a conclusive outcome. It also notes the trade-off of "prudence" and "calculated risk" stressed above.

American intelligence over the years obviously had been trying to track down bin Laden. But it was distracted by the priorities of the Bush administration and by its failures to follow through when it seemed to have had the al Qaeda leadership cornered near the Afghan-Pakistani border. At a press conference approximately six months after the attacks on the United States, President Bush indicated that getting bin Laden was no longer a priority, mainly because the administration had lost track of him. Despite Bush's tough words about bringing bin Laden to justice or justice to bin Laden, the lack of follow-through and clear operational procedures hindered that effort.

Obama renewed making the targeting of bin Laden a priority. As a candidate, during the first debate with John McCain, Obama stated that the United States would pursue bin Laden and would, if necessary, carry out operations in Pakistani territory. The change in priorities reflects Obama's persistence in achieving his ends and the need to force decisions on others in the chain of operational command. It also indicates how closely Obama pays attention to the capabilities of his operatives. He observed the precise performance of the Navy SEALS team in preventing Somalian pirates from holding hostages and possibly killing the American captain of a captured vessel. He knew the capabilities of those tasked with having to carry out an equally precise operation near Islamabad, the Pakistani capital, and he clearly indicated to his then CIA director, Leon Panetta, that the operation, once determined to be feasible, should be carried out.

In the end, Obama's decision-making style was characterized by a rare combination of deliberation, assessment of risks, delegation of operations to professionals, and decisiveness from the top. The presidency may be larger than the way a president goes about making decisions. But presidents are mainly about how they make decisions and follow through on them. This is what they have in their power to control. In this regard, Obama has not been found wanting.

Notes

1. Bert A. Rockman, "Does the Revolution in Presidential Studies Mean 'Off with the President's Head'?" *Presidential Studies Quarterly* 39 (December 2009): 786-794.
2. Herbert A. Simon, "The Proverbs of Administration," *Public Administration Review* 6 (Winter 1946): 53-67.
3. Barack Obama, *Dreams from My Father: A Story of Race and Inheritance* (New York: Three Rivers Press, 2004).
4. Compare Richard E. Neustadt, *Presidential Power* (New York: John Wiley, 1960), and Fred I. Greenstein, *The Hidden Hand Presidency: Eisenhower as Leader* (New York: Basic Books, 1982). The difference is partially attributable to when the authors wrote and what information was available to them, as Neustadt's 1990 edition of his book suggests.
5. Richard Cohen, "President Obama's Enigmatic Intellectualism," *Washington Post*, June 22, 2010, A19, http://www.washingtonpost.com/wp-dyn/content/article/2010/06/21/AR2010062103698_pf.html, last accessed April 24, 2011.
6. E. J. Dionne, "Obama Needs to Relearn the Art of Politicking," *Washington Post*, August 30, 2010, A13, http://www.washingtonpost.com/wp-dyn/content/article/2010/08/29/AR2010082902899_pf.html, last accessed April 24, 2011.
7. William F. Pewen, "The Health Care Letdown," *New York Times*, March 16, 2010, national edition, A21.
8. MSNBC host Chris Matthews publicly stated that he cried and felt a chill run up his legs while listening to Obama's speeches during the campaign.
9. David Brooks, "Not as Dull as Expected!" *New York Times*, February 26, 2010, national edition, A23.
10. Bert Rockman and Eric Waltenburg, "Obama at Mid-term," *Zeitschrift für Staats- und Europawissenschaften* (Journal for Comparative Government and European Policy) 8.2:177-201, 198.
11. Ibid. 180-182.
12. The so-called "A More Perfect Union" speech. Reportedly, Obama broke with his standard speech-writing format. Rather than providing his chief speechwriter, Jon Favreau, with an outline and then allowing Favreau to write a first draft, Obama dictated a first draft of the speech on March 15, which Favreau edited and returned to Obama. Obama then perfected the speech over the course of the next two days (Nedra Pickler, "From Greek Mythology, Obama Learned a Lesson," *USA Today*, June 4, 2008, http://www.usatoday.com/news/politics/2008-06-04-2310712963_x.htm, last accessed September 27, 2010).

13. Quoted in Kate Kenski, Bruce H. Hardy, and Kathleen Hall Jamieson, *The Obama Victory: How Media, Money, and Message Shaped the 2008 Election* (New York: Oxford University Press, 2010), p. 86.

14. This finally occurred at the end of April, after Wright repeated some of his most incendiary comments before a National Press Club audience.

15. The infamous "they cling to guns or religion . . . to explain their frustrations" comment at a San Francisco fundraiser on April 6, 2008.

16. We do not pretend to do justice to the complexity of the credit crisis in this chapter. An excellent treatment of it appears in Andrew Ross Sorkin, *Too Big to Fail* (New York: Viking, 2009).

17. Jonathan Alter, *The Promise: President Obama, Year One* (New York: Simon & Schuster, 2010), 11.

18. This section draws heavily on Rockman and Waltenburg, "Obama at Mid-term."

19. Massimo Calabresi, "Can Obama Regain Control of Congress's Stimulus Bill?," *Time,* February 5, 2009, http://www.time.com/time/politics/article/0,8599,1877192,00.html, last accessed September 29, 2010.

20. Carl Hulse and Adam Nagourney, "G.O.P. Leader Finds Weapon in Party Unity," *New York Times*, March 17, 2010, national edition, A1, A17.

21. Jeff Zeleny and Megan Thee-Brenan, "Poll Finds Hazards and Opportunities for Both Parties," *New York Times*, September 16, 2010, national edition, A1, A20.

22. Rockman and Waltenburg, "Obama at Mid-term," 190-191.

23. Ibid., 191.

24. Ibid., 192.

25. Senator Kennedy had lost his battle to brain cancer on August 25, 2009.

26. Polling data on the health care package are available at http://www.realclearpolitics .com/epolls/other/obama_and_democrats_health_care_plan-1130.html#polls, last accessed October 1, 2010.

27. Sheryl Gay Stolberg and David M. Herszenhorn, "Obama Weighs Paring Goals for Health Bill," *New York Times*, January 20, 2010, http://www.nytimes.com/2010/01/21/ health/policy/21health.html, last accessed October 1, 2010.

28. Vince Bzdek, "Why Did Health Care Reform Pass? Nancy Pelosi Was in Charge," *Washington Post*, March 28, 2010, http://www.washingtonpost.com/wp-dyn/content/ article/2010/03/26/AR2010032602225.html?sid=ST2010032603755, last accessed October 1, 2010.

29. Rockman and Waltenburg, "Obama at Mid-term," 192.

30. Ibid., 186; Nolan M. McCarty, Keith T. Poole, and Howard Rosenthal, *Polarized America: The Dance of Ideology and Unequal Riches* (Cambridge, MA: MIT Press, 2006).

31. Frances E. Lee, 2008. "Dividers, Not Uniters: Presidential Leadership and Senate Partisanship, 1981–2004," *Journal of Politics* 70:914-928.

32. Bob Woodward, *Obama's Wars* (New York: Simon & Schuster, 2010).

About the Contributors

Joel D. Aberbach is a professor of political science and policy studies and the Director of the Center for American Politics and Public Policy at UCLA. He is cochair of the International Political Science Association's Research Committee on Structure and Organization of Government. His books include *Keeping a Watchful Eye: The Politics of Congressional Oversight* (Brookings Institution, 1990) and (with Bert A. Rockman) *In the Web of Politics: Three Decades of the U.S. Federal Executive* (Brookings Institution Press, 2000).

Colin Campbell is the retired Canada Research Chair in U.S. Government and Politics and emeritus professor in political science at the University of British Columbia; and visiting professor at the U.S. Studies Centre at the University of Sydney. From 1983 to 2002, he was a professor at Georgetown University. He has published nine books, four of which have won awards.

James E. Campbell is a UB Distinguished Professor and chairman of the Department of Political Science at the University at Buffalo, SUNY. He previously served as an APSA congressional fellow and as a program director at the National Science Foundation. His research generally examines American macropolitics: presidential and congressional campaigns and elections, partisan realignments, public opinion, the policy performance of political parties, and election forecasting. In addition to the more than seventy journal articles and book chapters that he has published on various aspects of American politics, he is the author of *The American Campaign: U.S. Presidential Campaigns and the National Vote, The Presidential Pulse of Congressional Elections*, and *Cheap Seats*. He also coedited *Before the Vote* and has edited six journal symposia on forecasting American national elections.

George C. Edwards III is Distinguished Professor of Political Science at Texas A&M University and holds the Jordan Chair in Presidential Studies. A leading scholar of the presidency, he has written or edited 25 books on American politics. He is also editor of *Presidential Studies Quarterly* and general editor of the *Oxford Handbook of American Politics* series. Among his latest books, *On Deaf Ears: The Limits of the Bully Pulpit* examines the effectiveness of presidential leadership of public opinion; *Why the Electoral College Is Bad for America* evaluates the consequences of the method of electing the president; *The Strategic President* offers a new formulation for understanding presidential leadership; and *Overreach* analyzes leadership in the Obama presidency. Professor Edwards has served as president of the Presidency Research Section of the American Political Science Association, which has named its annual Dissertation Prize in his honor and awarded him its Career Service Award.

Christopher H. Foreman is a professor at the University of Maryland School of Public Policy and a nonresident senior fellow in the governance studies program at the Brookings Institution. His books include *Signals from the Hill: Congressional Oversight and the Challenge of Social Regulation* (Yale University Press, 1988) and *The Promise and Peril of Environmental Justice* (Brookings, 1998). From 1999 to 2005 he served as a member of the board of governors of The Nature Conservancy.

Diane J. Heith is associate professor and chair of government and politics at St. John's University. She is the author of several works on the presidency, public opinion and the media including, *Polling to Govern: Public Opinion and Presidential Leadership* (2004) and *In the Public Domain: Presidents and the Challenges of Public Leadership* (edited with Lori Cox Han, 2005). Her work has appeared in *Public Opinion Quarterly, Presidential Studies Quarterly, Political Science Quarterly, The Journal of Health Politics, Policy and Law, The Journal of Women, Politics and Policy, White House Studies and Congress and the Presidency.* She is currently completing *The Presidential Road Show: Public Leadership in a Partisan Era* (forthcoming, 2012).

Lawrence R. Jacobs is the Walter F. and Joan Mondale Chair for Political Studies and Director of the Center for the Study of Politics and Governance in the Hubert H. Humphrey School and Department of Political Science at the University of Minnesota. Dr. Jacobs has published 14 books and edited volumes and dozens of articles on presidential politics and American public policy including *Health Care Reform and American Politics* (with Theda Skocpol, Oxford University Press, 2010), and *Politicians Don't Pander: Political Manipulation and the Loss of Democratic Responsiveness* (with Robert Y. Shapiro, University of Chicago Press, 2000). Dr. Jacobs coedits the "Chicago Series in American Politics" for the University of Chicago Press.

Gary C. Jacobson is professor of political science at the University of California, San Diego, where he has taught since 1979. He previously taught at Trinity College, the University of California at Riverside, Yale University, and Stanford University. Jacobson specializes in the study of U.S. elections, parties, interest groups, and Congress. He is the author of *Money in Congressional Elections; The Politics of Congressional Elections,* 7th Edition; *The Electoral Origins of Divided Government: Competition in the U.S. House Elections, 1946-1988; Not a Uniter: George W. Bush and the American People;* and is a coauthor with Sam Kernel l of *Strategy and Choice in Congressional Elections,* 2nd Edition and *The Logic of American Politics,* 4th Edition. Jacobson is a fellow of the American Academy of Arts and Sciences.

Bert A. Rockman is currently a professor of political science and the department head at Purdue University. His books include *The Leadership Question,* which was awarded the Richard E. Neustadt Prize. He also has been a recipient of the Herbert A. Simon Award.

Andrew Rudalevige is the Walter E. Beach '56 Chair of Political Science at Dickinson College, and has held visiting posts at Princeton University and the University of East Anglia, England. His books include *The New Imperial Presidency* and *Managing the President's Program,* which was awarded the Richard E. Neustadt Prize.

Robert S. Singh is a professor of politics at Birkbeck, University of London. A graduate of Oxford University, he is the author of *The Congressional Black Caucus, The Farrakhan Phenomenon, American Politics: A Concise Introduction* and *Contemporary American Politics and Society: Issues and Controversies,* editor of *American Politics and Society Today* and *Governing America,* coeditor of *The Bush Doctrine and the War on Terrorism* and, most recently, coauthor of *After Bush: The Case For Continuity in American Foreign Policy.* His research interests are in the politics of contemporary U.S. foreign policy.

Barbara Sinclair is a professor emerita of political science at UCLA. She specializes in American politics and primarily does research on the U.S. Congress. Her publications include articles in the *American Political Science Review,* the *American Journal of Political Science,* the *Journal of Politics,* and *Legislative Studies Quarterly* and the following books: Congressional Realignment (1982), *Majority Leadership in the U.S. House* (1983), *The Transformation of the U.S. Senate* (1989), *Legislators, Leaders, and Lawmaking: The U.S. House of Representatives in the Postreform Era* (1995), *Party Wars: Polarization and the Politics of National Policy Making* (2006), and *Unorthodox Lawmaking: New Legislative Processes in the U.S. Congress* (2011). She has served as chair of the Legislative Studies Section of the American Political Science Association, president of the Western Political Science Association, and vice-president of the American Political Science Association. She is an elected member of the American Academy of Arts and Sciences. She was an American Political Science Association Congressional Fellow in the office of the House majority leader in 1978-79 and a participant observer in the office of the Speaker in 1987-88. She has testified before Congress on the legislative process, most recently before the Senate Committee in Rules and Administration on the filibuster in July 2010.

Eric N. Waltenburg is associate professor of political science at Purdue University. His research and teaching interests focus on judicial and state politics. He is the author or coauthor of three books, *Litigating Federalism* (Greenwood Press,

1999, with Bill Swinford); *Choosing Where to Fight* (SUNY Press, 2002); and *Legacy and Legitimacy* (Temple University Press, 2009, with Rosalee A. Clawson) as well as various articles. He is also the coeditor of *Politics, Groups and Identities.*

Stephen Weatherford is a professor of political science at the University of California, Santa Barbara. His research has ranged over questions of representation, political behavior and political economy, and he has written on presidential leadership in economic policymaking and on economic policy coordination between the U.S. and Japan. Two active research projects include a survey of U.S. economic policymaking in the post-WWII years and a study of deliberation and decision-making in education policy.

David A. Yalof is associate professor of political science at the University of Connecticut. His first book, *Pursuit of Justices: Presidential Politics and the Selection of Supreme Court Nominees* (University of Chicago Press, 1999), was awarded the American Political Science Association's Neustadt Award as the best book published on presidential studies in 1999. He is also the author of *Prosecution Among Friends: Presidents, Attorneys General and Executive Branch Wrongdoing* (forthcoming from Texas A&M University Press in 2012), *The First Amendment and the Media in the Court of Public Opinion* (Cambridge University Press, 2001), *The Future of the First Amendment: The Digital Media, Civic Education and Free Expression Rights in America's High* Schools (Rowman & Littlefield, 2008), and various articles and book chapters.